IELTS Washback in

Preparation for academic writing in higher education

IELTS Washback in Context

Preparation for academic writing in higher education

Anthony Green

CAMBRIDGE
UNIVERSITY PRESS

CAMBRIDGE UNIVERSITY PRESS
Cambridge, New York, Melbourne, Madrid, Cape Town, Singapore, São Paulo, Delhi

Cambridge University Press
The Edinburgh Building, Cambridge CB2 8RU, UK

www.cambridge.org
Information on this title: www.cambridge.org/9780521692922

First published 2007
Reprinted 2008

Printed in the United Kingdom at the University Press, Cambridge

A catalogue record for this publication is available from the British Library

ISBN 978-0-521-69292-2

For Sachiyo

Contents

Acknowledgements

I would like to express my thanks to the many individuals who have been involved with this volume as research participants, reviewers, colleagues and editors and who have supported and encouraged me in bringing it to print. Too many people have contributed for me to list them all by name, but I would particularly like to acknowledge the help of the following:

My PhD supervisors Cyril Weir and Roger Hawkey for their assistance and insightful criticism throughout the project and Arthur Hughes for getting me started and for encouragement during the early stages.

The British Council for funding elements of the study through the Joint Funded Research Programme and University of Cambridge ESOL Examinations for providing score data and forms of the IELTS Academic Writing test. In particular, I would like to thank Lynda Taylor, Rowena Akinyemi, Nick Saville and Mike Milanovic at Cambridge ESOL for their help with the manuscript and Chris Banks and Nick Charge for help with obtaining data and IELTS test forms.

The Department of Applied Statistics at the University of Reading for assistance with the choice of statistical analyses and to the many members of staff and fellow students at Roehampton and Reading who provided insights and support and who provided invaluable help with collecting the data.

Above all I am most grateful to the many students and teachers who participated in the study and without whose co-operation the research could not have taken place. I hope that this work will be considered worthy of their involvement.

The publishers are grateful to the copyright holders for permission to use the copyright material reproduced in this book. Cambridge University Press for Tables 2.1 and 7.1 from *Assessing Writing* by Sara Cushing Weigle, 2002. IELTS Australia for Table 2.2 from *IELTS Research Reports* (Volume 1), 1998.

Series Editors' note

The International English Language Testing System (IELTS) is a test of English for academic and vocational purposes managed jointly by three partners: University of Cambridge ESOL Examinations (a division of Cambridge Assessment), British Council and IDP:IELTS Australia. The test measures 'the language ability of candidates who need to study or work where English is the language of communication' (IELTS Handbook 2006: 4).

IELTS consists of four modules: Listening, Reading, Writing and Speaking. All candidates take the same Listening and Speaking modules, but there is a choice of Academic or General Training Reading and Writing Modules. If a candidate intends to enter undergraduate or postgraduate courses, they are advised to take the Academic Modules. If a candidate intends to continue their secondary education in English, to undertake work experience or training, or to emigrate, they are normally advised to take the General Training Modules. Test scores are reported, both for overall performance and on each of the four modules, in the form of 'bands' at nine defined levels from Non User to Expert User.

In recent years the IELTS candidature has grown exponentially, reflecting the increasing recognition of the test by higher education institutions and professional registration bodies around the world and by immigration authorities in Canada, Australasia and the UK. In 2006, over 700,000 candidates took the test and 70% of these entered for the Academic Modules. Most Academic Module candidates reported that they were taking the IELTS test for the purpose of entering higher education.

It is now commonplace to regard validity as a unitary concept with theory-based, context and criterion-related validation processes all having a part to play in contributing evidence to support the interpretation of test scores. High-stakes test providers such as Cambridge ESOL are also concerned with the ethical dimension of testing in terms of the effects and impact of a test on individuals and society and place as much emphasis on social values and social consequences as on traditional validity concerns in any consideration of the validity of test scores.

It is increasingly recognised that examination boards have a major impact on educational processes and on society in general because their examinations have widespread recognition and cash-in value. Such impact is often perceived as occurring at the 'macro' or social and institutional level. Effects may also occur at the level of the individual and such intended positive or unintended negative effects are normally referred to by the term 'washback' (or backwash). These effects are normally considered in relation to teaching practice or learning outcomes.

The study of IELTS impact, a major long-term programme of research initiated in 1995 by Cambridge ESOL, was among the earliest investigations into consequential validity. The project addresses a number of the issues at the macro level and is described in detail in Hawkey (2006). Green's volume focuses on micro issues of washback and as such can be seen as a valuable complement.

Despite widespread lip service to the mantra of washback in the international testing community, until recently only a limited number of research studies have been undertaken to investigate the effects of high-stakes language tests on teaching and learning. Even fewer studies have followed Messick's call and empirically grounded the impact of such effects on learners' resultant test performances.

The research reported by Green in this volume relates to work he conducted on IELTS for his PhD dissertation between 2001–2004. Green was looking at the influence of the IELTS Academic Writing Module on preparation for academic study and the equivalence between IELTS test preparation and other forms of English for Academic Purposes directed at university study. He investigated the general research question: *Is the washback model supported in relation to the role of the IELTS test in the context of preparation for academic study in the UK?* This general research question in turn implies a number of related questions.

1. Given the commonalities and discrepancies between IELTS and the EAP writing construct revealed in the literature review, do students and teachers regard themselves as engaging in IELTS test preparation rather than university preparation and do such beliefs give rise to practices, in relation to IELTS, which fail to address the EAP writing construct?

2. Do practices on courses which are not driven by IELTS better reflect this construct?

3. What are the characteristics of learners on different courses and how do these relate to the characteristics of the IELTS test-taking population?

4. Do instructional alternatives at points on a continuum from IELTS-driven to IELTS-unrelated EAP courses result in differential outcomes in terms of:
   - gains in scores on the IELTS Academic Module?
   - linguistic (lexico-grammatical) proficiency gains?
   - academic awareness and study skills gains?

5. Do facets of learners' individual differences interact with instructional differences in predicting outcomes?

Green's study informed the subsequent development of IELTS, contributing to the revision of the Writing module in 2005, in particular the rewording of task prompts. It confirmed the need for greater accessibility to information on the meaning of band scores; this has been provided in the form of increased information on score processing, reporting and interpretation being made on the IELTS website in recent years as well as the release in 2006 of the 'IELTS Scores Explained' DVD package. In addition, Green's work contributes to a better understanding of the relationship between test scores, periods of study and language gain.

His study has serious implications for all end users of IELTS test results and indeed the results of other high-stakes tests. It raises serious doubts over the conventional wisdom concerning the amount of language support required by EAP learners at different proficiency levels (as measured by the test) in order for them to meet minimally acceptable standards required for English medium tertiary study.

In the broader context, it adds significantly to our knowledge of the complexity of the mechanisms through which washback occurs and provides the field with a model that embraces this. As such it provides a valuable framework for carrying out further research in this oft-neglected area.

Recent validation projects in Sri Lanka (Wall 2005), Australia (Burrows 1998) and Hong Kong (Cheng 2005) have also addressed the question of washback in a variety of settings. Their work has established that washback is not one-dimensional or easily manipulated and that innovations in testing will not inevitably lead to changes in the classroom. It is clear that the interpretation and uses made of assessment procedures are not solely determined by testers, but depend on interactions involving the test and participants (such as test takers, teachers, administrators, materials developers and policy makers) with implications for teaching and educational policy. Green's work further grounds this critical relationship between the test, the test taker and test use.

Early research into washback from language tests (Hughes 1988, Khaniya 1990) was criticised for a lack of empirical data (Alderson and Wall 1993), relying instead on insights from interested participants. More recent research has therefore triangulated quantitative data with qualitative descriptions of educational practices derived through interviews, questionnaires and observations (Burrows 1998, Cheng 2005, Watanabe 1996). This has allowed the development of theoretical models of washback that recognise a wide variety of moderating variables interacting with test influence (Burrows 1998, Hughes 1993). At the same time, recent research has given insufficient attention to test design and learning outcomes and is therefore unable to relate the influence of tests on learning processes to test score gains. Green's work helps fill this gap.

A further important contribution of Green's work is the use he made of sophisticated quantitative and qualitative methods to investigate these effects. His main study is unique in the comprehensive range of data collection methods (classroom observation, individual and focus group interviews, staff and student questionnaires, document analysis and a range of test instruments) which provide multiple channels for the different voices to be heard. A combination of quantitative and qualitative methods of enquiry provides new insights into how washback to learners may be mediated by washback to the teacher.

Traditional correlation-based techniques such as multiple regression are limited as tools for investigating the wide range of variables implicated in washback, while experimental methods, in attempting to isolate the influence of test method, would distort the complex social reality of the setting (Bailey 1996, Larsen-Freeman 1997). An alternative which allows for the simultaneous investigation of large numbers of variables in interaction in natural settings is provided by a neural network approach (Garson 1998) which allows for non-linearity and is more flexible in handling missing data. This is one of the few studies to employ neural network methods in tandem with traditional linear regression analysis to investigate the multifaceted relationships between presage, process and product variables

Together with the three earlier volumes in this series on washback and impact – Volume 21 by Liying Cheng on the Hong Kong exam reforms, Volume 22 by Dianne Wall on the O level English examination in Sri Lanka, and Volume 24 by Roger Hawkey on the IELTS impact studies – this volume enriches our understanding of an under-researched area of validity and helps further ground the methodologies for investigating it. Volume 25 also complements two other IELTS-focused volumes in this series: one is a collection of research papers on IELTS Speaking and Writing (Volume 19, edited by Lynda Taylor and Peter Falvey, 2007), and the other is a historical overview of the development of ELTS and IELTS (Volume 23, by Alan Davies, forthcoming).

Cyril Weir
Mike Milanovic
January 2007

Abbreviations

ANOVA	Analysis of Variance
ARELS	Association of Recognised English Language Schools
ASI	Approaches to Studying Inventory
AWL	Academic Word List
AWM	(IELTS) Academic Writing Module
BALEAP	British Association of Lecturers in English for Academic Purposes
BASELT	British Association of State English Language Teaching
BICS	Basic Interpersonal Communicative Skills
CAE	Certificate in Advanced English
CALP	Cognitive Academic Language Proficiency
COLT	Communicative Orientation to Language Teaching
CPE	Certificate of Proficiency in English
CSWE	Certificates in Spoken and Written English
EAC	English through Academic Contexts
EAP	English for Academic Purposes
EGAP	English for General Academic Purposes
ELTS	English Language Testing Service
ESAP	English for Specific Academic Purposes
ESL	English as a Second Language
GSL	General Service Word List
IELTS	International English Language Testing System
IIS	IELTS Impact Study
IRT	Item Response Theory
LSP	Language for Specific Purposes
MANOVA	Multivariate Analysis of Variance
MCQ	Multiple Choice Question
MDI	Measurement Driven Instruction
MGLH	Multivariate General Linear Hypothesis
MLP	Multi-layer Perceptrons
MSE	Mean Squared Error
MTELP	Michigan Test of English Language Proficiency
NNS	Non Native Speaker
NS	Native Speaker
PEPS	Productivity Environmental Preference Survey
PEs	Processing Elements

PLSPQ	Perceptual Learning Style Preference Questionnaire
SILL	Strategy Inventory for Language Learning
SLA	Second Language Acquisition
SLC	Nepalese School Leaving Certificate
SOLO	Structure of Observed Learning Outcomes
SPQ	Study Processes Questionnaire
TEEP	Test of English for Educational Purposes
TL	Target Language
TLU	Target Language Use
TOEFL	Test of English as a Foreign Language
TWE	Test of Written English
UWL	University Word List
VLT	Vocabulary Levels Test

1 Wagging the dog? Towards a model of washback

Tests influence teaching and learning. Where a test is used for selection, as is IELTS, those who seek access will attempt to gain the skills they believe necessary to succeed on the test. Some of these skills are generally considered to be desirable, as they are required in the target language use domain. However, as all tests are limited in how much of the domain they can sample and involve a certain amount of measurement error, there is inevitably scope for the misrepresentation of test takers' abilities. The skills required to pass a test are not necessarily or comprehensively the skills required in a target language use domain (Bachman and Palmer 1996). Washback is thus grounded in the relationship between preparation for success on a test and preparation for success beyond the test, in the domain to which the test is intended to generalise and to which it may control access.

This chapter is devoted to discussion of different understandings of washback found in the literature. A conceptual model of washback is outlined that will serve to guide the research described in later chapters. In Chapter 2, the model is applied to the relationship between the IELTS test and theories of academic writing to make predictions about how the test might be expected to influence teachers and learners. These predictions are then tested against the evidence from the research studies described in Chapters 3 to 6.

Washback: definition and scope

In the literature (both in applied linguistics and in general education), the terms *backwash* and *washback*, are both used, and are invariably seen as interchangeable (Pearson 1988, Bachman 1990, Alderson and Wall 1993, Gipps 1994, Broadfoot 1996, Davies et al 1999, Hughes 2003). Dictionary definitions give *backwash* as a backward flow or movement of a fluid produced by a propelling force (as of an oar in rowing) with the meaning extending, figuratively, to the repercussions of a momentous event (Collins 1979, Merriam-Webster 2000, Oxford University Press 2000). Backwash carries technical meanings in fluid mechanics and in the economics of development where economic growth in an urban centre may have beneficial effects on the periphery (*spread*) or conversely, cause decline (*backwash*). As Spolsky

(1996) points out, in general usage the word is most usually applied to unintended and negative effects, and until the 1980s it generally carried a similarly negative meaning within applied linguistics (Khaniya 1990). However, *washback* has gained in currency and is now generally accepted in the applied linguistics literature. The term washback will therefore be used throughout, except where quoting from other writers.

In applied linguistics, washback is broadly defined as the effect of a test on teaching (Richards, Platt and Platt 1992, Davies et al 1999) and often also on learning (Shohamy 1993, Hughes 2003). It has been variously associated with effects on teachers, learners (Buck 1988, Messick 1996, Shohamy 2001), parents (Pearson 1988), administrators, textbook writers (Hughes 1993), instruction (Bachman 1990, Chapelle and Douglas 1993, Weigle 2002), the classroom (Buck 1988), classroom practice (Berry 1994), educational practices and beliefs (Cohen 1994) and curricula (Weigle 2002, Cheng 2005), although for Hughes (1993) and Bailey (1999), the ultimate effects on learning outcomes are of primary concern.

For Shohamy (1992, 1993, 2001) washback is an intentional exercise of power over educational institutions with the objective of controlling the behaviour of teachers and students. For Valette (1967), Wilkinson (1968) and Spolsky (1996) it represents only unforeseen and deleterious effects, while Cheng (1997, 2005) uses the term to refer exclusively to the intended curriculum changes associated with a testing innovation. More commonly, it is considered a neutral term (Alderson and Wall 1993) which may refer both to (intended) positive (Bachman and Palmer 1996, Davies et al 1999) or beneficial (Buck 1988, Hughes 2003) effects and to (unintended) harmful (Buck 1988) or negative effects (Bachman and Palmer 1996, Davies et al 1999, Hughes 2003).

A number of related terms, originating in the general educational measurement literature, have similar meanings and are sometimes equated with washback (Cheng 2005). Among these are *test impact* (Bachman and Palmer 1996, Shohamy 2001), *test influence* (Alderson and Wall 1993); *teaching to the test* (Madaus 1988); *measurement-driven instruction* (Popham 1987); *curriculum alignment* (Smith 1991a, Resnick and Resnick 1992), *systemic validity* (Fredericksen and Collins 1989) and the *consequential aspect of validity* (Messick 1989, 1996). There are often differences of approach implicit in the terminology and it is therefore important to differentiate between washback as operationally defined in this study and other similar terms as they are used in the literature.

Although the terms have been used to refer to the same concept, washback is distinguished from test impact by Bachman and Palmer (1996) who, with McNamara (1996, 2000), Hamp-Lyons (1998) and Shohamy (2001) locate washback under the umbrella of impact. While impact may occur at a *macro* or social and institutional level, washback occurs only at the *micro* level of the individual participant (primarily teachers and students). Bailey (1996, 1999) makes a further distinction between *washback to the learner* and *washback to the programme*. The former refers to effects on students, while the latter embraces effects on other participants such as teachers, materials writers and administrators.

For Brown and Hudson (2002), Bachman and Palmer (1996) and Bailey (1999) washback is not limited to preparation for taking a test, but may include the effects on an individual of actually sitting the test, of feedback received and of decisions taken on the basis of test scores (Bachman and Palmer 1996). However, these are excluded from other, narrower definitions (Weir 1990, Hamp-Lyons 1991, McNamara 2000), where washback is restricted to effects on the teaching and learning 'prior to', 'preceding' or 'leading up to' a test.

Although the terms have been used synonymously (Peirce 1992, Berry 1994), Shohamy (2001) distinguishes washback from Fredericksen and Collins' (1989) concept of *systemic validity*. Taking a systems approach – viewing test and curriculum as components in a constantly developing educational system – Fredericksen and Collins propose that a systemically valid test will be one that brings about curricular and instructional changes in an educational system that advance the development of the cognitive skills that the test is intended to measure (1989). Washback, for Shohamy (2001), following Alderson and Wall (1993), is more narrowly concerned with teachers and learners, but is equally dependent on comparisons made over time or between systems.

Washback is not generally considered to be a standard for judging the validity of a test. Although Morrow (1986), with support from Weir (1990) and Khaniya (1990), argues for *washback validity*, or the extent to which a test fulfils declared pedagogic aims, as a standard for the evaluation of language test development, Alderson and Wall (1993) and Messick (1996) contest this. Firstly, there are no agreed standards for evaluating washback and individual stakeholders may each regard the same effects differently (Hamp-Lyons 1987, Mehrens 1998). Secondly, washback can only be related to a test indirectly, as effects are realised through the interactions between, *inter alia*, the test, teachers and learners. A well-designed test may therefore be associated with negative consequences because of features of an educational system other than the test (Messick 1996). However, Messick suggests that tests which satisfy validity criteria are more likely to have a positive influence on teaching and learning, and so counsels that washback is not a sign of test validity, but that a valid test is likely to generate positive washback.

On the other hand, Messick (1989) argues that evidence of testing consequences, of which washback is one aspect, needs to be weighed with evidence supporting test inferences in validating test use, a view that has now been widely accepted in the educational measurement community (American Educational Research Association 1999). In this vein, Bachman (1990) recognises a potential for conflict between washback and other validity considerations so that even though a direct test of writing may have a lower predictive validity than a multiple-choice test in a university entrance test battery, the potential washback on instruction may outweigh this in deciding which test to prioritise (Bachman 1990).

While Popham (1987) views content as primary, holding that testing relevant skills, even through indirect test formats, will encourage those skills to be taught, advocates of communicative testing disagree. They argue that because test preparation involves training in the kinds of activities which appear in a test, maximal authenticity – the degree of correspondence between a given test task and a target language use (TLU) task (Bachman and Palmer 1996) – and directness – the extent to which a test entails a candidate performing precisely the skill(s) we intend to measure (Hughes 2003) – should be fundamental considerations in test design (Morrow 1986, Wesche 1987, Shohamy, Donitsa-Schmidt and Ferman 1996, Hughes 2003). The influence of sociolinguistics and pragmatics on the construct of communicative language ability (Bachman 1990) dictates the integration of skills in meeting test task demands.

Messick (1996) relates directness and authenticity to washback through the general validity criteria of *construct under-representation* and *construct-irrelevant variance*. He demonstrates that construct under-representation threatens authenticity, while construct irrelevant variance threatens directness. A test design which maximises authenticity and directness is therefore held to have the greatest likelihood of fostering positive washback. However, Messick also reminds us that both directness and authenticity are problematic qualities which cannot be fully realised in testing situations (see discussions in Bachman 1990, Lewkowicz 2000).

In construct under-representation (which jeopardises authenticity), a test is too narrow and fails to include important dimensions of the targeted construct (Messick 1996). A test, for both technical and practical reasons, can only address a limited sample of the focal test construct. Some areas of a test construct may not be readily accessible to measurement. Concern for reliability may also dictate a narrow consistency of content and format between testing occasions. As a result, participants are often able to predict test content and may direct their resources to the areas of the construct they anticipate are most likely to be tested at the expense of those that are least likely. Consequently, although users may interpret scores as indicating ability in all areas of the focal construct, the scores may, in fact, reflect a relatively limited knowledge or ability.

In construct-irrelevant variance (which jeopardises directness), the test is too broad, containing features that are not of relevance to the construct (Messick 1996). Examples of construct-irrelevant variance would be test formats that are vulnerable to test-wiseness coaching and so allow increases in test scores without development of the skills purportedly measured by the tests (resulting in invalidly high scores) or unfamiliar formats that cause confusion for some test takers (resulting in invalidly low scores).

Wiliam (1996) follows Messick (1989) in reversing the concept of wash-back validity. A test is not valid to the extent that it engenders positive wash-back, but is likely to engender positive washback to the extent that it is valid. Thus, a test will be valid if one would be satisfied for teachers to teach to the test. However, to be satisfied that teaching to the test would be beneficial, the test would have to meet the criteria for construct validity set out in Messick's (1989) four-faceted validity framework: a) the test would represent the whole of the target domain (within-domain inferences in Messick's frame-work); b) teaching to the test would also improve learners' performance on other assessments of the same abilities (beyond-domain inferences); c) the test would adequately represent our theoretical understanding of what was important in the domain (within-domain consequences); and d) the effects of teaching towards the test on teachers and students would be beneficial (beyond-domain consequences) (Wiliam 1996).

However, Wiliam recognises that no assessment can achieve such an ideal. Some negative effects are to be anticipated from any test. The relative extent to which different testing technologies are able to overcome the threats of construct under-representation and construct-irrelevant variance is central to discussions of washback and is recognised as a matter for empirical research, contributing to test validation (Linn, Baker and Dunbar 1991, Moss 1992, Alderson and Wall 1993, Shepard 1993).

In brief, most commentators associate washback with test preparation or teaching to the test, excluding broader questions of the social impact of test use and subsequent educational effects on individuals such as those resulting from diagnostic feedback or placement decisions based on test scores, although this limitation is not always made explicit (Valette 1967, Wilkinson 1968, Morrow 1986, Buck 1988, Hughes 1988, 1993, 2003, Pearson 1988, Davies 1990, Heaton 1990, Weir 1990, Watanabe 1992, McNamara 1996, Hamp-Lyons 1998). These constraints on washback studies have been the cause of some dissatisfaction for those language testers interested in explor-ing wider questions of test consequences (Hamp-Lyons 1997, 1998).

In accepting a relatively narrow definition of washback, exploration of *macro* issues (Bachman and Palmer 1996) of social impact and test use embraced by conceptions of the consequential aspect of test validity (Messick 1994, 1996) are excluded from this study. Also excluded are such *micro* issues as the degree to which test scores guide language support subse-quent to a test or how test design might affect students' learning *after* they have completed the IELTS test and progressed to academic study.

Although the IELTS candidature has increased rapidly over recent years with a concomitant rise in the number of preparation textbooks and preparation courses, the limited period available for the study also largely excludes the important question of how washback from the test has developed over time.

Washback by design: positive washback through authentic, direct testing

Washback is said to vary along at least two dimensions: *direction* (positive or negative) (Buck 1988, Alderson and Wall 1993, Brown and Hudson 2002, Hughes 2003) and *extent* (Bachman and Palmer 1996), *strength* (Gates 1995) or *intensity* (Cheng 2005).

The concept of washback direction encapsulates the principle that some effects of a test may be beneficial to the development of learners' abilities, while others may be damaging. For Bailey (1996), washback can be either positive or negative to the degree that it either encourages or inhibits the attainment of educational goals held by learners, educators or both. Thus washback is often evaluated as positive or negative according to how far it encourages or discourages forms of teaching or learning judged to be appropriate. Of course, what is considered to be appropriate will depend on the position adopted by the judge and the educational goals he or she espouses (Hamp-Lyons 1987, Mehrens 1998).

In reality, learners, teachers, administrators and other participants may have competing goals. Thus effects regarded as positive by one constituency within an educational system may be seen as negative by another: witness for example the impassioned debate over the merits of *measurement driven instruction* in the USA (Bracey 1987, Popham 1987, Airasian 1988, Ramirez 1999).

When tuition is geared to ensuring that students pass a test, at least some effects on teaching and learning are generally acknowledged to be positive. Among the potential benefits of test preparation are enhanced motivation and clearer, more focused instructional targets (Madaus 1988, Alderson and Wall 1993, Gipps 1994). Although some fear that these advantages may be brought through increased anxiety and intimidation (Stiggins 1999), at the least, preparation for a test motivates reflection about the material (Cohen 1994).

Nevertheless, washback has, historically, more often been associated with the negative effects of tests on teaching and learning (Spolsky 1996). Although much of the evidence is anecdotal (Alderson and Wall 1993) and the allegations have sometimes been contradicted by research findings (Wesdorp 1982, Watanabe 1992), the perception of damaging effects is widespread and well-established (Vernon 1956, Wiseman 1961, Cronbach 1963, Kellaghan, Madaus and Airasian 1982, Madaus 1988, Eisemon 1990, Khaniya 1990, Corbett and Wilson 1991, Haladyna, Nolen and Haas 1991, Smith 1991a, 1991b, Kellaghan and Greaney 1992, Gipps 1994, London 1997, Bailey 1999, Jones et al 1999, Shohamy 2001).

Based on perhaps the most thorough study on the subject to date (Bailey 1996, Hamp-Lyons 1998, Cizek 2001), involving a two year qualitative study carried out in US primary schools, Smith (1991b) finds support for the common allegations: testing programmes a) considerably reduce the time available for instruction, b) restrict the range of the curriculum and limit teaching methods, and c) potentially reduce the freedom of teachers to teach content or to use methods that are believed to be incompatible with the format of standardised tests. These findings are echoed in descriptions of testing programmes from payment-by-results in Victorian England (Holmes 1911, cited in Gipps 1994) through the 11-plus selection tests for English grammar schools (Vernon 1956, Broadfoot 1996) to state-mandated accountability testing in the USA (Corbett and Wilson 1991, Hermann and Golan 1993) and testing innovations in developing countries (Eisemon 1990, Chapman and Snyder 2000).

However, evidence from empirical research, as opposed to anecdote, is scanty and such evidence as does exist is not of a quality to support the inference that tests are *responsible* for teaching and learning practices (Mehrens 1998). Nonetheless, the proliferation of preparation courses and coaching materials and the testimony of teachers and students can leave little doubt that at least some tests do influence at least some individuals. It is less clear, however, why this happens and how far test design and use (as opposed to publishers, teacher trainers and school administrators or widely held beliefs about learning, for example) are implicated in any adjustment to behaviour (Hamp-Lyons 1998).

The objective underlying many test preparation practices is to exploit the format and content of a test to improve test scores quickly and efficiently. Apparent success in boosting scores has given rise to concerns that test-preparation activities threaten the interpretability of test scores. Tests do not (and probably cannot) include all of the abilities considered important in a domain (Wiliam 1996). Some skills are easier to test than others and these skills may come to be better represented on tests than other, perhaps equally important skills. Teachers may be able to predict test content and so become able to work efficiently to improve students' test scores by directing their efforts to the tested areas of a curriculum at the expense of untested areas (Crooks 1988).

Test scores are usually interpreted to represent ability in all areas of a domain, but where teaching has focused only on tested skills, such inferences may not be justified. As Cronbach (1963) observes, the knowledge that particular content will be tested encourages a concentration of effort, which is desirable, but learning the answer to a question is not the same as reaching an adequate understanding of the topic that the question represents.

Fredericksen (1984) charges that, as a result of this process, test results misinform the evaluation of educational systems. Performance in a school subject may *appear* to improve, because test scores rise, but the apparent improvements may simply result from the targeting of instruction towards tested skills and the growth in knowledge of test demands. The inference from improving test scores, that there has been a proportionate growth in student learning, may not be justified as the improvements may not generalise to areas of the focal construct that go untested. Empirical support for this view is provided by a series of studies in the United States which uncovered what became known as the Lake Wobegon effect (Koretz 1988). Improvements in school pupils' test scores over time, which resulted in all states performing above published national averages, failed to generalise to alternative measures of the same constructs (Cannell 1988, Koretz 1988, Linn, Graue and Sanders 1990).

Linn (2000) describes the effect of introducing a new test into an educational system. At first, scores are comparatively low, but during a period of adjustment in the school system, the scores rise steadily as teachers and learners adapt to the demands of the test. When the first test is replaced with a new, unfamiliar measure, scores fall. They then rise once again as teachers and learners adapt to the demands of the new test.

Score-boosting practices which fail to develop the range of construct skills have been dubbed *test score pollution* (Haladyna et al 1991) because they lead to mistaken inferences regarding ability. Haladyna et al list a variety of supposedly unethical test-preparation practices which may lead to score pollution including, among others, developing a curriculum or teaching objectives based on test items, presenting items similar to those on the test and using score-boosting activities. In their view such practices should be disallowed because they have led to a situation in which test results have come to misrepresent the outcomes of public education.

While many psychometricians may regard these test-preparation practices as questionable (Mehrens and Kaminsky 1989), unethical (Haladyna et al 1991) or immoral (Cannell 1988), this perspective places an unreasonable burden on teachers. Wiliam (1996) reminds us that teachers rightly consider it their duty to obtain the best test results for their students. Teachers and students often believe that tests contain what should be learned and therefore what must be taught: they do not distinguish between the target domain and test content. A view that Chapelle and Douglas (1993) regard as perfectly reasonable, given that a test such as IELTS represents the language hurdle students must clear before pursuing their academic careers.

Following this line of argument, Davies (1985, 1990) suggests that high-stakes proficiency tests, although founded on theoretical constructs and intended to be curriculum-free, will inevitably attract to themselves a syllabus and hence evolve into achievement tests. He considers any attempt to prevent teaching to the test both futile and misguided. Washback is so widespread that it is more rational to accept it and then work to make it as beneficial as it can be so that its influence on the classroom is transformed (Davies 1990). Based on the many examples of negative effects, it is assumed that similar mechanisms can be exploited to promote good practice when the technology of testing is reformed. This pragmatic notion of tests worth teaching to can be traced back at least as far as Thorndike (1921: 378), who writes, 'Students will work for marks and degrees if we have them. We can have none, or we can have such as are worth working for.'

In this spirit the distinction is often made between intentional, beneficial or positive washback associated with innovative test methods and negative washback engendered by inappropriate or outmoded forms of assessment which fail to keep pace with developments in pedagogy (Davies 1990, Bailey 1996, Hughes 2003).

As Chapman and Snyder (2000) point out, a number of features of test design may be manipulated in efforts to improve instruction. These include *item format* (multiple-choice, short-answer question, extended response etc.), *content* (topics and skills), *level of knowledge called for* (retention, understanding or use), *complexity* (the number of content areas and their interrelationship), *difficulty* (easy or challenging), *discrimination* (in terms of set standards of performance), *referential source* (criterion-referenced or norm-referenced), *purpose* (learner performance, curriculum evaluation, teacher evaluation) and *type of items* (proficiency, achievement or aptitude).

Although precise descriptions of how tests have been reformed to promote washback are often lacking (Cheng 2005, Wall 2005), Hughes (2003) devotes a chapter to achieving beneficial washback and Brown (2000) summarises suggestions for the promotion of positive washback from Hughes (2003), Heyneman and Ransom (1990), Shohamy (1992), Kellaghan and Greaney (1992), Bailey (1996), and Wall (1996). Brown categorises these prescriptions as *test design strategies, test content strategies, logistical strategies* and *interpretation strategies*.

Test design and content strategies are more closely identified with washback direction, while logistical issues are more closely identified with washback intensity (Kellaghan and Greaney 1992, Hughes 1993). Interpretation strategies may be viewed as indirect, policy-level means of ensuring standards of test design and logistical provision while the test design and content strategies relate most closely to Chapman and Snyder's (2000) test description categories of format, content, complexity and referential source. The following sections consider how these test design features are said to engender washback.

Test format

Madaus (1988) cites evidence of teachers limiting the tasks undertaken in the classroom to the types of task set in a test. He proposes as one of seven general principles for test impact that teachers will pay close attention to the format of questions on a test (for example, essay or multiple choice) and will adjust their teaching accordingly (Madaus 1988). Much of the criticism in EFL directed at tests such as the TOEFL has concentrated on the use of a multiple-choice item format and norm-referenced score interpretations (Spolsky 1995, Hughes 2003).

Multiple-choice tests have come in for particular criticism for negative washback on the grounds that they may restrict test content, atomise knowledge and encourage poor teaching practices (Wise 1985, Resnick and Resnick 1992, Prodromou 1995, Hughes 2003). However, others have rejected the assertions that the multiple-choice format is only capable of addressing *lower order* skills of recall or recognition and believe that recent test instruments employing multiple-choice items to test *higher order* analytical skills demonstrate their point (Wiliam 1996, Mehrens 1998).

On the other hand, Wiliam (1996) suggests that even where multiple-choice items have been designed to assess higher-order thinking, this is achieved by identifying *particular* higher-order skills. So even though the full breadth of a domain may be addressed, multiple-choice questions break it down into manageable, assessable units. Because the domain as a whole never gets assessed, teachers tend to concentrate on isolated elements. This criticism, which relates in Chapman and Snyder's (2000) terms to complexity as well as format, is of particular relevance to current conceptions of language use as 'the dynamic and interactive negotiation of meaning between two or more individuals in a particular situation' (Bachman and Palmer 1996: 62).

Aside from the constraints imposed by multiple-choice items on the content of a test, a further charge is that they affect teaching methods; that multiple-choice testing leads to multiple-choice teaching (Smith 1991a). Hughes (2003) argues that practice in taking multiple-choice items and test-taking strategies will not provide learners with the most effective means of improving their language ability and Smith (1991a, 1991b) cites examples of multiple-choice teaching among primary school teachers in the USA in response to the Iowa Test of Basic Skills. However, it is not immediately clear whether the preponderance of such practices should be attributed to test format or to other shortcomings in the educational system, for example, poor standards of teacher training (Hamp-Lyons 1998).

It is often asserted, as by Hughes (2003), that direct, constructed response item formats, such as the essay writing required in the IELTS Writing Modules, will yield more positive washback than multiple-choice items. However, direct tests of performance are not immune to narrow test-taking strategies. Linn, Baker and Dunbar (1991), in a discussion of validity issues surrounding performance assessment, see the potential for a narrow strategic approach to composition. They assert that more direct forms of assessment will not necessarily foster classroom activities that are more conducive to learning. A direct test of writing might, for example, encourage teachers to develop a formulaic approach that is effective in generating high-scoring essays within the time limit imposed by the test, but fails to develop learners' understanding of the material.

Madaus (1988) offers similar examples of essays written in response to different prompts, but employing the same memorised formulae. Gipps (1994) cites experience with GCSE coursework suggesting that performance tests can be associated with narrowing of the curriculum (a focus on assessed coursework at the expense of untested tasks) and score-polluting practices (such as assistance from parents). Brindley (1998) also reports concerns that criterion-referenced outcomes statements based on performance in regular classroom activities may, like traditional tests, come to narrow the curriculum and reduce the time available for teaching. Linn (1994) concludes that positive impact from performance assessments cannot be assumed, but must be demonstrated through empirical research.

Mehrens (1998) reviews a number of studies on the impact of performance assessments in the USA (Rafferty 1993, Khattri, Kane and Reeve 1995, Stecher and Mitchell 1995, Koretz, Barron, Mitchell and Stecher 1996, Lane and Parke 1996, Shepard et al 1996, Chudowsky and Behuniak 1997, Kane, Khattri, Reeve and Adamson 1997, McDonnell and Choisser 1997, Smith et al 1997). He quotes a series of findings from one investigation of a state-mandated portfolio assessment scheme. Teachers found the portfolio impeded their coverage of the regular curriculum and led them to neglect untested material; they reported negative effects on instruction almost as often as positive effects and felt that the use of rewards and sanctions caused them to ignore important aspects of the planned curriculum (Koretz et al 1996 quoted in Mehrens 1998).

These findings reflect quite closely the concerns raised by Smith (1991b) regarding the use of standardised multiple-choice tests and raise questions over the extent to which changes in test format can reform instruction. Based on his review of research into the impact of both multiple-choice tests and performance assessment schemes involving portfolios, Mehrens (1998) concludes, bluntly, that there is little evidence that item or test format matters for instruction.

However, if classroom tasks are to be limited, for whatever reason, to item formats derived from a test, it may be argued that it is preferable, from a language use perspective, to encourage language learners to practise writing even formulaic compositions than to practise responding to multiple-choice tasks.

During the 1980s, under the slogan of *work for washback* (Swain 1985), language testers increasingly argued for the benefits of direct tests of communicative performance relative to indirect tests of linguistic competence in promoting appropriate teaching and learning activities (Alderson 1986, Morrow 1986, Pearson 1988, Baker 1989, Davies 1990, Bailey 1996, Hughes 2003).

Indeed, the emphasis on promoting positive washback has been recognised as one of the criterial differences between more traditional language tests, which have a primary focus on a narrowly defined linguistic competence, and communicative language tests, which set out to assess the broader construct of communicative language ability (Bailey 1996). The question is not therefore simply one of item format, but rather of construct representation and hence of content and complexity.

Content and complexity

A recurrent theme in washback research is the relationship between test content and curriculum. The desire to relate tests more closely to valued classroom behaviours has been a major objective of the movement towards *communicative testing*, intended to support and reflect *communicative teaching* (Alderson 1986, Morrow 1986, Pearson 1988, Baker 1989, Weir 1993). For Pearson (1988), good tests will very closely resemble teaching-learning activities and Weir argues that the better test developers are able to incorporate key aspects of language use, including authentic activities performed under realistic conditions, the better the washback effects on teaching are likely to be (Weir 1993).

Tests, it is argued, should mirror the best practice of teachers, so that test practice will involve learners in activities which will develop a full range of skills in the target domain. Thus, for the best possible washback, there should be little distinction between language-learning tasks and effective test-preparation tasks (Messick 1996).

This influence between teaching and testing can be viewed as mutual. Resnick and Resnick (1992) suggest that *overlap*, or the extent to which the test and learning activities are the same, is critical to score outcomes. Where overlap is high, test scores are also high; when overlap decreases so do test scores. Under a process they term *curriculum alignment*, teachers may either adapt a curriculum to match the demands of a test (washback), or, alternatively, may adopt tests that match the requirements of a curriculum.

Tests may be reformed under pressure from teachers to reflect more closely, and so support, desired practices in teaching and learning. Hughes (2003) saw the introduction of the TOEFL Test of Written English (TWE) in 1986 as an example of this process. The TOEFL test, which had not previously offered a direct writing component, had been criticised on the grounds that writing was neglected by teachers because students were unwilling to devote time to skills which would not feature in the examination (Traynor 1985). Such complaints finally outweighed the objection that scoring of compositions would be impractical and unreliable.

Conversely, in measurement driven instruction (MDI) and similar initiatives, tests may be deployed as *curricular magnets* (Popham 1987) or *levers of change* (Pearson 1988) by external agencies to promote desired innovations in teaching and learning. Popham (1987) considered MDI to be the most cost-effective way of improving education and many language testers have shared this enthusiasm. Weir (1990) argues that a test can be a very potent tool for bringing about change in the language curriculum and Davies (1985), revising his earlier view, considers tests to be both a major and a creative influence for progressive change in language pedagogy.

This view of washback gained currency in language testing over the course of the 1980s and was incorporated into a number of test-development projects – although it received surprisingly little attention in the ELTS revision literature, describing the inception of the IELTS test (Criper and Davies 1988, Hughes, Porter and Weir 1988, Alderson and Clapham 1992). Hughes (1988) describes the benefits for learning associated with the introduction of a new test of EAP at a university in Turkey. Khaniya (1990) introduced a communicative test in Nepal in the hope of instigating beneficial washback. Pearson (1988) and Alderson and Wall (1993) document attempts to improve educational practices in Sri Lanka through reform of examinations. The Hong Kong Certificate in English investigated by Cheng (2005) was intended to influence and guide teaching and learning of English in Hong Kong secondary schools.

Ultimately, then, the key relationship determining the direction of washback is not that between test and curriculum, but that between both test and curriculum and the construct to which they are directed. The better a test represents target skills (whether these are based on a specified curriculum or a target domain), through content, complexity, format, scoring procedures and score interpretation, the more beneficial the washback effect is predicted to be (Messick 1996). Arguments over washback direction are, at root, variations on arguments over construct definition.

Weir (1993) advocates that tests of English for Academic Purposes designed to measure whether students have the language ability to cope with the demands of English-medium academic study should be made as realistic and direct as possible so as to reflect the performance conditions and operations that apply in the target language use domain. This has, broadly, been the approach taken by the developers of the IELTS (Clapham and Alderson 1997), which, in the words of the *IELTS Handbook*, 'provides an assessment of whether candidates are ready to study or train in the medium of English' (IELTS 2005: 4).

In its Academic Modules, the IELTS is intended to reflect the target needs of prospective undergraduate and postgraduate students, needs identified through target situation analyses such as Weir (1983) and Geoghegan (1983). In short, the better the IELTS Academic Writing Module represents the writing skills required in the university, the more likely it is to engender positive washback.

Hence a basic model of washback direction might appear as in Figure 1.1. The more closely the characteristics of the test reflect the focal construct as understood by course providers and learners (the greater the overlap), the greater the potential for positive washback. The smaller the overlap, the greater the potential for negative washback. There is controversy, however, as to whether test design alone is responsible for the direction of washback. In addition to test format and content, it has been argued that test use and test stakes, or the (perceived) consequences of test scores will also affect the direction of washback.

Figure 1.1 A basic model of washback direction

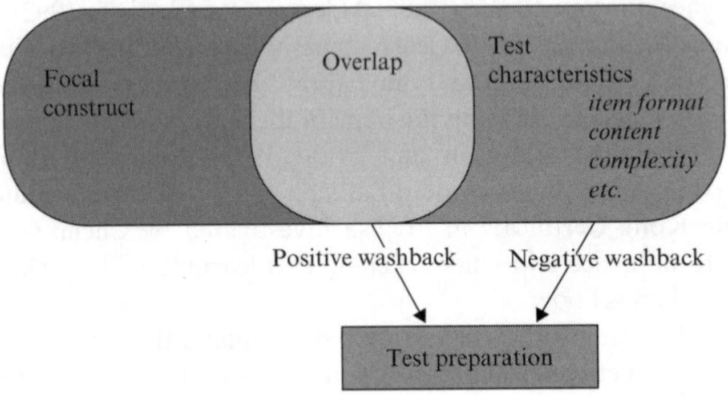

Test purpose and test stakes

If there is a broad consensus that test content and its relation to criterion skills is central to washback, the related questions of test purpose and test stakes are more controversial. From a constructivist perspective, emphasising the role of the learner in processes of organising and restructuring knowledge, some have expressed scepticism over the potential for high-stakes tests to exert a positive influence on a curriculum (Gipps 1994, Haertel 1999).

The use of rewards and sanctions to control teachers and learners is seen to reflect behaviourist theories of learning and to encourage teachers to conceive of learning in the same terms (Shepard 1991, 1993). The suspicion is that narrow, programmatic approaches will emerge in response to a high-stakes test, regardless of its content; when the teacher's professional value is measured through exam scores, teachers will distort the targeted skills by reducing them to strategies and drilling the learners in these (Madaus 1988).

Advocates of beneficial washback (Swain 1985, Hughes 1988, Bachman and Palmer 1996) suggest that this be accomplished through the involvement of teachers in test development. However, for some constructivists, a more radical recasting of the relationship between teaching, learning and testing is required. Madaus (1988) believes that the highest test stakes induce the most damaging forms of test impact. He argues that when test results become the major determinant of future educational or career opportunities, societies will tend to regard success on tests as the principal goal of school-based education, rather than as a convenient, but imperfect indication of academic achievement.

This preoccupation with outcomes is said to have an impact on student learning. Wiggins (1998) believes that a results-focused attitude will encourage students to believe that performance means simply making an effort to do what one has been taught. Crooks (1988) and Gipps (1994) argue that it is the current social role of tests as well as their format, that encourages *shallow learning*, typically marked by the rote learning of content without understanding (Biggs 1993), over *deep learning* based in an interest in the subject matter with the objective of maximising understanding. Students are encouraged to focus on accumulating facts in order to pass examinations, but these facts are often simply discarded after the test or exam has been passed (Gipps 1994).

If improvements in education are to be realised, assessment – a term sometimes used to indicate alternatives to standardised testing (Burrows 1998, Gardner 1989, Gipps 1994) – should be employed principally in support of learning processes, rather than in measuring and comparing learning outcomes (Gipps 1994, Broadfoot 1996, Shepard et al 1996, Wiggins 1998, Stiggins 1999, Shohamy 2001). The aim of assessment is said to be to develop and improve student performance, not just to measure it (Wiggins 1998). This may only be achieved where assessments are, in Goldstein's (1989) terms, *connected* to teaching and learning processes through processes of feedback, and are not *separate* measures which avoid connection with specific learning environments. A primary objective of this connected approach to assessment is to improve instruction: classroom practice will be based on a clear knowledge of learners' understanding of content and teachers can select appropriately challenging tasks that are consistent with curricular goals (Shepard et al 1996).

In language testing, this thinking is shared by Shohamy (1992) who argues that a focus on outcomes impedes improvements to teaching and learning processes in the classroom. It follows that, if schooling is to be reformed, high-stakes testing must be minimised. The potential danger for IELTS, as a high-stakes test, would be that the need to succeed on the test by whatever means would displace the need to develop the range of skills required in the target domain.

Haertel (1999) attributes restrictions of format in high-stakes assessments to requirements for comparability and fairness imposed by the uses to which they are put as well as the practical constraints on the time available, viability of item formats and methods of scoring. He argues that connected uses of assessment to support teaching and learning must be adaptable to local conditions and involve feedback to the learner with opportunities for self-correction. Such uses are incompatible with testing for accountability or certification, which impose standardised conditions and cast the teacher in the role of invigilator. Such restrictions have led to calls for psychometric standards for validity and reliability to be reconceived and for greater recognition to be given to multiple perspectives on performance and the knowledge of individual abilities built up by teachers (Fredericksen and Collins 1989, Linn et al 1991, Gipps 1994, Haertel 1999).

As noted above, studies of performance testing in high-stakes settings offer some empirical support for the view that high stakes are damaging, regardless of format and content. Brindley (1998) and Teasdale and Leung (2000) provide reviews of the negative pressures generated by efforts to reconcile formative and summative uses of assessment to inform high-stakes accountability or certification decisions.

In his review, Mehrens (1998) concludes that, in high-stakes contexts, performance assessments are equally open to charges of narrowing and distorting instruction and encouraging unethical behaviour as more traditional formats. He concludes that high stakes are likely to have both damaging and beneficial impacts: dissatisfaction, cheating, fear and lawsuits increase with the stakes, but, given adequate test design and tight security, student learning is also encouraged.

Others have criticised as anti-democratic the use of tests, regardless of format or content, as instruments for social and educational control (Hanson 1993, Shohamy 2001) with implications, in some EFL settings, of cultural insensitivity as innovations developed by professionals from one culture are imposed on teachers and learners from a different tradition (Heiman 1994).

In conclusion, there are no agreed standards for judging the direction of the influence of test purposes and associated test stakes on teaching and learning. If it can be agreed that raising the stakes for participants increases their extrinsic motivation, this is not regarded by all as a benefit for teaching and learning. As with other sources of motivation and anxiety (Skehan 1989, Spolsky 1989, Alderson and Wall 1993, Dörnyei 2001), it seems likely that individuals will be differently affected and that benefits for one educational context may be deleterious to another. Indeed, the same effects that are judged to be beneficial by some observers may be judged to be damaging by others.

High stakes may have an indirect role in the washback model outlined above, acting to restrict test format, content and complexity. Additionally, decisions associated with important consequences may help to motivate learners to succeed, but may also contribute to a social climate in which education is reduced to credentialism (Lee 1991) where an emphasis on test scores overcomes education as the mission of the school (Mabry 1999). Test purpose and stakes contribute to individual perceptions of, and attention to, test demands and to their conceptions of the relationship between test, curriculum and construct. Where individual participants come to value success on a test above construct knowledge and understanding, negative effects appear more likely.

On the basis of the above discussion, the basic model of washback can be redrawn to incorporate the influence of test stakes and participant characteristics on test method and test preparation (Figure 1.2).

Figure 1.2 Model of washback direction, incorporating test stakes

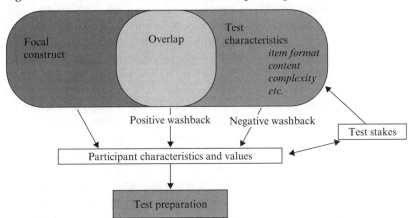

Participants set the test stakes according to their awareness (or lack of awareness) of the uses to be made of test results. The stakes associated with the test influence the behaviour of those preparing for the test; high stakes encouraging greater adjustment on the part of participants. They also affect test design issues as higher test stakes impose stricter attention to questions of test fairness and encourage techniques that support objectivity.

Variability in washback

While the model outlined above pictures washback as an external force, bearing on test preparation, even the proponents of high-stakes test-driven change have allowed that tests cannot, of themselves, reform instruction. Hence they acknowledge that washback (at least in its intentional form) is not deterministic.

Popham (1987) suggests that additional support for instruction will be needed if measurement driven instruction is to fulfil its potential. Pearson (1988) similarly sees limitations in the use of tests as deliberate washback-generating devices. Davies (1985) warns of the dangers both of the *excessive conservatism* of tests that fail to reflect current practices in pedagogy, and of *unthinking radicalism* in introducing tests that demand too much adaptation on the part of teachers and learners.

If tests pose challenges that teachers and learners are not equipped to meet, benefits are unlikely to be realised. Such interdependence implies a challenge for researchers of washback in isolating the effects of a test from the effects of teacher training, curriculum reform or other variables in the setting.

A disappointed attempt to exploit the power of tests to support curricular innovations in Sri Lanka led to an influential critique of washback by Alderson and Wall (1993). Their report on the Sri Lanka 'O' level project (Wall and Alderson 1993) found washback to be both more elusive and more complex than had been anticipated. Problems arose in attempting to discriminate between behaviours provoked by the test and those provoked by the textbook. It was also clear that some behaviour evaluated as negative, which might, prior to the innovation, have been blamed on poor test design, such as teachers explaining all the vocabulary in a reading passage, could not be attributed either to the new examination, or to the new textbooks.

As evidenced by a combination of observation and interview/questionnaire data, washback occurred most obviously to the content of classes, but there was little apparent impact on methodology. The authors concluded that other variables in the setting, besides the test, such as the familiarity and acceptability of the test and texts for teachers, beliefs about effective learning, resourcing, and the wider social context all influenced the success of the educational innovation.

In face of this complexity, they suggested that the *washback hypothesis* that tests influence teaching and learning could be broken down into a set of logically separate propositions. The resulting 15 washback hypotheses involve the influence of tests on attitudes towards teaching and learning, on the methods, content, rate, sequencing, degree and depth of teaching and learning, the relationship between the importance of test consequences and washback and differences in the washback effects experienced by individuals.

Similar limitations on the benefits of external tests to those encountered in Sri Lanka are described by Chapman and Snyder (2000) who review research into a variety of educational development projects (Bude 1989, Schiefelbein 1993, Burchfield and Allen 1995, Chapman and Leven 1997, London 1997, Snyder et al 1997). They conclude that changes to national assessments introduced with the aim of changing instructional practices can be effective, but that their impact is less direct than is usually understood, and their success is not assured.

Attempts at educational reform through testing may be hampered by a general lack of resources; a lack of understanding on the part of teachers about how to improve test scores; a lack of content knowledge or pedagogical skills on the part of teachers; conservatism on the part of participants who perceive the innovations as threatening their current advantages and the failure of real changes in instructional practices to improve student performance. Reviews of testing initiatives aimed at improving teaching and learning in the USA such as Mehrens (1998) and Linn (2000) have reached similar conclusions.

Following the criticisms and questions raised by Wall and Alderson (1993), subsequent studies of washback in ESL contexts have explored individual variation in responses to tests with the focus on how teachers respond to innovations in testing (Alderson and Hamp-Lyons 1996, Watanabe 1996, Burrows 1998, Cheng 2005, Wall 2005). A common finding has been that individual teachers bringing different experiences and beliefs to the classroom respond differently to tests.

Alderson and Hamp-Lyons (1996) and Watanabe (1996) both find differences between teachers contributing as much to the variation between classrooms as differences in the role of test preparation. Alderson and Hamp-Lyons (1996) found teachers adopting narrower multiple-choice teaching strategies in response to the TOEFL test when compared with their General English classes, but further discovered that teacher variables contributed at least as much to the variation in practices as did the test/non-test distinction. Interviews with students also seemed to undermine teacher assertions that learners preferred to study for TOEFL in this way.

Watanabe (1992, 1996) has raised questions concerning both positive and negative washback. In the Japanese context, college entrance tests have long been censured for being a negative influence. Buck (1988) and Brown and Yamashita (1995), for example, blame the poor standards of validity exhibited by these tests for negative effects on classroom practice. Watanabe (1992), however, found that learners preparing for college entrance tests unexpectedly employed a wider range of learning strategies than those admitted to college by recommendation (and hence exempted from the tests). Although Watanabe concluded that the tests might be having a positive washback effect, methodological concerns undermine the value of the findings.

Firstly, use of a greater number of strategies may not be indicative of greater learning; it may be that the narrower range of strategies was being used more effectively. Secondly, the study was conducted after the participants had entered college and not while they were preparing for the test. Thirdly, it is not clear how far the two groups of students could be considered to be equivalent, especially as the samples were not controlled for proficiency. Indeed, even if Watanabe's findings are taken at face value and we accept that test preparation encouraged a wider range of strategy use, this might not be considered evidence of a wholly positive effect. An equally plausible interpretation would be that, in a context where the learning of English is dominated by the university entrance tests, the exempted students simply lost their primary incentive for learning (and hence for employing strategies).

The lack of strategy use on the part of exempted students might, for that reason, be attributed to the damaging role of tests in the Japanese educational system.

Watanabe (1996) investigated washback to teachers. University entrance tests had been criticised for focusing on translation, with the supposed result (based on a literature review, media reports and interviews with teachers) that a grammar-translation methodology came to dominate in the classroom. However, following the introduction of a listening component into some entrance tests in the course of the 1990s, Watanabe found that teachers did not necessarily adjust their teaching to accommodate to the demands of the new tests, as had been intended. Some continued to use translation (even where this was not included in the target examination) and did not teach listening skills (even where listening was included in the examination). Teacher variables including beliefs about teaching and learning, knowledge of effective techniques and knowledge of test demands apparently contributed most to the variation in test preparation practices.

Burrows (1998), reflecting a similar classification of teacher responses (to the Arizona Student Assessment Program) in Smith et al (1997), identified teachers as *adopters*, *adapters* and *resisters* according to their reaction to the Certificates in Spoken and Written English (CSWE) scheme. Teachers had divergent views of the benefits or detriments of the scheme and the depth of the change it represented. Some immediately adopted the Certificates, others more gradually adopted and adapted them as time passed and others resisted the Certificates and the assessment scheme as far as they were able. Burrows (1998) accounts for teachers' reactions as an expression of the encounter between the philosophy underlying the Certificates and teachers' own beliefs about teaching and learning.

As Burrows (1998) observes, this evidence of free will on the part of teachers implies that washback can only occur to the extent that participants allow. However, given the apparently low stakes associated with the scheme, it is not clear that teachers in the contexts addressed by Burrows were subject to strong pressures for success from other stakeholders (such as administrators, students, teachers, parents, the media, funding bodies and policy makers) and may as a result have been better placed to resist the innovation, if they chose to, than teachers in contexts where higher stakes apply.

The recent EFL/ESL research has made it clear that washback is not straightforwardly a function of test design. The effects of a test may not, as Alderson and Wall (1993) point out, be assumed, but must be established through investigation. This raises the issue of how washback may best be observed and measured. It is now widely acknowledged that because of the intervening variables, washback is far more complex than the simple definition – the effect of testing on teaching and learning – would suggest (Bachman and Palmer 1996).

This introduces a second major consideration in washback theory: washback intensity (Cheng 2005), the degree of washback associated with a test or the extent to which participants will adjust to its demands.

Washback intensity

As noted above, washback appears to occur in response to some tests and in some settings, but not in others. Washback theory needs to account for the observed differences in test influence. Hughes (1993), responding to the issues raised by Alderson and Wall (1993), lists a number of conditions that will need to be met for washback to be fully realised. Success must be of real importance to participants; participants must have sufficient understanding of the design of the test and its implications for learning; and the resources required to support test preparation (including teacher expertise, learning materials etc.) must be in place.

The stakes associated with a test are often regarded as a strong indicator of washback intensity, although, as Madaus (1988) has argued, it is the perception of stakes, rather than the reality that will influence behaviour. In short, the more that teachers and students consider a test to control access to rewards or to threaten sanctions for failure, the more likely they are to change their behaviour to do things because of the test that they would not otherwise do (Alderson and Wall 1993).

For Popham (1987), the higher the stakes associated with a test, the greater the potential for washback. However, others take issue with the assumption that high-stakes accountability pressures will be needed in conjunction with performance assessments to drive instructional change (Shepard et al 1996). Indeed, as discussed above, high stakes in themselves are sometimes said to have deleterious effects regardless of the qualities of a test.

Hughes' (1993) notion of test importance does not, of course, necessarily imply high stakes in the sense used by Popham (1987), but could also encompass low-stakes assessments which are appreciated by teachers or learners for other reasons, such as their value in informing learning, as proposed by Crooks (1988) and Black and Wiliam (1998).

However, while Hughes (1993), Bailey (1999) and others (Pearson 1988, Messick 1996) suggest that both positive and negative washback are generated by essentially the same mechanisms, rooted in test design, and would thus equate the influence of high test stakes with other forms of test importance, this is not the view taken by constructivist critics of high-stakes testing (Crooks 1988, Gipps 1994, Shohamy 1992). These critics consider test use and associated consequences (above test design issues) to be the dominant factors influencing teaching and learning.

Also implicated in the question of test importance is the acceptability of the test to participants. Davies (1985) uses the term *unthinking radicalism* to describe situations in which teachers may be unwilling or unable to adjust their behaviour to meet the demands of a new test. In testing innovations, teachers may feel unsympathetic towards novel methods or may be ill equipped to understand how to accommodate their teaching to the new test tasks.

The failure of teachers to adapt their practices to the demands of innovations in testing in the Burrows (1998), Wall and Alderson (1993) and Watanabe (1996) studies might be attributable, at least in part, to a degree of such radicalism in testing, unsupported by sufficient training and consultation. In light of these experiences, Wall (1996) identifies washback research with innovation theory (Fullan and Stiegelbauer 1991, Markee 1993). In particular, she points to the need for testing innovations to take account of local contexts, to allow time for adaptation, and to recognise that new ideas will be assimilated and interpreted in many different ways by participants.

Resistance from teachers is not limited to testing innovations, however. Smith (1991b), for example, found that some teachers resisted the perceived pressure to teach narrowly to the content of established standardised tests because this conflicted with their sense of what the students needed to learn. Hence, where participants' beliefs regarding appropriate teaching objectives conflict with the ostensible focus of a test, and where these objectives are valued more highly (or are at least better understood) than success on the test, washback would seem to be less probable.

Gates (1995) points to further issues affecting the perception of a test's importance. He suggests that the prestige of a testing organisation and the degree of monopoly it enjoys in a marketplace will also contribute to washback intensity. For Gates, washback from IELTS may be diluted because learners seeking entrance to British universities are able to select from an array of alternative tests such as the TOEFL or the Certificate of Proficiency in English (CPE). This has implications for washback in at least two respects. Firstly, the availability of alternative tests may allow course providers to select one which best reflects their curriculum or beliefs regarding language ability, allowing for optimal overlap (Resnick and Resnick 1992). Secondly, it may affect perceptions of the stakes associated with IELTS as test takers who fail to reach their target band score may have opportunities to sit for alternative tests or to repeat the IELTS.

Alongside the question of importance in motivating learners to succeed on a test, assumptions 2 to 5 in Hughes' (1993) list, and most of the *logistical strategies* for promoting washback abstracted by Brown (2000) are concerned with participants' awareness of test demands and the availability of resources for meeting these demands. If teachers and learners are unaware of test content, are unable to access test-related materials, or simply do not comprehend what the test demands of them, the washback effect is not likely to be great; a point both Hughes (1993) and Wall (1996) raise in relation to the Sri Lankan study (Wall and Alderson 1993), noting that teachers had not been provided with necessary resources. This framework may also go some way to explaining the lack of impact reported for low-stakes standardised tests in studies such as Kellaghan et al (1982), Shohamy et al (1996) and Wesdorp (1982). Conversely, if teachers are more aware of test demands and preparation techniques than of the skills required in the target domain, washback is likely to be intensified.

A further consideration in washback intensity is test difficulty, as perceived by participants. Echoing a point made by Airasian (1988) in connection with basic skills testing, Crooks (1988) notes that research has consistently suggested that learners will achieve most and gain most on key motivational variables when standards are attainable, but challenging. If teachers and learners believe that test standards are easily achieved, they will not consider that they need to devote attention to meeting those standards (Mehrens 1998). However, the relationship between test difficulty and washback is not linear. If standards are seen as unattainable because they are too high, teachers and test takers may come to feel that preparation is hopeless and so overlook test demands.

It also appears logical to suggest that participants will only adapt their behaviour if they believe that this makes success on a test more likely. Mehrens (1998) argues that when teachers do not see a connection between test results and their instructional approaches, the test is unlikely to impact on teaching. If test results are not influenced, or rather if participants do not *believe* results are influenced by the choice of teaching or learning strategies, they will not be motivated to alter their behaviour to accommodate to the test.

Alderson and Hamp-Lyons (1996) question whether teachers give sufficient consideration to the success of their test preparation strategies, relying too readily on test format imitation on the assumption that this will bring success. On the grounds that there is little evidence that TOEFL cramming boosts scores (although she is equally unable to cite evidence that it does not), Hamp-Lyons (1998) suggests that poor teaching practices associated with TOEFL classes should, perhaps, be attributed more to a pervasive culture within the English language teaching profession, than to the format and content of the test itself. Alderson and Hamp-Lyons (1996) conclude that in addition to stakes and the relationship between the test and current practice, washback intensity will be influenced by the extent to which educators reflect on methods for test preparation, and the extent to which they are prepared to innovate.

Although the claims made by publishers and course providers for their test preparation products are rarely substantiated by any empirical research (Hamp-Lyons 1998, Powers 1993), the studies in the Lake Wobegon tradition (showing that test scores improve over time, but that the improvements fail to generalise to alternative measures) (Cannell 1988, Koretz, Linn, Dunbar and Shepard 1991, Mehrens and Kaminsky 1989, Linn et al 1990) demonstrate that there may be some justification for the belief that teacher strategies can be successful in boosting test scores.

In sum (Figure 1.3), washback intensity varies in relation to participants' perceptions of test stakes (now incorporated into *importance*) and test difficulty (Hughes 1993). Washback will be most intense where participants:

Figure 1.3 Model of washback, incorporating intensity and direction

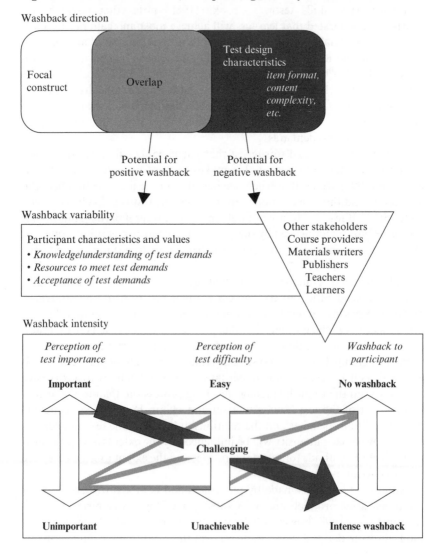

a) value success on the test above developing skills for the target language use domain

b) consider success on the test to be challenging (but both attainable and amenable to preparation)

c) work in a context where these perceptions are shared (or dictated) by other participants.

As these conditions are most likely to be met when a test is imminent, the intensity of washback is likely to be seasonal, increasing with the approach of the test date (Bailey 1999, Watanabe 1997). It may also change as a test, and the implications of success or failure, become established in an educational system (Shohamy et al 1996, Wall 1996).

Washback research methodology: issues of measurability

In the previous section, the scope of washback and the mechanisms through which it is believed to operate were investigated. This section explores the value of the washback model arrived at above as a framework for investigating the effects of a test. The nature of evidence required to support claims of a washback effect is also considered.

The model proposes that the nature of washback from language tests flows from overlap, the distance between test method characteristics (the range and types of test tasks) and the characteristics of the target language use (TLU) domain. The greater the distance between test tasks and the skills required for success in the TLU domain, the greater the potential for unintended washback. The greater the congruence, the more likely positive washback becomes. However, washback is not simply a matter of test design, it is realised through, and limited by, participant characteristics. Differences among participants in their perceptions of test importance and difficulty, and in their ability to accommodate to test demands, will moderate the strength of any effect, and, perhaps, the evaluation of its direction.

Investigating overlap

Overlap can, in part, be addressed through comparison of test design characteristics with analyses of the TLU domain: in language testing terms, the gathering of content-related evidence for test validity. However, overlap is not synonymous with content-related validity. Where validity concerns the theoretical bases for the interpretation of test scores, overlap involves participants' interpretation of test task demands, their understanding of test content and of its relationship to their construction of the TLU domain.

In addition to considering the relationship between test and TLU as conceptualised in the literature, the researcher must therefore also gather participants' views of the extent to which the test reflects the TLU domain.

In this study, the relationship of the IELTS Academic Writing component a) to theories of academic literacy and b) to analyses of the writing needs of international students in higher education is addressed in Chapter 2. Participant perceptions of overlap are taken up in Chapters 3 and 5.

Establishing dependent variables in washback research

As apparent preconditions for washback, participant knowledge of test demands, beliefs regarding the value of success and assessments of the level of challenge posed must also be investigated. These issues are examined through the survey studies reported in Chapters 3 and 5.

Establishing that the supposed conditions for washback are in place is not a sufficient basis for the assumption that washback will in fact occur. There is a need to uncover empirical evidence of the phenomenon. This raises the issue of how washback can be recognised: of the dependent variables appropriate to washback research efforts.

Wall and Alderson (1993) argue the need for clarity in defining dependent variables in washback research and their 15 washback hypotheses suggest predictions regarding content (*what*), methods (*how*), rate, sequence, degree and depth of teaching and learning as potential dependent variables for investigation.

Following this call for explicitness, various symptoms have been suggested as evidence for washback. Bailey (1999) remarks that washback studies can broadly be divided into those focusing on perceptions and those concerned with actions.

Hughes (1993) provides a model of washback process as a basis for research which encompasses both perceptions and actions and links these to learning outcomes. This model has been further developed by Bailey (1996), who presents it in the form of a flow diagram. Where the conditions outlined for washback intensity are met, washback will occur to participants, affecting their attitudes towards their work. Participant attitudes will affect processes, including both what participants do, and how they do it. Processes could include providing test-directed courses, preparation of materials and teaching and learning strategies. In their turn, these processes will influence the critical product: the content and extent of learning.

In similar vein, Messick (1996) proposes firstly, that test design must be evaluated in terms of the construct it represents. Secondly, he insists that products must be of central importance in washback research, suggesting, in the context of TOEFL 2000, that researchers should relate teaching and learning practices to TOEFL scores (Messick cited in Bailey 1996). Similarly Hughes (1993) recommends that research should start from the identification of the skills intended to be developed, with washback being evaluated in light of the degree to which these skills improve or decline when a test is introduced.

Dependent variables in this study will include the effects of the IELTS test on participant attitudes and beliefs, the content and methods of teaching and learning and course outcomes, in the form of learners' test scores and self-assessed learning gains.

Washback must be conceived as a comparative phenomenon, contingent on the degree to which a test influences participants to do things that they would not necessarily do otherwise (Alderson and Wall 1993, Messick 1996). Research has often evaded the issue of comparison by posing it as a hypothetical question. Participants may be asked 'what would you do if there were no test?' This approach is unconvincing. Speculation about how we might act in new circumstances, given the chance, may not reflect our behaviour when the opportunity in fact presents itself (Alderson and Wall 1993).

Concrete comparisons have involved either baseline: what participants did before a test was introduced (Hughes 1988, Burrows 1998, Cheng 2005, Wall 2005), or concurrent studies: what participants do in alternative settings such as courses without tests, or preparing for different tests (Khaniya 1990, Alderson and Hamp-Lyons 1996, Watanabe 1996, Brown 1998).

The selection of treatments for comparison is critical in washback research as this is likely to have a significant bearing on findings. In the context of established EAP tests such as the IELTS Academic Writing Module (AWM), which had been offered in the form described here since 1995, baseline comparisons are ruled out. An important question is thus whether research should focus on differences between IELTS preparation and situations where no testing occurs, between preparation for alternative tests as between IELTS and TOEFL preparation courses, or between different methods of preparation for the same test.

The present study encompasses comparisons between different types of IELTS preparation provision and between IELTS preparation and other forms of English for Academic Purposes (EAP). It does not, for practical reasons, consider preparation for other external tests of EAP, less widely offered in the UK than IELTS, such as the TOEFL test. For similar reasons, comparisons involving an absence of instruction are not feasible in this context. Students intending to enter university, but not studying on any course are not readily accessible to research and are, in any case, likely to represent quite different populations from those studying for a test.

Each of the facets of washback to be considered – participant attitudes, content and methods of teaching and learning and course outcomes – poses its own challenges for the researcher.

Accessing participant attitudes

Surveys of participant attitudes have been a popular means of investigating washback, often with no other forms of evidence. Wall and Alderson (1993) point to the inadequacies of relying on survey data in isolation, but acknowledge that surveys can help to explain teacher behaviour by probing understanding and beliefs.

Bailey (1996) doubts whether washback is accessible to measurement as understood in the tradition of experimental research. Pointing out that washback is a *real-world* phenomenon which inevitably involves non-random samples of participants in naturally occurring, hence uncontrolled, settings, she suggests that triangulated ethnographic approaches are most suitable, a conclusion that is shared by recent researchers (Burrows 1998, Wall 2000, Hayes and Read 2004, Watanabe 2004, Cheng 2005).

Although many washback and impact studies have relied exclusively on questionnaire data, and selected-response questionnaires allow for the efficient comparison of views obtained from large numbers of respondents, results obtained in this way may lack ecological validity. Because the researcher provides the response options, these may not reflect participant understandings of the study context. More flexible methods are required in order to explore participant understandings and reveal some of the complexity of participant experiences.

Watanabe (2004) points to a number of advantages of qualitative methods such as interviews in understanding washback in context. Interviews can provide access to the world view of the participants and are flexible enough to allow the progress of the research to be restructured to reflect participant values. Qualitative interview data can also assist the researcher both in the design of more quantitative instruments and in the interpretation of results.

Accessing processes

Along with Watanabe (2004), Shohamy (1993, 2001), Turner (2001) and Alderson and Wall (1993) stress the need for triangulation of data derived through qualitative and quantitative methods and garnered from a variety of sources. They also recommend the triangulation of perspectives, incorporating the views of teachers and students as well as the researcher. Hence they suggest that questionnaire responses and interview data will need to be supported by direct observation.

Although surveys and interviews provide insights into how participants believe they have been affected by a test, direct observation of behaviour in the classroom, it is argued (Wall and Alderson 1993), can inform interview and questionnaire design and contextualise otherwise incomprehensible responses. It can also provide a corrective to potentially misleading interview/questionnaire data. Wall and Alderson (1993) could find no evidence of observable changes in instructional methodology, despite the teachers' assertions that the new test affected how they taught. Cheng (1997), citing Bailey (1999) agrees that observation allows for a richer understanding of washback than surveys alone and argues for a combination of *asking* – through surveys and interviews – and *watching* – through observation. For Wall and Alderson (1993) observation is not limited to classroom events, but also involves inspection of teacher-devised materials and assessments of students.

Accessing outcomes

For Hughes (1993), the product – the English skills that candidates develop – is the ultimate concern. Hence the measure of washback of greatest interest will be the extent to which criterion abilities improve as a result of test preparation. In spite of this, Wall (2000) acknowledges that there is a dearth of outcomes measures in washback research. The reasons for the lack of consideration given to test results include the problems of comparing non-equivalent, often temporally distant groups and the selection of alternative outcome measures.

In evaluating outcomes, it is important to bear in mind Madaus' (1988) warning regarding the circularity of evaluating test impact through score gains. A rise in scores may reflect increasing test-wiseness rather than improving skills, but this will be masked if test scores are used as the index of improvement. It is therefore important to incorporate alternative measures of the criterion abilities to provide a point of comparison, as was done in the Lake Wobegon studies (Koretz 1988, Linn et al 1990). Improvements in test scores may of course imply no more than test-wiseness. More robust designs will include the use of at least one alternative measure of the focal construct.

Previous studies addressing test gains illustrate the challenges involved. Khaniya (1990) was only able to provide pre/post instruction comparisons for one of the two tests he researched. There were no significant gains on a *communicative* test that Khaniya devised following a year of preparation for the Nepalese School Leaving Certificate (SLC), a fact interpreted as evidence that washback from the SLC was preventing learning of valued skills. However, it is not clear that any gains did occur on the SLC itself, as this was not administered at the beginning of the year. In the current study, measures are administered both at course entry and exit. Hughes (1988) found that language ability, as measured by the Michigan Test of English Language Proficiency (MTELP) improved following the introduction of a new, EAP proficiency test developed from a target situation analysis. However, the MTELP, as Alderson and Wall (1993) indicate, is unlike the EAP test in content and method and the extent to which it could be said to test the skills intended on the course is not clear.

For this reason, Alderson and Wall (1993) imply that, because students now had to pass a test to enter university where previously they had been able to enter without succeeding on the test, the gains in MTELP scores could be attributed to the raised stakes of testing, regardless of test method, rather than any innovation in the content or format of the EAP test. Bailey (1999), however, points out that Hughes (1988) did obtain supporting testimony from receiving instructors that criterion skills had indeed improved. Bailey suggests that obtaining a variety of evidence from a range of perspectives in this way enhances the validity of the conclusions.

In the current study, self-assessment of learning gains and measures of grammatical/lexical proficiency supplement Writing tests at course entry and exit. These cannot provide a comprehensive alternative measure of academic literacy in English, but do offer additional perspectives on student learning, serving to contextualise the gains made on the Writing tests. If test preparation courses resulted in greater gains on the IELTS test, but failed to deliver equivalent gains on other measures, this would suggest that score-boosting practices were successful. Findings of this nature would constitute the kind of evidential link between test design issues and test score interpretation called for by Messick (1996).

The following chapter provides a review of the literature relating to the construct of academic writing for international students in tertiary education. The degree of overlap between academic writing as conceived in this literature and the IELTS AWM is explored. The washback model serves as a basis for predictions about participant attitudes, teaching and learning processes and learning outcomes. These questions are then taken up in the main study.

Implications of washback research

If washback involves not so much a deterministic (Alderson and Wall 1993) influence of tests *on* teaching and learning, as an interaction *between* tests, teaching and learning, washback research may have connotations for educational administration, textbook development, teacher training and resourcing as much as for test development and revision (Wall and Alderson 1993, Alderson and Hamp-Lyons 1996, Shohamy et al 1996, Watanabe 1996, Hamp-Lyons 1998). It is therefore important to gain ecologically grounded understandings of how a test operates within an educational context, rather than (or in addition to) seeking to isolate the effects of testing in experimental fashion.

When test data is combined with descriptions of test preparation practices, comparisons can more readily be drawn between those practices which result in increased test scores and those which do not. Where test scores improve in line with criterion abilities, judged by other measures, positive washback is implied. Where test scores improve, but criterion abilities do not, the washback is likely negative. Where preparation practices fail to boost either test scores or criterion abilities, we might look to other variables such as participant beliefs or availability of resources to explain the outcomes.

2

Academic writing

Overlap between IELTS and academic writing

According to the model of washback delineated in Chapter 1, washback flows from *overlap*, or the degree of congruence between a test and the construct it represents. The IELTS Academic Writing Module (AWM) is based on the assumptions that writing is separate from other language skills and that it is possible to differentiate between academic writing and the global construct of writing (Hamp-Lyons 1987). Evaluating the potential for washback from the test involves a consideration of the construct of academic writing and of how this is represented in the IELTS AWM.

In this chapter, we will consider the nature of academic writing and draw comparisons with the content of the IELTS Writing component. In other words, we will look for content-based evidence relating to the overlap between IELTS and the target language use domain.

The nature of academic writing

Academic writing is classified by its educational purpose and resists any but a circular definition; it may be described in relation to but cannot be isolated from other forms of writing. Weir (1983) provides a broad definition embracing context and content: 'institutional writing circumscribed by conventions' (Weir 1983: 226), while Jordan (1997) simply acknowledges that it is a 'wide umbrella term embracing considerable variation'.

Indeed, even if we follow Hamp-Lyons and Kroll (1997) in restricting our definition to the writing produced by students within higher educational institutions for purposes of assessment, we are still faced with 'a wide range of different types of text, ranging from undergraduate essays produced under timed examination conditions, to laboratory reports, and, further, to dissertations and theses. The products are highly diverse, and the resemblances are in some cases almost impossible to find' (Thompson 2001: 14).

Although academic writing may be resistant to definition, students at universities in L1 English countries write assignments in English as a basis for academic assessment and there is a practical need to prepare L2 learners to fulfil the requirements of their courses. The obligation for receiving institutions to ensure that learners entering academic courses have the linguistic resources to meet course demands has motivated the development of language courses and tests of proficiency in English for Academic Purposes (EAP) such as the IELTS and TOEFL. EAP course and test design has motivated research into the demands made of students in their academic work at university and the difficulties encountered by international students in meeting these demands.

In both teaching and testing of EAP (as in other forms of English for specific purposes) there is a tension between close specification of the tasks learners are likely to face in their academic work and the practical need to cater to divergent needs within common courses. Learners may benefit from attention to language associated with their field of study, but, as Alderson (1988) points out, there are logistic constraints on English for Specific Academic Purposes (ESAP) (Blue 1988); it is not generally feasible to provide material closely tailored to the needs of the individual learner.

At the other end of a continuum in EAP provision, English for General Academic Purposes (EGAP) seeks to abstract common skills that can be transferred across contexts. In vocabulary learning, for example, EGAP would involve learning *core* vocabulary (words occurring with high frequency in a wide variety of texts) and *subtechnical* vocabulary (words found more frequently in academic than general texts, but occurring with similar meanings across disciplines). ESAP would involve learning the technical vocabulary specific to a field of study.

The ESAP/EGAP distinction is related to the specificity continuum described by Douglas (2000) between the narrowly field specific and the relatively general test of language for specific purposes. For Douglas, the IELTS falls towards the general or EGAP end of this continuum as it does not, since the 1995 revision, assume any field-specific background knowledge on the part of the test taker.

The abstraction of academic writing skills can be approached from a variety of perspectives, depending on how writing is conceived by the researcher. The word 'writing' may be understood to refer both to a formal product and to a process and this ambiguity is reflected in the breadth of research across disciplines.

From the perspective of *cognition*, cognitive psychology and ethnography have explored the process of writing, emphasising the role of internal composing processes. *Text description* employing techniques from rhetoric, discourse analysis, register analysis, genre analysis and functional grammar has provided insights into patterns of textual organisation. Sociologists, anthropologists and sociolinguists have examined the contribution of writing from a *social* perspective. They consider how texts and the act of writing contribute to the construction and reproduction of social relationships.

This chapter will outline the relevance of current theories of writing, within these three broad traditions, to EAP provision, and then consider how the IELTS Academic Writing Module (AWM) relates to each.

Cognition

Psychological accounts of writing have explored cognitive processes internal to the individual. Flower and Hayes (1981, 1984) synthesised protocol analysis research with L1 learners to construct a cognitive model of writing. They propose three components: the writer's long-term memory, the task environment and a *composing processor* which incorporates three related elements (*planning*, *translating* and *reviewing*) managed by a controlling *monitor*. Although empirically grounded, the model has attracted criticism on three counts: it fails to allow for differences between individual writers in how they approach the writing process, it is too vague to be tested against empirical evidence and it is too narrowly based on a single research strategy (protocol analysis) (Grabe and Kaplan 1996).

Knowledge telling and knowledge transforming

Bereiter and Scardamalia (1987) respond to some of these criticisms by providing two empirically testable models, arguing that different models are required to account for the different approaches taken by novice and expert writers. Bereiter and Scardamalia distinguish *knowledge telling* from *knowledge transforming*. This is an opposition that resonates throughout the EAP literature and is worth exploring in some depth.

Knowledge telling is a task-execution model involving the retrieval of content knowledge from memory and the shaping of this information to fit a formal schema or internalised set of expectations regarding the writing task requirements (Bereiter and Scardamalia 1987). It is dependent on pre-existing knowledge of content and form and is efficient enough that given a specification of topic or genre, a writer can quickly produce an essay that will relate to the topic and conform to expectations of the type of text that is called for. Indeed, the knowledge telling strategy is so successful, Bereiter and Scardamalia argue, that it can account for much writing even at post-graduate levels and beyond.

Knowledge transforming, on the other hand, is a more controlled, problem-solving model, in which the thoughts come into existence through the composing process itself (Bereiter and Scardamalia 1987). In knowledge transformation there is continuous interaction between developing knowledge and developing text so that problems are raised and solved by the writer. Knowledge transforming writers problematise the text. They adopt a critical relationship with the text as they construct it, engaging a problem-solving executive to question whether the text they have written says what they want it to say and whether they themselves believe what the text says. In the process they are likely to consider changes not only in the text, but also changes in what they want to say (Bereiter and Scardamalia 1987).

The distinction between knowledge telling and transforming resembles the distinction made by Cummins (1984) between social and academic uses of language (BICS and CALP). However, Bereiter and Scardamalia (1987) do not envision a direct relationship between writing purpose and process.

Although academic uses of language are more likely to involve the problem-solving, rethinking and restating involved in knowledge transforming, this may be closer to an ideal for academic writing than a minimum requirement. Knowledge transforming may not result in a product that will be judged more successful, nor is textual evidence conclusive with regard to which process of composing has been applied (Bereiter and Scardamalia 1987).

The knowledge-transforming approach to writing does not exclude knowledge telling, but rather subsumes it. Knowledge telling may be integrated with knowledge transformation where information is held to be unproblematic or may precede knowledge transformation in the form of an initial draft. Furthermore, with important implications for the ESAP/EGAP distinction, knowledge-transforming writers may be unable to transfer their skills across contexts. Unfamiliarity with either text type or topic may inhibit the operation of knowledge-transforming processes (Bereiter and Scardamalia 1987).

The strength of the Bereiter and Scardamalia (1987) models is that they are able to account for observed differences in composing processes and provide for testable hypotheses. Supporting evidence for the dual models is not limited to verbal protocols, but also comes from direct observation of writers and from the characteristics of texts written by novice and expert writers. In think-aloud protocols, novice writers report little goal setting, planning or problem solving. Brief start-up times for novice writers, revealed by observation, indicate a lack of planning time. Novice texts often meet basic structural requirements, but fail to fulfil functional aims, are not adapted to audience and lack internal coherence, all of which require a problem-solving approach.

Writing processes and L2 writers

The work of Flower and Hayes (1981, 1984) and Bereiter and Scardamalia (1987) in describing writing processes for L1 learners has been taken up by L2 researchers. Studies by Zamel (1982, 1983), Raimes (1985) and Jones and Tetroe (1987) found close similarities between L2 participants' composing strategies, whether observed or recalled, and those identified for L1 writers. There is evidence that L1 composing processes may transfer to L2, although L2 proficiency may inhibit such transfer, suggesting a threshold level below which L1 strategies cannot be deployed in L2 (Jones and Tetroe 1987, Grabe and Kaplan 1996).

There is also evidence from process research for the multidimensionality of writing skills. Some areas of writing ability appear to be largely independent of grammatical proficiency (Krapels 1990). Grammatical monitoring and correction of student work has been found to be less effective in improving the quality of the product than feedback on content and organisation (Raimes 1985, Radecki and Swales 1988, Fathman and Walley 1990).

Cognitive models of this kind, although based on L1 research, have had a powerful influence on L2 pedagogy and are associated with *process approaches* to writing instruction (Krapels 1990, Jordan 1997). Process approaches stress the importance of planning, multiple drafting and revising in text construction, which is seen as a recursive, non-linear process. They often involve students in collaborative activities such as conferencing and peer review and involve ongoing feedback from instructors, stressing content and expression over grammar and usage.

Drawbacks of the Bereiter and Scardamalia (1987) models of particular relevance to EAP include their failure to account for the interrelationship of the two models, or how writers progress from knowledge telling to knowledge transforming (Grabe and Kaplan 1996). Bereiter and Scardamalia suggest that features of the writing task (familiarity and complexity of content and genre) may cause writers to modify their strategies, but the theory does not allow for any mechanism for, or constraints on, model selection.

More fundamentally, the Bereiter and Scardamalia (1987) models fail to account for the social nature of writing. Restrictions imposed on processing by cultural values or power relationships are not explored. We must therefore look elsewhere – to functional linguistics, contrastive rhetoric and critical applied linguistics – to discover how far knowledge transforming, expectations of text structure and the status of topic knowledge are controlled by social factors.

Text description

There is a long tradition of research into the distinctive nature of academic text: the written *product*. This has identified features that are more frequently found in texts for academic audiences, written either by professionals or by students, and has raised questions in the matter of advice commonly given in style manuals and handbooks (Lea and Street 1999).

Early research in register analysis identified syntactic or lexical features occurring more frequently in published texts written for academic purposes (West 1953, Herbert 1965, Ewer and Hughes-Davies 1971). This work continues today in, for example, the word frequency lists generated by Xue and Nation (1983) and Coxhead (1998), but has been supplemented by the emergence of discourse analysis in the 1970s and 1980s (Coulthard and Sinclair

1975, Brown and Yule 1983) which allows for the investigation of patterning in text beyond the sentence level.

Attention to apparent differences in the structuring of texts across cultures, or *contrastive rhetoric*, has indicated a number of challenges that L2 learners of academic writing in English are likely to face in composing texts that will be positively evaluated by their subject teachers. Although questions have been raised as to whether the different features observed in learner text are caused by transfer from L1, or by the developmental process of learning to write in a second language (Mohan and Lo 1985), the implications for instruction are little affected. Knowledge of discourse features will help learners to understand and adapt to (or challenge) the expectations of their teachers.

Thompson (2001) follows Trzeciak (1996) in outlining four areas of contrastive rhetoric research of relevance to EAP learners. These are: macro-discoursal patterns, coherence and style, degrees of commitment and detachment, and the use and attribution of source material.

Macro-discoursal patterns

At the macro-discoursal level, researchers have discovered that writers from different language backgrounds tend to organise their text in different ways. In a study widely regarded as the foundation of contrastive rhetoric, Kaplan (1966) compared the introductions to 600 student essays and observed that learners from a variety of language backgrounds organised these according to distinctive patterns, which Kaplan represented in the form of diagrams.

In the wake of this discovery, a large body of research has grown up around the organisation of L1 and L2 English writing and that of texts written in other L1s. Hinds (1983, 1990), for example, suggested that Japanese writing follows rhetorical patterns derived from classical Chinese poetry. Discourse-level differences have been identified between L1 English texts and L2 English texts produced by L1 Japanese (Connor-Linton 1995, Kobayashi and Rinnert 1996, Sasaki and Hirose 1996), Chinese (Tsao 1983, Hinds 1990, Shi 2001) and Korean writers (Eggington 1987, Hinds 1990) among others.

Functional differences in how rhetorical units are used across languages have also been found. Hinds (1983) notes that Japanese essays often end with a question or an inconclusive statement that would not satisfy the expectations for a conclusion in English essays; Cmejrkova (1996) found that Czech writers of research articles tended not to follow the common pattern found in English of referring to principal findings and describing the structure of the article in their introductions.

Given the discrepancies observed in the composition of apparently similar text types in other languages and in English, the organisation of English academic texts is likely to pose problems for L2 writers.

Coherence and style

Academic style is said to involve more frequent use of passive forms, use of impersonal pronouns and phrases, qualifying words and phrases, complex sentences and specialised vocabulary. It typically involves less frequent use of contractions, phrasal verbs, colloquialisms, personal pronouns and vagueness in word choice (Biber 1988, Elbow 1991, Clanchy and Ballard 1992, Jordan 1997).

Academic style is linguistically demanding and it is difficult for L2 learners to achieve, with evidence of avoidance, misuse and overuse of features such as passives, expressions of personal opinion and contractions (Granger and Tyson 1996, Shaw and Liu 1998). Coherence and cohesion are a further source of difficulty, with learners overusing a limited range of connectors relative to L1 writers (Ventola and Mauranen 1991, Milton and Tsang 1993, Granger and Tyson 1996, Altenberg 1998).

Differences in academic writing styles across cultures may relate to culturally rooted expectations of the roles of reader and writer. Hinds (1987) suggests that Japanese is more *reader-responsible* than English. In other words, Japanese writing is less explicit than English and readers are expected to make a greater contribution to the generation of meaning. This distinction between reader-responsible and *writer-responsible* text, in which the writer gives more explicit guidance to the reader, has also been made for other languages such as Chinese (Reid 1990a) and Finnish (Mauranen 1993).

Degrees of commitment and detachment

Signalling degrees of commitment and detachment through devices such as vague or cautious language (*hedging*) has been identified as a distinctive feature of academic style in English (Selinker 1979, Hyland 1994) and this is said to be problematic for L2 writers (Makaya and Bloor 1987).

Also relating to questions of detachment, the writer's stance (neutral/objective or emotional/subjective) and propositional responsibility (the extent to which writers identify with, or distance themselves from propositions expressed in a text) have been identified as further areas of difficulty (Miyahara 1986, Clanchy and Ballard 1992, Jordan 1997, Groom 2000).

Use and attribution of source material

One area in which incompatibility between tutor and student expectations may lead to very severe consequences is that of plagiarism. Jordan (1997) observes that the extent of collaboration in learning accepted in some traditions may be interpreted as cheating in Western education. In addition to the sharing of ideas between learners, the relationship between the student writer and textual sources may be a source of difficulty for learners from traditions that do not share Western conceptions of textual authority and the individual ownership of intellectual property.

It has been remarked that traditional Western views of plagiarism are both simplistic and inconsistent (Cortazzi 1990, Bloch and Chi 1995, Scollon 1995, Pennycook 1996). Nonetheless, learners are expected to work through the confusing distinctions that are made between originality of thought and originality of word (Pennycook 1994).

Cammish (1997) suggests that plagiarism is often attributable to the fear of making mistakes in English. The pressures of a heavy workload and the need to use appropriate technical vocabulary, combined with a lack of confidence in their language ability and knowledge of the subject may lead learners to rely too heavily on source texts or peer support (Mohan and Lo 1985, Campbell 1990, Pennycook 1996, Currie 1998).

Two longitudinal studies of individual L2 learners making extensive use of textual 'borrowing' illustrate how plagiarism can be a response to cultural, linguistic and cognitive factors. Spack (1997) and Currie (1998) both found that their East Asian informants, rather than continuing to struggle to produce originally worded material in English in the face of poor grades, were using extensive copying from sources as an efficient method of producing assignments that would satisfy their tutors. In both cases, the learners adopted copying as an acceptable strategy to cope with the most cognitively demanding academic tasks, but eschewed copying on occasions when they felt more confident. For both learners, the strategy was rewarded with higher grades, without attracting sanctions from teachers.

Even where they avoid copying, L2 writers may experience difficulty in integrating sources into their texts. Thompson and Tribble (2001) found that learners were often unable to distinguish between the rhetorical function of different forms of citation and relied too heavily on a limited repertoire of devices. They may also have difficulty in adequately distinguishing between their own ideas and those of the sources they cite (Groom 2000).

Needs research in academic writing: task description

Needs analysis research

Pragmatically motivated needs analyses have approached textual description from a different angle. They investigate the tasks required of tertiary students and derive taxonomies of the types of writing tasks students will encounter.

A number of studies have explored, with increasing sophistication, the variety of writing tasks encountered by international students in universities in the UK, North America and Australasia and hence the types of texts learners are expected to produce. Methods of data collection have included faculty and student surveys (Ostler 1980, Bridgeman and Carlson 1983, Weir 1983, Leki and Carson 1994), the collection of corpora of academic writing tasks (Horowitz 1986a, Hale et al 1996, Moore and Morton 1999) and to a more limited extent, judgements applied to student-produced texts (Vann, Meyer and Lorenz 1984, Santos 1988). Much of this research has been associated with test development, particularly of the TOEFL test (Bridgeman and Carlson 1983, Hale et al 1996) and the Test of English for Educational Purposes (TEEP) (Weir 1983). The primary concern has been to identify the task types most often encountered at university, although attention is sometimes also paid to features of written text believed by participants to cause the greatest difficulties for L2 writers.

In their influential study, Bridgeman and Carlson (1983), contributing to the development of the TOEFL Test of Written English (TWE), surveyed faculties involved in undergraduate and postgraduate programmes in 190 academic departments in Canada and the USA, asking them to report on the types of writing task undertaken by their students. They found that, while the amount of writing required varied, students in all faculties were required to undertake some written work and that it was generally felt to be at least moderately important to academic success. Significant differences between native and non-native student writing were found for ratings of sentence-level skills, vocabulary knowledge and overall writing ability. Faculty assessment of student writing on the other hand was mostly concerned with discourse-level features, which were felt to be fairly similar between native and non-native writers.

Included with the questionnaires were 10 sample tasks. Faculties were asked to rate the task types according to how effectively they might elicit writing samples providing the information about a candidate required by the receiving department (Bridgeman and Carlson 1983). Two of the tasks most favoured by faculties were Type H: Describe and interpret a graph, chart etc., and Type E: comparison/contrast plus take a position. These were subsequently incorporated into the TWE (Waters 1996). It should be noted that these task types correspond closely to the IELTS Academic Module Writing Tasks 1 and 2.

While Bridgeman and Carlson (1983) found some common ground between disciplines, it was apparent that there were substantial differences in terms of the importance, frequency, volume and types of writing being demanded in different study contexts, a finding repeated in subsequent studies (Weir 1983, 1984, Horowitz 1986a, Moore and Morton 1999).

Horowitz (1986a) criticised research in the Bridgeman and Carlson (1983) tradition for a lack of empiricism: 1) in supplying preconceived categories, rather than categories based on tasks collected from the setting, and 2) in relying on questionnaire or interview data – asking faculties what tasks they set – rather than direct observation. In an attempt to address the perceived failings of the Bridgeman and Carlson methodology, Horowitz garnered tasks from the actual handouts in university lectures and then derived a classification scheme.

Both Waters (1996) and Moore and Morton (1999) point out, however, that this solution – to categorise a corpus of university writing tasks – simply transfers the burden of classification from the faculty to the researcher who brings a set of notions of what is salient in a task, which may or may not be identical with those of the task designer. Hence the discrepancies between Horowitz's (1986a) taxonomy of tasks and the corpus-driven Canesco and Byrd (1989) version, or the substantial disagreement between researchers employing the classification system of Hale et al (1996). Hartill (2000) points out the additional danger that the schema (Bartlett 1932), or formal and content expectations of what is meant by terms such as essay or paper may not be shared by researcher, academic department and student: words such as dissertation or term-paper have different meanings even within institutions.

So, relying on departmental descriptions of tasks is potentially just as misleading as using predefined categories. Nonetheless, Horowitz has proved influential in promoting the direct analysis of tasks, and his taxonomy has been taken up by other researchers examining the tasks required by faculties in other settings (Braine 1989, Casanave and Hubbard 1992, Jenkins, Jordan and Weil 1993).

Although the response to Horowitz's questionnaire was only 5% (38 faculties – apparently mostly in the social sciences – of 750 surveyed), raising serious concerns about representativeness, he was able to identify seven broad task types. Of these, the category *synthesis of multiple sources* proved to be the most popular, and occurred across a range of faculties (Horowitz 1986a), underlining the importance of writing from source material as a feature of academic writing across disciplines.

In drawing conclusions for pedagogy, Horowitz combines his seven categories into a description of the generalised academic writing task:

> Given a topic, topicless thesis statement or full thesis statement, an indication of the audience's expectations (in terms of what questions are to be covered and in what order they should be answered), specified sources of data, and a lexis constrained, to some extent, by all of the above, find data which are relevant to each question and then reorganise and encode those data in such a way that the reader's expectations of relevance, coherence and etiquette are fulfilled (Horowitz 1986a: 455).

He uses this generic task as the basis for recommendations for a genre-based teaching approach. He favours the grouping of students with shared or similar majors in order to simulate the subject classroom, and in order to practise the constituent skills of academic information processing that include:

1. Selecting data, which is relevant to the question or issue from a source or sources.
2. Reorganising that data in response to the given question or issue.
3. Encoding that data into academic English (Horowitz 1986a: 455).

Horowitz argues that maximum transferability (Horowitz 1986a, 1986b) of taught skills will be achieved if teachers understand the information processing burdens imposed by academic writing tasks, and set out to simulate these in the classroom. Transferability in teaching contexts would, of course, equally imply generalisability in testing tasks.

Research of the type illustrated by Bridgeman and Carlson (1983) and Horowitz (1986a), notwithstanding the difficulties of task description, has proved successful in describing the variety of writing tasks demanded at university. However, it has had relatively little to say about tutors' and students' assumptions concerning written work and the standards for assessment applied to it. Task description tells us even less about the composing processes engaged in by student writers.

Academic writing as socialisation

The relative merits of formal (product) and process-based approaches have been a major issue in EAP pedagogy. Weaknesses of the two approaches identified by opponents may be summarised briefly as follows. Product-based approaches risk reducing writing instruction to the provision of simple, formulaic templates for composition, encouraging conformity and reifying current practices (Widdowson 1983, Benesch 1996). Process approaches, on the other hand, have been associated with an asocial, romantic view of writing as a creative process, neglecting its social character and failing to acknowledge the distinctive formal conventions of academic writing (Horowitz 1986a).

As is now widely recognised, there is no fundamental incompatibility between product and process approaches (Bamforth 1992, Silva 1993), rather they may be viewed as complementary. The Bereiter and Scardamalia (1987) models include knowledge of genre as a necessary component and there is no denial of cognitive process in genre descriptions. For Grabe and Kaplan (1996) the theories have coalesced into a *socio-cognitive* paradigm (Flower 1994); the instructional implications being that students are to be initiated into discourse communities through exposure to genres, but that the development of writing skills is cognitive, prioritising self-reflection over imitation.

Inherent, although to varying degrees and with varying implications, in socio-cognitive views of writing is a consideration of the relationship between text and participants: the writer and the reader as actors within a given social space. The interactionist (Johns 1990) views writing as not only expressive of, but also constitutive of power relationships. This analysis may be traced to Marxist theory (Gramsci 1971, Volosinov 1973, Bakhtin 1981), and to the sociology of Bourdieu (1991). It is also expressed through recent work in the sociology of science (Bazerman 1988, Geisler 1994, Berkenkotter and Huckin 1995), drawing on the social-constructionist work of Kuhn (1970) in which social realities, and hence genres, are co-constructed and supported by communities of individuals with common interests (Johns 1990).

These writers show that both register and genre in scientific texts are informed by a set of underlying assumptions about what constitutes knowledge within a disciplinary culture. All scientific writing both reinforces and redefines topic knowledge – what is known – and how knowledge is to be communicated – the nature of scientific writing (Grabe and Kaplan 1996).

In common with the cognitive psychologist, although for very different reasons, the social-constructionist does not consider texts in isolation (Myers 1988), but weighs the historical and social forces shaping the writer's conception of a writing task. Communicative purpose is not always explicit and recoverable from text, but may be covert, camouflaged by genre requirements (Myers 1999).

Longitudinal research into student writing

The acquisition of academic writing is perceived not only as the mastery of certain instrumental skills, but also as a process of acculturation. In line with this view, there have been attempts to define elements of culture of relevance to EAP. Flowerdew and Miller (1995) distinguish four levels: ethnic, local, academic and disciplinary. Ethnic culture is social and psychological, while local culture involves knowledge of a local setting. Academic culture involves institutional values, assumptions and expectations while disciplinary culture refers to the theories, concepts, norms and terms of a particular culture with which lecturers working in the field are familiar and students, as apprentices, by definition, are not (Flowerdew and Peacock 2001b).

In their *cultural synergy model*, Cortazzi and Jin (1997) approach the difficulties of international students from a different perspective. They describe three forms of *cultural distance* affecting academic language use: *social distance, psychological distance* and *academic distance*. Social distance includes racism, knowledge of other societies, cultural orientation and cultural congruence; psychological distance involves culture shock, language shock (attitudes to language learning, confidence), identity maintenance, financial anxiety and character attribution of other societies; academic distance refers to academic orientation (active/passive participation, independence/dependence), tutor–student relationships, academic language use (discourse patterns, referencing, turn-taking) and academic culture shock (motivation for study, knowledge of education systems).

While these models have not been validated empirically, they do provide a framework for understanding difficulties that international students can face in addition to issues of lexico-grammatical language proficiency. An alternative approach to needs analysis has grown up in response to the growth of socio-cognitive perspectives on writing. This involves a greater attention to learning processes and individual experience with an emphasis on qualitative case study or ethnographic research techniques. Objects of enquiry include how students engage with writing tasks and how teachers evaluate student text. This research is reviewed under the categories proposed by Cortazzi and Jin (1997) of psychological distance, social distance and academic distance.

Psychological distance

Longitudinal studies and introspective reports written by students reveal that acquiring competence in academic writing in a second culture requires sometimes profound psychological adjustment. It is notable that such adjustment is not confined to L2 writers, but is shared by other 'outsiders' (Bizzell 1987); those who, for reasons of race or class, are traditionally excluded from academic communities.

Accounts of the psychological distance students may have to traverse to enter the academic discourse community are provided by Canagarajah (2001) and Shen (1998). Shen describes developing an English identity in her academic writing to complement her Chinese identity, a necessary process in meeting the conflicting demands of her culturally rooted beliefs about learning and the alien academic culture, each being associated with competing constructs of what is natural in discourse. Canagarajah (2001), in a longitudinal study of students at a university in Sri Lanka, describes how one outsider student writer engages with academic discourse. She regards the tension between discourses as a force for creativity, lending the writer a critical voice.

A point often made in the literature is that questions of cultural difference do not conform to a strict L1/L2 distinction and that there is no deterministic relationship between first culture and beliefs about learning (Brew 1980). Resembling Shen (1998), a Chinese student engaging with writing in a new culture, Mellix (1998) writes of the tremendous emotional and psychological conflict involved in mastering academic discourse. However, Mellix writes, not as an international student, but as a black woman in the United States. Turner (1999) suggests that the distinction between so-called native and non-native speakers of English is evolving into a continuum, redirecting attention to the cultural rather than linguistic specificity of higher education and its associated values.

Social distance

Leki and Carson (1994) and Imber and Parker (1999) argue for the inclusion of learner beliefs in needs analysis procedures, on the basis that what learners believe about what they are learning, and about how they need to learn, strongly influences their receptiveness to learning (Leki and Carson 1994). Learner perspectives can reveal areas of need obscured in faculty surveys or task descriptions. Imber and Parker (1999) found that their informants (Asian graduate engineering students in the USA) felt that they lacked social speaking skills and tended, like the non-European students in Blue and Archibald's (1999) study, to be isolated from social interaction in English.

Harris and Thorp (1999) describe the learning experiences of ethnic minority students at a catering college in London, finding that, beyond the overt racism of some instructors, different cultural expectations amongst students and staff about such aspects of university life as roles, social distance, duties, rights and obligations seriously affected students' learning. The researchers note similarities with Kinnell's (1990) study of overseas students and conclude that EAP cannot be seen as a set of technical skills in isolation, but rather is a blend of language, culture and affect.

Academic distance

Leki and Carson (1994) asked students to rate EAP writing skills. They found that task management strategies – including, managing text (e.g. brainstorming, planning, outlining, drafting, revising, proof-reading), managing sources (e.g. summarising, synthesising, reading, using quotes), and managing research (e.g. library skills, research skills) – were considered to be of greatest assistance in content classes and to contribute most to success. On the other hand, echoing Bridgeman and Carlson's (1983) and Leki's (1995) findings regarding lacks, students felt that their EAP classes had failed sufficiently to develop their grammar and vocabulary skills.

Research into the social processes by which students are inducted into discourse communities has tended to reject the division of reading and writing skills, and argues for treating these as inextricably related in the acquisition of academic literacy in L2. Benson (1991) used an ethnographic approach to questions of cultural difference in EAP literacy with respect to content and text type. In a case study of one EAP reader, 'Hamad', he observed which types of text the student encountered and how he integrated the reading into his learning.

Benson (1991) concluded that extensive reading must take a central position in EAP provision not only because it requires a particular set of skills (he cites reading for general information and maintaining concentration), but also because it can initiate students into Western academic modes of thought. Extensive reading provides examples of how expert writers use sources of authority (such as statistical data or texts produced by other writers).

Finally, Benson (1991) suggests, reading for comprehension is qualitatively distinct from reading for learning, the latter involving the integration of new information into existing schemata. Hamad, in his academic work, applied the ideas from his reading to familiar situations to draw conclusions. For this reason, Benson advocates content courses as a means of promoting EAP literacy and intertextuality skills.

More recent constructivist studies have questioned the generalisability of the academic literacy construct. Superficial similarities in the tasks required of students may mask fundamental differences of purpose. Academic disciplines, with divergent ontologies, make quite different assumptions about the nature and purposes of writing (Biglan 1973, Becher 1989, Lewis and Starks 1997, Candlin and Plum 1999, Clarke and Saunders 1999, Creme and Lea 1999).

In this research, the discourse community is revealed, not so much as a stable community of like-minded peers as a site of conflict and contradiction (Harris 1989). Starfield (2001) describes the power relations apparently underlying assessment decisions at a South African university. Clarke and Saunders (1999) and Candlin and Plum (1999) describe some of the problems caused for students in adapting to different expectations when they switch between disciplines on modular courses. Creme and Lea (1999) offer a list of the divergent criteria applied by academic staff in a range of disciplines in judging the quality of an essay.

Expectations may also vary between educational levels. Entering a university from secondary school or advancing from undergraduate to postgraduate study involves a form of academic culture shock as learners face different expectations (for knowledge transforming rather than knowledge telling). Brew (1980) remarks that overseas students entering five Open University courses from colleges of Further Education appeared to be disadvantaged, raising the possibility that study practices that had brought success in Further Education could not readily be transferred to the university.

For Clarke and Saunders (1999), adapting to the expectations of disciplinary writing imposes a *double burden* on international students as they are not only faced with multiple academic discourses, but also bring their own expectations and values based in different national educational cultures which may conflict with the expectations both of their teachers and of their fellow students.

Educational experiences in other societies may lead students to harbour false expectations of the British university. Turner (1999) notes that students from some cultures expect more support from their lecturers than is usually forthcoming in the Western university, perhaps underestimating the cultural value attached to the notion of independent study and hence independence of choice (Turner 1999). Bloor and Bloor's (1991) survey of 48 non-native speaker (NNS) students at the University of Warwick revealed discrepancies between students' expectations and those of the institution; 50% of students had expected to be assessed only through examinations (and for these to be objective tests) rather than the written assignments in fact required in all courses. In a similar study, Jordan (1993) describes questionnaire responses from 82 postgraduate pre-sessional students, which indicated that many lacked study-skills training in their own language and had no experience of finding books in libraries. A majority expected subject tutors to tell them precisely what to read, to correct their mistakes in written English and to meet with them more than once a week; expectations Jordan claims are likely to be disappointed in the British university.

Where a student's previous experience of using English has been in an EFL setting, with attention given to form over content, expectations regarding English language requirements may also play an inhibiting role, preventing students from focusing on their subject in their written work. One of Zamel's (1998) informants, an English Department instructor, observed that a student was apparently fixated on surface form, but that once he stopped being so concerned about this became a better writer. However, the difficulties experienced by this student could, perhaps, be attributed to the kinds of cultural misapprehensions described by Ballard and Clanchy (1991), given the tendency they describe for subject instructors and students to collude in attributing culturally rooted writing problems to linguistic inadequacies. On the other hand, Brew (1980) suspects that students are embarrassed to confess to linguistic difficulties and instead ascribe these to the volume of reading demanded or a lack of background knowledge.

It has been suggested that the process of acculturation is too often assumed to be unidirectional. International students are expected to adjust to the host institution. Following Bizzell (1987), critical applied linguists have begun to question the *pragmatism* (Pennycook 1996) of EAP teaching on the grounds that it requires learners to adapt to the institutional requirements of the university, without demanding that the university become more inclusive and accommodating to its members and to recognise the value of the experiences they may bring with them (Benesch 1996, Pennycook 1996). Starfield (2001) for example, criticises Casanave (1995) for failing to observe – in her ethnographic needs analysis study of a sociology programme – how the discursive practices of this community made inclusion relatively easy for some and exclusion likely for others.

Conclusions: the nature of academic writing in English

In sum academic writing in English (in the tradition of Aristotelian rhetoric most typically encountered in the UK) may be described in the following broad terms.

Academic writing is the pre-eminent means for the assessment of student learning outcomes in Higher Education. It is based on (and may be limited to) *specified external sources of data* and is typically, perhaps paradigmatically, displayed through the *essay* or related genres involving the marshalling of evidence to indicate or test a conclusion or set of conclusions. This may involve *induction, abstraction, deduction* and *generalisation from given knowledge to new situations* (Biggs and Collis 1982).

Topic understanding is both built and assessed through the process of academic writing. The *selection, reorganisation, analysis, synthesis* and *evaluation of data* (Bloom 1956) constitute both writing processes and learning processes (writing to learn).

Academic writing is constrained by expectations of:

* text length
* comprehensibility and coherence
* technical vocabulary use
* formal register
* textual organisation.

Successful (positively evaluated) academic writing is said to be based on a common understanding of *terminology, assumptions, issues, modes of argument*, and *legitimate evidence* (National Committee of Enquiry into Higher Education 1997) between student and assessor in a given discipline. However, understandings of the legitimacy of objects and/or methods of inquiry may not readily generalise across disciplines.

Successful (positively evaluated) academic writing in non-timed settings typically involves recursive processes of *drafting, editing* and *reformulation*.

Judgements applied to academic writing principally concern *topic knowledge and understanding, relevance to task set, coherence* and due *observation of* discourse domain *conventions*.

Overlap between L2 academic writing theory and academic writing as operationalised in the IELTS AWM

Language testing: socio-cognitive models of academic writing

A *direct* test of writing (a test of writing which requires the test taker to produce an extended piece of writing) is a form of performance test: a test that involves either observing activities in the real world or observing activities in a simulation based on real life (Weigle 2002). This contrasts with *indirect* tests which might assess writing ability through multiple-choice grammar items.

The use of performance tests for the assessment of language ability reflects the belief that *knowledge about* language, which might be accessed by indirect tests, is not a sufficient basis for predictions about a candidate's *use* of language to accomplish tasks outside the classroom or the examination room. Since the 1970s, efforts have been underway to develop models of language ability that represent both knowledge about language and the ability to put language resources to use to accomplish specified tasks (notably by Hymes 1972, Canale and Swain 1980, Bachman 1990, Bachman and Palmer 1996).

McNamara (1996) criticises these models for their inadequate conception of *ability for use*, in Widdowson's phrase, or what people are actually able to do with their language abilities (Widdowson 1989). McNamara suggests that the consideration of cognitive variables and performance conditions already accounted for in models of communicative language ability must be supplemented by attention to the social variables involved in communication such as the relationship between the speaker and interlocutor in spoken communication, or between writer and reader in written.

Hamp-Lyons (1990), proposes that four components need to be considered in the validation of writing tests: the task, the writer, the scoring procedure, and the reader(s), but McNamara (1996), like Kenyon (1995) and Skehan (1998), sketches a somewhat more complex model of interaction. In this model he outlines factors that, in combination with the physical conditions under which performance occurs – and, as Weigle (2002) adds, the institutional and wider social context within which a test is used – will impact on proficiency as realised in the test score or rating.

In addition to the four components suggested by Hamp-Lyons, McNamara (1996) includes as a separate element, the test candidate's performance: the text he or she produces in response to the task. It is also helpful to conceive of the reader in Hamp-Lyons' (1990) framework in relation to two quite different roles accounted for by the McNamara model. Firstly, a text is usually intended for a (more or less explicitly) defined audience or addressee. Secondly, performance may be judged by a rater (who may or may not also be the intended addressee of the text). The rater applies criteria in judging the text, perhaps in accordance with a defined rating scale. As all elements in the model are interrelated, changes to any one of them may affect the judgement made by the rater (the rating) and hence the test score that is awarded. The following section describes the design features of the IELTS AWM in terms of this extended version of McNamara's (1996) model. Relevant research on the IELTS and similar tests will be reviewed and the possible implications of the test design for washback are delineated.

Target candidature

The IELTS Academic Modules are intended to 'assess whether a candidate is ready to study or train in the medium of English at undergraduate or post-graduate level' (IELTS 2005: 2). However, figures from the IELTS partners published in the *IELTS Annual Review* show that the uses made of the test are not always limited to these purposes. One alternative use made of the Academic Modules is to inform professional recognition decisions by bodies such as the UK's General Medical Council. As a result a proportion of candidates are not intending to enter university after taking the test. If learners do not share an academic purpose beyond the test, course providers may be less inclined to integrate IELTS preparation with EAP instruction directed beyond the test towards academic language use.

Task characteristics

Research into the characteristics of EAP writing tasks, described on pp. 39–43 in this chapter, has provided increasingly elaborate frameworks for task description. Weigle (2002) synthesises earlier frameworks produced by Purves (1984) and Hale et al (1996) (Table 2.1).

Table 2.1 Dimensions of tasks for direct writing assessment (from Weigle 2002: 63)

Dimension	Examples
Subject matter	self, family, school, technology, etc.
Stimulus	text, multiple texts, graph, table
Genre	essay, letter, informal note, advertisement
Rhetorical task	narration, description, exposition, argument
Pattern of exposition	process, comparison/contrast, cause/effect, classification, definition
Cognitive demands	reproduce facts/ideas, organise/reorganise information, apply/analyse/synthesise/evaluate
Specification of:	
• audience	• self, teacher, classmates, general public
• role	• self/detached observer, other/assumed persona
• tone, style	• formal, informal
Length	less than half-page, half to 1 page, 2–5 pages
Time allowed	less than 30 minutes, 30–59 minutes, 1–2 hours
Prompt wording	question vs statement, implicit vs explicit, amount of context provided
Choice of prompts	choice vs no choice
Transcription mode	handwritten vs word-processed
Scoring criteria	primarily content and organisation; primarily linguistic accuracy; unspecified

Performance conditions: length and time allowed

The IELTS AWM specifies that candidates should complete two tasks within 60 minutes (the task instructions advise them to spend 20 minutes on Task 1 and 40 minutes on Task 2). Candidates are advised to write at least 150 words for Task 1 and 250 words for Task 2. The *IELTS Handbook* (IELTS 2005) states that scripts under the required minimum word limit will be penalised.

Banerjee (2000) notes that the writing samples obtained through the IELTS AWM are comparatively short, and may not therefore show how far a test taker could produce coherent, appropriate and accurate texts of the length of a normal academic assignment. Preparation for the test might be expected to focus on the production of short texts and to neglect distinctive features of lengthier text.

Timed writing tests, because of the constraints they place on the interaction between writer and reader (and on the role of writer-as-reader), are said to be poorly suited to the assessment of the process of writing (Hamp-Lyons and Kroll 1997). It is the written product that is scored, and this provides scant evidence of how the text was composed.

For this reason it has been claimed that the IELTS AWM writing tasks may discourage process approaches. Cresswell (2000) compares process approaches to writing to the timed writing test; in class, students engage in pre-writing activities, plan and draft their essays, request feedback and revise the emerging text. In a test, in contrast, students are segregated from each other and engage, silently, in writing an impromptu timed essay. To the extent that preparation for the IELTS AWM encourages test-like activities, participants may seek to learn as much as possible about managing the time limits imposed by the test and may overlook the revision and reshaping of text.

Subject matter and stimulus

The subject matter of the IELTS AWM was described in the following terms in the *IELTS Handbook*: 'Texts have been written for a non-specialist audience. All the topics are of general interest. They deal with issues which are interesting, recognisably appropriate and accessible to candidates entering undergraduate or postgraduate courses' (IELTS 2005). The general nature of the tasks implies a decisively EGAP approach to instruction, excluding content related to a specific academic discipline.

In conception, the precursor of the IELTS, the ELTS test, was a test of English for Specific Academic Purposes (ESAP). Both test content and method were derived from an analysis of a (hypothetical) specific language use situation. The test construct was based on a quasi-Munbian (Munby 1978) needs analysis undertaken by Carroll (1981), although this was criticised for failing to follow Munby's empirical data gathering methods (Alderson 1981).

In development of the IELTS, the Munbian model was rejected because it had proved inadequate as a basis for developing test item specifications (Weir 1983, Alderson and Clapham 1992). Instead, in a reverse of the Munbian approach, teams of item writers developed sets of specifications, which were distributed to stakeholders for comment and revision (Alderson and Clapham 1992). However, in the absence of an alternative, the underlying construct of the IELTS remained, as Hamp-Lyons (1991) described it: there was a division of the language proficiency of students into *general proficiency* and *study proficiency* and study proficiency was further divided into different proficiencies for different disciplinary areas.

Despite the reduction of subject-specific modules from five to three in 1989, the question of subject specificity raised by Hamp-Lyons (1987, 1991) proved as problematic for IELTS, as it had for its predecessor. Research by Clapham (1996) into the role of background knowledge in reading comprehension found that although topic knowledge could be seen to affect comprehension in some circumstances, there was no clear fit between general discipline areas and the kinds of background knowledge that could be assumed. Administratively it was often unclear which of the subject modules an individual candidate should take and whether the choice should relate to prior experience or future intentions. Partly on this basis, and in the context of growing numbers of undergraduate applicants taking IELTS, the test was revised in 1995 and the provision of subject-specific modules discontinued (it being assumed that undergraduates, a growing proportion of the test-taking population, have more general language learning needs) (see Charge and Taylor 1997).

The retreat from subject specificity and the ending of the link between the Reading and Writing Modules, which took place at the same time, represents a decisive move towards EGAP and away from ESAP. Although Davies (2001) considers that the revision strikes a better balance between specificity and generality of purpose, Blue (2000) and others (Nettle 1997, Wallace 1997) have expressed concern at the removal of the optional link between the Reading and Writing components. Moore and Morton (1999) contrast the IELTS Task 2 requirement that test takers use *prior knowledge* as a source of information – personal ideas, knowledge and experience – with the observation from faculty informants that the only valid opinions in university writing are those based on reading and research.

Like Moore and Morton (1999), Nettle (1997) and Wallace (1997), suggest that the ending of the reading–writing link will reduce attention to the use of sources in academic writing in IELTS preparation courses. Blue (2000) suspects that incompatibility between the level of specificity preferred in EAP teaching and the generality of the revised IELTS may result in a negative washback effect on instruction.

On the other hand, although the revisions of IELTS, rejecting subject specificity and the reading–writing link, appear to have been driven primarily by practical concerns (Charge and Taylor 1997), language testers have begun to question the theoretical assumption that EAP tests should be based on specific purpose language use domains. The debate can be traced back to discussions surrounding the proposals for the Business and Social Science module of IELTS (Coleman 1991).

In defending the draft specifications, Coleman draws a distinction between the linguistic and cultural challenges involved in functioning in an alien academic system (Coleman 1991). The specifications simulate an academic writing task, requiring students to read extensively (including irrelevant material), and synthesise the information in their essays. Scoring would employ the SOLO (Structure of Observed Learning Outcomes) taxonomy (Biggs and Collis 1982) designed for use by academic staff in evaluating the quality of learning.

For Coleman (1991) the test, because of its supposed authenticity, would almost certainly have a very important and beneficial washback effect. The more closely the test tasks parallel real academic tasks, the more likely it will be that test preparation will resemble preparation for the activities that candidates will have to engage in once they have entered their academic courses.

The proposals were rejected by the reviewing stakeholders on the grounds that they confounded future conditions with pre-entry status; the tasks were too difficult and would be better suited to students who had already started on a course and who had learned the appropriate study skills (Clapham 1997). It would be unfair to demand that NNS applicants should display an awareness of academic discourse that is not required of their native-speaker (NS) counterparts (Waters 1996, Clapham 2000).

Fulcher (1999) is also concerned by problems of construct definition in EAP tests and the disagreement between expert judges on what constitutes the content of academic English. He believes that IELTS remains committed to an assumption that there should be a direct link between the content of academic courses and the content of an EAP test and cites what he describes as mounting evidence of the inadequacy of this assumption as a basis for the interpretation of test results. This evidence largely consists of the failure of research to justify subject-specific modules (Weir 1983, Hamp-Lyons 1987, Clapham 1996) and the unexpectedly high correlations found between ESAP tests and those aiming at an underlying linguistic competence through grammar and lexis: the draft IELTS grammar subtest (Alderson 1993), for example.

Davies (2001) agrees with Fulcher (1999) that the language-for-specific-purposes (LSP) construct underpinning the IELTS has proved untenable. Nevertheless, he argues for the retention of a specific purpose approach to test construction on the grounds that, while such tests have not been demonstrated to be of any greater validity than general proficiency tests, they have not proved to be any less valid either and, in view of their supposed positive washback, the approach is worth maintaining.

Fulcher (1999) takes a more radical view, arguing that LSP tests can no longer be justified. However, he acknowledges Davies' arguments to the extent that he envisages the inclusion of academic *settings* in the tests of English through Academic Contexts (EAC) that he believes will come to replace EAP tests. He proposes that academic settings should be included for washback purposes, suggesting that a positive washback effect can be achieved by incorporating academic content without seeking to measure EAP *knowledge*. Fulcher argues that the surface features of a test including the title and labels of subtests may have a significant washback effect upon what teachers do in classrooms.

This implies a radical reinterpretation of the concept of washback. Messick (1996) sets out the hitherto widely accepted view that, for optimal positive washback there should be little if any difference between activities involved in learning the language and activities involved in preparing for the test. For Fulcher (1999) and Clapham (2000), however, positive washback is in tension with construct validity; students who learn study skills and the discourse conventions of their intended subject will be better placed to succeed, but it would be inequitable to require that all applicants display these skills before entry to the university. For Clapham and Fulcher washback is to be achieved by a kind of sleight of hand; learners will be hoodwinked by the appearance of academic titles and content into pursuing EAP skills, although these will not be a focus of measurement in an EAC test.

The utility, if not the validity, of IELTS as a test of EAP may thus rest not only on its value in predicting the degree of language-related difficulty that students are likely to face in their academic studies, but also on the degree to which it encourages students to develop skills of relevance to the academic domain, whether directly, by measuring these skills, or indirectly, through the inclusion of features that encourage teachers and learners in the belief that these skills will help them to succeed.

A further objection concerns the representativeness of the range and types of tasks undertaken in the IELTS AWM. Two timed Writing tasks cannot adequately reflect the range of writing activities typically required in academic study. This is a point often made by advocates of portfolio assessment (Belanoff and Dickson 1991, Cresswell 2000, Brindley and Ross 2001) which allows for compilation of a wider range of text types than a timed essay test. The limited range of tasks is likely to be reflected in the choices made in test preparation courses.

Genre, rhetorical task and pattern of exposition

Not only has the range of the IELTS AWM tasks been called into question, but also their authenticity as representative academic writing tasks. Working in the tradition of task description for needs analysis, and adapting the framework used by Hale et al (1996), Moore and Morton (1999) carried out an investigation into the tasks required of university students in Australia in order to evaluate the IELTS AWM Task 2. Comparing typical Task 2 prompts (sourced from sample tests and practice materials) with a corpus of university writing assignments, they found broad similarities between this task and the most common university genre, the essay.

Moore and Morton (1999) observed that IELTS tasks called for a relatively restricted range of rhetorical functions: most (70%) included a very infrequent function among the university tasks (occurring in 15%), *hortation*, involving judgements about the desirability of given phenomena such as actions or states of affairs. Where university essays were typically concerned with abstract, *metaphenomenal* objects of enquiry (theories, ideas, methods), the IELTS tasks investigated more typically involved concrete, *phenomenal* entities (situations, actions, practices).

Moore and Morton (1999) spell out the implications of their findings for washback, concluding that the implicit Task 2 curriculum is narrow. The task implies a number of important features of academic writing – including structuring paragraphs, writing coherently and arguing a case – other key areas are unlikely to attract coverage in test preparation – especially linguistic and cognitive skills associated with integrating other writers' ideas. The authors also point to restrictions on the range of genres likely to be encountered in IELTS preparation.

To improve the supposed effects on instruction, Moore and Morton (1999) advocate restoration of the (pre-1995) thematic link between the Reading and Writing test modules and the option to refer to a Reading passage in the Writing test. They also suggest elicitation of a wider range of rhetorical functions and the inclusion of attributed propositions (e.g. *some psychologists argue*) to encourage a more academic, *metaphenomenal* style of response. For a response to these recommendations from the perspective of the IELTS partners see Taylor (2007).

Cognitive demands

Task 1 of the IELTS AWM calls on candidates to transfer information from a diagram or graph to a written text. According to the *IELTS Handbook*, this task may require candidates to 'organise, present and possibly compare data; describe the stages of a process or procedure; describe an object or event or sequence of events; explain how something works' (IELTS 2005). The task appears to be straightforwardly a knowledge-telling exercise. Candidates are called on to select and reorganise data, but not to evaluate them.

Task 2 calls on prior knowledge in the construction of an argument. According to the *IELTS Handbook* (IELTS 2005: 8), this task requires candidates to 'present the solution to a problem; present and justify an opinion; compare and contrast evidence, opinions and implications; evaluate and challenge ideas, evidence or an argument'. The task requires integration of the task prompt with the candidate's comprehension and internal representation of the topic.

However, there is little opportunity for knowledge-transformation, given the limitations on the time available and on the sources of input. What is required by the task is precisely that the writer will be able to start work immediately and then quickly produce an essay that addresses the topic and that conforms to expectations of the type of text called for by the task instructions (Bereiter and Scardamalia 1987). In other words, the writing process required for successful completion of the task is primarily knowledge telling rather than knowledge transforming.

Hamp-Lyons and Kroll (1997) suggest that impromptu tasks of this type will access linguistic and rehearsed genre competence, but may fail to engage additional discourse, sociolinguistic and metacognitive abilities of relevance to academic language use. Success on the test is likely to indicate that the writer has good control of grammar and vocabulary and is able to organise ideas within a template or *model text*. However, such tasks may provide little information about the writer's ability to work within genres other than the five-paragraph essay, or to shape texts to meet the demands of academic addressees within the university context.

Mickan and Slater (2003) provide some empirical support for this position in relation to the IELTS AWM. The researchers interviewed L1 and L2 writers as they tackled an IELTS AWM Task 2. They found that time constraints and anxiety added to the complexity of text production. Candidates who could quickly identify the topic and purpose underlying the task prompt would have more time available for composing their response.

Participants in search of success on the test might focus on building knowledge of the kind of text expected by the examiners; on building a template for composing IELTS texts. On the other hand, Mickan and Slater (2003) argue that the type of text expected in Task 2 – which they identify after Gerot and Wignell (1994) as *analytical exposition* – is not sufficiently clearly specified in the task instructions and the *IELTS Handbook*. If participants do not appreciate what kind of text is called for, they are unlikely to be able to meet the rhetorical expectations implied or to work towards developing an adequate template for text construction.

Both Mickan and Slater (2003) and Thorp and Kennedy (2003) have found that IELTS responses written by non-native speakers, even those awarded high scores, may lack the features of well-developed writing such as transparent organisation, academic objectivity and impersonal voice. Thorp and Kennedy describe IELTS Task 2 essays awarded a band score of eight as having rather the tone of letters to a newspaper editor than academic essays.

The addressee

Reflecting the understanding of the importance of audience and communicative purpose in functional grammar and discourse analysis, both IELTS AWM tasks at the time of the study provided the writer with an imaginary addressee. In Task 1 this was 'a university lecturer' and in Task 2 'an educated reader with no specialist knowledge'. The specification of audience has subsequently been removed from the task rubrics for reasons outlined below.

Douglas (2000) considers IELTS AWM Task 1 (Write a report for a university lecturer describing the information given below) to be a reasonably authentic academic task. He is pleased that a putative audience is specified in the task rubric. However, the imaginary 'lecturer' may also serve to confuse participants. It is not made clear whether the tasks are to be evaluated in the manner of the imaginary 'university lecturer' and 'educated reader' to whom the text is supposedly addressed – and who might be expected to prioritise content and organisation over grammar (Weir 1993) – or in the manner of an English language teacher, perhaps with opposing priorities.

Although it may be objected that there is no reason for students (particularly undergraduates) who are yet to enter university to be aware of the kinds of text a university lecturer would expect (Clapham 2000), it is possible that specifying a lecturer as the addressee of Task 1 will encourage attention to the expectations of academic staff in preparation courses. On the other hand, participants may be aware that the rater responsible for scoring the script will probably be an English language teacher. As a result, participants may be more interested in learning about the criteria to be applied by the rater than those more typically applied by academic staff.

Raters

Language testing handbooks advocate that, in order to ensure reliability, at least two ratings should be obtained for each writing sample (Weir 1993, Bachman and Palmer 1996, Hughes 2003). However, for practical and financial reasons (Alderson and Clapham 1992) the IELTS employs a single rater for each script (the same marker scoring both tasks), supplemented by a second rater in cases of *jagged profiles* where writing scores are inconsistent with other parts of the test.

The IELTS test partners have been criticised, particularly in America, for failing to publish sufficient evidence of reliability (Grabe and Kaplan 1996). The partners have responded by placing more information, including reliability estimates, on the IELTS website (www.ielts.org). An inter-rater correlation for such paired sample (double rated) scripts reported by Cambridge ESOL at the time of the study was .85 (Taylor 2002). In addition, a number of procedures are in place to assure the quality of test scores. Chalhoub-Deville and Turner (2000) observe that IELTS raters are trained and recertified every two years, that writing scripts are re-rated when there is an inconsistency in the profile of the scores and that centres are regularly monitored. Although Chalhoub-Deville and Turner describe the training, certification and monitoring procedures as reassuring, others (McNamara and Lumley 1995 for example) contend that re-certification can be no substitute for multiple rating.

If, in spite of the procedures employed by Cambridge ESOL, participants lack faith in the reliability of the test, any washback effect may be moderated. If participants come to attribute scores on a test to chance, rather than effort, they are less likely to devote resources to passing – an effect remarked by Watanabe (2004) in relation to poorly designed multiple-choice items in Japanese university entrance tests.

Hamp-Lyons and Zhang (2001) show that cultural differences might account for some of the variation in scores between raters. In their study, L1 English and L1 Chinese teachers of English rated essays differently, being affected by the (culturally mediated) rhetorical structures of the texts and ideologies expressed by the writers. Hinkel (1994) and Kobayashi and Rinnert (1996) have made similar findings. This raises questions regarding the fairness of ratings obtained across cultures.

As IELTS is locally scored by test centre staff, any systematic variation between raters from different backgrounds, or between raters with different levels of exposure to local rhetorical norms, could lead test takers to seek out the test location where they might hope to receive the most generous marks.

Rating scales and criteria

The IELTS AWM is rated on a nine-band scale against task-specific criteria. These criteria were updated in 2005 since the study was completed and the updated scales are now made available on the IELTS website (www.ielts.org). On the scales in use at the time (first developed in 1995), there were three criteria for each task (see Appendix 8). Details of the scales used by raters were not disclosed, but the criteria themselves were published in the *IELTS Handbook*. These criteria are reproduced in Appendix 8. Task 1 was rated for *Task Fulfilment, Coherence and Cohesion and Vocabulary* and *Sentence Structure*. Task 2 was rated for *Arguments, Ideas and Evidence, Communicative Quality* and *Vocabulary and Sentence Structure*.

The washback model suggests that these features would be given particular attention in preparation classrooms, to the extent that they were understood by teachers and learners (Mickan and Slater 2003) and to the extent that they were felt to be appropriately challenging. In this respect, the shortage of information on how the scale levels were defined may have limited the effect on teaching (Banerjee 2000, Douglas 2000).

Hamp-Lyons (1991) and others (Weir 1983, Santos 1988, Wall et al 1988, Brown 1991, Daborn and Calderwood 2000) have questioned how far rating scales employed in tests like the IELTS AWM reflect the ways in which written work is evaluated at university. Hamp-Lyons notes similarities between the IELTS scale criteria and the features of writing most valued by English teachers in their responses to the Bridgeman and Carlson (1983) survey. In this survey, English teachers valued paper organisation, development of ideas and paragraph organisation; they also considered sentence structure important. Academic staff, in contrast, prioritised quality of content, assignment requirements and addressing the topic, giving a low rating to sentence structure (Weir 1983 supports this). Hamp-Lyons (1991) found that English teachers did not attend to the quality of content in discipline-related essays and on these grounds questioned the validity of the IELTS as a test of discipline-specific language use (ESAP) (even though, at the time, specific purpose modules were provided).

Rignall and Furneaux (2002), in a study of the effects of rater training on trainees, found that their judgements appeared to be more influenced by some criteria than others. *Coherence and cohesion* was apparently given relatively little attention even at the end of the training period. Mayor, Hewings and Swann (2003), in a study of the features of IELTS responses at different levels, found that raters seemed to be responding to scripts in a holistic rather than strictly analytic way.

These findings are consistent with Lumley's (2002) research into the Australian *step* test, which suggests that even trained raters will use their own, idiosyncratic values in applying scale criteria and that aspects of the training may be partially or wholly ignored, or may take on unintended qualities. If teachers, who usually lack training as raters, are similarly idiosyncratic in their interpretation of the scale criteria, the design of the test may be of less relevance to the instruction they provide than the beliefs about the qualities of successful writing that they bring to the preparation classroom.

Existing evidence for washback from the IELTS test

In accordance with the washback model outlined in Chapter 1, on the basis of the design of the IELTS AWM, a number of predictions can be made regarding the likely effects of the test on teaching and learning. A small body of research is now available which addresses the question of washback from the IELTS test. This has included case studies of IELTS preparation courses including observational studies and both quantitative and qualitative surveys of teacher attitudes. However, none of these studies has explored in any depth the relationship between course content and course outcomes.

Brown (1998) collected information relating to two courses; one an IELTS preparation course, the other a more broadly defined EAP course. The differences between the two courses are summarised in Table 2.2. In short, he found that the IELTS preparation course placed less emphasis on research skills and the writing process and instead concentrated narrowly on task types required by the test.

Table 2.2 Comparison of EAP- and IELTS-focused courses at Hawthorn Institute (from Brown 1998: 34)

	IELTS preparation course	EAP course
Frequency of classes in writing instruction	7 hours/week × 10 weeks = 70 hours per course.	3 hours/week × 10 weeks = 30 hours per course.
Objective of writing instruction on course	Develop skills in Task 1 and Task 2 short essay writing.	Plan, prepare & present one 1,000 word assignment on project topic.
Knowledge of IELTS writing assessment criteria	Students given a summary of IELTS writing assessment criteria in course week 2.	No reference made to writing assessment.
Practice of Task 1 and Task 2 writing on course	All students complete 1 × Task 1 and 1 × Task 2 essay/week = 10 Task 1 + 10 Task 2 practices/course.	No task practices of writing during course. Emphasis on student research skills.
Timed practice test writing	3 timed practices of both Task 1 and Task 2/course.	No practice timed writing test on course.
Writing homework	Students encouraged to complete extra Task 1 and Task 2 essays as weekly homework.	No requirement for writing homework, except the completion of course project.
Feedback on writing	Correction code distributed to students in week 2. All writing subject to teacher application of code. Student self correction encouraged.	Feedback system informal. Teachers correct draft of project writing. Emphasis on content rather than accuracy.
Instructional focus on structure of essay writing	All writing instruction oriented to short IELTS Writing Task 1 and Task 2 requirements.	Writing instruction oriented to long essay planning, research preparation and organisation.
Instructional focus on strategies for timed writing in tests	Emphasis on strategies for writing in examination conditions continuously maintained throughout the course.	Emphasis on strategies for writing in academic contexts, as in note-taking and summarising.
Type of instructional materials	Majority of teaching material drawn from 'IELTS Preparation' textbooks.	Majority of teaching material selected from 'Academic Writing' coursebooks.

The IELTS AWM was administered twice: at course entry and exit. The nine learners on the 10-week IELTS preparation course made an average gain of 0.94 of a band on the Academic Writing Module. On the other hand, a group of five students on a second EAP course, without IELTS-related content, saw their scores decline by 0.6 of a band over the same period.

Brown (1998) shows the value of comparing IELTS-directed courses with alternative forms of preparation for academic study, and the importance of considering whether narrow preparation activities provide a benefit in the form of enhanced score gains. Unfortunately, the limited number of participants restricts the generalisability of the results. Brown acknowledges additional problems in comparing the two groups; students on the IELTS preparation course may have been better motivated as they were due to take the test immediately after the course, while EAP students were still several months away from university entry.

Everett and Coleman (2003) evaluated IELTS preparation materials. Although the main focus was an analysis of reading and listening materials, the study also included a questionnaire survey of students preparing for IELTS and an interview with teachers. Everett and Coleman found that few teachers felt students made connections between IELTS and academic study, a viewpoint supported by student comments about the limitations of IELTS training. Teacher informants working at universities were critical of the relationship between test materials and academic study, although some preferred the inclusion of current issues as topics for the classroom in the belief that these could promote interaction.

The study also revealed that, rather than simply practising for the test, teachers selected materials that they believed would develop learners' skills and strategies as a means of enhancing test performance. On the basis of a programme evaluation, Hayes and Watt (1998) agree that a pedagogically motivated syllabus, rather than one driven by test practice alone, would be more effective in improving test scores for 'intermediate' level learners.

Evidence of the effectiveness of test preparation courses is inconclusive. In a comparative study involving both TOEFL and IELTS candidates, Geranpayeh (1994) offers evidence that students do make improvements when given explicit examination preparation materials. The finding was most striking for those attending TOEFL preparation courses (whose score gains on TOEFL were not matched by equivalent gains on IELTS), but was also noticeable for students provided with a sample IELTS test. On the other hand, a study in Malaysia by Celestine and Ming (1999) found no comparative benefit for learners taking brief (30–48 hour) test preparation courses in terms of test score gains.

Archibald (2001), employing an IELTS-related nine-point scale (Hamp-Lyons and Henning 1991), found a mean band score improvement of 1.1 (from 4.49 to 5.59) on an essay-writing task (similar to IELTS AWM Task 2) for 50 students following an eight-week pre-sessional course (although it is not stated whether the students were provided with test preparation materials). The greatest mean gain was on the *Organisation* sub-scale and the lowest for *Linguistic Accuracy*. Archibald suggests that the pattern of gains reflects the discourse skills focus of the course. Unfortunately, the study does not report reliability estimates, so it is unclear how much faith can be had in the appearance of differential gains across criteria.

In contrast to Brown's (1998) small-scale case study approach, Deakin (1996) used questionnaire and interview data to explore washback from the IELTS on EAP course providers in Australia. Approximately 120 institutions involved in IELTS preparation were surveyed, with a 51% response rate. A qualitative follow-up survey was administered at 42 centres. Next, the language-related problems experienced by students in the course of their studies were investigated through 105 case studies. Finally, focus group meetings with representatives of the centres involved in the second survey discussed implications for good practice in relation to IELTS.

From the survey data, Deakin was able to classify course provision. He found that more than 50% of centres offered IELTS preparation within EAP, either integrated within it (36%) or as a test preparation option (17%). Overall, 29% ran dedicated IELTS preparation courses (Deakin 1996). Comments on IELTS were generally positive, and respondents regarded it as playing a moderately useful role in EAP preparation (Deakin 1996). However, 57% of respondents to the initial survey mentioned teaching-related problems, with 37% of these mentioning the negative washback effect of IELTS on EAP teaching and university preparation. These results were supported in the more qualitative follow-up survey, with concerns being voiced over the test's lack of focus on academic English or broader EAP skills, and the prevalence of teaching to the test.

Although IELTS was regarded as the best available English test for helping to determine if students are ready for tertiary studies, a number of concerns were voiced. Among these were the technical qualities of the test, particularly the reliability of the Writing and Speaking Modules, the over-reliance on IELTS scores in university entry decisions and the need to provide students with a broader range of EAP skills than those addressed by IELTS. Particular areas of content felt to be under-represented by the test included (in order of frequency):

* listening to lectures and taking notes
* presenting and participating in seminars
* participation in academic discussions
* coping with the volume of reading
* writing long assignments
* study skills.

The case study phase of the research also identified a number of skills deficits supposedly experienced by students after entering university in areas not covered by IELTS:

• understanding subject-specific concepts
• specialised language and vocabulary
• interpreting assessment tasks
• time management and organisational skills
• research skills
• cognitive skills/critical skills
• understanding academic requirements
• cultural understanding – interacting with Australian students
• citing references in writing/plagiarism
• seminar presentations
• organising and writing longer papers
• participating in tutorials
• communicating with lecturers/supervisor (Deakin 1996).

There is therefore a concern that the need for students to develop the range of EAP competencies required for university study is not well addressed in IELTS preparation courses. Such skills may be better supplied by courses which are not primarily directed towards IELTS; students who enter tertiary studies via an EAP course or foundation programme are generally said to be better prepared than those entering solely on the basis of IELTS results.

The possibility of negative washback in this context is apparent in one teacher respondent's comment that their EAP class was, in spite of its name, an IELTS preparation class as unless students could succeed in attaining the required IELTS band scores, they would be unable to enter a university and benefit from EAP training (Deakin 1996).

A failing of the Deakin (1996) study is that students were not surveyed or tested directly, but information on skills deficits was collected instead from their teachers. There was also a lack of direct evidence from classrooms in the form of observations or examples of student work to support the reports collected from teachers and course providers.

Read and Hayes (2003) combined a similar survey approach to that of Deakin (1996), first surveying course providers and then interviewing a selection of these to gain a picture of the range of IELTS provision in New Zealand and of attitudes towards the test. The study also incorporates classroom observation, demonstrating the value of combining interview and survey data with direct classroom observation, as recommended by Alderson and Wall (1993), to provide mutual corroboration of findings. The researchers were particularly concerned that the learners they encountered on IELTS preparation courses did not have the linguistic resources to cope with academic language use. Even some of those able to achieve the minimum requirements set by institutions for entry were felt by their teachers to be poorly equipped to deal with the linguistic demands of an academic course.

Read and Hayes (2003) conclude that preparation for the test often becomes an end in itself, rather than part of the process of equipping learners from a variety of linguistic and cultural backgrounds to cope with academic study in New Zealand.

Conclusions

This review has pointed to a number of discrepancies between the design of the IELTS Academic Writing Module and the construct of academic writing in English at universities in the UK and elsewhere. In keeping with the wash-back model, critics of the IELTS have expressed concern that, under pressure from the stakes associated with gaining admission to university, learners may focus on the demands of the test tasks at the expense of broader academic writing skills. There is consistent concern that IELTS preparation may involve:

- an undue focus on rehearsal in composing a limited range of text types
- composition of texts based on personal opinion.

There is also concern that IELTS preparation may, in following the design of the test, pass over valued areas of EAP including:

- the integration of source material
- subject-specific knowledge and vocabulary
- coping with the length of university-level written assignments
- the requirement to shape texts to meet the expectations of university staff.

There is research evidence to support at least some of these assumptions. Studies have suggested that participants do shape their behaviour to prepare for the test. Projects in Australia and New Zealand involving surveys of course providers and teachers and some direct classroom observation have found that teachers do tend to concentrate on the test tasks and that some are concerned important EAP skills may be under-represented in IELTS preparation.

Researchers have suggested that learners preparing for IELTS may not acquire the range of skills they will need to maximise their chances of success in their academic studies. A shortcoming of these studies, however, is that they have failed to locate IELTS preparation in the wider context of preparation for academic study. As a result, the anecdotal comparisons with EAP provision lack empirical support.

There is no adequate evidence that dedicated IELTS preparation yields a premium in terms of IELTS Writing score gains. If it is possible to make greater improvements in IELTS Writing scores by concentrating on the idiosyncrasies of the test, this will have implications for their interpretation. The question of score gains is therefore of central importance in this study.

Research questions

Given the high-stakes use of the IELTS as a screening test for university entrance, the washback model described in Chapter 1 predicts that the test is likely to have a powerful washback effect. According to the model, participants preparing for the test will adjust their behaviour to accommodate to the demands made by the test tasks.

Chapter 2 has reviewed the extent of overlap between the Academic Writing Module and the construct of academic writing at UK universities. Although the IELTS Academic Writing Module is a direct test of writing which is based in analyses of academic writing requirements, the review has identified a number of discrepancies between the test and the academic writing construct. The washback model predicts that these areas of discrepancy will give rise to test preparation practices associated with features of the test design that will be of limited relevance to the construct of academic writing.

General research question

The overall concern of this study is with the influence of the IELTS Academic Writing Module on preparation for academic study and the equivalence between IELTS test preparation and other forms of English for Academic purposes directed at university study. This leads us to the general research question:

> Is the washback model supported in relation to the role of the IELTS test in the context of preparation for academic study in the UK?

Specific questions

The washback model outlined in Chapter 1 provides a framework for exploring this general research question. The model suggests a number of related questions that will be of relevance. The model places participant beliefs regarding the overlap between test content and focal construct at the centre of the washback process. If there are features of the test that are not seen by participants to overlap the focal construct (construct–irrelevant variance) or features of the focal construct that are not seen to be represented in the test (construct under-representation), the model predicts that preparation for the test and the development of academic writing skills for university study will not be equivalent. Hence the first specific research question:

1. Given the commonalities and discrepancies between IELTS and the EAP writing construct revealed in the literature review, do students and teachers regard themselves as engaging in IELTS test preparation rather than university preparation and do such beliefs give rise to practices, in relation to IELTS, which fail to address the EAP writing construct?

Courses which are more directly concerned with preparation for university study might be expected to better reflect the academic writing construct. This gives rise to the second research question:

2. Do practices on courses which are not driven by IELTS better reflect this construct?

It is important to allow that there are likely to be differences between the kinds of learners attracted to the various course types on offer. Those who choose to study on an IELTS preparation course may have different characteristics from those who study on other forms of EAP course. Such differences may interact with the influence of the test and impact on course outcomes. Consideration of differences between learners gives rise to the third research question:

3. What are the characteristics of learners on different courses and how do these relate to the characteristics of the IELTS test-taking population?

If preparation programmes are successful at exploiting the characteristics of the test, we would expect to see greater improvement in IELTS scores on dedicated test-preparation courses. Taking into account pre-existing differences between groups of learners, we would expect to observe higher gains in IELTS scores on test-preparation courses in relation to gains in lexico-grammatical language proficiency, but with little growth in academic awareness and study skills. Conversely, we would expect to see greater growth in awareness of academic writing demands and study skills on courses directed at university preparation. This leads us to the fourth research question:

4. Do instructional alternatives at points on a continuum from IELTS-driven to IELTS-unrelated EAP courses result in differential outcomes in terms of:
   • gains in scores on the IELTS Academic Module?
   • linguistic (lexico-grammatical) proficiency gains?
   • academic awareness and study skills gains?

The washback model predicts that the influence of the test will vary according to the characteristics of the learner. Learners, according to the model, will be influenced by the test to different degrees and effects on score gains will not be uniform. This study sets out to explore learner characteristics that may interact with instructional differences and the role of the test to influence score outcomes. This leads to research question five:

5. Do facets of learners' individual differences interact with instructional differences in predicting outcomes?

A summary of the research questions and their relationship to the study phases is set out in Appendix 1.

3

Pilot studies

Preliminary studies of IELTS and EAP provision in the UK

This chapter describes the findings from a series of preliminary studies investigating components of the washback model described in Chapter 1 (Figure 1.3). The range of methods used will be briefly described, followed by a summary of the findings and their implications for the main study.

The key aims of these studies were to:

- provide an overview of the context of EAP provision in the United Kingdom and the role of IELTS therein
- identify variables believed by participants to affect student learning and the probability of success on the test
- trial methods and instruments for data collection with groups drawn from the intended population.

In line with the washback model described in Chapter 1 (Figure 1.3), it was important to place IELTS in the context of the range of courses open to students intending to enter Higher Education in the UK as a means of understanding the role of the test and its potential influence on teaching and learning. How is an IELTS preparation course different from other forms of preparation for academic study?

The overlap between the test and participants' conception of the focal construct of academic writing lies at the heart of the washback model. It was therefore important additionally to establish how participants understood this relationship and to trace whether and how they believed that the test affected their behaviour.

Following an iterative process suggested by Watanabe (1997), a developing understanding of these questions was used to refine each phase of the study. First, course directors, students and teachers involved in IELTS preparation and other EAP courses were approached informally. Next, course outlines were gathered to allow for the identification of similarities and differences across providers. On this basis a tentative categorisation of course types was developed to be further refined through a nationwide survey of course providers and a set of research strategies that would elicit data of relevance to the research questions.

The relationship between participants, test instruments and testing and learning constructs lies at the heart of the washback model. Accordingly, the area of participant perceptions has long been a cornerstone of washback studies, with an emphasis on survey (Madaus 1988, Haladyna et al 1991, Jones et al 1999) and interview (Smith 1991b) methods. Key questions suggested by the model include the value placed by participants on a test (test stakes and importance), the perceived difficulty of the test, and beliefs about the relationship between test content and desired learning outcomes.

Although Alderson and Wall (1993) are critical of an earlier over-reliance on survey methods, without supporting empirical data from observations, they nonetheless agree with Bailey (1996) that they are essential components in washback research designs. Surveys remain the most effective means of accessing the views of participants and are therefore included in the current study.

It is likely that groups of participants will experience test preparation in different ways. Just as teachers set out with certain goals in mind, so learners come to EAP courses with their own beliefs and objectives and so tend to value aspects of the course which best fit their preconceptions and objectives (Brookes, Grundy and Young-Scholten 1996). Unfortunately, the surveys described in the washback literature, while proving successful in revealing teachers' attitudes, have largely failed to capture the relationships between the perceptions of classroom events expressed by the individuals concerned, and the impact these may have on learning.

Appropriate methods for the study would capture the participants' own approach to and interpretation of the learning context, yet allow principled comparisons between individuals. This suggests that quantitative questionnaire data and qualitative interview data might each contribute to an understanding of the effects of the test on teaching and learning. Through these preliminary studies, as advocated by Alderson and Wall (1993) and Bailey (1999), there was a concern to triangulate both data sources and methods; that is, to obtain evidence through a variety of data collection methods and instruments and to compare results obtained from a range of informants.

In addition to collecting data on participant perceptions, a sense of how much improvement learners might be expected to make in their IELTS Writing scores from one testing occasion to the next was also sought. This would allow a comparison with the gains observed in the main study and help to contextualise any dividends provided by dedicated IELTS preparation. With this aim, results for over 15,000 IELTS Academic Module candidates who had taken the test on more than one occasion were obtained from Cambridge ESOL. Comparisons among these test results provided further evidence relating to score gains and possible moderating influences including age, gender and nationality.

Following the research questions outlined in Chapter 2, a series of studies were undertaken, experimenting with a variety of both quantitative and qualitative data collection instruments, investigating course provider, teacher and student perceptions and empirical evidence relating to the following features. In this chapter, findings from the range of pilot studies (PS1 to PS7) are briefly summarised in relation to each of the key areas listed here:

- variation in learning aims between courses and between participants
- overlap between IELTS preparation and EAP needs
- test importance and difficulty
- characteristics associated with successful learners on these courses
- learning and teaching strategies bringing IELTS Writing success
- length of time required for specified score gains.

The methods and data sources employed in the pilot studies are set out in Table 3.1.

Table 3.1 Summary of pilot study methods

Pilot Study	Institutions	Participants	N	Methods (instruments)
PS1 Review of course outlines	Institutions offering IELTS preparation (IP) and/or pre-sessional English (PE) courses	n/a	45 course outlines	Documentary analysis (corpus of course outlines obtained from worldwide web)
PS2 Student survey	University (pre-sessional English with IP strand) Sixth-form college (foundation course with IP) Language school (dedicated IP course)	Learners preparing for IELTS	31 students university: 15 foundation course: 6 language school: 10	Survey (paper-based questionnaire including both selected response and open response items)
PS3 Teacher interviews	University	Teachers with experience of both IP and PE courses	5 teachers	Interview (repertory grid-based interview procedure)
PS4 Teacher survey	Various EAP/ IELTS course providers	Teachers including interview participants	16 teachers 4 of 5 earlier interview participants 12 additional teachers from various institutions	Survey (paper-based questionnaire developed from interview responses)

Table 3.1 (Continued)

PS5 Student focus groups	University	Learners on PE course with experience of both IP and PE	9 students	Interview (Repertory grid-based group interview procedure)
PS6 Course providers survey	Course providers	Course directors/ teachers with responsibility for course content	76 institutions 36 ARELS[1] members 23 BALEAP[2] members 17 BASELT[3] members	Survey (online and paper-based question-naire)
PS7 Test score analysis	IELTS partners	Test takers	15,300 IELTS test candidates	Test/survey (IELTS Writing test and Candidate Information Sheet)

[1]*ARELS:*   *Association of Recognised English Language Schools (the representative body of private accredited language schools in the UK)*
[2]*BALEAP: British Association of Lecturers in English for Academic Purposes (a national organisation of centres where EAP (English for Academic Purposes) is taught within British universities and providers of higher education)*
[3]*BASELT: British Association of State English Language Teaching (a group of UK universities and colleges, offering English Language courses for leisure, work and as preparation for further academic and vocational studies)*

Variation in learning aims between courses and between participants

The washback model predicts that tests may affect the goals that partici-pants set for themselves in their learning and teaching and that the need to succeed on a test may, to some extent, come to displace the development of criterion abilities as a learning goal (Alderson and Wall 1993, Bailey 1996, 1999). It is also well-attested that washback is experienced differently by participants in different contexts and with different beliefs about testing and its relation to learning (Alderson and Hamp-Lyons 1996, Shohamy, Donitsa-Schmidt and Ferman 1996, Wall 1997, Watanabe 1997, Burrows 1998).

In the preliminary studies, evidence was sought of how learners, teachers and course providers conceptualised their respective tasks. Of particular interest were differences between participants in this regard and methodolo-gies that would access these.

Informal interviews and the inspection of course outlines (Pilot Study One) provided an overview of the range of EAP provision available to international students in the UK. Courses for students intending to enter further education seemed to lie on a continuum between the extremes of *IELTS preparation* – courses aimed primarily at success on the IELTS test – and *pre-sessional English* – courses focused more directly on preparation for tertiary academic study.

Course publicity material analysed in Pilot Study One reflected these differences. Pre-sessional English courses offered English language skills (the four skills of Writing, Reading, Speaking and Listening), supplemented by study skills: library and research skills, note-taking from lectures, note-making from written sources, IT skills, referencing, bibliography compilation and report writing. IELTS preparation courses also offered four skills instruction, but did not generally prioritise study skills. Publicity for IELTS preparation courses bore a close resemblance to that for other test preparation courses such as the Cambridge FCE or the TOEFL: providing a brief description of the content and purpose of the test and promising opportunities for test practice. Pre-sessional course publicity, in contrast, emphasised the value of the courses for university preparation and outlined the range of skills to be developed. As predicted by the washback model, apparent differences in course aims and content were closely related to the relationship between course and test.

IELTS preparation took a variety of guises, often being offered as a strand within other courses. Outside the university sector, IELTS preparation was offered by some institutions as a part-time option alongside *General English* courses. In these courses, there seemed to be little acknowledgement of a specifically academic purpose in language learning. Within universities, IELTS preparation was more usually provided in the context of English for Academic Purpose instruction.

Participants across surveys concurred that IELTS preparation courses were primarily driven by the test content and format. Students interviewed in Pilot Study Five were very clear that preparation for IELTS was 'only for the test' and that this was different from their goal on their pre-sessional course to prepare themselves for their university studies. Students, teachers and course providers agreed that preparation courses (or the test preparation strands of combination courses) should be directed above all towards ensuring that students would pass the test and that practice with test tasks and instruction in test-taking techniques would contribute to their chances of success.

The evidence from the pilot studies was consistent with the prediction of the model that the IELTS, as a high-stakes gate-keeping test, would have a strong influence on the content of test-preparation courses, which could be clearly distinguished from their pre-sessional counterparts. Teachers and students preparing for the test tended to regard success on IELTS as the key short-term goal for their learning (Table 3.2).

Table 3.2 Summary of Pilot Study findings relating to course aims

	Students	Teachers	Course providers
Course aims	IELTS courses should be directed towards the test and test-relevant skills.	IELTS courses are directed towards the test and test-relevant skills. Students lobby for test-related activities.	IELTS courses are directed towards the test and test-relevant skills.

The pilot studies highlighted the importance of combining quantitative with qualitative methods and of involving a range of participants in an iterative process of exploration. Course providers, teachers and learners did not necessarily share an understanding of course aims. Interviews provided rich insights both into areas of shared understanding and into disputes, but could not indicate how widely any individual's goals were shared by other participants. For this, quantitative data was required, proving most informative where grounded in the qualitative phases of the study. Quantitative outcomes in turn pointed towards interesting avenues to be pursued through further open-ended interviews.

Overlap between IELTS preparation and EAP needs

According to the washback model, where participants take success on a test as their goal for learning and where they perceive discrepancies between test content and the focal construct, they will tend to adapt their behaviour to meet the test's demands. The pilot studies sought evidence for participants' understanding of this relationship and the influence this had on their teaching and learning practices.

In this context, differences in course aims and their relationship to the test, as understood by participants, did appear to give rise to differences in practices across courses. Data from each of the pilot studies indicated that students, teachers and course providers perceived differences between preparing for IELTS and preparing for university study which impacted on their attitudes towards and selection of teaching or learning activities.

In Pilot Study Two, students used five-point Likert scales to rate both the frequency of activities in their classes (*How often did you do this in your classes?*) and their relevance to success on IELTS (*Does this activity help you to pass IELTS?*), see Box 3.1.

Very similar ratings of activities were obtained across groups (university, foundation course and language school) in relation to their value for IELTS preparation. However, as might be expected, the reported frequency of

Box 3.1 Questionnaire given to students in Pilot Study Two

	How often did you do this in your classes? Very often ... Never					Does this activity help you to pass IELTS? Very much ... Not at all				
Listening and taking notes.	⑤	④	③	②	①	⑤	④	③	②	①
Listening and writing short answers.	⑤	④	③	②	①	⑤	④	③	②	①
Grammar exercises.	⑤	④	③	②	①	⑤	④	③	②	①
Discussions with small groups of students.	⑤	④	③	②	①	⑤	④	③	②	①
Writing short essays (500 words or less).	⑤	④	③	②	①	⑤	④	③	②	①
Discussions with the whole class.	⑤	④	③	②	①	⑤	④	③	②	①
Writing long essays (1,000 words or more).	⑤	④	③	②	①	⑤	④	③	②	①
Giving spoken presentations.	⑤	④	③	②	①	⑤	④	③	②	①
Reading longer articles or books.	⑤	④	③	②	①	⑤	④	③	②	①
Reading short texts (one page or less).	⑤	④	③	②	①	⑤	④	③	②	①
Spoken projects.	⑤	④	③	②	①	⑤	④	③	②	①
Written projects.	⑤	④	③	②	①	⑤	④	③	②	①
Taking practice IELTS tests.	⑤	④	③	②	①	⑤	④	③	②	①
Vocabulary exercises.	⑤	④	③	②	①	⑤	④	③	②	①
Taking practice IELTS tests (or parts of IELTS tests).	⑤	④	③	②	①	⑤	④	③	②	①

activities in class showed greater variation, likely reflecting institutional differences in syllabus and teacher choices. Certainly, teachers on all three courses, including the language school course, seemed to be presenting a wider variety of activities than mere test practice might dictate.

Principally, activities considered to be the most helpful for passing the test tended to resemble the test tasks: *writing short essays, listening and writing short answers, reading short texts*. However, *grammar exercises* were ranked third by the university group and fourth by the language school group, even though the IELTS does not include a grammar subtest. This suggests that test format is not the only factor influencing learner preferences among test preparation activities, but that prior beliefs about effective language learning (and the value of grammar knowledge in this respect) also play a role.

The reported frequencies also indicated that teachers were not limited to imitating the format of the test in their classes. A number of task types which do not occur on the test (*listening and taking notes, grammar exercises, small group discussions*) were apparently more frequent as class activities than other tasks, which do occur (*short essay writing*). Again, this indicates limitations on the influence of the test format on the content of classes. However, the least frequent activities (*lengthy writing assignments, spoken projects*) were also considered by learners to be of least value for IELTS preparation.

Learner responses suggested that a preference for interaction in the classroom could compete with the impact of the test as an influence on learning choices. When asked which skill they would like to spend more time on, the largest number (n = 9) nominated speaking, although none rated speaking activities as being of the greatest importance for their success on IELTS. Three students justified selecting reading or writing as an activity they would like to do less of in class on the grounds that these were better suited for independent study. However, there was also demand for more test practice (n = 6) and writing (n = 6), the second most popular responses.

Teachers, for their part, also reported that IELTS influenced their choice of activities. The teachers interviewed and surveyed in Pilot Studies Three and Four identified activities either with EAP or IELTS preparation and located these on a nine-point scale with EAP placed at one extreme and IELTS preparation at the other. The results of the follow-up survey of 16 teachers are displayed in Figure 3.1. This shows that taking practice tests, memorising relevant phrases or structures and learning about the description of graphs and diagrams (required in IELTS Academic Writing Task 1) were particularly identified with IELTS preparation. On the other hand, a number of activities including note-taking, summarising and referencing were not generally considered relevant to IELTS preparation and were less often included in classes directed towards the test.

In spite of the differences they observed between their IELTS preparation and other EAP classes, teachers interviewed in Pilot Study Three nonetheless

Figure 3.1 Activities identified with IELTS preparation and EAP courses by 16 teachers

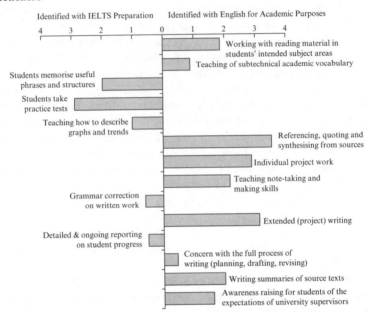

endorsed the statement that, 'IELTS preparation develops skills relevant to the academic (university) context'.

Students interviewed in Pilot Study Five shared some of the teacher percep-tions of differences between course types. Table 3.3 summarises the differences identified by these learners between their previous experiences of IELTS prepa-ration courses and the pre-sessional EAP course on which they were studying. Like the teachers, they identified IELTS preparation with more test practice and memorisation of useful phrases. They also found a greater emphasis on grammar in their IELTS classes. EAP was seen to involve a greater volume of reading and writing and included the integration of source material.

Students agreed that the skills they had developed in IELTS preparation were useful for university study, particularly in reading and writing. However, IELTS-related skills were not felt to be sufficient. One student had come to study on the pre-sessional course despite obtaining a high enough IELTS band score (7.5) for unconditional acceptance to her intended course. She commented that she did not feel that studying for IELTS in her home country had given her all the skills she needed in preparing for university study and had overcome resistance from her cost-conscious parents to attend a pre-sessional course.

The Course Providers' Questionnaire (CPQ) (Pilot Study Six) provided a further means of quantifying differences in class activities between course types. Item 17 on the CPQ asked how frequently certain statements were true

Table 3.3 Student views of IELTS preparation in relation to pre-sessional EAP (N = 9)

Number of students	Associated with IELTS preparation	Associated with pre-sessional EAP	Number of students
4	Studying grammar	Greater volume of reading and writing	4
3	Studying model essays	Quotation and referencing skills	4
3	Memorising phrases	Summarising and paraphrasing	4
3	Test-like activities	Process writing, involving multiple drafts	2
2	More 'general' writing topics	Specifically 'academic' writing (in terms of content, structure, or both)	7

of the targeted courses. Response options ranged from 'Typically true' to 'Almost never true'.

The statements were drawn from the earlier pilot studies, see Box 3.2 for some examples.

Box 3.2 Course Providers' Questionnaire used in Pilot Study Six

17. How often are the following statements true of this course? (please circle your answer)

Student essays are expected to be longer than 500 words [*Extended writing assignments*].

Typically true	Often true
Sometimes true	Not often true
Almost never true	Unknown

Students engage in a wide range of writing activities [*Wide range of writing activities*].

Typically true	Often true
Sometimes true	Not often true
Almost never true	Unknown

Students undertake extended project work involving independent research [*Project work*].

Typically true	Often true
Sometimes true	Not often true
Almost never true	Unknown

Students take practice IELTS tests (or sections of IELTS tests) [*IELTS test practice*].

Typically true | Often true
Sometimes true | Not often true
Almost never true | Unknown

Instruction is given in test-taking strategies [*Test-taking strategies*].

Typically true | Often true
Sometimes true | Not often true
Almost never true | Unknown

Instruction is given in writing descriptions of graphs and diagrams [*Describing graphs and diagrams*].

Typically true | Often true
Sometimes true | Not often true
Almost never true | Unknown

Instruction is given in integrating source material and referencing the work of others [*Writing from sources*].

Typically true | Often true
Sometimes true | Not often true
Almost never true | Unknown

Listening tasks include extended lectures (15 minutes or more) [*Extensive listening*].

Typically true | Often true
Sometimes true | Not often true
Almost never true | Unknown

Students give oral presentations [*Giving presentations*].

Typically true | Often true
Sometimes true | Not often true
Almost never true | Unknown

Opportunities are provided to practise social and informal conversation [*Social conversation*].

Typically true | Often true
Sometimes true | Not often true
Almost never true | Unknown

Opportunities are provided to participate in group discussions [*Group discussions*].

Typically true | Often true
Sometimes true | Not often true
Almost never true | Unknown

Opportunities are provided for students to work in their chosen discipline (e.g. economics students have opportunities to study language specific to economics) [*Work in own discipline*].

Typically true	Often true
Sometimes true	Not often true
Almost never true	Unknown

In order further to explore the distinction between courses and to reveal whether certain activities might be related to different instructional strategies, a factor analysis was carried out on responses to these items. This involved principal factors extraction with Varimax rotation using SPSS 11.5 for Windows. Although the number of participants is barely adequate for factor analysis (Comrey and Lee 1992), the strength of the factor loadings obtained and the essentially descriptive purpose of the analysis may be said to justify the procedure in cases such as this (Tabachnik and Fidell 2000).

Principal components analysis and a scree test were employed before the factor analysis to estimate the appropriate number of factors. Three factors were extracted with eigenvalues greater than one, identified with IELTS test-preparation focus, broader EAP skills and speaking skills (Table 3.4).

Table 3.4 Rotated factor matrix based on factor analysis of class activities on EAP courses

Rotated Factor Matrix

	F1	F2	F3
	46.97%	16.17%	9.65%
Writing from sources	.840		
Project work	.794		
Extensive listening	.749		
Extended writing assignments	.747		
Work in own discipline	.649		
Wide range of writing activities	.615		
Instruction in IELTS format		.756	
IELTS test practice		.856	
Test-taking strategies		.955	
Describing graphs and diagrams		.649	
Giving presentations	.510		.653
Social conversation			.804
Group discussions			.546

Extraction Method: Principal Axis Factoring.
Rotation Method: Varimax with Kaiser Normalisation.

As shown in Table 3.4, *Instruction in IELTS format, IELTS test practice, Test-taking strategies,* and *Describing graphs and diagrams* (items identified with IELTS preparation by teachers and students in Pilot Studies Two, Three and Four) load on one factor (F2), while *Extended writing assignments, Wide range of writing activities, Project work, Work in own discipline, Extensive listening* and *Writing from sources* (all previously identified with EAP) load on a second (F1). *Social conversation* and *Group discussions* load on a third factor (F3), identified with speaking skills, while *Giving presentations* loads both on this factor and on the EAP skills factor (F1).

Figure 3.2 Frequency of three activity types on IELTS and EAP courses

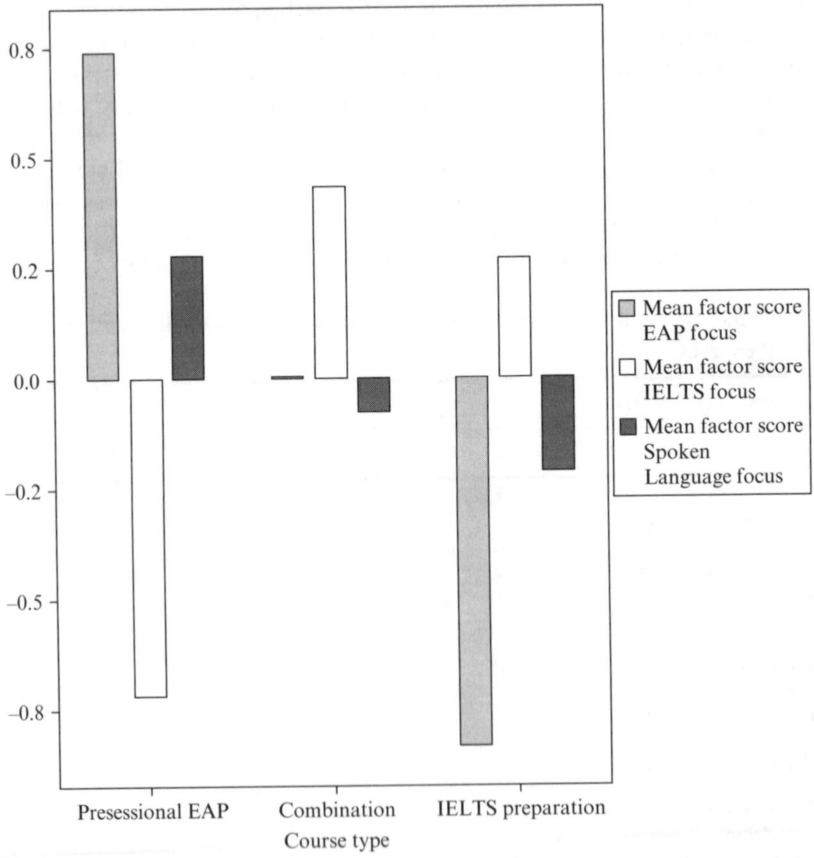

As might be expected, courses scoring highest on the IELTS focus factor tended to be dedicated IELTS courses, while those scoring lowest were pre-sessional courses with no IELTS component (Figure 3.2). Those scoring highest on EAP focus also tended to be pre-sessional or combination courses. Combination courses scored moderately high on both IELTS and EAP factors, but the pattern of responses (higher scores for IELTS, lower scores for speaking skills and EAP) associated them with the IELTS courses rather than the pre-sessionals.

Table 3.5 summarises the findings of the pilot studies relating to the overlap between IELTS and academic-writing needs as perceived by course providers, teachers and learners. It appears that, although skills tested by IELTS are regarded as relevant and useful for university study, all three groups of stakeholders noted a number of discrepancies between the test and writing in the university as they understood it. Although teachers and course providers were better able to articulate some of these differences, learners seemed to share at least some of their perceptions of a narrower focus in test preparation.

Table 3.5 Summary of pilot study findings relating to overlap between IELTS preparation and EAP needs

	Students	Teachers	Course providers
Overlap between IELTS preparation and EAP needs	English skills learned for IELTS (e.g. basics of essay organisation) are useful for future studies. EAP courses involve a wider range of skills (including use of sources, extensive reading). IELTS writing topics are more general. Relationship of Task 1 to university writing questioned. Future language needs and learning preferences were considered to be important in dictating learning choices (in addition to test demands).	IELTS preparation develops many skills relevant to university study. IELTS preparation tends to exclude: • broad range of writing tasks • work in learners' own discipline • individual project work • referencing and use of sources • teaching of subtechnical academic vocabulary • awareness of the expectations of academic staff.	IELTS preparation tends to exclude: • range of writing tasks • work in learners' own discipline • project work • writing from sources.

Test importance and difficulty

The importance attached to the test by the participants is suggested to be a key determinant of washback intensity (Hughes 1993). The more important a test is considered to be, the more likely it is to engender washback. At the same time, if participants believe a test to be either too difficult to allow them a reasonable chance of success, or if it is so easy that success seems assured, they may not consider test preparation to justify a substantial investment of resources. Although it may appear self-evident that the IELTS, as a high-stakes test, would be important to learners, and challenging enough to encourage them to invest in a preparation course, it was important to establish whether this was equally true for all and the extent to which perceptions of test importance and difficulty influenced test-preparation behaviour.

Although teachers reported that the test was very important to their students, in responses to the student questionnaire (Pilot Study Two) there was considerable variation in reactions to the test, both in terms of attitudes and in the effect reported on study habits. The question, *How important is it for you to pass IELTS?* (with response options on a Likert scale ranging from 1: *very important* to 5: *not important*) attracted an average rating of 1.77 with 17 of the 31 respondents rating the test at 1, compared to four rating it at 5.

However, the perceived importance of the test did not consistently motivate learners to spend time on independent study. Although the test date was approaching for learners on all three courses in the study, not all of the participants dedicated much time to studying outside class. One reported spending 40 hours a week, but over half (16 of 31) reported spending 5 hours or less each week, with five of these claiming not to study at all outside class. This data suggested an important role for maturity in learning choices. The students who did no extra work were all prospective undergraduates aged 20 or under (of various nationalities), while postgraduates (of all nationalities) tended to be more conscientious, making up 10 of the 15 who claimed to do more than 5 hours of extra work.

Generally, the tasks students claimed to practise independently were among those they considered most important to their success at IELTS. Of students who did work at home, test taking was not usually the only activity (only four reported tests as their only form of additional study), but more typically made up between one third and two-thirds of self-study time. Five students reported doing additional study with no test practice.

Respondents across studies shared the view that learners would require a certain level of ability at the outset in order to benefit from IELTS preparation courses. In Pilot Study Two a student commented that, 'it [success on the preparation course] depends how good one's English was before he takes this course' (foundation course respondent). This view was echoed both by teachers and by course providers who suggested that learners with low levels of proficiency at course entry might not gain very much from a preparation course.

Table 3.6 provides a summary of pilot study findings relating to test importance and difficulty. The studies suggested that, as the model predicts, the importance of the test did make it a source of motivation for learners. However, the belief that the test was both important and challenging did not necessarily provoke intensive test preparation. Learner background variables, notably age, appeared to play a role in mediating the effect of beliefs about the importance and level of challenge of the test.

Table 3.6 Summary of pilot study findings relating to perceptions of test importance and difficulty

	Students	Teachers	Course providers
Test importance and difficulty	Test generally seen as important.	Test seen as important.	Test importance has a motivational effect.
	Sufficient level of ability needed to benefit from prep. courses.	Learners should be placed in a class of suitable level to benefit.	Learners need to be at an 'intermediate' level of ability to benefit from prep. courses.
	Concern about marker reliability; perceived that the test is easier in home country.	Concern about marker reliability; perceived that the test is easier in home country.	
	Concern about the role of topic knowledge in writing performance.		

Characteristics associated with successful learners on these courses

Two related questions about learners are central to washback, but have rarely been addressed in research: a) which learner characteristics and behaviours are believed to yield test success? and b) are these beliefs justified by results? Understanding participants' beliefs about how to succeed can help to explain their teaching and learning behaviours and help to relate these to test demands. Exploring the relationship between beliefs, behaviours, other learner characteristics and observed outcomes, including gains in test scores, can help us to understand whether participants are in fact able to boost their scores, with implications for test validity. In short, do learners and teachers who do adapt to test demands – the adopters and adapters in Burrows' (1998) categorisation of teachers – outperform those resisters who choose, for whatever reason, not to conform to test demands? Or are other variables, unrelated to test demands, of greater importance in determining score outcomes?

In the pilot studies, the differences between learners and teachers in their attributions of success seemed to reflect their roles in the learning process. Students, in both Pilot Study Two and Pilot Study Five, almost invariably attributed success on the test to diligence, or, as one student (Pilot Study Two) expressed it, 'I have to give up pub and disco if I want to be a good IELTS student'. Teachers, on the other hand, emphasised that success also required openness to instruction and a willingness to follow the teacher's guidance. In this context, cultural distance between teacher and learner was nominated as a possible cause of resistance, giving rise to the different rates of improvement some teachers claimed to have observed between Western European and East Asian learners.

Responses from course providers also pointed to a wide range of factors that could contribute to success. Motivation was mentioned most frequently, but other factors included aptitude and ability, educational experience, cultural background, first language, nationality, social problems, flexibility, intelligence and maturity among others.

In Pilot Study Seven, supplementing the earlier pilot studies investigating participants' beliefs about success, Cambridge ESOL Examinations provided extensive data to inform an investigation of score gains on the official IELTS test and allow these to be related to a number of candidate background variables.

This data comprised the results for 15,380 candidates who had taken the Academic Writing Module of IELTS on two or more occasions between January 1998 and June 2001. As Cambridge ESOL also routinely collects background data on all candidates, it was possible to relate score gains to candidate gender, nationality (consolidated to regional origin to limit the number of groups), age, test location, number of years studying English and educational status. Unfortunately, this background data does not include details of whether candidates have spent the period between tests engaged in any form of English study (although the IELTS partners do recommend this). Hence score gains could not be related to instructional variables.

Repeated measures analysis of covariance revealed significant effects for age, gender, educational status, number of years studying English, region of origin, test location, and for the interaction between region and test location. Younger candidates tended to make greater gains than older, women made more rapid gains than men (but scored lower on both tests) and there was a slight advantage for non-students over students. Those studying English for longer tended to score higher on both tests, but made less gain.

Candidates were classified into four regional categories (reflecting those to be used in the main study); China/Taiwan, Other East Asian, Western European and Other. East Asians, on average, scored lower on both tests than Western Europeans and Others (the highest-scoring group on both measures) and appeared to make least improvement overall.

The data showed that many candidates had travelled to an L1 English-speaking country for their second test; the proportion of candidates taking the test in an L1 English country rose from 38.3% on the first to 46.4% on the second. There was apparently an advantage for candidates moving to L1 English countries, who gained more than those remaining in the same country or moving away from L1 English countries. However, the interaction between region of origin and test location indicated that Western Europeans gained more from this, in terms of IELTS Writing scores, than did their East Asian counterparts.

The evidence gathered from the pilot studies pointed to a complex interaction of factors that might influence score gains (Table 3.7). Interesting differences also emerged between participants in their attributions of success, reflecting their identities in the educational process. Students stressed personal qualities such as effort and diligence, while teachers and course providers envisaged a greater role for learner background variables and for acceptance of instruction. The limited candidate background information available with IELTS scores indicated that age, gender, nationality, educational status, English language experience and residence all had some influence on score gains. Again, the combination of qualitative interview and survey data and quantitative test-score and questionnaire-response data appeared to provide complementary perspectives that could enrich understanding.

Table 3.7 Summary of pilot study findings relating to the characteristics of the successful IELTS learner

	Students	Teachers	Course providers	Test score data
Characteristics of the successful learner	Be diligent, need to study hard in and out of class.	Be intelligent, adaptable and diligent. Western Europeans tend to outperform East Asians.	Wide variety of variables, affect, effort, maturity, cultural background and aptitude.	Evidence of slower gains for: older candidates, East Asians, males, students. Faster gains for: Western Europeans, those moving to L1 English countries for second test, those with less experience of learning English.

Learning and teaching strategies bringing IELTS writing success

Having explored the question of which learner characteristics might bring test success, the focus in this section will be on the specific teaching and learning behaviours believed by participants to boost their chances. Where course aims involved test preparation, how was this reflected in the choice of content and methods? And how closely were these choices related to test content?

In Pilot Study Two, where respondents on IELTS preparation courses were provided with a closed list of options, activities considered by learners to be most helpful for passing the test tended to be those that most resembled the test tasks: *writing short essays, listening and writing short answers, reading short texts.* However, *grammar exercises* were ranked third by the university group and fourth by the language school group, even though the IELTS does not include a grammar subtest.

In Pilot Study Five, involving open-ended interviews with learners on a pre-sessional course who had previously taken IELTS, students again most often suggested test practice, but also nominated extensive reading, social interaction with local people, having a clear purpose for studying and asking questions in class. There was some disagreement among these learners over the efficacy of IELTS preparation courses. One student felt that his preparation course (at a UK language school) had not been useful and that studying alone with preparation books had been of more value. However, most felt that test preparation had been of considerable benefit and were pleased that they had taken courses. One student who had not attended a formal course, but had prepared for the test alone, was clearly impressed by some of the test-preparation strategies being described (such as memorising stock phrases of comparison) and commented that he wished he had been more aware of these when readying himself for the test.

In the Pilot Study Three interviews, teachers agreed that activities closely based on test content were of value in boosting test scores, including memorisation of phrases, question analysis and direct test practice, but there were areas of disagreement about activities less closely related to the test content. Some teachers believed that discussion of listening strategies, teaching academic vocabulary and summarising written texts in their IELTS preparation classes would help to improve test scores, while others did not. Overall, four of the five teachers interviewed agreed with the comment of one that, 'IELTS test preparation is an effective strategy for improving students' scores on the test, although such score gains might not be matched by gains in ability'.

Course providers in Pilot Study Six also suggested test practice together with 'memorising formulaic structures', learning exam techniques and use of IELTS revision books (one suggested providing preparation materials in learners' own first languages). In common with the students, they also suggested a wide range of activities that could help to improve their scores. These included regular class attendance and engaging with the language outside the classroom through self-directed study, extensive reading, vocabulary study, exposure to English in the media, mixing with English speakers and using English rather than their L1 outside class.

Similarly to the responses from learners in Alderson and Hamp-Lyons (1996), behaviours encouraged by the test included both those obviously related to the test format, such as intensive test practice and memorising stock phrases and more general language learning strategies, such as spending more time interacting in English (Table 3.8). This implies at the same time that the test could encourage both narrow test-preparation strategies and greater engagement in language learning activities apparently unrelated to the design of the test. Behaviours that have been regarded respectively as evidence for negative and positive washback.

Table 3.8 Summary of pilot study findings relating to strategies bringing about success

	Students	Teachers	Course providers
Strategies bringing IELTS writing success	The following encourage success on IELTS:	The following encourage success on IELTS:	IELTS success is promoted through:
	Memorising stock phrases Taking practice tests Learning test-taking strategies Learning grammar Preparing essays on anticipated topics Studying model essays Reading widely Talking to local people Being engaged in class	Providing instruction in how to describe graphs Rehearsing test tasks Teaching test-taking strategies Providing grammar correction on written work Predicting likely writing topics and building knowledge of these	Familiarity with the test Test-taking techniques Practice in taking IELTS tests Use of IELTS revision books Memorising formulae Extensive reading in English Use of English outside class Additional reading Vocabulary learning

Length of time required for specified score gains

An important consideration for teachers and learners, relating to the level of challenge a test represents and beliefs about the attainability of success, is the length of time needed to improve performance to the required level. Learner behaviour may be guided by their beliefs, perhaps mediated by advice from teachers or test providers, about the time needed for them to reach the level required for a passing grade.

In the context of the use of the IELTS test in the UK, the length of time required for learners to progress is a key concern. Candidates are often under pressure to obtain a score at a given level before they can be accepted onto an academic course. This may mean that they have a limited period within which to reach the required level. Although this restriction has since been lifted, at the time of the study the IELTS partners required candidates to wait for three months before attempting it for a second time. In this context, obtaining accurate guidance on the length of time that a candidate might require to make a specified score gain was considered to be important.

At the same time, university departments are often flexible in admitting international students who fail to obtain the required IELTS scores on condition that they complete an English language course. The length of the course that a student is required to take is related to the distance between the IELTS score they present and that required for admission. At the time of writing, the British Association of Lecturers in English for Academic Purposes (BALEAP) provides guidelines to institutions, based on recommendations formerly made by the IELTS partners, that two months of intensive English study is broadly equivalent to one band on the nine-band IELTS scale (Bool et al 2003).

For washback, a key question is whether dedicated test preparation is able to accelerate score gains. Hamp-Lyons (1998) is critical of unscrupulous publishers of test preparation materials who claim, without empirical support, to facilitate rapid score gains. However, if test preparation is successful, there may be implications for learners, for admitting departments and for the validity of the test.

Course providers surveyed in Pilot Study Six were divided about how many contact hours it would take for learners to make a gain of one band on IELTS. Five reported that they were unable to judge. The most optimistic estimate was 10 hours (of instruction on a part-time course) and the most pessimistic 500 hours. The variation in estimates was considerable, did not show any clear clustering around numbers of hours and seemed to demonstrate the difficulty for respondents of predicting gains in this context.

Respondents also disagreed on whether it would be easier for learners to advance from Band 4 to 5, 5 to 6 or from 6 to 7. Of the 40 who made estimates, 15 saw progress as a steady process, estimating equal numbers of hours at each level. Of the other 25, 4 believed it became steadily more difficult with each band advanced and 5 saw the period of study required growing more dramatically. The remainder regarded progress as variable, with four considering that it would accelerate at certain levels (although there was no agreement about which level or levels this would be).

The test score data supplied by Cambridge ESOL provided evidence of the score gains possible on the official IELTS test. As no candidate was at that time permitted to retake the IELTS test within a three-month period (a restriction lifted in May 2006), the interval between tests was at least 12 weeks.

Figure 3.3 shows that repeating candidates with Writing scores at Band 5 or below on the initial test tended to improve their results on the second test. Those obtaining a Band 7 or 8 on the first occasion tended to receive a lower score on the second, while those starting on Band 6 tended to remain at the same level. Longer periods between tests did not appear to yield much greater score gains. However, as noted above, it is not clear from the data how far different lengths of time between tests might relate to periods of instruction or other language learning opportunities.

Figure 3.3 Mean score gains on IELTS Writing component for repeating candidates (Academic) 1998–2001

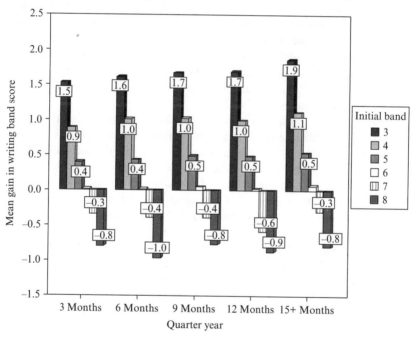

Table 3.9 summarises findings relating to the time required for specified score gains. The data suggests that there is limited consensus among professionals regarding the time required to make score gains. This may reflect the considerable variation in score gains observed among repeating candidates. Data from these repeating candidates further suggested that score gains were related to score on the first testing occasion, with low scorers making relatively greater gains than high scorers.

Table 3.9 Summary of pilot study findings relating to time required for score gain

	Course providers	Test score data
Time required for score gain	Disagreement on time required for score improvements.	Evidence from test scores that gains vary by level and may be more limited than anticipated.

Conclusions

The preliminary studies confirmed that IELTS plays an important role in university admissions (although it is not without competitors), being linked to entry requirements and to recommendations for periods of pre-sessional study in English for Academic Purposes. However, where both are available, preparation for the test is usually offered separately from other EAP course strands. IELTS preparation in the UK could occur in the form of intensive, often very brief, self-contained courses, or as a component within courses with rather broader aims. Such courses included those – often provided by universities – explicitly designed to prepare students for university study; and courses – often provided by language schools – aimed at developing a more general language ability.

Course providers, teachers and students shared the belief that the design of the IELTS test dictated practices on preparation courses. IELTS preparation courses appeared to share a set of features that marked them apart from other forms of EAP provision. These included, but were not limited to, test-taking practice, memorising phrases of relevance to the test tasks, studying model essays, and focusing on the language of description of graphs and diagrams. There was also some evidence that IELTS preparation classes tended to place a greater emphasis on grammar than did other EAP classes, a feature that would not seem to be directly related to test content. Some strategies for success reported by learners and encouraged by teachers, such as meeting local people and seeking opportunities to interact in English, also bore little direct relation to features of the test, but were apparently directed at a more general improvement of language abilities. Nevertheless, these strategies were seen to be of relevance to test performance.

For participants, IELTS preparation was set apart from other forms of EAP not so much by what it included as by what it excluded. Although the IELTS test was compared favourably with alternatives because it was felt to better reflect academic language use, teachers and learners with experience of both IELTS preparation and other EAP courses nonetheless remarked on the relatively narrow focus of the IELTS classroom. IELTS preparation was said to be relevant to university study, but tended to exclude such features as research and note-taking skills, integration of source material in written work, technical and subtechnical language and the (discourse) features of texts longer than 500 words. These effects are consistent with the predictions of the washback model in relation to limited overlap between test and target.

Both teachers and learners generally believed that success on the test was achievable for learners, unless they entered the programme at too low a level. Although learners generally regarded the test as important and many saw it as difficult, this did not necessarily lead to the kind of behaviour that might be implied by the washback model. While many did, some learners did not study for the test outside class, in spite of anxiety about their results. Again this suggests the importance of including participant characteristics in the washback model as they play a key role in mediating the influence of the test. In this context, maturity seemed to be an important factor with older post-graduate students readier to give up their leisure time in pursuit of their goal of succeeding on IELTS.

Participants pointed to a wide range of variables besides test preparation that might facilitate or inhibit score gains. Students tended to prioritise dedication and hard work, while teachers and course providers pointed to a much wider range of biographical, cultural, cognitive and affective variables. Suggestions from teachers and course providers that IELTS candidates from East Asia tend to make slower gains were supported by evidence from score data, with the caveat that there were no controls for instructional treatment. As a group, the East Asian IELTS retake population seemed to progress more slowly and to reap less benefit, in terms of Writing score gains, from moving to an (L1) English-speaking environment than its counterparts in Western Europe and other regions.

Regarding methodology, the studies suggested that a combination of quantitative and qualitative data could serve to relate the behaviour of participants to the influence of the test as a motivating factor on one side and to score outcomes on the other. The claims of participants about how the test influenced them in their teaching and learning provided input to questionnaires developed for the main study and suggested areas for more detailed probing in participant interviews.

Documentary evidence gathered in the first instance indicated that providers drew clear distinctions between IELTS directed courses, as test preparation, and other forms of EAP. The course providers' questionnaire provided extensive quantitative data relating to the areas of difference between course types, as well as indicating areas of variation among courses with similar aims. However, the data gave only a limited indication of how differences in course aims might relate to classroom practices. The initial surveys were also limited in the insights they offered into the relationship between course provision and the expectations and experiences of teachers and learners. It was not clear from this initial data whether the course outlines might reflect the practices of teachers and learners, their beliefs about how they should prepare either for the test or for academic study and their perceptions of overlap between these aims.

Qualitative interviews offered data with greater explanatory power. The face-to-face, open-ended nature of the interviews made it possible to probe teacher and learner beliefs about how their behaviour might impact on their chances of success on the test and intervening variables that might interact with the influence of the test. The structure provided by personal construct theory proved effective in generating ideas and focusing the scope of discussion. Themes emerging from these interviews could then be incorporated into the development of questionnaires, as in the follow-up survey of teachers, enabling an evaluation of the prevalence of the views expressed in the wider EAP teaching profession in the UK.

The pilot studies provided input to the main study in:

- Research methods: in the pilot phase, a combination of survey and interview methods proved effective in providing multiple perspectives on the teaching/learning context. In the main study, features such as the expectations of course content held by teachers and learners were investigated through questionnaire surveys, as well as focus group interviews with teachers and learners. The design of survey and interview instruments employed in the main study built on those used in the pilot studies.

- Content of main study instruments: following an iterative process of development, by which issues raised in one study could be pursued in the next phase, factors said by participants to affect examination success, such as familiarity with test content, were further investigated in the main study.

- Analysis and interpretation: the pilot studies demonstrated that the integration of evidence from multiple sources could usefully inform interpretation. In the main study, teacher and student beliefs, for example, could be accessed through surveys and questionnaires and considered together with direct classroom observation to build a multifaceted understanding of classroom events.

4 Main study methods and instruments

Chapter 1 indicated that washback is a complex phenomenon, and this complexity was confirmed through the pilot studies reported in Chapter 3. To reflect and address the complexity of the research focus, building on the outcomes of the pilot studies, the main study involved a range of participants, including both teachers and learners on a variety of courses. As in the pilot studies, diverse methods of data collection and analysis were employed. This chapter focuses on the methods used in the study in three areas, providing descriptions of:

- the participants involved and the recruitment procedures
- the content, rationale for and development of the research instruments
- the techniques used to analyse the data.

Participants and settings

Table 4.1 provides an overview of the participants in, and settings for, each stage of the main study. This table shows the extent of participation in each phase of the study for each of the 18 courses and 15 institutions involved. Course length is operationally defined in this study as the period between the administration of entry and exit tests. The actual length of the courses involved was usually one or two weeks longer than this period.

Student participants in the main study represented an opportunity sample of international students preparing for academic study at 15 institutions in the UK. On the basis of responses to the Course Providers' Survey (Pilot Study Five), a number of institutions were approached to request their involvement. It was intended to include institutions representing each of the course types identified in the Course Providers Survey: IELTS preparation, combination and pre-sessional EAP. Each student participating in the study signed a consent form allowing the use of their anonymised data.

Of 24 institutions approached, eight universities, two colleges of further education (FE) and seven private language colleges agreed to take part. Of these, one university (which offered an IELTS preparation option for large numbers of students within a pre-sessional EAP course) had to be excluded from the main study on the grounds that they were unable, for logistical and

Table 4.1 Overview of participants and settings

Institution	Course type†	IELTS AWM	Student surveys	Student number	Observation	Teacher focus group	Teacher survey	Student focus group	Course length (weeks)	Course intensity (hours)
University A	EAP	✓	✓	53			✓		4	23
University A	EAP	✓	✓	48			✓		8	23
University A	EAP	✓	✓	54	✓		✓		12	23
University B	EAP	✓	✓	104			✓		4	28
University B	EAP	✓	✓	60	✓		✓	✓	8	28
University C	EAP	✓	✓	12	✓		✓		10	21
University D	EAP	✓	✓	27			✓		4	21
University E	COM	✓	✓	4	✓	✓		✓	8	23
University F	COM	✓	✓	13	✓	✓		✓	10	20
University G	COM	✓	✓	1	✓	✓		✓	8	25
College A	IEL	✓	✓	33			✓		10	18
College B	IEL	✓	✓	12		✓	✓		10	2–21*
College C	IEL	✓	✓	25	✓	✓	✓	✓	6	25
College D	IEL	✓	✓	2					10	15
College E	COM	✓	✓	15	✓	✓			14	25
College F	IEL	✓	✓	1	✓	✓		✓	10	23
College G	IEL	✓	✓	4	✓	✓		✓	10	21
College H	IEL	✓	✓	8	✓	✓			4	21

Research Focus

* Some students on this course were studying full-time, others attended only for 2 hours each week.
† EAP = Presessional EAP Course, IEL = IELTS Preparation Course, COM = Combination Course

administrative reasons, to complete all parts of the study. In addition, take-up on some dedicated IELTS preparation courses was much lower than had been anticipated, with one IELTS preparation course at College B and a second at a private college being cancelled altogether for lack of students. As a result, fewer participants from IELTS-related courses were included than had been intended. The initial plan to include equal numbers of IELTS preparation and non-IELTS preparation students was therefore disappointed. In all, 663 students volunteered to participate in the research with 476 of these completing both entry and exit forms of the IELTS Academic Writing Module (AWM): an overall response rate of 71.8%.

The largest groups of student participants were studying on six pre-sessional English courses provided by three universities (referred to as Universities A, B and C). These comprised two courses of four weeks' duration, two of eight weeks, one of 10 weeks and one of 12 weeks. Smaller groups studying at other universities were attending an IELTS preparation option on presessional EAP courses (University D to University G: with courses ranging from four to 10 weeks). Others were attending colleges of further education (College A – F/T 10 weeks; College B P/T 10 weeks) or private sector language schools (College C to College G: courses ranging from four to 14 weeks). Full-time courses included between 15 and 28 hours per week of classroom instruction.

According to the categories established in Pilot Study Five (Chapter 3), the courses included in the case study at Universities A to C could all be classified as pre-sessional EAP (with no IELTS component). Courses at Universities D, E, F and G, and College E, were combination courses (EAP courses incorporating an IELTS preparation strand). The remaining courses were all categorised as IELTS preparation.

In all, 50 student nationalities were represented, with 73% of students (n = 349) being from East Asia (Table 4.2). The largest cohort was from China (162), with large numbers (94) also coming from Taiwan and a handful from Hong Kong (5). For the purpose of analysis, based on distinctions made by course providers in predicting score gains in Pilot Study Six, four regional groups were distinguished: China/Taiwan, Other East Asia, Western Europe and Other. The majority of the Other East Asia group was Japanese (54 of 88) with 19 from Thailand; the largest single group in the Western European cohort was Greek (23 of 61) with a further seven from Cyprus. In the Other cohort the largest groups were from Russia and Kazakhstan (10 and 11 of 66).

Data for the overall UK IELTS candidature for the period January 2000 to December 2002 shows that proportions were similar for all groups except the Other cohort. The higher proportion of candidates in the Other category among the IELTS candidature no doubt reflects the greater diversity of the national candidature, but also reflects the 16% of UK candidates taking the test for reasons of professional registration. This group is largely made up of candidates from outside the regions of East Asia and Western Europe.

Table 4.2 476 participants responding to IELTS AWM at course entry and exit by Nationality and Region of Origin

Country	N	%	Country	N	%
China/Taiwan			Ethiopia	3	4.57
China	162	62.07	Iran	2	3.03
Hong Kong	5	1.91	Jordan	1	1.52
Taiwan	94	36.02	Kazakhstan	11	16.67
Total	*261*	*100.00*	Latvia	1	1.52
			Lebanon	1	1.52
Other East Asia			Libya	3	4.55
Indonesia	2	2.27	Mexico	3	4.55
Japan	54	61.36	Mozambique	1	1.52
Korea	12	13.64	Nepal	3	4.55
Malaysia	1	1.14	Oman	3	4.55
Thailand	19	21.59	Pakistan	2	3.03
Total	*88*	*100.00*	Palestine	1	1.52
			Peru	1	1.52
Western Europe			Russia	10	15.15
Belgium	1	1.64	Saudi Arabia	2	3.03
UK	1	1.64	Slovakia	2	3.03
Cyprus	7	11.48	Slovenia	1	1.52
Finland	2	3.28	Sri Lanka	1	1.52
France	2	3.28	Tanzania	1	1.52
Germany	6	9.84	Ukraine	1	1.52
Greece	23	37.70	Venezuela	1	1.52
Italy	11	18.03	Yemen	1	1.52
Norway	1	1.64	*Total*	*66*	*100.00*
Spain	5	8.20			
Turkey	2	3.28			
Total	*61*	*100.00*			
Rest of the World					
Argentina	2	3.03			
Bahrain	1	1.52			
Belarus	1	1.52			
Bhutan	1	1.52			
Bolivia	1	1.52			
Brazil	1	1.52			
Colombia	1	1.52			
Egypt	2	3.03			

Table 4.3 Regional origin of students in current study compared with UK IELTS candidature 2000–2002

Region (%)	UK candidature 2000–2002	Current study
China/Taiwan	44.34	54.83
Other East Asia	13.58	18.49
Other	32.29	13.87
Western Europe	9.79	12.82

First languages (Table 4.4) were closely identified with region of origin. 'Chinese' was given as the first language of 254 learners. There were also 54 speakers of Japanese, 19 of Thai, 18 of Russian and 15 of Arabic.

Table 4.4 476 participants responding to IELTS AWM at course entry and exit by First Language

L1	N	%	L1	N	%	L1	N	%
Amharic	2	.4	Greek	28	5.9	Punjabi	1	.2
Arabic	15	3.2	Hungarian	1	.2	Russian	18	3.8
Binna	1	.2	Indonesian	1	.2	Sinhalese	1	.2
Cantonese	4	.8	Italian	11	2.3	Slovak	1	.2
Chinese	254	53.4	Japanese	54	11.3	Slovenian	1	.2
Chope	1	.2	Kazakh	5	1.1	Spanish	14	2.9
Dzongkha	1	.2	Korean	12	2.5	Taiwanese	5	1.1
Farsi	2	.4	Latvian	1	.2	Thai	19	4.0
Finnish	2	.4	Nepali	3	.6	Turkish	4	.8
French	4	.8	Norwegian	1	.2	Urdu	1	.2
German	6	1.3	Portuguese	1	.2			

Ages ranged from 15 to 48 with a mean of 25.4 and a standard deviation of 5.39 (Figure 4.1). IELTS preparation students were the youngest with an average age of 21.9 years, while combination course students averaged 25.1 and EAP students 26.4. Overall, 50.6% of students were female, 45.6% male, and 3.8% did not respond to the question. The highest proportion of females was on the IELTS preparation courses (61.3% of respondents) and the lowest was on the combination courses (48.7%).

Previous educational achievement varied across courses. Of students on IELTS preparation courses, 45.7% were educated to undergraduate level and a further 3.5% had already completed postgraduate studies. In contrast, 74.9% of pre-sessional EAP students had completed undergraduate and 10.9% had completed postgraduate studies. Of all students (33% of IELTS preparation, 64% of combination and 90% of pre-sessional) 69.5% intended to go on to study at postgraduate and 10.7% intended to study at undergraduate level (20% of IELTS, 29% of combination and 9% of pre-sessional students). Three students (0.6% of the total number) did not intend to progress to any form of academic study.

Of those on IELTS preparation courses, 81.8% reported that they were intending to take an official IELTS test within the next six months, as did 69.1% of students on combination courses and 18.7% on pre-sessional EAP courses. Of all students, 41.6% reported having taken an official IELTS test before (15% on IELTS preparation, 33% on combination and 49% on pre-sessional courses). The mean IELTS band scores reported by these students (representing their overall band scores on the test as a whole, not the Writing component alone) were 5.27 on IELTS preparation, 5.58 on combination

Figure 4.1 Histogram of distribution of student age

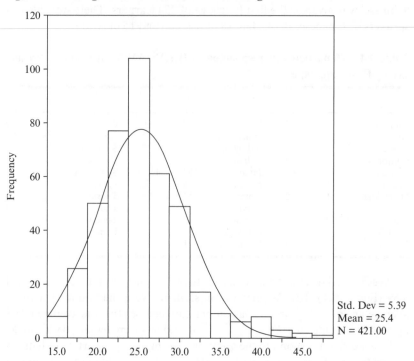

and 5.87 on EAP courses. In short, learners on dedicated IELTS preparation courses tended to be younger, educated to a lower level and with lower levels of language ability than their pre-sessional counterparts. They were also less likely to have taken an IELTS test previously.

Constraining factors on the research methods

The nature of the study necessarily placed constraints on the kinds of investigation that could be undertaken. The co-operation of a variety of course providers and of teachers and learners was essential to the success of the study. From the earliest stages it was clear that the integration of the research with operational exigencies was a necessary precondition for access to the data. A process of negotiation with participants and progressive piloting of instruments was required to establish how much time could be made available for completing the tests and surveys and ways in which the study instruments could be made useful to the participants as well as the researcher.

As a result of this process, the instruments were developed with the needs of the participants in mind. Writing tests were employed by institutions for placement purposes and for the ongoing assessment of student progress. Grammar and vocabulary tests were also used for placement purposes and as diagnostic tools. Questionnaires A and B were each accompanied by guidelines on the interpretation of the final section, so that they could be exploited in class after completion.

Instruments

The instruments used with students in the main study consisted of:

* four linked forms of the IELTS Academic Writing Module (AWM)
* two student questionnaires (Questionnaire A and Questionnaire B) probing background and affective variables considered likely to impact on score gains (Appendices 5 and 6)
* a test of grammar and two tests of vocabulary knowledge
* two brief questionnaire forms administered before and after each administration of the IELTS AWM, addressing knowledge of the IELTS Writing component, perceptions of task difficulty and use of test-taking strategies (Appendices 2 and 3).

Groups of students also participated in focus group discussions, based on the questionnaire sections, concerning their courses and their reaction to taking the IELTS test.

In addition, teachers on the focal courses were either administered a Teacher Questionnaire (Appendix 4), or participated in focus group interviews, based on the same set of questions, probing their attitudes towards the test and influences on teaching methods and course content.

In addition to the tests and surveys, classroom observations were carried out at selected centres. The observation schedule used in these sessions appears in Appendix 7.

Following a distinction made by Dunkin and Biddle (1974), the instruments were intended to assemble data from a variety of perspectives with bearing on:

a) presage variables: those that learners brought to the course such as age, L1 and previous experiences of learning English

b) process variables relating to experiences during the course such as course type and extra-curricular exposure to English, and self-assessments of learning gains

c) product variables to do with course outcomes such as gains in IELTS Academic Writing band score.

The development of the instruments and the manner in which they were intended to tap these three categories of variable is described in the following sections.

Development of the instruments for the main study: (i) Questionnaires

In addition to length of study, numerous learner characteristics affect language-learning gains (Skehan 1989, Spolsky 1989, Larsen-Freeman and Long 1991, Ellis 1994, Mitchell and Myles 1998). Informants in the pilot surveys also supported the notion that IELTS score gains are related to a range of variables. The testimony of course providers in particular (Pilot Study Six), points to a wide range of learner characteristics affecting how successful an individual is likely to be in making IELTS score gains.

This raises the issue of whether a single recommendation for required periods of study can be made for all learners, regardless of background. If not, refinement of recommendations rests on the collection of relevant information concerning test takers and the relating of this information to score gains.

To this end, in addition to administering the IELTS AWM, background and affective features that might impact on student learning were also measured. A set of questionnaire instruments was developed for administration in parallel with the IELTS AWM. This was an iterative process, which drew on the available literature, the pilot studies described above, personal judgement and informal contacts with study participants and other language-teaching professionals. The instruments were then piloted and further refined before being employed in the main study.

The final versions of the questionnaires probed students' biographical details (age, L1, nationality, gender, highest level of education completed, exposure to English, previous experience and knowledge of IELTS, sources of motivation, orientation towards the learning context, expectations and experiences of study, learning channel preferences, approaches to learning, self-assessment of learning gains, learning strategies and test-taking strategies).

Questionnaire development

From the literature it is apparent that a wide range of factors have been found to influence the rate and degree of second language acquisition (Spolsky 1989, Skehan 1991, Ellis 1994). In a review of research, Spolsky (1989) lists some 79 variables that may exert such an influence and suggests that these interact in complex ways. Factors that have been investigated include features of a learner's background such as age, social class and L1, and psychological factors including intelligence, personality, motivation, language aptitude and language-learning strategies.

Skehan (1989) unifies a number of research traditions concerned with individual differences in a model of language learning. In conjunction with age, gender and other features of a learner's background, this study employs Skehan's model as a preliminary framework for the investigation of how learner variables may interact with test features in determining outcomes. In addition, addressing the relationship between test taker and test task, this study also considers task characteristics, test anxiety, test familiarity and test-taking strategies.

There is evidence that individual learner differences are an important factor in EAP success for NNS. Weir (1983) incorporated a number of social and psychological indicators, finding features such as age and educational experience to be significant predictors of performance. Hawkey (1982) included personality and attitude factors. Although he found language proficiency to be a strong predictor of EAP success in second language settings, cognitive style and attitude also proved to be significant factors.

While Hawkey (1982) uses correlational techniques, the need for explanatory models and the complexity of the interrelationship between large numbers of learner variables have led to innovation in statistical analysis. In recent years, techniques such as path analysis or structural equation modelling (Gardner 1985, Wen and Johnson 1997, Purpura 1999), cluster analysis (Skehan 1991) and neural networks (Boldt and Ross 1998, Hughes-Wilhelm 1999) have been employed to accommodate a wide range of interacting variables and to model their relationships.

Hughes-Wilhelm (1997, 1999), taking an exploratory approach, investigated an array of 70 student background features, including 57 language-learning variables, as predictors of success (measured by class grades, rate of progress and course completion) on an English course which builds from a General English focus to an EAP focus for students preparing to enter US universities. Although entry proficiency (TOEFL test score) was the best single predictor of success, accuracy of prediction was considerably enhanced by the inclusion of other learner characteristics.

Among features contributing most to the prediction of success (defined as rate of progress and level of final achievement on a university language programme) were:

- communicative use of English both in school (reading and writing) and outside formal education (speaking and listening)
- school success and prior experience of academic study
- type and source of exposure to English and
- individual characteristics (self-confidence, attitudes and motivations when learning English) (Hughes-Wilhelm 1999).

Interestingly, low-success learners were more likely than high-success learners to indicate they were learning English to obtain a required TOEFL score, while high-success learners were more likely to cite work-related reasons in addition to academic purposes (Hughes-Wilhelm 1997).

Hughes-Wilhelm (1999) intends to expand her research agenda to incorporate preferred cognitive, learning and work styles, predicting that such features are likely to influence both progress and outcomes and could be important indicators of learning needs. The present study will need to take account of such factors, bearing in mind that the relationship between learner attitudes and strategies may be both disjunctive – different combinations of background features may lead to the same outcomes – and reciprocal – a test may motivate, but prior motivation may determine how a test affects learning choices (Skehan 1989).

Rationale for questionnaire items

The questionnaire instruments were developed to probe three areas of the Skehan model: opportunities for TL use, the learner and learning. However, the nature of the study dictated that there were aspects of the model that could not be addressed directly through the questionnaires. Among features of the learner that could not readily be measured in this context, or that raised objections from participants, were intelligence, aptitude and personality variables.

Questionnaire A: presage variables

The first questionnaire (Questionnaire A), for administration at course entry, set out to gather background information on learners, including prior experience of studying English, orientation towards studying in the target context, expectations of course content and the learning style preferences the students brought to their courses. A second questionnaire (Questionnaire B) to be administered at course exit was targeted retrospectively at actions and beliefs relating to the period of study (see Appendix 6).

Introductory items: learner background

Respondents were asked to provide their names as the primary means of organising and combining data. While the lack of anonymity may have influenced some students to provide answers designed to elicit approval from teachers or administrators, complete exclusion of names from the responses was considered both impractical and undesirable for the following reasons. Firstly, data from the different instruments would need to be combined for analysis and names would provide the simplest means of tracking the responses. Secondly, as agreement for centres to participate had been secured on the basis that all instruments should serve some pedagogic purpose, the questionnaires would be administered in class by teachers and true anonymity of response would therefore be unrealistic. Alternative, less direct means of tracking data via code numbers or similar means might suggest to respondents some clandestine motive for identifying their responses. During the pilot study (including Pilot Study Two and piloting of the learning strategy inventory) and trial phases, no participants displayed any reluctance to give their name or other personal details, so this approach was maintained for the main study. Participants were given the option of withdrawing from the project at any stage.

A standard selected response format for the entire questionnaire was preferred over open ended questions to allow for quantitative comparisons. However, to accommodate the variety of information, a range of item types proved necessary. These included yes/no responses, 5-point Likert scales and 9-point rating scales (the justification for each is discussed below). Instructions and examples were provided at every stage and pilot studies demonstrated that the multiple response formats were not generally problematic for the learners.

Taking previous exposure to English as a potential predictor of gain, the first section of the survey asked respondents about their experiences of learning English. A list of the items with a brief commentary on each follows.

4. In your country, or before moving to Britain, how often have you used English in your work (including all the jobs you have done)?
    I have worked mainly in   I have not used English
    English (1)   at work (9)
       1   2   3   4   5   6   7   8   9

The pilot version of the item had called for a binary response: *In your job, did you have opportunities to use English? Yes/No.* The wording was refined during piloting in response to queries from students about whether this related to their most recent job and to the likelihood that even very minimal English usage at work would elicit a positive response. A 9-point scale was selected to discriminate between a wide range of positive responses, from very occasional use of English to a predominantly English working environment.

This and the following item targeted extra-curricular use of English, a variable found to be significant by Hughes-Wilhelm (1999). The limitation of responses to experience in the 'home country' was designed to prevent overlap with later items targeting experience in the UK or other English-speaking countries.

5. At home or at work, in your country, how often do you use English for socialising (talking to friends)?,
    I usually socialise in   I usually socialise using my
    English (1)   own/other language (9)
       1   2   3   4   5   6   7   8   9

This item also addressed extra-curricular use of English, replacing a number of pilot items including, *how many hours each week do you spend talking English outside school?* It appeared likely that at this early stage in a course, any pattern of using L2 outside class would not yet be established and that question would be better posed at course exit. However, socialising in English in the home country could be a factor promoting learning gains and might additionally be associated with positive attitudes towards the English language.

The next item targeted the use of written English:

6. At home or at work, in your country, how often do you write in English?
    I write in English every day (1)   I never write in English (9)
    $\quad$ 1 $\quad$ 2 $\quad$ 3 $\quad$ 4 $\quad$ 5 $\quad$ 6 $\quad$ 7 $\quad$ 8 $\quad$ 9

Clearly experience of writing in English could contribute to performance on written tasks and to rate of progress. Home and professional writing are distinguished from school or academic writing, which is addressed in a later section. It might also have been desirable to have gathered information on the nature of the writing students had experienced, but any distinction between forms of writing in additional items would have added to the length of the survey and could have proved confusing for students with limited knowledge of writing genres and varying conceptions of the meaning of terms used in typologies of writing tasks such as reports, memoranda and personal letters.

Also of potential relevance to L2 writing is exposure to L2 written text:

7. At home or at work, in your country, how often do you read in English?
    I read in English every day (1)   I never read in English (9)
    $\quad$ 1 $\quad$ 2 $\quad$ 3 $\quad$ 4 $\quad$ 5 $\quad$ 6 $\quad$ 7 $\quad$ 8 $\quad$ 9

Again, although such information would have been of interest, for reasons of brevity and clarity no attempt was made to distinguish between reading text-types or reading purposes.

The next set of items, prefaced *About studying English*, targeted exposure to English in the home and at school.

8. As a child, did you live with a parent, guardian or other close relation who was a *native speaker* of English (English was their first language)?
    YES ☐   NO ☐

Having a native speaker of English as a caregiver might contribute to proficiency, affect and rate of progress (Spolsky 1989). The earliest questionnaire form had included a number of additional items on family background, which Hughes-Wilhelm (1999) found to predict progress. These included home location (urban/rural), parental occupation, parental level of education and study overseas by other family members. Course teachers and directors consulted during the development process regarded these items to be unacceptably personal in a questionnaire of this nature (Hughes-Wilhelm employed data which had been gathered in hour-long personal interviews). In response to the objections, given the need to secure the co-operation of participants in the study, the family background items were excluded in advance of piloting.

> 9. As a child, did you live with a parent, guardian or other close relation who could have a conversation in English (although English was not their first language)?
>   YES ☐   NO ☐

Parental knowledge of English may contribute to learning and might also be an indirect indicator of social class – a variable that could not be addressed more directly for the reasons given above.

The next series of items sought information on formal language-learning experience. Hughes-Wilhelm (1999) reports that hours of study alone were not a good predictor of success on an intensive English programme and suggests that the nature of instruction should also be addressed. While asking learners how many hours of instruction they had received under which method of instruction was felt to be unrealistically detailed for a paper-based survey; a single question such as that used on the IELTS Candidate Information Sheet (*How many years have you been studying English?*) would be uninformative and perhaps misleading as it includes no indication of settings or intensity of study.

For the purpose of this study, divisions were made between levels of formal schooling and between English language instruction and English-medium content instruction. General indications were sought of teachers' use of English (direct method instruction), exposure to NS teachers of English and the role of writing in English language classes as well as instruction in writing in the L1.

> 10. Did you study English in . . .?
>   Kindergarten ☐   Primary school ☐   Secondary school ☐
>   (age 3–6)   (7–11)   (12–17)
>   University/college ☐   Extra language classes outside school ☐

Students responded by marking any that applied. This item was intended to indicate approximately how long students had spent studying English in formal schooling. Not all school systems fit the age bands set out here, and there is no indication of the number of hours studied. However, it was felt that respondents could not be expected to recall the details of how many hours they had studied each subject in school and more detailed responses might therefore prove less reliable.

Pilot versions of this item required participants only to mark those levels at which they had attended English classes. Respondents tended to mark only their earliest level of English classes. As a result, the data was ambiguous as to whether or not they had attended English classes at later stages. The items were therefore revised to require a yes/no response for each level.

11. Did you study English as your main/major subject at university?
     YES ☐   NO ☐   I have not been to university ☐

English majors would probably receive more exposure to the language at university than others, and might have greater intrinsic motivation for studying English than their peers.

12. Have you ever been taught other subject classes (for example science or maths) in English?
     Yes, at school ☐   Yes, at university ☐   Never ☐

In addition to the advantages claimed for studying academic subjects in the medium of English for learning the language (Ellis 1994), experience of learning English in this way might prove better preparation for the demands of university study than classroom language learning. Greater exposure to technical vocabulary and experience of using study skills in English might enable more rapid progress on EAP courses.

13. How many of your English lessons in your country were given by native speakers of English?

Most classes (1)	More than half	About half (5)	Less than half	None (9)
1 2	3	4 5 6	7 8	9

Exposure to L1 English-speaking teachers may contribute to the effectiveness of school language provision (Weir 1983). In the initial pilot, this item, following Weir (1983) and Hughes-Wilhelm (1999), read, *How many teachers did you have who were native speakers of English?* However, the number of native speakers (who could be short-term teaching assistants or long-term class teachers) seems less relevant than the proportion of classes given by such teachers; hence the item was reworked for the purposes of the main study.

14. How much of the time in class did your English teachers speak to you in English?

All the time (1)	More than half	About half the time (5)	Less than half	Never (9)
1 2	3	4 5 6	7 8	9

This item attempted to capture differences of instructional approach. Grammar-translation methodology is typically associated with the use of the learners' L1 in the classroom (Watanabe 1997), while more direct methods require the use of English. More use of English in the classroom at school has been associated with more rapid progress in university English programmes (Hughes-Wilhelm 1999).

15. How often did you practise writing in English in your classes?

In most classes (1)	More than half	About half (5)	Less than half	Never (9)
1	2 3	4 5 6	7 8	9

As noted for item 6 above, previous experience of writing in English might be considered likely to contribute to success on an EAP writing course.

16. How often do you usually write essays and reports in your own language?

Often (about once a month) (1)	Quite often	Sometimes (once a year) (5)	Occasionally	Never (9)
1	2 3	4 5 6	7 8	9

Experience of writing in the L1 could make a significant contribution to writing in L2 to the extent that composing skills are transferable across languages (Grabe and Kaplan 1996). There are variations between countries in the value placed on academic writing with some international students apparently having very little experience of writing even in their national languages (Jordan 1997).

17. Since leaving school/university have you studied English with a teacher in your own country?
    YES for _____ *years* ☐   NO (→ *GO TO 19*) ☐
    ↓

18. Since leaving school/university, in your country, how many hours did you study English with a teacher each week?
    about _____ *hours*

Items 17 and 18 target experience of studying English after completion of formal education. Again, the information is likely to be rather crude, given the range of study modes available, but experience of studying with a teacher might facilitate the return to study for mature students and continued language study might prove an advantage for all.

19. Have you stayed in any English-speaking countries for more than two weeks (including this trip, if you are in Britain now)?

YES for a total of _____ years, _____ months ☐
NO (➔ *GO TO 22*) ☐
⬇

20. How long have you studied English in any English speaking coun-
     tries (including this school, if you are in Britain now)?
     For a total of _____ *years,* _____ *months*

21. If you studied English in an English speaking country, how many
     hours did you study each week on average?
     about _____ hours

Items 19 to 21 target experience of living and studying in an English-speaking
country. Those with greater experience might be expected to suffer less from
initial culture shock, and perhaps to have an advantage in language learning.
Conversely, one of the course providers (Pilot Study Six) suggested that
those with exposure to intensive English programmes immediately before
entry might benefit less from pre-sessional English in improving their IELTS
scores. Spending time in the UK as a language student might thus be an
inhibiting factor on score gains.

22. Have you ever studied on an IELTS preparation course before?
     YES for _____ weeks ☐   NO ☐

This item sought information on which students had previous experience of
IELTS courses. It was anticipated that those with prior experience of IELTS
preparation might make less gain on IELTS preparation courses, having
already benefited from test familiarisation. On the other hand, such students
on non-IELTS pre-sessional courses might be better able to relate their newly
acquired knowledge to the demands of the IELTS tasks.

The next three sections of the survey shared the same format.
Respondents were presented with a series of statements each accompanied
by a 5-point scale with a choice between *definitely agree, tend to agree, tend to
disagree, definitely disagree* and, alternatively, *I don't know/cannot answer the
question.* A 5-point scale was chosen on the grounds that the use of more
points encourages precision (Hatch and Lazaraton 1991), but that respondents may have difficulty in making distinctions between more than five categories of response (Hopkins, Stanley and Hopkins 1990). At the end of each
section, open-ended comments were invited to allow learners to add personal
views unaddressed by the selected response items.

Section 1: Motivation for study

The first set of items addressed motivation for studying English and for
entering higher education in the UK. Sources of motivation have been shown

to affect language acquisition (see for example Ehrman and Oxford 1995, Gardner, Tremblay and Masgoret 1997). In university settings, Blue (1991) and Blue and Archibald (1999) have shown that students may be motivated to study in the UK as much by a desire to improve their English as by interest in studying an academic subject. More language learning occurs within the university when learners are as motivated to learn the language as they are to learn about their academic subject. It may be that progress on a preparatory language-learning course is similarly affected; those who prioritise an academic subject over the aim of learning English may make less improvement in their English skills.

In trialling, responses had involved a ranking from *my most important reason* to *not at all important*, however, a number of respondents ranked several items as being most important. In order to establish which of the items was most important to the learners, items RE6 and RE12, which force a choice between the listed reasons, were added to the survey (see Box 4.1).

Section 2: Orientation to the language study context

In the next section, items targeted affective factors including self-perception of language-learning aptitude, test-related anxiety, orientation towards writing in English and attitude towards the host culture and study context. The intention was to gain general indices of orientation towards the study context. This included self-confidence in studying English and living in the UK both at the level of a general self-confidence in language learning and cultural adjustment and at the more specific level of self-confidence and enjoyment of writing in English.

In the matter of satisfaction with the study context, items SC02, SC04, and SC11 built on Hawkey (1982) and were aimed at orientation to the host culture with SC08 and SC18 focused on the school. Items SC01, SC03 and SC12 targeted a general self-perception of aptitude, or self-confidence for language study. Other items were based on Cheng, Horwitz and Schallert (1999), tapping the L2 writing anxiety dimensions of *aversiveness of writing in English* (SC06, SC09 and SC19) and *low self-confidence in writing in English* (SC05, SC07, SC14, SC15), which is also taken to be an indicator of aptitude. Thus SC05, SC06, SC07, SC09, SC14, SC15 and SC19 were directed at a construct of *Self-Confidence in English Writing Ability*. Items SC10, SC13, SC16 and SC17 tapped *Test Anxiety* and were developed from Sarason's (1980) Test Anxiety Scale. This scale is based in interference theory, which postulates that test anxiety causes learners to underperform on test tasks by interfering with their capacity to process information. High test anxiety would therefore be expected to suppress a student's IELTS AWM band score relative to ability and might also inhibit measured gains. (See Box 4.2.)

Box 4.1 Questions RE1 – RE12

In this section, we would like to find out about your reasons for taking this course and for studying in an English speaking country.

	I definitely agree	I tend to agree	I tend to disagree	I definitely disagree	I don't know / I cannot answer the question
RE1 I am taking this course because I want to get a good grade on IELTS (or other test/assessment called: _____).	4	3	1	0	2
RE2 I am taking this course because I want to learn useful skills for studying at university.	4	3	1	0	2
RE3 I am studying on this course because I want to improve my general ability to use English.	4	3	1	0	2
RE4 I am required to take the course by my employer, my parents, or other authority. (_____)	4	3	1	0	2
RE5 I have a different reason for taking this course (write your reason here): (my reason is: _____).	4	3	1	0	2
RE6 Which reason for taking this course (RE1 – RE5) is most important for you (circle one)?	RE1 RE2 RE3 RE4 RE5				
RE7 I am going to college/university in an English-speaking country to improve my English.	4	3	1	0	2
RE8 I am going to college/university in an English-speaking country to help me get a good job in the future.	4	3	1	0	2
RE9 I am going to college/university in an English-speaking country to study a subject that interests me.	4	3	1	0	2
RE10 I am required to attend university/college by my employer, my parents, or other authority. (_____)	4	3	1	0	2
RE11 I have a different reason for going to college/university in an English speaking country: (my reason is: _____).	4	3	1	0	2
RE12 Which reason for going to college (RE7 – RE11) is most important for you (circle one)?	RE7 RE8 RE9 RE10 RE11				

Box 4.2 Questions SC01 – SC19

In this section, we would like to find out how you feel about learning languages and about taking tests.

		I definitely agree	I tend to agree	I tend to disagree	I definitely disagree	I don't know / I cannot answer the question
SC01	People say that I am good at language learning.	4	3	1	0	2
SC02	I feel happy about living in an English speaking country.	4	3	1	0	2
SC03	I usually did better than other students at my school in English classes.	4	3	1	0	2
SC04	I do NOT really like the British way of life.	4	3	1	0	2
SC05	I am NOT good at writing in English.	4	3	1	0	2
SC06	I feel I will never really enjoy writing in English	4	3	1	0	2
SC07	Writing classes are difficult for me.	4	3	1	0	2
SC08	I am pleased I chose to study at this school.	4	3	1	0	2
SC09	I like writing down my ideas in English.	4	3	1	0	2
SC10	If we had no tests, I think I would actually learn more.	4	3	1	0	2
SC11	I usually enjoy meeting British people.	4	3	1	0	2
SC12	I think learning languages is more difficult for me than for the average learner.	4	3	1	0	2
SC13	During an important test, I often feel so nervous that I forget facts I really know.	4	3	1	0	2
SC14	I DON'T think I write in English as well as other students.	4	3	1	0	2
SC15	It is easy for me to write good English essays.	4	3	1	0	2
SC16	Even when I'm well prepared for a test, I feel very worried about it.	4	3	1	0	2

SC17	I don't study any harder for final exams than for the rest of my course work.	4	3	1	0	2
SC18	I think the Writing classes will be useful for me.	4	3	1	0	2
SC19	I enjoy writing in English.	4	3	1	0	2

Section 3: Expectations for language study

Section 3 focused on the expectations students brought to their courses. This was intended both to provide a point of comparison between courses – do students hold different expectations of IELTS and EAP focused courses? – and to indicate whether individual preference for IELTS preparation would predict score gains on the test.

Items were drawn from syllabus documents and publicity for pre-sessional EAP courses derived from Pilot Studies One and Five, teacher comments from Pilot Study Four on activities occurring with greater frequency on either EAP or IELTS courses, IELTS preparation textbooks, responses to the pilot student survey (Pilot Study Two) and previous surveys of EAP courses (Jordan 1997). Item CE27 was introduced following trialling as respondents tended to mark all items as important. (See Box 4.3.)

Section 4: Learning style preferences

Skehan describes learning style as a 'general predisposition, voluntary or not, towards processing information in a particular way' (Skehan 1991). Although a wide variety of learning styles have been investigated, the most consistent findings have been for perceptual learning preferences. Bailey, Onwuegbuzie and Daley (2000) used Dunn, Dunn and Price (1991) *Productivity Environmental Preference Survey* (PEPS), finding that students with the highest levels of achievement in a foreign language were likely to favour informal classroom designs, to be responsible in completing their work, to prefer not to receive information in the kinesthetic mode, and to require mobility in learning environments.

Questioning whether instruments devised for North Americans could be used with international students, Reid (1987) developed her Perceptual Learning Style Preference Questionnaire (PLSPQ) to investigate the learning styles of 1,234 ESL learners at university-affiliated intensive English centres in the US and a comparison group of 154 native English-speaking university students. The PLSPQ was developed on the basis of existing learning style instruments, with modifications suggested by NNS informants and consultants in the field of linguistics, education and cross-cultural studies. The

Box 4.3 Questions CE01 – CE27

In this section, we would like to learn about what you want to study during this course, and what you expect to do in your classes.

		I definitely agree	I tend to agree	I tend to disagree	I definitely disagree	I don't know / I cannot answer the question
CE01	I expect to learn specialist vocabulary for my university subject.	4	3	1	0	2
CE02	I expect to learn general vocabulary.	4	3	1	0	2
CE03	I expect to learn about the kinds of writing tasks students do at university.	4	3	1	0	2
CE04	I expect to learn about differences between university education in my country and in Britain.	4	3	1	0	2
CE05	I expect to learn ways of improving my English Language test scores.	4	3	1	0	2
CE06	I expect to learn words and phrases for describing graphs and diagrams.	4	3	1	0	2
CE07	I expect to learn how to use evidence to support my written arguments.	4	3	1	0	2
CE08	I expect to learn how to organise an essay to help the reader to understand.	4	3	1	0	2
CE09	I expect to learn how to communicate my ideas effectively in writing.	4	3	1	0	2
CE10	I expect to learn grammar.	4	3	1	0	2
CE11	I expect to learn how to write university essays and reports.	4	3	1	0	2
CE12	I expect to learn how to find information from books to use in writing essays.	4	3	1	0	2
CE13	I expect to learn how to use quotations and references in academic writing.	4	3	1	0	2
CE14	I expect to learn how to edit and redraft my written work.	4	3	1	0	2
CE15	I expect to learn how to use ideas from text books or academic journals in my writing.	4	3	1	0	2
CE16	I expect to learn how to write long essays or reports of 1,000 words or more.	4	3	1	0	2

CE17	I expect to learn how to organise my time for studying.	4	3	1	0	2
CE18	I expect my teacher to correct my grammar mistakes in my written work.	4	3	1	0	2
CE19	I expect the activities we do in class will be similar to the ones on the IELTS test.	4	3	1	0	2
CE20	I expect to learn quick and efficient ways of reading books in English.	4	3	1	0	2
CE21	I expect to learn how to write successful test essays.	4	3	1	0	2
CE22	I expect to read books and articles about my specialist subject area.	4	3	1	0	2
CE23	I expect to learn how to write in a formal, academic style.	4	3	1	0	2
CE24	I expect to take practice tests in class.	4	3	1	0	2
	Other points you expect to study.					
CE25	_____	4	3	1	0	2
CE26	_____	4	3	1	0	2
CE27	Which of these items (CE01 – CE24) do you think is most important for you? _____					

process of development and the issues arising from it are described in greater detail in Reid (1990b).

The instrument consists of 30 items made up of randomly distributed sets of five items each targeting one of six learning styles. Four of these are perceptual – visual (effectively reading), auditory, kinesthetic and tactile – the remaining two indicate preferences for group or individual study. Items consist of a statement, to which students respond by indicating their degree of agreement on a 5-point Likert scale.

As learning style preferences are held to be relatively invariant features of the individual learner, the instrument was integrated into a course entry questionnaire to provide an indication of how far such preferences might affect progress.

For the purposes of this study, the PLSPQ was trialled with 45 EAP learners, who were able to comment on the items both in writing and in oral discussion. It was also critiqued by three experts in applied linguistics, and four course directors responsible for EAP programmes.

The student respondents apparently found the PLSPQ the most difficult section of the course entry questionnaire, with four of the 41 respondents indicating that they found items from this section difficult to answer. Further, in discussion following the administration, three students expressed disagreement with the conclusions suggested by the PLSPQ regarding their learning style preferences.

Two of the three applied linguists objected to items on the survey on grounds of ambiguity, a complaint taken up by two of the course directors. These objections centred on the comparative language employed. During the process of revision, dependent comparative clauses were removed for the sake of simplifying the items. Unfortunately, although Reid's (1987) ESL informants apparently found the final wording clear and unambiguous (Reid 1990b), the resulting statements appear somewhat vague. Item 7, for example is worded '*When someone tells me how to do something in class, I learn it better.*' This is ambiguous as it is unclear whether the respondent should compare their learning with occasions when they are told nothing at all, or with occasions when they are given written instructions or visual demonstrations. Comparative language is used – '*better*' – but no basis for comparison is provided. Just three items; 9, 24 and 29, provide points of comparison: Q4. *I remember things I have heard in class better than things I have read*, Q24. *I learn better by reading than by listening to someone* and Q29. *I learn more by reading textbooks than by listening to lectures.* The problem here is that it is unclear whether these items tap a positive preference for reading or a negative preference for listening.

Further problems with the PLSPQ were found by Wintergest, DeCapua and Itzen (2001) who conducted a factor analytic study with 100 university ESL learners in New York. Similarly to my experience in trialling, their interview data sometimes contradicted the PLSPQ results. Furthermore, the factor analysis failed to support the six style preferences hypothesised by Reid (1987) and the authors proposed an alternative interpretation based on individual, group and project preferences (Wintergest et al 2001). Although the emergence of a simple factor structure appears encouraging with respect to group and individual preferences (also the least problematic scales for Reid 1990b), the project factor does not reflect any previously established category of learning style, nor is it clear how a project learning style preference would relate to the individual or group preferences.

A further issue, acknowledged by Reid (1990b), involves the narrowing of the visual preference scale to items addressing only reading. Visual preference scales normed on NS participants incorporate charts, diagrams, maps and other forms of visual representation. Reid, however, was unable to build reliable scales for NNS employing the full range of items. Her response, later regretted, was to eliminate all but the reading items from the scale, effectively narrowing the visual preference scale to one addressing reading alone. The possibility that reading preference might form a separate scale for NNS, distinct from a broader visual preference, thus remained unexplored.

Having raised these questions regarding the validity of the PLSPQ, it followed that the instrument was inadequate in its original form and would need to be revised, removed or replaced. As discussed above, however, no alternative instrument could match the PLSPQ for ease of administration and no additional administration time could be made available for a lengthier or more complex form. Equally, within the terms of the research, insufficient time would be available for the development of an adequately trialled replacement questionnaire. On the other hand, the complete abandonment of the PLSPQ would have deprived the study of a potentially significant predictor.

The most acceptable solution was felt to be the modification of the PLSPQ in line with the criticisms and questions raised by the trial respondents and expert advisors.

To accomplish this, the response format was modified. Firstly, to disambiguate the bipolar comparisons implicit in the PLSPQ, Reid's (1987) statements were adapted and combined into dyads, forming the poles of 20 9-point rating scales. Nine-point, rather than 5-point rating scales were employed to allow for discrimination between strengths of attitudes on either side. Secondly, items causing difficulty to NNS in trialling were reworded or replaced. In this way, a randomly ordered 20-item questionnaire was constructed made up of 16 items targeting sensory learning style preferences and four targeting group/individual preferences. The two items discussed below illustrate the process of item revision.

> LP06 *I learn better by participating in role plays – I learn better when the teacher tells me something.*

This item was adapted from items 19 and 1 (*I understand things better in class when I participate in role playing* and *When the teacher tells me the instructions, I understand better*) on the PLSPQ. The wording was adapted so that both statements open with the same phrase: *I learn better*. The wording was also simplified in response to the comments of three NNS informants in pre-trialling.

A second item (*I enjoy making models or doing crafts – I enjoy reading for pleasure*) was adapted, again in consultation with NNS informants, to reflect the broader interpretation of learning style found in many instruments devised for NS students, such as Dunn et al's PEPS (1991), and acknowledged by Reid (1990b) with respect to items tapping the visual learning preference. See Box 4.4 for LP01–LP20; and Appendix 5 for the complete set of instructions that accompanied the questions.

Timing for Questionnaire A completion ranged from 15 minutes for the fastest to 30 minutes for the slowest respondents, with most, even at the lowest levels of proficiency completing all items within the 25 minutes recommended. In trialling, learners generally indicated that they had found the questions straightforward to answer and did not feel that the form was too long or too demanding.

Box 4.4 Questions LP01 – LP20

LP01 I prefer to study by making or building things (TP)   I prefer to study by looking at charts, maps or diagrams (VP)

1	2	3	4	5	6	7	8	9

LP02 I learn better when the teacher tells me something (AP)   I learn better when I can touch the things I am learning about (TP)

1	2	3	4	5	6	7	8	9

LP03 I learn better when I work alone on assignments (IP)   I learn better when I work on group projects (GP)

1	2	3	4	5	6	7	8	9

LP04 I understand things better when I practise a new skill (KP)   I understand things better when the teacher gives a lecture (AP)

1	2	3	4	5	6	7	8	9

LP05 I understand more when I work on an assignment with two or three classmates (GP)   I understand more when I work by myself on assignments (IP)

1	2	3	4	5	6	7	8	9

LP06 I learn better by participating in role plays (KP)   I learn better when the teacher tells me something (AP)

1	2	3	4	5	6	7	8	9

LP07 I remember images and pictures (VP)   I remember things that I have heard people say (AP)

1	2	3	4	5	6	7	8	9

LP08 I understand better by reading books (VP)   I understand better by doing experiments or practical activities (KP)

1	2	3	4	5	6	7	8	9

LP09 I learn more when I write down my ideas (VP)   I learn more when I build something for myself (TP)

1	2	3	4	5	6	7	8	9

LP10 I enjoy reading for pleasure (VP)   I enjoy listening to people talking on the radio or on tape (AP)

1	2	3	4	5	6	7	8	9

LP11   I remember things better when I
work with other students (GP)

I remember things better when I
work independently (IP)

1	2	3	4	5	6	7	8	9

LP12   I learn more when someone tells
me instructions (AP)

I learn more when I can make
something for a class project (TP)

1	2	3	4	5	6	7	8	9

LP13   I learn when I write down my
ideas (VP)

I learn more when the teacher
gives a lecture (AP)

1	2	3	4	5	6	7	8	9

LP14   I prefer listening to the
teacher (AP)

I prefer doing things in
class (KP)

1	2	3	4	5	6	7	8	9

LP15   I understand better when someone tells me what to do (AP)

I understand better when I look
at visual instructions (VP)

1	2	3	4	5	6	7	8	9

LP16   I remember better when I do
experiments or practical
activities (KP)

I remember better when I look at
diagrams or pictures (VP)

1	2	3	4	5	6	7	8	9

LP17   I prefer to solve my problems
by myself (IP)

When I have a problem, I usually
ask for help from other people (GP)

1	2	3	4	5	6	7	8	9

LP18   I understand better when the
teacher gives a lecture (AP)

I understand better when I read
books (VP)

1	2	3	4	5	6	7	8	9

LP19   I enjoy making models or
doing crafts (TP)

I enjoy reading for pleasure (VP)

1	2	3	4	5	6	7	8	9

LP20   I understand better by writing
about a topic (VP)

I understand better by doing
activities in class (TP)

1	2	3	4	5	6	7	8	9

IELTS Awareness Forms

Before taking the IELTS AWM, learners were asked to complete a brief questionnaire – the IELTS Awareness Form (IA). Form A of the IA addressed their experience of taking IELTS, their anxiety relating to the test and their knowledge of the AWM test format and scoring. IA, Form B, administered at course exit, replaced questions on Form A relating to experiences before the course with items on the subject of extra-curricular exposure to English through independent study, use of the media and socialising in English (see Appendices 2 and 3).

Test Knowledge

The Test Knowledge section was made up of six selected response items with three options (*Yes/No/I don't know*), the items being identical on both occasions. These items were adapted from a similar set designed for use in the IELTS Impact Study (Banerjee 1996), but, to reflect the focus of the current study, addressed knowledge of the Writing component of the IELTS test only (see Box 4.5).

Box 4.5 Questions 15–20 from the IELTS Awareness Form

Are the following statements about the IELTS Writing test true?	Yes	No	I don't know
15 The IELTS Writing test is 60 minutes long.	☐	☐	☐
16 There are two sections in the Writing test.	☐	☐	☐
17 The Writing test is worth more marks than the Speaking test.	☐	☐	☐
18 The topic for one of the Writing tasks comes from one of the texts in the Reading test.	☐	☐	☐
19 The Writing test also includes some grammar questions.	☐	☐	☐
20 In Task 1, you should write 150 words.	☐	☐	☐

Test-taking strategies

Following each administration of the IELTS AWM, learners were asked to complete a brief questionnaire – the Test Strategy Report (TSR) relating to the time they had spent on each section, their perception of how well they had understood and been able to respond to the tasks and the test-taking strategies they had used. Items for the TSR were based on test-taking strategy items from Purpura (1999) and Herington (1996), descriptions of strategy use written by six candidates preparing to take IELTS and a review of test strategy 'tips' in IELTS preparation textbooks (see Appendices 2 and 3).

The first set of questions addressed overall planning and the time allocated to each task (Box 4.6).

Box 4.6 Questions relating to test-taking strategies

At the beginning, did you plan how much time to spend on each section of the test? Yes ❏ No ❏	
The test takes 60 minutes, about how many minutes did you spend on Task 1?	_____ minutes
And about how many minutes did you spend on Task 2?	_____ minutes

The following eight items (Boxes 4.7–4.9) were presented twice, to target strategy use on both Task 1 and Task 2. The first three items of this set addressed students' ability to manage task demands.

Boxes 4.7–4.9 Questions relating to test-taking strategies

Tick (✓) the boxes on the right to show how far you agree with each statement.
If you definitely agree, tick 4.
If you definitely disagree, tick 0.

		I definitely agree	I tend to agree	I tend to disagree	I definitely disagree	I don't know / I cannot answer the question
1	I understood the question	4	3	1	0	2
2	I had enough ideas to write about this topic	4	3	1	0	2
3	I had enough time to write about the question	4	3	1	0	2

The next four items reflected common strategy tips gleaned from test preparation textbooks.

4	I read the question carefully and underlined or highlighted key words	4	3	1	0	2
5	I made an outline plan before writing	4	3	1	0	2
6	I tried not to write more than the required number of words	4	3	1	0	2
7	I checked my answers for grammar and spelling mistakes	4	3	1	0	2

The final item was included to reflect a negative strategy; a tactic cautioned against in IELTS preparation texts.

| 8 | I wrote a draft essay first, then wrote the essay again neatly | 4 | 3 | 1 | 0 | | 2 |

Questionnaire B: Course exit

The course exit questionnaire, Questionnaire B (see Appendix 6), addressed learning processes and outcomes, requesting learners to retrospect on their course of study. Bearing in mind that approaches to learning and strategy use are said to be affected by context and task demands (Entwistle and Ramsden 1983, Oxford 1990), these could only validly be addressed in relation to specific learning experiences, i.e. a completed course of study. Sections of this questionnaire addressed the nature of activities on the antecedent course, learning strategy use, satisfaction with the experience of living and studying in the UK, sense of improvement in general language and writing abilities, expectations of future study and the students' approach to learning during the courses.

Section 1: Course outcomes

Section 1 reprised Section 3 of the course entry questionnaire, but with the statements transformed from future to past. Here students were asked to look back over their course and indicate what they felt they had learned. The first item is given here as an illustration:

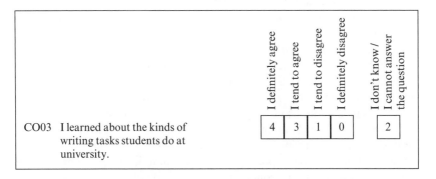

	I definitely agree	I tend to agree	I tend to disagree	I definitely disagree		I don't know / I cannot answer the question
CO03 I learned about the kinds of writing tasks students do at university.	4	3	1	0		2

This would serve as an indicator of student perceptions of course focus and as a means of comparing expectations with outcomes. The intention here was to capture student perceptions of what they had gained from their courses, including an element of evaluation with the understanding that skills may have been studied, but not learned.

Section 2: Learning strategies

Section 2 targeted learning strategies. Learning strategies have been described as 'the special thoughts or behaviors that individuals use to help them comprehend, learn, or retain new information' (O'Malley and Chamot 1990: 1). In second language acquisition they are defined by Purpura (1999: 23) as 'specific actions, activities or behaviours that are directly linked to some processing stage of language acquisition, use or testing.' Although distinctions have sometimes been made between communication strategies (strategies directed at facilitating communication) and learning strategies, (strategies directed at gaining knowledge) Purpura (1999) follows Oxford (1990) in rejecting this distinction on the grounds that both may contribute to language acquisition.

The primary source for this section of the questionnaire was the Strategy Inventory for Language Learning (SILL) (Oxford 1990), a widely used and reliable research instrument (Oxford 1996). However, numerous strategy questionnaires have been developed and a number of these were also considered in developing this section. Most important among these were Purpura's (1999) cognitive and meta-cognitive strategy questionnaires and the instrument derived from these produced by Herington (1996) for the IELTS impact study.

Version 7.0 of the SILL employs a series of 50 statements relating to strategy use, each of which is rated on a 5-point Likert scale ranging from *Never or almost never true* to *Always, or almost always true*. For ease of response, the format was adjusted to fit with the other sections of Questionnaire B; but with wording altered to reflect frequency rather than agreement as the intention was to learn how often strategies had been used. The choices were *Usually, Quite often, Occasionally, Never, I don't know/I cannot answer the question*.

On the SILL the statements are divided into two sections, each made up of three sub-scales. The direct strategies section includes memory strategies (to remember target language features), cognitive strategies (to use the language and uncover principles), and compensation strategies (to overcome difficulties in communication). The indirect strategies section includes meta-cognitive strategies (planning, organising and evaluating learning), affective strategies (ways of finding a positive value in language learning), and social strategies (looking for opportunities for communication). Emphasis was placed on compensation, cognitive and meta-cognitive strategies as these have generally been found to be most frequently used and have been linked to higher proficiency (Peacock 2001).

The development of the section involved triangulation of a number of data sources. First, following a procedure suggested by Peacock (2001), the SILL was given to a group of 15 students on a pre-sessional course. These students indicated not only which strategies they had used, but also which they regarded as potentially useful for learning on a pre-sessional course and listed strategies they did not use, but would like to develop. The group also kept diaries in which they logged strategy use over a 12-week course. A second group of six students preparing for IELTS completed a guided writing assignment in which they described strategies that they believed would help them to succeed on the IELTS Academic Writing Module. These two exercises suggested additional strategies for inclusion in the question-naire and implied that affective strategies, with the exception of risk-taking, were rarely used and little valued, perhaps because they were not immedi-ately associated by the learners with language learning.

Of the 30 items in Section 2, 21 were derived or adapted from the SILL:

Direct

	memory:	PS15, PS22
	cognitive:	PS01, PS02, PS04, PS08, PS19, PS26
	compensation:	PS14, PS18, PS25
Indirect		
	meta-cognitive:	PS09, PS11, PS21, PS27, PS28, PS30, PS03
	affective:	PS17
	social:	PS05, PS16

Four additional items were adapted from Purpura (1999): PS06, PS13, PS23 and PS29. These correspond to items on Purpura's questionnaires loading on factors associated with self-evaluation (EVAL46, EVAL69), monitoring (MON74) and analysing inductively (item AI39). These items were added to the questionnaire because they corresponded to strategies mentioned by learners in their diaries and were felt to reflect academic language-learning needs.

Items PS07, PS10, PS12, PS20 and PS24 were included to reflect the importance placed on effort and hard work by student respondents in the pilot studies. These items addressed the amount and kinds of extra-curricular study that students might undertake to supplement their coursework.

For the items selected for inclusion in the questionnaire see Box 4.10.

Section 3: orientation to language study and self-assessment of gain

This section reiterated section 2 of the entry questionnaire, excluding items on test anxiety, but including items requiring learners to assess their own progress (IM01, IM03, IM05, IM09, IM16, IM17, IM18, IM19 and IM21) as well as their confidence regarding IELTS (IM01) and university writing tasks (IM17). (See Box 4.11.) These items were based on the IELTS scoring criteria and EAP writing demands identified in the review of the lit-erature (see Chapter 2).

Box 4.10 Questions PS01 – PS30

In this section, we would like to find out about **how** you learned during this course and your feelings about your studies.
How often did you do the following? Mark your answer from 4 (usually) to 0 (never).

	Usually	Quite often	Occasionally	Never	I don't know / I cannot answer the question
PS01 I memorised English words by saying or writing them several times.	4	3	1	0	2
PS02 I tested my knowledge of new English words by using them in different ways.	4	3	1	0	2
PS03 I tried to find better ways of learning English.	4	3	1	0	2
PS04 I looked for words in my own language that look or sound similar to new words in English.	4	3	1	0	2
PS05 I tried to improve my writing by asking others (e.g. teachers, students, friends) to correct my mistakes.	4	3	1	0	2
PS06 I noticed mistakes in my writing, and used that information to help me do better.	4	3	1	0	2
PS07 I took IELTS Writing or other practice writing tests in my free time.	4	3	1	0	2
PS08 I tried to find grammar patterns in English.	4	3	1	0	2
PS09 I looked for people I could talk to in English.	4	3	1	0	2
PS10 I studied vocabulary in my free time.	4	3	1	0	2
PS11 I thought about my progress in learning English.	4	3	1	0	2
PS12 I studied extra English outside school.	4	3	1	0	2
PS13 I tested myself on new words or phrases I learned.	4	3	1	0	2
PS14 If I couldn't think of an English word, I used a word or phrase that means the same thing.	4	3	1	0	2
PS15 I reviewed my class notes or text book in my free time.	4	3	1	0	2

PS16	I tried to learn about the culture of English speakers.	4	3	1	0		2
PS17	I encouraged myself to use English even when I was afraid of making a mistake.	4	3	1	0		2
PS18	I read English without looking up every new word.	4	3	1	0		2
PS19	When reading in English, I tried to translate into my language to help me understand.	4	3	1	0		2
PS20	I studied grammar in my free time.	4	3	1	0		2
PS21	I was NOT sure how to improve my English skills.	4	3	1	0		2
PS22	I used new English words in sentences so I could remember them.	4	3	1	0		2
PS23	When I learned a grammar rule, I tested myself to make sure I really knew it.	4	3	1	0		2
PS24	I tried to improve my writing by doing extra writing activities at home.	4	3	1	0		2
PS25	To understand unfamiliar English words, I tried to guess their meaning.	4	3	1	0		2
PS26	When writing in English, I tried to translate from my language.	4	3	1	0		2
PS27	I thought about the goals I wanted to achieve on this course.	4	3	1	0		2
PS28	Before studying, I planned what to do, so I could use my time well.	4	3	1	0		2
PS29	I tried to improve my writing by analysing the work of other writers.	4	3	1	0		2
PS30	When I received corrected work from the teacher, I thought about how to improve next time.	4	3	1	0		2

Section 4: Expectations of tertiary education in the UK

This section addressed expectations of studying at university in the UK. Studies by Bloor and Bloor (1991) and Jordan (1993) indicate that international students may bring quite unrealistic expectations to their academic study in the UK. Although the diversity of disciplines and institutions precludes any realistic comparison between learners' expectations and the reality that an individual will encounter, a general awareness of prevailing expectations in the UK tertiary sector is taken here as a measure of pragmatic competence (Bachman 1990) in EAP settings. (See Box 4.12.)

Box 4.11 Questions IM01 – IM21

In this section, we would like to find out about how much progress you have made and how satisfied you are with the course.

		I definitely agree	I tend to agree	I tend to disagree	I definitely disagree	I don't know / I cannot answer the question
IM01	After studying on this course, I would feel more confident about taking an IELTS Writing test.	4	3	1	0	2
IM02	I feel I will never really enjoy writing in English. (*Questionnaire A SC06*)	4	3	1	0	2
IM03	My ability to write quickly in English has improved during this course.	4	3	1	0	2
IM04	After studying on this course, I feel that I am **NOT** good at writing in English. (*SC05*)	4	3	1	0	2
IM05	My ability to organise my ideas in my written work has improved during this course.	4	3	1	0	2
IM06	The Writing classes were difficult for me. (*SC07*)	4	3	1	0	2
IM07	I do **NOT** really like the British way of life. (*SC04*)	4	3	1	0	2
IM08	I enjoyed writing in English. (*SC19*)	4	3	1	0	2
IM09	I feel that my general ability to use English has improved during this course.	4	3	1	0	2
IM10	I think the Writing classes were useful for me. (*SC18*)	4	3	1	0	2
IM11	I am pleased I chose to study at this school. (*SC08*)	4	3	1	0	2
IM12	I usually enjoy meeting British people. (*SC11*)	4	3	1	0	2
IM13	I don't think I write in English as well as other students. (*SC14*)	4	3	1	0	2
IM14	I like to write down my ideas in English. (*SC09*)	4	3	1	0	2
IM15	It was easy for me to write good English essays. (*SC15*)	4	3	1	0	2

IM16	My ability to use evidence to support my written arguments has improved during this course.	4	3	1	0	2
IM17	After taking this course, I would feel more confident about writing assignments at university.	4	3	1	0	2
IM18	I feel that my ability to write in English has improved during this course.	4	3	1	0	2
IM19	My ability to use grammar and vocabulary in my writing has improved during this course.	4	3	1	0	2
IM20	I feel happy about living in an English speaking country. (*SC02*)	4	3	1	0	2
IM21	My ability to write using information from books or articles I have read has improved during this course.	4	3	1	0	2

Box 4.12 Questions EU01 – EU15

In this section, we are interested in your expectations of studying at university in an English-speaking country.

		I definitely agree	I tend to agree	I tend to disagree	I definitely disagree	I don't know / I cannot answer the question
EU01	I feel that I have a good knowledge of what university study in Britain is like.	4	3	1	0	2
EU02	I do **NOT** expect university teachers to show students examples of good essays and reports.	4	3	1	0	2
EU03	I expect university teachers to tell the students exactly which books they should read.	4	3	1	0	2
EU04	I expect students should read all the books their university teachers recommend.	4	3	1	0	2
EU05	To get a good grade for their writing at university, students must show that they have remembered facts from lectures.	4	3	1	0	2
EU06	I expect I will have difficulties studying at university because of problems with the English language.	4	3	1	0	2

EU07	I expect the style of teaching at university will be different from the teaching in my country.	4	3	1	0	2
EU08	To get a good grade, in their writing, students should **NOT** criticise the work of their teachers or other experts in their specialist subject.	4	3	1	0	2
EU09	I expect my university grades will mostly come from tests or examinations rather than from essays or coursework.	4	3	1	0	2
EU10	I expect my university subject teachers to correct the English grammar mistakes in my essays.	4	3	1	0	2
EU11	I expect my university tests will follow a **multiple-choice** style (in multiple-choice questions you choose the correct answer from a list: a, b, c or d).	4	3	1	0	2
EU12	I expect university teachers to tell students exactly what to do when the students prepare an essay or report.	4	3	1	0	2
EU13	I expect I will have difficulties studying at university because the style of education in my country is different to the style of education in Britain.	4	3	1	0	2
EU14	I expect the writing tasks students do at university are similar to the writing tasks I have done on this course.	4	3	1	0	2
EU15	I expect my university teachers will give me all the facts and information I need to get a good grade.	4	3	1	0	2

Section 5: Approaches to learning

This final section addressed approaches to learning (Entwistle and Ramsden 1983). In Britain, Sweden and Australia, a tradition of both qualitative (Marton and Saljo 1976a, 1976b) and quantitative (Entwistle and Ramsden 1983, Biggs 1987a) research into student approaches to learning in higher education has yielded a distinction between deep and surface approaches. The founders of the distinction, Marton and Saljo (1976a) define the deep learner as one:

> directed towards the intentional content of the learning material (what is signified), i.e. he is directed towards comprehending what the author wants to say about, for instance, a particular scientific problem or principle. The surface learner, in contrast, adopts a "reproductive" conception

of learning which dictates a rote-learning strategy. Such a learner will fail to integrate ideas, but seeks to learn the material itself. He is thus confined to the level of the sign, failing to integrate material with experience or with other sources of knowledge (Marton and Saljo 1976a: 7–8).

This is effectively the same distinction made by Bereiter and Scardamalia (1987) between knowledge-telling and knowledge-transforming processes in writing. A writing strategy based in knowledge telling alone expresses a surface approach to learning, while one based in knowledge transforming indicates a deep approach to learning.

The deep, or meaning-based approach is associated, in the UK at least, with academic success and entails looking for meaning, active interaction with learning material and interest in topics and courses for their own sake. The surface approach, on the other hand, involves syllabus-boundedness, attempts to memorise and an attention to the demands of examinations.

There are clear parallels with the distinctions that have been made between supposedly Confucian conceptions of learning and Western academic values (Ballard and Clanchy 1991, Flowerdew and Miller 1995). Confucian (East Asian) cultures of education are said to embrace a knowledge-telling role for students at tertiary levels, while Western systems envisage tertiary level students as knowledge-transformers (although see Biggs 1993, 1996 and Kember and Gow 1991 for a vigorous questioning of these assumptions).

Two questionnaires have been widely used in studies of approaches to learning: the Approaches to Studying Inventory (ASI) (Entwistle 1981) and the Study Processes Questionnaire (SPQ) (Biggs 1987b) and these are evaluated by Richardson (1994). Although a Chinese language version of the SPQ has been widely used with Chinese learners in Hong Kong (Tang 1992), and might therefore appear well suited to the requirements of the present study, Richardson (1994) observes that the constituent structure of the six subscales of the instrument has not been well supported beyond a broad distinction between surface and deep approaches (Biggs 1987a, Watkins and Akande 1992, Kember and Gow 1991). In the ASI, deep and surface approaches are subsumed into a *meaning-based orientation*, which includes deep approaches to learning, intrinsic and academic motivation (Entwistle 1981); *reproducing orientation* involving surface approaches to learning, extrinsic motivation and syllabus-boundedness and a third orientation; *achieving orientation* incorporating well-organised study methods, competitiveness and hope for success.

The original 64-item ASI has been abbreviated to 30 items by Entwistle (1981) and to 18 items by Gibbs (1992). Richardson (1994) advocates a 32-item questionnaire he developed based on the only unequivocal distinction established for the full form of the ASI: that between meaning orientation and reproducing orientation.

However, Richardson's (1994) rejection of the achievement orientation scale may be contested. As both the SPQ and the ASI are concerned with approaches to specific study contexts, we should not perhaps anticipate an unvarying factor structure across studies. Learners might adapt their approaches to meet the demands of different modes of study and this adaptation may be expressed through their responses to the questionnaires.

In factor analytic studies undertaken in different countries the deep/surface distinction is supported, arguing for the cross-cultural validity of the questionnaires (Watkins 1994). However, items measuring achievement on both the ASI and SPQ load in some countries on a deep approach/meaning orientation factor, but in others have been associated with surface approach/reproducing orientation. Thus, in the studies described by Watkins, he speculates that Australian, Nepalese and Nigerian school students and Brunei university students believe that academic success comes through a combination of deep and achieving strategies, hence achievement and deep items load on the same factor for these cohorts. However, Hong Kong school and Nepalese university students believe that success in their academic contexts requires principally a surface-level approach to learning and this is reflected in the loadings of surface and achievement items.

Hence, depending on the learning context, students with an achieving orientation may decide either to adopt a deep or a surface approach, according to their perceptions of which would be more likely, in the circumstances, to yield the higher grades. Tang (1992) regards washback as more closely related to the students' perceptions of the demands of the assessment than to what the teacher intends to assess. If learners perceive that an assessment requires only accurate reproduction of details, students will likely adopt a surface approach and employ low level cognitive strategies including rote learning, concentrating on facts and details. If they believe the assessment requires high-level cognitive processing to demonstrate a thorough understanding, integration and application of knowledge, then they are more likely to engage a deep approach to address the task.

In Tang's (1992) results (obtained with tertiary students of physiotherapy from Hong Kong), surface approaches (as measured by the SPQ) were associated with success on a short essay test of lecture content, but not with an assignment requiring the exploration of a single topic. Further, where students were aware of assessment task demands and motivated to succeed, they adjusted their approach to meet the demands of the assessment.

Given that deep and surface approaches have been identified with differential success in higher education (Entwistle 1981), that surface approaches reflect the supposed pathologies of learning from which international students are said to suffer (Ballard and Clanchy 1991, Flowerdew and Miller 1995) and that evidential links have been discerned between assessment task demands and approaches to learning (Tang 1992, Scouller 1998), it was decided to incorporate a measure of approaches to learning into the current study.

Unfortunately the ASI could not be administered unaltered to a NNS student population as the wording of a number of items appeared likely to pose difficulties of comprehension. Further, the 64-item version would be too lengthy for inclusion with other sections within a 20-minute questionnaire. Practical concerns thus dictated that a choice would have to be made between the various alternative short forms of the inventory.

Of these, the 32-item version developed by Richardson (1994) was the most promising as it had been developed, on the basis of factor analysis, directly from the original 64-item form. It also had been successfully validated for NS university students in a replication study. Balancing this, the Richardson (1994) form excluded items addressing achievement orientation, potentially a key explanatory element in linking choices between the meaning-based or reproducing orientation of the learner to test washback (Watkins 1994, Tang and Biggs 1996).

Restoring the six items measuring an achievement orientation from Entwistle (1981) and Gibbs (1992) would have generated a 38-item inventory. However, this would have proved too lengthy, taking the course exit questionnaire beyond the maximum number of items that could be administered in the limited time available. Indeed, to meet the practical constraints on questionnaire length, a reduction from the 32-item form rather than an increase in length was preferred.

The next stage of development involved reducing the number of items and simplifying the language of the remainder to make them more meaningful to NNS. To this end, the 38 items were first presented to a group of three teachers of EAP who were asked to indicate those they felt would pose difficulties for their learners. This information was then combined with item-scale correlations from the Richardson (1992) survey (obtained with a population of NS undergraduates) to compile a 20-item form, striking a balance between the practical requirement for brevity and the necessity for sufficient items to form adequate scales.

Three EAP students commented on the wording of the resulting draft. A form of wording was sought that would retain the sense of the original, but pose minimal difficulties for students with IELTS Academic Reading scores at Band 4 or 5. In piloting with 30 participants this section appeared to cause little difficulty, although the two groups involved included a number of lower-proficiency learners. No students indicated that they had failed to understand any items in this section and few selected *I do not know/I cannot answer the question* as a response to any of the statements.

The items used in the main study are set out in Box 4.13. Items marked R represent the *reproducing orientation*, consisting of *surface approach* (SA), *improvidence* (IP), and *syllabus-boundedness* (SB). Items marked M indicate a *meaning orientation* (*deep approach* DA, *use of evidence* UE, and *relating ideas* RI), and items marked A an *achieving orientation* (*extrinsic motivation* EM, *strategic approach* ST, *organised study methods* OS, and *achievement motivation* AM).

Box 4.13 Questions A01 – R07

In this section, we are interested in finding out about your attitude to studying. When you answer, please think about your experience on **this course**.

			I definitely agree	I tend to agree	I tend to disagree	I definitely disagree	I don't know / I cannot answer the question
A01	When I am doing an assignment, I try to think about exactly what the teacher of that class seems to want.	(ST)	4	3	1	0	2
A02	I find it easy to organise my time for studying.	(OS)	4	3	1	0	2
A03	It's important for me to do really well in this course.	(AM)	4	3	1	0	2
A04	If the situation is not right for me to study, I usually manage to do something to change it.	(ST)	4	3	1	0	2
A05	When I am doing a piece of work, I try to think about exactly what that particular teacher seems to want.	(ST)	4	3	1	0	2
A06	It is important to me to do things better than my friends.	(AM)	4	3	1	0	2
M01	When I am trying to understand new ideas, I often try to connect them to real-life situations.	(RI)	4	3	1	0	2
M02	I often think about and criticise things that I hear in lessons or read in books.	(DA)	4	3	1	0	2
M03	I need to read a lot about connected ideas before I am ready to write about a topic.	(RI)	4	3	1	0	2
M04	I like to try to find several different ways of explaining facts.	(UE)	4	3	1	0	2

M05	I usually try hard to understand things that seem difficult at first.	(DA)	4	3	1	0	2
M06	I usually try to understand completely the meaning of what teachers ask me to read.	(DA)	4	3	1	0	2
M07	I am very interested in puzzles or problems, particularly when I have to study the information carefully to reach a logical conclusion.	(UE)	4	3	1	0	2
R01	When I am reading, I try to memorise important facts that may be useful later.	(SA)	4	3	1	0	2
R02	I usually study very little except what I need for assignments or tests.	(SB)	4	3	1	0	2
R03	Teachers seem to like making the simple truth more complicated.	(SA)	4	3	1	0	2
R04	I find I have to memorise a lot of what we study.	(SA)	4	3	1	0	2
R05	Teachers seem to want me to use my own ideas more.	(IP)	4	3	1	0	2
R06	I like teachers to tell me exactly what I must do in essays or other coursework.	(SB)	4	3	1	0	2
R07	I prefer courses that are structured and highly organised.	(SB)	4	3	1	0	2

Asking: the teacher survey

The teacher questionnaire (Appendix 4) was developed in tandem with the student instruments and was trialled with a group of five teachers during the summer of 2000. In all, 52 teacher questionnaires were distributed at nine centres of which 33 were returned (a response rate of 63.5%) from seven centres. Of these seven returns came from courses including IELTS preparation, the remainder were from pre-sessional EAP courses. Teachers' ages (for the 27 who supplied their ages) averaged 43 and ranged from 28 to 58. They had between two and 30 years of EFL experience. Sixteen had some experience of IELTS preparation, while five claimed no previous experience of EAP teaching and the others ranged in EAP experience from less than a year up to 25 years. The survey was not repeated during 2002 as most teachers participating in the later phase of the study were both interviewed and observed and it was felt that a survey form covering similar ground to the interviews might prove burdensome to participants.

Development of the instruments for the main study: (ii) Interviews

Asking: interviews with course directors and teachers

Following Pilot Study Five, a number of centres providing IELTS preparation courses were approached to participate in a further round of data collection. In order to extend the coverage of the project, institutions which had not participated the previous year were preferred.

In all, a total of 21 course directors and teachers at eight institutions, including one centre which had participated the previous year, took part in the focus group phase of the study. The number of participants in the interviews ranged from one to five and the sessions lasted for between 28 and 76 minutes.

Interviews were semi-structured and were based on findings from the more detailed, and lengthier, Repertory Grid interviews employed in Pilot Study Three (see Chapter 3). The intention was to gain a qualitative description from course providers of course aims and of how these related to the IELTS test and to the language needs of students in higher education. Of specific interest were the effects of the test on course content and on teaching methods.

Table 4.5 Participants in teacher focus group interviews

Institution	Name*	Course director	Teacher on course	IELTS Examiner
College H	Belinda		✓	
College H	Andrew		✓	✓
College H	Charles		✓	
College D	Geoff	✓		
College C	Fiona	✓	✓	✓
College C	Harry		✓	✓
College C	Imogen		✓	✓
College G	Julia	✓		
College F	Marvin	✓		
College F	Trevor		✓	
College F	Kim		✓	
College F	Edgar		✓	
College F	Laura		✓	
University F	Penny	✓	✓	
University E	Frank	✓	✓	
University E	Ursula		✓	
University G	Olivia	✓	✓	
College E	Ken	✓	✓	
College E	Bill		✓	
College E	Joanna		✓	
College E	Kate		✓	

* All names have been changed to preserve anonymity.

Although Pilot Study Four had provided a rich source of data, application of the full Repertory Grid procedure was not a practical option for the main study. The technique would simply be too time-consuming to apply in busy school offices. However, the usefulness of dyads (opposed pairs of elements) in generating insights and the importance placed on allowing participants to articulate their own construction of the role of the test were both seen from Pilot Study Four to be valuable features of the Repertory Grid technique that should be retained in a modified interview method based on Burr and Butt (1997).

The focus group interviews were based on, but not limited to, a set of key questions. These questions were derived from Pilot Study Four, but were also intended to provide opportunities for the participants to steer the discussion into areas of personal concern.

All interviews were recorded in real time in the form of field notes, which were transcribed and reviewed later on the same day. Although tape recording of interviews was preferred, participants in the first round of focus groups, given the choice, preferred not to be recorded on tape and so field note recording alone was used for the remaining interviews.

Following the data collection phase, responses were summarised and compared with responses to a similar exercise conducted as a component in the IELTS Impact Study (IIS) sponsored by Cambridge ESOL (Hawkey 2006). This provided a measure of researcher triangulation and revealed that the responses obtained in the current study were in line with those obtained in the IIS. The summary was also circulated to participants in the original focus groups for their comments. A total of three responses were received. None included any disagreement with the content of the summary.

Asking: interviews with students

Groups of students were also interviewed during their courses in order to garner their views of IELTS preparation and its relationship to their academic and language studies. The key questions for these interviews were whether the test had influenced learners' approaches to their learning and their choices concerning what to study.

The sessions took the form of semi-structured focus-group interviews based on the model developed in 2001 (Pilot Study Five). As the time available for these sessions was very limited, the decision was taken not to introduce students to the Repertory Grid technique, but to adapt the PCT approach in developing an interview schedule based on Pilot Study Three.

In all there were eight such focus groups: two on IELTS preparation courses of six and 10 weeks duration, four on pre-sessional EAP courses with an IELTS preparation component and lasting for between eight and 10 weeks, and two on an eight-week pre-sessional course with no IELTS preparation component. Details of participants in the student focus groups are set out in Table 4.6.

Table 4.6 Students participating in focus group sessions

Focus Group	Institution	Home Country	Sex	Intended Level of Study	Subject	Name*
1	College C	Russia	M	PG	Law (LLM)	Andrei
1	College C	Russia	M	UG	Law	Dmitri
1	College C	China	M	PG	MBA	Bei
1	College C	Russia	F	PG	PhD Child Psychology	Agafya
2	College F	Palestine	M	PG	Financial Markets	Ahmed
2	College F	Saudi Arabia	M	UG	Business	Omar
2	College F	Russia	F	PG	LLM	Svetlana
2	College F	Italy	F	–	–	Maria
2	College F	Japan	F	PG	Management	Chika
2	College F	Japan	F	PG	MBA	Takako
2	College F	China	F	–	–	Yuan
3	University B	Taiwan	F	PG	MSc Financial Markets	Tai
3	University B	China	F	PG	MSc Management	Qian
3	University B	Taiwan	M	PG	MBA	Wen
3	University B	Taiwan	M	PG	MSc Accounting and Finance	Chun
4	University B	China	F	PG	MSc Accounting and Mgmt	Ping
4	University B	Taiwan	F	PG	MSc Accounting and Finance	Kung-Li
4	University B	China	M	PG	MSc Accounting and Mgmt	Wu
4	University B	Indonesia	M	PG	MBA	Hasan
5	University E	Taiwan	F	PG	Music	Jia
5	University E	Japan	F	PG	Interactive Media	Ai
5	University E	Korea	F	–	(To monitor progress)	Hyun
5	University E	Korea	F	–	(To improve English)	Jung
5	University E	Japan	F	Visiting Student	Art history	Keiko
6	University F	Japan	M	PG	MBA	Nobuo
6	University F	China	M	PG	Business	Bo
6	University F	Taiwan	M	PG	Business	Jian
6	University F	Spain	F	PG	MBA	Isabella
6	University F	Japan	F	PG	Politics	Fujiko
6	University F	Japan	F	PG	Accounting	Harumi
6	University F	China	F	PG	Business	Xiang
6	University F	China	F	PG	Business	Ju
6	University F	Korea	F	PG	Business	Yung
7	University G	China	M	PG	MBA	Wei
7	University G	Taiwan	F	PG	MA Cultural Studies	Chi-Hua
7	University G	Japan	F	PG	MA Applied Linguistics	Mariko
7	University G	Japan	F	PG	MSc Environmental Science	Natsuko
8	University G	Libya	F	PG	MSc Epidemiology (also for medical recognition)	Asma
8	University G	China	F	PG	MSc International Mgmt	Jing

Table 4.6 (continued)

Focus Group	Institution	Home Country	Sex	Intended Level of Study	Subject	Name*
8	University G	China	F	PG	MSc International Mgmt	Lin
8	University G	China	F	PG	Law (LLM)	Qian

Totals					
Institution	Home Country	Sex	Study Level	Intended Subject	
College C (4)	12 China	13 M	34 PG	7 MBA	
College F (7)	9 Japan	28 F	2 UG	6 Business	
University B (8)	7 Taiwan		1 Visiting	5 Law	
University E (5)	4 Russia		4 None	2 International Mgmt	
University F (9)	3 Korea			2 Financial Markets	
University G (8)	1 Saudi Arabia			2 Accounting and Mgmt	
	1 Palestine			2 Accounting and Finance	
	1 Libya			2 Management	
	1 Italy				
	1 Indonesia				

* *All names have been changed to preserve anonymity.*

Development of the instruments for the main study: (iii) Observation instruments

Watching: the COLT observation schedule

As noted elsewhere (Alderson and Wall 1993, Bailey 1996, 1999), data obtained by asking participants about their behaviour does not provide sufficient evidence to demonstrate that washback occurs to teaching and learning processes; empirical evidence of what occurs in classrooms is also required. As Bailey (1999), Alderson and Hamp-Lyons (1996) and Watanabe (1996) have discovered in a variety of contexts, evidence from the classroom may contradict or recast the claims made by participants.

One observation instrument that has been widely used in washback studies (Watanabe 1996, Cheng 1997, 2005, Burrows 1998, Read and Hayes 2003) is the Communicative Orientation to Language Teaching (COLT) observation schedule (Spada and Fröhlich 1995). The COLT consists of two Parts (A and B). Part A is designed for use in real time and describes classroom events at the level of *activities* and their constituent *episodes*. Spada and

Fröhlich explain that activities include such things as drills, translation tasks, discussions or games. Three episodes of *one* activity might be: 1) teacher introduces dialogue 2) teacher reads dialogue aloud 3) individual students read parts of dialogue aloud.

Part B is designed to describe features of the interactions between teachers and students in greater detail. It is completed retrospectively from transcripts or recordings and includes features of classroom communication identified with communicative methods, such as use of the target language, information gaps and the amount of sustained speech.

The COLT has been used extensively in classroom process research since its development in the early 1980s and is designed to capture instructional variables that might impact on language learning; particularly in relation to the goals of *communicative* language teaching and the balance of attention to form and opportunities for meaningful interaction in the classroom (Spada and Fröhlich 1995). The authors recommend that the schedule be adapted to the specific purpose of defined research objectives, stressing that observation schemes are tools which should serve rather than direct research. Taking heed of this advice, a number of adaptations were made to the instrument to reflect the academic writing construct and predictions regarding the effects of testing on teaching.

As Part A of the COLT is explicitly designed to relate quantified classroom processes to differential learning outcomes, it is better suited to the needs of the current study than more ethnographic observational approaches. This is perhaps the main reason why the COLT has proved to be such a popular tool in washback studies. It has been used by Burrows (1998), Watanabe (1996), Cheng (2005) and Hayes and Read (2004) and has been influential in the development of the observation schedules used by Alderson and Hamp-Lyons (1996) and refined for the Cambridge ESOL IELTS Impact Study (IIS).

Read and Hayes (2003, Hayes and Read 2004) used the COLT (Part A), unadapted, in conjunction with Part 2 of the draft IIS instrument to capture differences between two IELTS preparation courses. This use of the COLT demonstrates its value in capturing broad similarities and differences in classroom organisation, instructional focus and student modality. However, as in piloting for this study, a need to supplement or adapt the COLT to meet the needs of an investigation of the influence of the IELTS test became apparent.

Firstly, the COLT does not capture references to test-taking strategies, or the relationship between class activities and activities included on a focal test, clearly important considerations for washback studies.

Secondly, the description of materials provided for by the COLT is not sufficiently sensitive. The distinction made in the COLT between minimal – word or sentence length – and extended – paragraph length or longer – material cannot capture a crucial distinction made by teachers in criticism of the IELTS Writing test (Pilot Study Four). Teachers express the concern that

IELTS preparation may not require integration of the very extensive – multipage, even multi-volume – reading material that is required for much academic writing. Thirdly, the COLT includes no section for homework activities, while the intensive nature of much IELTS preparation (and of pre-sessional EAP courses) dictates that students do a high proportion of their written work outside the classroom.

A further issue raised by Read and Hayes (2003) is that the COLT schedule is better adapted to teacher- than to student-centred classrooms; capturing the primary focus of a class, but lacking the flexibility to record instances of different groups working on diverse activities. In practice this did not prove to be a handicap for this study, as there were few instances of students working on different activities concurrently or of other variations that called for a more flexible recording tool.

A further adaptation to the COLT intended to better reflect questions of overlap between IELTS and EAP content involved the *topic* category. The COLT distinguishes *narrow* topics (relating to the immediate context or personal experience) from *broad* topics (such as international events, subject-matter instruction and imaginary events). In Pilot Studies Four and Five IELTS was criticised by teachers for the use of topics of general interest, while writing at the university was said to involve more 'academic' topics. On the COLT there is no provision for such a distinction; both would constitute *broad* topics on the COLT. To assess whether the criticism from teachers was reflected in differences between courses, more sensitive distinctions were required between topic types.

Read and Hayes (2003) supplemented the COLT with the draft IIS observation schedule (Part 2). This instrument was commissioned by UCLES from the University of Lancaster in 1995 at the inception of the IELTS Impact Study (IIS), but was not employed in its original form in the operational phase of the IIS. This schedule includes lists of text types and activities anticipated to occur in preparation classes and is specifically designed to record instances of IELTS preparation.

Although it was developed to record events identified with IELTS preparation and is, as Read and Hayes (2003) note, a useful tool for capturing the occurrence of IELTS directed activities, the draft IIS instrument was not used in the present study. The draft IIS instrument is designed to test hypotheses regarding the occurrence of predicted IELTS-directed activities in a classroom, with any such activities being taken as evidence for washback. For the current study, the requirement was not only to observe IELTS preparation classes, and to capture instances of test preparation, but also to compare test-directed activities with activities in classes that were not directed towards the test.

There are areas of common ground between the COLT and draft IIS instruments in the approach to recording classroom episodes and in recording instances of grammar and vocabulary instruction. Following Read and

Hayes (2003) in using both would involve a good deal of duplication as well as making the observation task more complex.

For this reason an adaptation of the COLT Part A, incorporating features of the IIS instrument, and henceforth referred to as the COLTeap, appeared most promising as a means of recording comparative data on the courses at the centre of this study.

Piloting and modifications to the COLTeap

Descriptions of the COLT categories and coding conventions are given in Spada and Fröhlich (1995). Categories are grouped under the headings of Time, Activities and Episodes, Participant Organisation, Content, Content Control, Student Modality and Materials. Below the uses made of the COLTeap are described as well as the modifications made to the instrument during piloting to bring it into line with the purposes of the study.

Initial familiarisation with the observation scheme involved observing videotapes of EFL classes unrelated to IELTS, intended for teacher training purposes. Once familiar, the COLTeap was piloted through observation of five classes, including 240 minutes of pre-sessional EAP, and 150 minutes of IELTS preparation (60 on an IELTS intensive course and 90 on a course offering IELTS preparation together with pre-sessional EAP). Two of these classes – 206 minutes of class time – were video recorded and reanalysed at the end of the observation cycle to provide an estimate of internal consistency.

Between the two occasions, there were only minor differences in the COLTeap recording. On the first occasion, one brief activity was recorded that was not subsequently recorded as a separate activity on the second occasion. The discrepancy can be attributed to the difficulty of accurately determining the length of an activity; on the second occasion I had decided that the activity (an introduction to the topic by the teacher) took less than one minute and should not therefore be separately recorded. The level of agreement between the two sets of observations (the ratio of coinciding marks on the two forms to the total number) was 82.5%. This suggests that the instrument was being used consistently during the study. As only minor modifications were made as a result of the trials, these pilot study observations were integrated into the analysis.

Following discussions with Roger Hawkey, a consultant to the IIS, the adapted COLTeap instrument was taken up as the primary data collection instrument for this study and made available for use in the IIS and other Cambridge ESOL impact studies, such as the Italian Progetto Lingue 2000 study (Hawkey 2006).

Time

Observations were recorded in real time and the approximate time in hours and minutes was entered at each episode boundary. Determining episode and activity boundaries was sometimes less straightforward than the COLT manual suggests, as some students might, for example, become engaged in a new activity while other students completed an earlier task, or a teacher might interrupt an activity that they had just launched to clarify the task. Following the suggestion given by Spada and Fröhlich (1995), a minimum threshold of one minute was set for separately coded episodes. This undoubtedly led to a certain loss of information. Some teachers gave brief instructions initially, and then supported individual students with further instructions as they began work on a task. Other teachers spent longer on setting up a task, but then needed to offer less support. Although the two teachers might, in fact, have spent an equal amount of time on task instructions, the latter would appear on the schedule to have spent longer on procedural matters. However, such discrepancies were accepted; the objective here was a specification of the balance of activities rather than a detailed description of teaching styles.

Activities and episodes

The COLT A allows for the recording of a brief text description of each teaching/learning activity. In piloting it became apparent that teachers and students could each engage in activities in different ways. Teachers, for example, could sometimes closely monitor students' work, offering individual correction or advice; on other occasions they might leave students to work independently while they remained apart. Where students are asked to take practice tests, it is to be anticipated that teachers play a less supportive role and so it was important to address the relationship between teacher and student behaviour more explicitly.

Such differences in behaviour are better captured by the IIS draft which divides the description of teacher and student actions, each being recorded in a separate field. This format was therefore adopted for the COLTeap, with the *Activities and Episodes* section of the COLT being divided into *Teacher Actions* and *Student Actions*.

Participant organisation and content

No changes were made to the *Participant Organisation* section of the schedule which describes the interaction between participants. In the *Content* section, *Management: Discipline* and *Procedure* and the division of *Language* into *Form, Function, Discourse* and *Sociolinguistics* were also retained.

Distinctions between *Form, Discourse* and *Sociolinguistics* were sometimes difficult to sustain where tasks touched on all three. Where students were working on the description of a diagram, for instance, the teacher might introduce vocabulary and syntax (*Form*), including cohesive devices (*Cohesion*) appropriate to a formal description (*Sociolinguistics*). Coding activities involved judgements regarding which of these potentialities was being realised in the context, and which was being given primary focus.

As Read and Hayes (2003) found in New Zealand, most topics were categorised as *Broad* on the COLT and the *Other Topics*: *Broad/Narrow* section
of the schedule was adding little useful information. To reflect distinctions
made by teachers between academic and more general topics, an additional
category of *Academic* was introduced to the schedule to cover topics that
were identifiably derived from an academic discipline. Discussion of a
current news story would be coded as *Broad*, while a discussion of urban
planning, for example, would be coded as *Academic*. However, during piloting, it was apparent that these topic categories were not mutually exclusive;
issues such as urban traffic congestion, for example, could be treated both as
a topic for analysis (which appeared to be *Academic*) and as news/current
affairs (which was considered to be *Broad*).

A more useful distinction could be made in this context when considering
how a topic is approached by teachers and learners. A topic may be used in a
language class either as an object of inquiry in its own right, as in subject
instruction, or as a prompt for an activity in which language is the main
focus, a distinction which is not made explicitly by the COLT schedule.
Hence, in the adapted observation instrument a distinction between
Academic and *Broad* was retained. An *Academic* topic would be indicated
where teachers and students were primarily engaged in discussion of content,
treating the topic as academic subject matter. The *Broad* category would be
indicated where a topic was used primarily to introduce questions of form,
discourse or sociolinguistics. Thus the *Academic* category was used to
describe activities in which the primary focus was learning about the topic,
rather than exploiting topics as a means to learn about language.

The COLT includes no reference to tests or test-taking strategies. To
reflect the assertions by teachers and students that IELTS preparation
involves a dominant focus on test-taking strategies and activities which
emulate test tasks, the COLTeap would need to record references to the
IELTS (or any other tests or assessments that may be included in EAP
classes) and any instances of test-strategy instruction. A *Test References*
section was included, with three categories; *IELTS, Other* and *Test
Strategies*. The *IELTS* section was used to record any mention of the IELTS
test, with a separate record being made of the context. *Other* was used to
record any mention of tests or assessments other than IELTS such as the
TOEFL test or course exit tests. The *Test Strategies* category was used as a
record of any test-taking strategy instruction. A separate note was made of
the specific test-taking strategies being mentioned in class.

Student Modality and *Content Control* were retained unmodified from the
COLT. To reduce the requirement for real-time coding, materials were
treated on a separate form of the COLTeap. The COLT requires coding of
materials for each activity, but piloting revealed that this often involved the
repetitive entry of the same set of details. Copies of all materials used in class

were collected for later analysis and the details were recorded separately under the COLT headings of *Type: Minimal/Extended, Audio/Visual* and *Source: L2-NNS/L2-NS/L2NSA/Student Made.* The title and page number of any printed materials (or the source of any reproductions) were also recorded.

In addition to the COLTeap analysis, as suggested in the COLT manual (Spada and Fröhlich 1995), additional notes were kept of observations made in class that were of interest, but fell outside the parameters of the schedule. These notes included a variety of points such as the arrangement of students in the class, items written on the board by teachers and details of specific test-taking strategy suggestions.

In order to provide a cross section of courses, a range of institutions were approached to participate in the observation phase of the research. Although it was originally intended that each course would be observed on three occasions, in practice this could not be arranged as course providers were reluctant to accommodate so many observation sessions in a limited period in addition to the other strands of the project. As a compromise, a minimum of one class for each month of a course was targeted. In this way, the co-operation of 12 institutions was secured. In all, some 36 classes were observed. These were given by 20 different teachers; 14 EAP classes (nine on EAP and five on combination EAP/IELTS courses) and 22 IELTS pre-paration classes (11 on dedicated IELTS courses and 11 on combination EAP/IELTS courses).

Following each observation, teachers were briefly interviewed about the class. The interviews focused on five questions; teachers were asked about the aims of the class, the extent to which the aims had been met, the place of the focal class in a teaching sequence, the extent to which the class could be described as typical of writing classes on the course and the influence of the IELTS test on the class. Because teachers sometimes did not have time to take part in these interviews, it was not always possible to obtain this feed-back. Nonetheless, 22 of the classes were accompanied by interview data (eight EAP and 14 IELTS).

In addition to the checks on intra-rater consistency outlined above, the inter-rater reliability of the instrument was investigated, in co-operation with the IIS. Roger Hawkey, a consultant to the IIS (see Hawkey 2006), was trained in the use of the COLTeap observation schedule and independently observed two of the videotaped classes. These observations showed complete agreement on the number of activities observed with minor discrepancies on timing. These discrepancies reflected the subjectivity of determining boundaries between activities where teachers begin an activity with some students before others or where they spend time relating two activities to each other. There was agreement on 72% of the observed categories, with most of the differences being on the minor focus of an activity.

For example, I recorded that one activity was led by the teacher, but the second observer also recorded that this involved learners working in small groups.

Development of the instruments for the main study: (iv) Test instruments

The rationale for development and trialling of the tests of grammar and vocabulary used in the main study are described in this section. In common with the IELTS Academic Writing test, these were administered at course entry and exit, providing an alternative perspective on language growth to compare with Writing score gains.

Measuring: rationale for and development of vocabulary and grammar tests

As a comparison measure for the IELTS Academic Writing Module for use in the main study, a comprehensive measure of the construct of academic writing skills that fully reflected the EAP construct explored in Chapter 2 would have been of great interest. Unfortunately, a number of concerns argued against the inclusion of such a measure.

Any alternative measure of academic writing that more fully reflected the construct would need to include features identified in the review of the literature: features such as the integration of source material and opportunities for redrafting. A measure of this nature would inevitably be more time-consuming than the IELTS and might be difficult to integrate into intensive language programmes. Participating institutions offering IELTS preparation, precisely because of their focus on the IELTS test, might be reluctant to involve their students in lengthy alternative measures. Given the lack of fit with the IELTS test, it might also prove difficult to obtain valid responses from students. Those preparing for IELTS might react negatively to being asked to take a demanding assessment that did not closely resemble the IELTS and so fail to treat it seriously. In light of these issues, no alternative measure of academic writing was developed for the main study.

At the same time both academic writing and the IELTS Academic Writing Module both require lexico-grammatical competence: a central area of overlap between the two and one that is accessible to relatively practical test instruments. If IELTS preparation courses are successful at exploiting features of the test to boost scores, the gains should not extend to independent measures of grammar and vocabulary. In order to explore the relationship between writing score gains and underlying knowledge of grammar and lexis, tests of grammar and vocabulary were included in the study.

The vocabulary test

Background: academic vocabulary

Weir (1983) sees copious problems in testing EAP vocabulary. These problems include selection – identifying which vocabulary to test – and methods – deciding what types or degrees of knowledge to test (receptive or productive knowledge) and how best to achieve this.

Recent corpus-based work has gone some way towards answering the first of these concerns: selecting which words to test. A distinction is often made, on the basis of frequency counts, between *general service* (West 1953) words encountered across a wide range of text types, *subtechnical* or academic words encountered in university texts across disciplines, and *technical* vocabulary encountered more frequently in texts concerning a specific discipline (Xue and Nation 1983, Coxhead and Nation 1998).

West's (1953) General Service Word List (GSL) of 2,000 of the most frequent words in English offers 75% *coverage* (percentage of words, including repeats, in a corpus) of non-fiction texts and 90% in fiction texts (Nation and Hwang 1995). The University Word List (UWL) of 800 academic word families (Xue and Nation 1983) provides 8.5% coverage of academic texts, 3.9% coverage of newspapers and 1.7% coverage of fiction (Nation and Hwang 1995), while Coxhead's (1998) Academic Word List (AWL) – a corpus-based collection of words occurring frequently across academic texts, but not represented on the GSL – includes 588 word families and provides a slightly fuller coverage of academic text than the UWL at 10.8% (Coxhead and Nation 1998). Technical words, on the other hand, may occur frequently in a limited range of texts, or in a single text. Nation and Hwang (1995) suggest a further possible distinction between technical vocabulary, which is often explained on first appearance, and topic vocabulary, which has no technical meaning, but occurs with high frequency throughout an individual text.

Academic vocabulary may cause more difficulties for NNS students than the technical vocabulary associated with their discipline and has therefore been identified as a focus for EAP instruction (Ghadessy 1979, Nation 1990, Cunningham and Moore 1993, Parry 1993, Coxhead 2000). Nation and Hwang (1995) advocate a vocabulary learning sequence which starts from a general service list of around 2,000 words, then stresses academic vocabulary as the most efficient route to a level of knowledge which will provide the 95% coverage said to be necessary for adequate comprehension (Nation and Hwang 1995). Similarly, Coxhead and Nation (1998) advocate a graded approach, introducing academic words through adapted texts and building up to extensive reading of authentic academic texts both within students' own discipline and across disciplines. Unfortunately, the depth, as opposed to the extent, of vocabulary knowledge required for academic study is still not well understood. It is not clear what degree of word knowledge is required at the various frequency levels to support academic literacy.

Questions have also been raised regarding the nature of the vocabulary required for academic study. Liu and Nesi (1999) question the assumption that academic subtechnical vocabulary is the area of greatest importance for EAP classes. Classifying technical and academic terms on the basis of frequency and range in texts employed on a sample of courses, Liu and Nesi tested engineering students on their knowledge of technical and academic *procedural* (Widdowson 1983) or subtechnical vocabulary, finding that the former were significantly less familiar to the students. Given that learning technical vocabulary is closely related to learning the academic subject (Coxhead and Nation 1998) their findings have worrying implications. To help learners to deal with technical vocabulary, Liu and Nesi, like Coxhead and Nation (1998) and Flowerdew (1993), suggest that they should be given training in recognising and interpreting definitions and in determining whether or not a technical word should be learned.

The implications of the limited research into academic vocabulary needs are that students entering university will require:

1. A working (receptive and productive) knowledge of general service and academic vocabulary in order to access and generate academic texts.
2. The ability to identify and acquire, when they encounter it, the technical vocabulary associated with their discipline.
3. The ability to recognise and interpret spoken or written definitions.

Item 1 is clearly an essential prerequisite for academic study across disciplines, while 2 and 3 are closely related to disciplinary knowledge and may transfer less easily across topic areas. Although the evidence for the role of topic knowledge in reading and writing is inconclusive, it seems logical to suggest that the ability to recognise and interpret definitions in one area of knowledge may not generalise well to others. Thus, while 2 and 3 are of interest and point to important areas for EAP pedagogy, no instrument could be found that adequately addresses these abilities. It was concluded that the development of a comprehensive test of EAP vocabulary skills was beyond the scope of this study and that, as a result, the vocabulary test would be restricted to the first of the three.

There are a number of diverging estimates of how much vocabulary knowledge is enough for academic study. Laufer (1992) concludes that a threshold knowledge of 3,000 word families is required for independent reading while Sutarsyah, Nation and Kennedy (1994) suggest that a receptive vocabulary of around 5,000 words is required to understand a first-year economics textbook. Hazenberg and Hulstijn (1996), working in Dutch, found that a vocabulary of 10,000 words may be required for university study. The inconsistency between these estimates may reflect both differences among disciplines and institutions and of research method, including methods for determining thresholds considered acceptable for comprehension.

Coxhead and Nation (1998), along with Beglar and Hunt (1999), suggest that knowledge of the General Service Word List (West 1953) level of 2,000 words plus the University Word List (or Academic Word List) level provide a minimum requirement for accessing academic text. Coxhead and Nation (1998) found that the Academic Word List provided 10% coverage of an academic corpus of 3,500,000 running words and, when combined with the General Service Word List would give readers 90% coverage. On the other hand, Schmitt, Schmitt and Clapham (2001) in their review, suggest, less optimistically, that a vocabulary of 5,000 words will allow readers to access authentic text, while additional subtechnical or academic vocabulary will also be required for academic study.

In short, given the concern with determining how far students preparing for IELTS are also prepared for academic study, the main study called for a measure of vocabulary knowledge that would (a) indicate whether learners had acquired a threshold of vocabulary knowledge that might allow them to access academic text, (b) reflect EAP vocabulary needs across disciplines, (c) capture differences in gains in vocabulary knowledge made during courses of study and (d) be practical and straightforward for teachers to administer and score.

Trialling of vocabulary test instruments

Of available measures, the Vocabulary Levels Test (VLT) (Xue and Nation 1983, Nation 1990) seemed the most promising candidate to meet at least the first and third of the above criteria. It has been described as the best available measure of vocabulary size (Schmitt et al 2001) and has been widely used both in research and as a diagnostic tool for teachers (Read 2000). Permission was given by the author for its use here. The original test, published in Nation (1990) has 30 words at each level sampled from a number of published wordlists. The test is based on word frequency count levels with subtests at the 2,000, 3,000, 5,000 and 10,000 word levels. There is an additional subtest directed at academic or subtechnical vocabulary based on the Campion and Elley (1971) university wordlist. The test consists of clusters of six options to be matched to each of three brief definitions (see Nation 1990).

Vocabulary test trial

Before deciding whether to use the VLT in the main study, a trial of the instrument was conducted. A total of 79 students on a pre-sessional EAP course were administered the VLT: 32 on a 12-week course and 47 on an eight-week course. Forms of the VLT (Nation 1990) were administered to students on 12- and eight-week pre-sessional courses during June, July and August 2000. Pre-tests were given within the first three weeks of each course, and the post-test was administered in the last week of classes (before a final week of testing and project presentations). Thus, there were at least eight weeks between administrations on the 12-week course and at least four weeks on the eight-week course.

There was no time limit for the test (although the time required was noted in each instance) and teachers administered it in regular classes. Teachers and learners were encouraged to use the results diagnostically, to guide vocabulary learning and were informed that the results would not be used for formal assessment purposes.

Differences in test means between forms were of concern in the development of equivalent forms for the main study. The largest differences on the VLT were found between the 5,000 word frequency level forms (1.84 points). ANOVA revealed significant differences between forms at the 3,000 and 5,000 word levels, while no two test forms at the same level satisfied Henning's (1987) three criteria for equivalence through means, variance and covariance (Schmitt et al 2001). It was clear that the equivalence of forms could not be assumed.

Given the low levels of reliability on the test sections and the lack of equivalence between forms, any conclusions regarding gains would have to be tentative. Nevertheless, consideration of gains at the group level could provide valuable insights into the suitability of the two tests for the purposes of the study.

A two-way ANOVA was carried out to explore gains made in vocabulary test scores and differences in gains between the two courses. This revealed significant ($p < 0.05$) gains on both, with significantly higher gains on the longer course. Gains on both courses were very much in keeping with their length, with the 12-week classes having approximately twice as long (eight to nine weeks) between administrations as the eight-week classes (four to five weeks). The tests did therefore appear to reflect greater vocabulary gains occurring over the longer period of instruction. However, the 12-week students as a group failed on either post-test to attain the level of knowledge displayed at entry by the eight-week students.

Implications

With respect to the requirements for vocabulary testing in the main study, the Vocabulary Levels Tests did appear to reflect learning gains made over the course of instruction, and to reflect the greater gains made by learners over the longer of the two courses. The trial also offered evidence for two additional possibilities with implications for the main study. Firstly, the students on the longer of the two courses did not, in general, reach even the entry level of the students on the shorter, although both groups might expect to be at the same level at course exit. Secondly, there appeared to be a minority of students who learned very little new vocabulary during the 12-week course.

The VLT was thus potentially a useful addition to the main study. However, two 60-item vocabulary tests, each taking over 20 minutes to administer, when added to the other instruments, would clearly place too much of a burden on learners and so fail to satisfy the third criterion: for ease and practicality of administration.

The AWL level of the VLT, although it may only access initial knowledge of a word's most frequent meaning (Schmitt et al 2001), seemed to offer a useful measure of vocabulary knowledge within a framework of academic literacy. Under the model of EAP writing outlined in Chapter 2, learners need to be able to access vocabulary in their reading that will allow them to generate source text-based written work. Such knowledge represents one of the areas identified in Chapter 2 where the IELTS AWM may not adequately represent academic writing skills. Thus the VLT might be expected to highlight relevant differences between IELTS preparation and pre-sessional EAP courses.

While it had been determined that the VLT was best suited to the requirements of the main study, there remained a need to generate equated forms; a task that remained unfulfilled, despite the widespread use of the VLT in research (Beglar and Hunt 1999). Fortuitously, while the pilot study was under way, Schmitt et al (2001) made available two equated forms of the VLT made up of 30 items at each level, and it was decided to employ the AWL level of this test in the main study. While it would have been useful to include items at the 3,000 and 5,000 word levels in addition to the academic, this would have created either too lengthy a test form, or reduced the number of items at each level, jeopardising the reliability of the measurement.

Although Schmitt et al (2001) indicate that the two forms of the test may not be truly equivalent at the AWL level, there were arguments for using two forms rather than a single repeated measure. Firstly, the participation of teachers and learners in the study would be encouraged by the provision of diagnostic information in support of learning and, for this reason, the provision of feedback on test performance was encouraged. Use of the same test form at entry and exit would preclude this. Secondly, the tests were being used for the purpose of group comparisons, rather than for high-stakes decisions about individuals and, for this purpose, use of the two forms was considered justified.

Grammar test development

A measure of grammatical competence provides a programme-neutral objective measure of academic language proficiency to set against the gains made in IELTS AWM scores. Significant gains in Writing scores without accompanying gains in grammatical competence scores would lend support to claims that the focal courses were more successful in developing students' writing abilities in areas other than grammatical competence (such as test-taking strategies or discourse organisation).

Grammatical competence has long been recognised as a key enabling skill (Weir 1993) for writing ability, although the extent of the relationship is a matter for debate. Morley (2000) compares writing performance, judged on an adaptation of the IELTS 9-point scale, with the Chaplen test, a speeded 100 item test of structure and lexis developed for the purpose of screening international students at the University of Manchester in the 1960s. He finds that the Chaplen test is broadly predictive of writing test performance, correlating at .812 with writing test results (on an internally developed placement measure, n = 60). At the same time, individual students' performances on the two tests displayed considerable variability. Some learners scored at quite different levels on the two tests.

While Morley's (2000) study suggests a limited relationship between grammar and academic writing, the conclusions are not well supported. Morley interprets the disparity in learners' scores as an indication of the limitations of speeded grammar tests. However, they might, equally, raise questions about the qualities of the writing test. Unfortunately, Morley provides no indication of the stability of scores between forms of the writing and grammar tests; it may be that an equal lack of concordance would be found between individuals' scores on two forms of the Chaplen test or on two writing samples.

Trialling of the Grammar test

In developing the Grammar and Vocabulary tests, validated, but flexible and efficient instruments were sought. These instruments would need to address language proficiency in specifically academic settings, be practical to administer and to have been developed for the international student population.

During the development of IELTS, a Grammar subtest was developed (Clapham and Alderson 1997). This test of lexis and structure, published in Clapham (1996) was innovative in its focus on cohesion and coherence in the context of continuous texts. However, it was dropped from the IELTS battery during development because it correlated so highly with the IELTS Reading and Listening subtests, raising the question, for Alderson and Clapham (1992) of whether it was simply an indirect measure of reading skills.

The draft IELTS Grammar test was not used in the current study for the following reasons. The use of continuous texts, while providing a context for each item, restricted the focus of the test. While reference and cohesion were well addressed, the only other structures which could be tested were those occurring in the passages, rather than those targeted by the test developers (Clapham 2000).

The use of continuous passages also constrained opportunities for rapid item revision. The restricted time frame for development on this project meant that any problematic items would have to be quickly revised or replaced. Where items were embedded in extended text, revisions might prove unworkable, while deletions would further reduce the limited pool of items, threatening test reliability.

The test consisted of 38 items to be administered in 30 minutes. As it involved learners of divergent proficiency, but with limited time available, the study called for a test that could be delivered in a shorter time, but that would likely require more items in order to provide a sufficient spread of scores.

Although the IELTS Grammar test targeted both structure and lexis, only the first section, consisting of four items, was restricted to lexical items, while one other included *lexical sets* (see Clapham and Alderson 1997 for an overview of the test content). The intention in the study was to gather more extensive evidence of learners' lexical knowledge.

Weir (1983) also developed a grammar test for use with an EAP test battery: the TEEP. This test is constructed on a principled basis of relevance to the current study – the common structural errors made by international students in their academic writing. Thus it is well aligned to the intention in EAP writing instruction to reduce the incidence of such errors and could be expected to point to differences between IELTS preparation and EAP courses in meeting this aim.

A number of considerations argued for the further development of the test before it could be employed in the study. Firstly, shifts in the international student population since the early 1980s implied that the test might not operate in the same fashion today as it had 20 years earlier (Alderson 2000). Secondly, Weir (1983) reports unacceptably low item-total correlations (r_{pbi}) for some items, suggesting that the test could, in any case, be improved by revision.

Trials involving a total of 150 learners with two overlapping 50-item versions of the test were carried out in 2000 and 2001. These trial forms were made up of a total of 85 items (including some added to the item bank for the purpose of the study). The trials revealed that some items were not performing adequately and that, to provide adequate discrimination at the targeted level, additional items would be required. Although the intention had been to develop two parallel forms, the trials yielded too few items with the required levels of difficulty and discrimination. Instead, a single 50-item form was produced for use in the main study. As all learners in the main study were to be tested at intervals of three weeks or more, and as no detailed feedback would be provided on performance on the first of the two test administrations, it was assumed that there would be no significant practice effect (Henning 1987, Brown 1996).

Following the first round of administrations, comparison of results from the operational version with the trial version showed that the operational version was better adapted to the level of the test population, although it remained a little easier than preferred with a mean of 33.06 and a standard deviation of 6.32 for this higher proficiency group of learners (n = 223). Reliability was also disappointing; the reliability index for this administration being 0.796. However, the fact that this figure was lower than those obtained for Proficiency Group-A and Proficiency Group-B may simply have reflected the comparatively narrow range of scores on this administration of the test.

An Item Response Theory (IRT) analysis was carried out on the operational form. In this analysis three items were identified as questionable. Item 15 ('We STILL have not discovered what causes certain illnesses') had an infit mean square value of 1.26, indicating relatively poor fit to the model. Analysis of the distractors revealed that, on this item, option A (*yet*) was somewhat more popular with high scorers than the correct response, option C (*still*). Additionally, two items had unexpectedly low infit mean square values (items 28 and 42). According to McNamara (1996), such *overfit* can indicate that the item lacks stochastic independence, that the response may in some way be influenced by responses to neighbouring items. Indeed, item 28 targeted a construction which also appeared in the following question [*so* adv. *that*]. Item 42 ('The number of students WHO ARE SUCCESSFUL HAS not been worked out') seemed similarly vulnerable to clues from a neighbouring item: item 43 was 'NEITHER of the students has started the course'. However, as the fit statistics for all three of these items were considered acceptable, and their exclusion would have required re-scoring of all grammar answer forms, they were retained on the test and included in the subsequent analyses.

The operational form of the Grammar test (GT) thus consisted of 50 four-option multiple-choice items to be administered in approximately 25 minutes. In all, a period of 35 minutes was allowed for both the GT and VLT, which were administered together. The timings were derived from trialling and were based on the maximum time taken by test takers to respond to the tests of 30 seconds per item. The combined tests were administered within five days of the initial and exit IELTS AWM and were scored locally by teachers so that results (raw scores) could be reported to students and used for local purposes (such as placement of students into class levels).

Development of instruments for the main study: (v) The IELTS AWM

Test instruments

The IELTS AWM requires two writing samples. The test taker must respond to both tasks and has no choice of topic. The first Writing task involves a description of a table, graph or diagram for a specified audience: a university lecturer. The second task is a discursive essay on a single given topic, based, in the words of the task rubric, on the test taker's 'own ideas, knowledge and experience'. The first task (Task 1) requires a minimum response length of 150 words and the second (Task 2) requires 250 words. Scoring is task-specific, but utilises the IELTS 9-band scale descriptors. Although the scoring criteria have since been updated, at the time of the study Task 1 was rated on *Task Fulfilment, Coherence and Cohesion* and *Vocabulary and Sentence Structure*. Task 2 shared this criterion of *Vocabulary and Sentence Structure*, but was also rated on *Arguments, Ideas and Evidence* and *Communicative Quality*. Details of these criteria were not made public by the IELTS partners at that time, but are provided in Appendix 8. The new criteria are provided on the IELTS website (www.ielts.org).

Two operational forms of the test, IELTS Academic Module Writing, Versions 37 and 40, were provided by Cambridge ESOL for the purposes of the study. The test forms are statistically equated for level of difficulty by Cambridge ESOL. The tasks from the two tests were combined to create four test forms (Table 4.7).

Table 4.7 Component tasks for the Writing tests employed in this study from IELTS AWM versions.

Form	Version	Task		Version	Task
A	37	1	and	37	2
B	40	1	and	40	2
C	37	1	and	40	2
D	40	1	and	37	2

Task 1 tasks included one table of figures for educational achievement among school children at different ages and one bar chart displaying household consumption figures. Task 2 tasks involved a discussion of the problem of traffic congestion in modern cities and a question relating to punishment through imprisonment or community service.

The mean score for the IELTS AWM reported in the *IELTS annual review* for 2001–2002 (IELTS 2002) is 5.67 and the overall mean band score was 5.95 for academic candidates. Historically, mean band scores for the IELTS Writing test range between 5.33 and 5.86. Although IELTS scripts are usually scored by a single rater, for monitoring purposes a proportion of scored scripts are reviewed by a senior, experienced examiner. An inter-rater correlation for such paired sample (double rated) scripts reported by Cambridge ESOL (Taylor 2002) is .85.

Procedures

Scoring

All IELTS tasks were scored by two independent raters using the official IELTS Writing Assessment Guide (IELTS 2000). The raters employed for the study were all currently certified IELTS examiners who, in accordance with IELTS practice, had been re-certified as examiners by Cambridge ESOL within the previous two years. To preclude any bias resulting from expectations of gain following instruction these raters were given no indication of whether any given script had been written at course entry or at course exit.

Scoring employed the IELTS 9-band scale, following the official guidelines (IELTS 2000) in all but two respects. Firstly, all rating was both global – providing an overall impression score for each script – and analytic – employing the full range of three scoring criteria for each task. This approach excluded the option, available at that time in operational scoring of IELTS, of awarding a single global score without reference to the analytic criteria. The advantages of analytic rating include greater reliability – it provides more ratings for each candidate – and greater discrimination across bands. An extensive review of research evidence in Weir (1990) and, in an IELTS context, an investigation of trainee rater behaviour by Rignall and Furneaux (2002) suggest that raters are more consistent when employing an analytic rating scale than when making a single, global rating.

Secondly, in this context the gains anticipated following instruction are relatively small; perhaps half a band for each month of study (Bool, Dunmore and Tonkyn 1999). Unfortunately it is impossible to register small gains using the official IELTS band scores for Writing as these only allow raters to express scores in whole numbers. As a result, if possible, there was a need to make the scoring criteria more sensitive than the nine bands would allow. To achieve this, raters were asked to use half bands to indicate a relatively good performance within a band. Thus a rater awarding a band of 5 to a script on the basis of the official guidelines could, for the purposes of this project, indicate a good performance within the 5 band by awarding a score of 5.5. The raters employed for the study considered that they would be able to score scripts in this way, so a half-band scoring strategy was adopted.

Inter-rater correlations for global ratings (Pearson's r) were modest: .70 for Form A, .81 for Form B, Task 2; .74 for Form C and .74 for Form D. As gain scores are highly sensitive to the reliability of the instruments employed, these figures were disappointingly low when compared with inter-rater correlations of .85 reported for the IELTS Writing test by Cambridge ESOL (Taylor 2002).

A relatively low figure for inter-rater consistency was, perhaps, only to be expected given the rather narrow range of scores under consideration and the use of single, global ratings applied by each examiner. Indeed, when the analytic scoring was used (with ratings summed across criteria), the figures were considerably higher: .94 for Form A, .91 for Form B, .87 for Form C and .98 for Form D.

To reduce the effects of inter-rater variability, and hence to improve the reliability of the individual scores, these were corrected for the effects of task difficulty and rater severity through a multifaceted Rasch procedure using FACETS Version 3.22 for MS-DOS. FACETS, in the four-faceted model employed for this study, offers estimations of test-taker ability, rater harshness, task difficulty and scale criterion. These facets of the test are all reported on the same scale, expressed in logits.

Logit scores are also translated in the FACETS output onto the scale used by the raters (the IELTS band score scale) in the form of *fair average* scores (Table 4.8). It is assumed that the steps of the rating scale are equivalent across criteria. Rating was carried out according to a predetermined matrix to ensure multiple connections between raters and tasks. This enabled the programme to adjust scores by taking into account rater harshness and any variation in task difficulty.

Reliability figures are generated by FACETS for each of the four facets considered in the model: persons, items, raters and scoring criteria. According to Linacre (1988), the reliability figure for persons can be interpreted as an index of inter-rater reliability for the person ability scores generated by the model in the same way as Cronbach's α. In this case, the figure was 0.94.

The correlation between the *fair average* scores generated by FACETS and scores obtained by averaging observed scores across two raters was 0.923.

Of the 952 scripts, 57 were identified as misfitting using the criterion of MSq > 2.0 (Myford and Wolfe 2000). Cases of misfit were investigated to ensure that scores had been entered correctly and to find reasons why aberrant ratings should have been awarded.

The adequacy of the FACETS model is assessed through two measures of fit: the infit and the outfit mean squares. The raters displayed infit and outfit mean squares ranging from 0.7 to 1.3, tasks ranged between 0.9 and 1.0 and scale criteria from 0.8 to 1.4. All were judged to be within an acceptable range according to criteria suggested by Wright and Linacre (1994).

Results were less satisfactory for persons (the test takers). Setting limits on acceptability of infit of 0.4 as suggested by Wright and Linacre (1994), 71 test takers were identified as overfitting. Overfit indicates unexpectedly consistent performance and is potentially a problem in selected response tests as it may indicate collusion on the part of candidates or a lack of independence between items. For a test of performance of this kind, however, it is less of a concern as consistent performance across tasks is unlikely to be attributable to either of these causes.

Setting a boundary for misfit of 2.0 (Myford and Wolfe 2000), 57 test takers were identified as misfitting the model. Inspection of the FACETS output revealed that most of these cases involved differential performance on the two test tasks.

These cases were not excluded from the study for two reasons. Firstly, the IELTS AWM involves completion of both test tasks and differential performance is allowed for in the test design. The adjusted scores could still, on this basis, be interpreted as the best available estimates of learners' writing ability. Secondly, the intention of the study was to predict learning gains for all learners, and not only for those who demonstrated adequate fit to the model. Candidates are not excluded from courses or denied IELTS scores on the basis of lack of fit. Excluding cases from the study on purely statistical grounds could have distorted the results.

Table 4.8 FACETS Tasks Measurement Report (arranged by N)

Obsvd Score	Obsvd Count	Obsvd Average	Fair-M Average	Model Measure	S.E.	Infit MnSq	Infit ZStd	Outfit MnSq	Outfit ZStd	N	Tasks
43015	3996	5.4	5.44	−.07	.01	1.0	0	1.0	0	1	37T1
42311	4020	5.4	5.29	.13	.01	1.0	1	1.0	1	2	40T1
42328	3984	5.3	5.34	.06	.01	1.0	1	1.0	1	3	37T2
44025	3996	5.5	5.48	−.13	.01	0.9	−3	0.9	−3	4	40T2
42919.8	3999.0	10.7	10.77	.00	.01	1.0	−0.0	1.0	−0.1	Mean	(Count: 4)
698.5	13.1	0.2	0.15	.10	.00	0.0	2.0	0.0	2.0	S.D.	

RMSE (Model)   .01   Adj S.D.   .10   Separation   7.94   Reliability .98
Fixed (all same) chi-square: 256.4   d.f.: 3   significance: .00
Random (normal) chi-square: 3.0   d.f.: 2   significance: .22

Scores for persons, expressed in logits, ranged from −2.84 to 2.66 and rater harshness ranged from −.77 to .93, indicating that raters were working to a similar standard in their ratings, falling within one band of each other. Task difficulty (Table 4.9) ranged from −.13 (Version 40 Task 2) to .13 (Version 40 Task 1). Criteria ranged from −.10 logits (*Coherence and Cohesion*) to .19 logits (*Task Fulfilment*). The range in candidate scores was 5.5 logits, while the range of rater severity was 1.7 logits. The difference in range may be interpreted as an indicator of the impact of rater harshness on candidate performance (Myford and Wolfe 2000, O'Sullivan 2002). As the range of candidate performance is three times that of rater severity, the effect of rater severity can be seen to be relatively small.

The mean error score was 0.2 logits, which may be calculated as 0.14 of a band. Thus we may be 95% confident that a student with a fair average score of 6.0 on the IELTS AWM has a true score of between 5.72 and 6.28.

Table 4.9 FACETS summary 'rulers' showing rater harshness, task difficulty and criteria difficulty

```
|Measr  |+Candidates  |Raters          |Tasks       |Criteria*        |S.1   |

+ 3   +             +               +           +                + (9.0)+
                    .
                                                                  7.5
                                                                  ---
              .
              .                                                   7.0
+ 2   +       .      +               +           +                +      +
              *
              .
              **.                                                 6.5
              **.
              **.
              *.                                                  ---
+ 1   +       ****.  +               +           +                +      +
              ****.     R6i
              ******.                                             6.0
              *****.
              ******.   R5                                        ---
              ******.
              ********. TF
              ********.   R2i         40T1                        5.5
* 0   +  * ********.  * R2ii R3i R4ii R4i* 37T2   * AIE Global VSS *      *
              ********.   R3ii        40T2 37T1   CC      CQ
              ******.   R6ii
              ******.                                             ---
              *******.   R1i                                      5.0
              ******.
              ****.     R1ii
              ****.                                               ---
+ -1  +       ****.  +               +           +                +      +
              **.                                                 4.5
              **.
              **.
              *.                                                  ---
              .
              **                                                  4.0
              .
+ -2  +       .      +               +           +                + ---  +
              .
              .                                                   3.5
              .
              .                                                   ---
              .
+ -3  +       +     +               +           +                + (1.0)+

|Measr   * = 7      |Raters          |Tasks       |Criteria         |Scale |
```

```
* Criteria:
Task 1            TF Task Fulfilment
                  CC Coherence and Cohesion
                  VSS Vocabulary and Sentence Structure
Task 2            AIE Arguments Ideas and Evidence
                  CQ Communicative Quality
                  VSS Vocabulary and Sentence Structure
```

On the basis that the results were adequate for the purposes of the study and that the FACETS fair average scores were more dependable than the averages of scores from two raters, these were employed as the preferred estimates of writing ability in the main study.

Trialling

A full trial of instruments and procedures was carried out with a total of 50 candidates on two courses and refinements were made on the basis of these trials, including:

- reformulation of questionnaire items (see above)
- adjustment of time available to respondents
- development of administration procedures and instructions for teachers
- presentation of both IELTS AWM Writing tasks on a single page.

The IELTS AWM was administered, together with the grammar and vocabulary tests, at course entry and exit. In addition, brief questionnaires were administered before (IELTS Awareness Forms A or B – IA) and after (Test Strategies Report form – TSR) the IELTS Writing tasks. The IA administered before the test, posed questions relating to familiarity with and attitude to IELTS. The TSR, administered after the test, addressed test-taking strategies.

All tests were administered at course entry and exit according to guidelines provided to invigilators. However, some variation in conditions was inevitable as the project had to accommodate local needs. Some administrations were undertaken by teachers in class, while others were held collectively, in lecture theatres.

Initial results were used by institutions for decisions regarding placement, diagnosis and achievement. Courses incorporating IELTS preparation offered the Writing tests as IELTS test practice, others included the tests in exit test batteries or as components in a scheme for continuous assessment. These variations were unavoidable given the different course objectives and the practical need to meet local needs. It is possible that the differences may have influenced test performance and they must be weighed when considering the results. Nonetheless, all students did have a clear reason to take the tests and all completed the test tasks. This suggests that the tests were treated seriously across courses.

To control for any effect for task characteristics, a crossover design was employed. Each test taker responded to all four test tasks, but would encounter one of the four possible configurations (see Table 4.10) of tasks at course entry and exit (Form A to B, B to A, C to D or D to C) according to the institution he or she was attending. The design is set out in Table 4.10.

Questionnaires A and B, addressing a range of attitudinal and background variables (see above), were administered on the same occasion as the

Table 4.10 Forms of the IELTS AWM by institution

Institution		Initial Writing test	Exit Writing test	N
University	A	FORM C	FORM D	53
University	A	FORM C	FORM D	48
University	A	FORM C	FORM D	54
University	B	FORM B	FORM A	104
University	B	FORM B	FORM A	60
University	C	FORM A	FORM B	12
University	D	FORM A	FORM B	27
University	E	FORM D	FORM C	4
University	F	FORM C	FORM D	13
University	G	FORM D	FORM C	1
College	A	FORM B	FORM A	33
College	B	FORM D	FORM C	12
College	C	FORM C	FORM D	25
College	D	FORM D	FORM C	2
College	E	FORM D	FORM C	15
College	F	FORM D	FORM C	1
College	G	FORM D	FORM C	4
College	H	FORM D	FORM C	8

tests, or within a few days. They were either administered by teachers in class or (on short courses) as a take-home activity.

Questionnaire A and B responses were obtained from a total of 454 of the 476 students participating in the study. Of these, 454 (87%) responded to Questionnaire A and 348 to Questionnaire B (77%).

Analyses

Through the data collection a total of nearly 300 data points had been assembled on each student involved in the study. The next step was to consolidate the data and to relate it 1) to group differences and 2) to gains on the IELTS AWM. Analysis was undertaken in two phases. The objective of the first phase was to explore group differences among the students. In the second phase the data was explored for relationships between the variables and IELTS AWM score gains.

The first phase of the analysis related the assembled presage and process variables to group differences. As a preliminary, it was necessary to establish whether learners in the case study had improved their scores from time one to time two. Paired sample t tests for repeated measures were used to determine whether score gains (or losses) by learners on each of the three Course Types were significant or whether observed differences in scores might have occurred by chance alone.

Analysis of covariance was used to explore the relationship between Course Type (pre-sessional EAP, IELTS preparation or combination) and other variables. Analysis of covariance allows the researcher to hold the values of one or more variables constant in seeking significant differences between the values of a second variable for two or more groups. For example, if age were seen to be strongly related to test scores, and the distribution of student ages were not equivalent across Course Types, it would be important to take age into account when comparing scores across courses. Analysis of covariance can be used to investigate whether there are significant differences between scores obtained by learners on the three Course Types when age is held constant.

Appropriate use of analysis of covariance depends on certain assumptions regarding the data. It is assumed that data is continuous and that results are normally distributed. As item responses were typically ordinal ratings, item-level data did not meet these assumptions. Non-parametric alternatives were therefore used to explore group differences at the item level. The *Wilcoxon signed rank sum test* is the non-parametric equivalent to the paired samples *t* test. It is not based on the assumption that the difference between two variables is interval and normally distributed, but is calculated on the basis of the rank order of values. Like the *t* test it is used to determine the significance of differences *within* groups between scores obtained through the same measure on two occasions. Where comparisons are to be made between two groups and assumptions of normality of distribution and interval measurement are not met, a *Mann-Whitney* test is used. The *Kruskal Wallis test* is used when one independent variable has two or more levels and the dependent variable is measured on an ordinal scale (as with the item-level data in this study). In other words, the Kruskal Wallis test is a non-parametric alternative to analysis of variance and may be used to evaluate the differences between more than two groups.

Correlation analysis was used to explore the degree of association between the independent variables and score gain. The correlation coefficient (r) is a number that serves as an indication of the extent to which two things are related (Guilford and Fruchter 1978). A significant positive correlation shows that increases in one variable are associated with increases in another while a significant negative correlation shows that increases in one variable are associated with decreases in another. A positive correlation between age and gain scores would indicate that older people tend to make higher score gains, a negative correlation would show that older people tend to make lower gains.

As with analysis of covariance it is possible to remove the effects of one variable in exploring the relationship between two others. Partial correlations, which removed the effects of initial scores, were used to further analyse the relationship between independent variables and score gains.

Both traditional and partial correlations are based on the assumption that relationships between variables are linear; that increases in one variable are always associated with increases in the other. This assumption might not be justified for all data in this study. Increasing levels of test anxiety, for example, might be associated with higher scores, as anxiety engenders the motivation to succeed, but above a certain level, anxiety might become debilitating and so be associated with lower scores. To reveal any such non-linear relationships between variables and score gains, data was also plotted graphically. On the basis of the correlations and data plots, variables associated with score gain were selected as candidates for the development of a model capable of predicting Exit Writing scores.

The second phase of analysis involved the construction of prediction models to identify which constellation of variables might provide for the most accurate prediction of Exit Writing scores. This involved two methods of model development; a neural network method through *NeuroSolutions 4.16* (NeuroDimension Inc. 2001) and traditional linear prediction through multiple regression in *SPSS 11.5 for Windows* (SPSS 2002).

The choice of a neural network method of analysis was dictated by the large number of interrelated variables addressed by the study. Neural networks differ from more familiar Multivariate General Linear Hypothesis (MGLH) methods such as multiple regression or MANOVA in several respects. The MGLH is programmatic, involving a model determined by the researcher and tested against the data. In contrast, neural networks are adaptive; data is presented to the network case by case and parameters are adjusted through an automatic process of feedback, governed by learning rules. Somewhat different outcomes with varying levels of predictive accuracy will be obtained on each training occasion.

The advantages of neural networks for studies of this kind lie in this adaptivity. Unlike the MGLH, they make no assumptions regarding the linearity of relationships between variables or about patterns of distribution in the data. They are robust with respect to missing or incomplete data and can operate with large numbers of variables relative to the number of cases: a liberal rule of thumb being 10 cases for each variable (Garson 1998).

Multi-layer perceptrons (MLP) – the form of neural network selected for this study – may be used for a wide range of data analysis applications including classification, data reduction and regression. They have been widely used in a number of areas including financial forecasting and engineering, but are becoming increasingly popular in the social sciences. Applications related to language include their use in *connectionist* psychology (Rumelhart and McClelland 1986, Elman 1996), text recognition and generation (Taschman 1993, Bullinaria 1995) and the prediction of item difficulty on language tests (Perkins, Gupta and Tammana 1995). They have also been used as an alternative to multiple regression or analysis of covariance in predicting language course outcomes from multiple sources of data (Hughes-Wilhelm 1997, 1999, Boldt and Ross 1998).

Although MLPs are more flexible than MGLH methods in handling large numbers of input features, generalisation may be poor if too many are used.

Following the initial correlation studies, two sets of MLPs were developed, one based on presage features, the other on process. In this way it was possible to establish how far it might be possible to predict outcomes on the basis of each. A series of two- and three-layered backpropagation MLP networks were constructed. Two-layer networks are effectively linear regressors, while three-layer networks allow for non-linear relationships between the input and desired sets. It was thus also possible to compare linear with non-linear prediction.

In determining the most appropriate architecture for the networks, the number of input and output processing elements (PEs) is determined by the problem. The number of PEs in the input layer is equal to the number of features in the input set (the number of independent variables). The number of PEs in the output layer is equal to the number of features in the desired set (the dependent variables). The number of PEs in the hidden layer is not determined by any theory or set of guidelines, but is established through experimentation with the aim of finding the simplest architecture capable of solving the problem. In this case, the number of PEs at input ranged from just one (initial IELTS AWM score) to 34 (for the widest range of presage, process and product features). A single PE formed the output layer, corresponding to the single feature being predicted (scores on the exit IELTS AWM). The number of PEs in the central, hidden layer was determined for each case through experimentation.

Each network was trained with randomised sequences of input vectors. Of the input set, 20% (95 cases) was used as a cross-validation set and a further 20% retained as a testing set. The remaining 60% (286 cases) of the input vectors formed a training set. The networks were initially trained by passing these training sets through the networks, so that they *learned* the problem.

If the process of training continues unchecked it is possible for a network to *overtrain*, obtaining very accurate results which are limited to the specific set of data under consideration. To prevent such an outcome, the training was halted at the point of optimum generalisation; the point at which there was least error in estimation of the cross-validation set. This point is reached when the mean squared error (MSE) calculated between the predicted values generated by the MLP and the actual values in the desired set reaches its lowest value for the cross-validation set. If overtraining occurs, the MSE will continue to decline in the training set, but will increase for the cross-validation set as generalisation of the predictions declines.

The next two chapters describe the results of the main study. The first explores differences across courses through questionnaire, interview and observation data, relating these to the influence of the IELTS Writing test. The second relates course and learner variables to differences in score outcomes through linear and non-linear predictive models.

Main study results I

The main study took the form of a triangulated case study involving both quantitative and qualitative methods. It is presented in two parts, the first being concerned with differences between groups of participants and the second with the prediction of score outcomes.

This chapter is primarily directed towards the following research questions:

1. *Given the commonalities and discrepancies between IELTS and the EAP writing construct revealed in the literature review, do students and teachers regard themselves as engaging in IELTS test preparation rather than university preparation and do such beliefs give rise to practices, in relation to IELTS, which fail to address the EAP writing construct?*

2. *Do practices on courses which are not driven by IELTS better reflect this construct?*

In making comparisons between the aims and content of courses, differences between learners populating the courses must also be taken into account. If this is not done, it is possible that differences of practice resulting from learner characteristics might be wrongly attributed to divergent course aims or the effect of test preparation. This methodological concern raises a third question to be addressed in this chapter:

3. *What are the characteristics of learners on different courses and how do these relate to the characteristics of the IELTS test-taking population?*

Evidence regarding the nature of the courses came from extensive questionnaire data, interviews with participants, observation of classes and inspection of classroom artefacts. Quantitative evidence for inter-group differences came from questionnaire data and test measures.

Asking: large-scale survey data from teachers and students

Learner background variables

Questionnaire data provided a demographic overview of the learners included in the study. This was helpful in identifying features of the population which might contribute to differential outcomes. There was variation in the balance of gender, age and nationality groups on the three course types investigated.

The genders were evenly represented in the study population, with women slightly outnumbering men (54% to 46%), but there were differences between course types. There was a higher proportion of women on IELTS preparation courses: 63.5% of participants compared with 48.3% on combination and 52.6% on pre-sessional courses.

IELTS preparation students were generally younger than their counterparts on pre-sessional and combination courses (Figure 5.1). The average age for IELTS preparation students was 21.9 years, while the average age for pre-sessional students was 26.4 years and for combination courses it was 25.1. A larger proportion of IELTS preparation students (32.5%) were aged under 18. There was a relatively small proportion of 19 to 22 year-olds on pre-sessional courses (13.3% against 30.6% on IELTS and 30.0% on combination courses).

Figure 5.1 Distribution of student age by Course Type

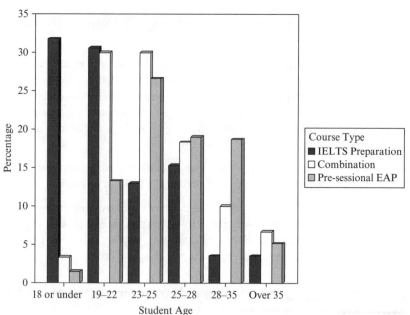

Figure 5.2 shows that the largest proportion of students overall were from China/Taiwan (54.8%). However, on combination courses, the largest numbers came from other East Asian countries, with Japan and Korea

Figure 5.2 Distribution of student Region of Origin by Course Type

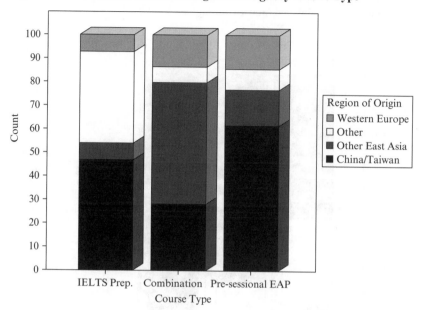

contributing 50% of the participants. IELTS preparation courses had the highest proportion of students from regions outside East Asia and Western Europe (38.8%). These came mostly from the former Soviet Union with 12.4% of learners on IELTS preparation courses coming from Kazakhstan, and 10.6% from Russia.

Learners on pre-sessional courses had completed the highest levels of education with most having completed at least undergraduate education (Figure 5.3). Learners on IELTS courses, being the youngest of the three groups, were evenly divided between those who had graduated from university and those who had completed only secondary-level education.

Reflecting the differences in educational attainment, over 40% of the learners on IELTS preparation courses were intending to go on to study on 'A' level, foundation or university preparation courses rather than entering university directly (Figure 5.4). It is interesting that these students were all preparing for the Academic Modules of IELTS rather than for the General Training Module which is directed at secondary education and non-degree level training programmes and so might appear more appropriate. Most learners on pre-sessional and combination courses were planning to enter postgraduate programmes, in common with a third of those on IELTS preparation courses.

Figure 5.3 Bar chart showing frequency of responses to Item 7. 'What level of education have you finished (mark your highest level)?'

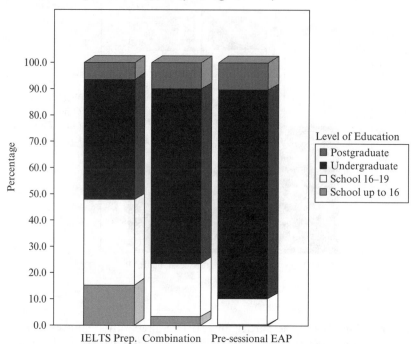

Questionnaire A: About how often you use English

Responses to the four items asking learners how often they used English at work and for socialising and how often they spent writing or reading in English are displayed in Figure 5.5. Learners generally reported spending more time reading than writing in English and reported using English for work more often than for socialising.

Making the comparisons between courses, a Kruskal Wallis test for the non-parametric comparison of groups revealed that learners on pre-sessional and combination courses reported spending significantly ($p<.01$) less time socialising in English than their peers on IELTS preparation courses. Although the question specifies 'in your own country', the difference may reflect the longer periods spent in the UK by these students and accommodation with local host families. Differences on items 4, 6 and 7 were not significant.

Questionnaire A: About studying English

Questions 8 and 9 asked whether students had a parent or close relative who spoke English as a first or second language. Only 1.5% of learners across

Figure 5.4 Bar chart showing frequency of responses to Item 11. 'At what level are you planning to study after this course?'

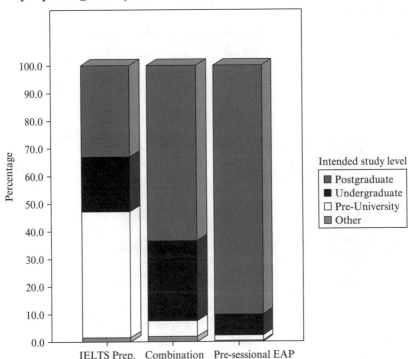

courses claimed that a parent or close relative spoke English as a first language. Of IELTS preparation students 20% reported having a parent or close relative who spoke English as a second language, compared with 13% of combination and 14% of pre-sessional students. This may be a reflection either of differences in the international distribution of L2 English speakers, or in how learners defined the ability to 'have a conversation in English'.

Learners were asked to indicate whether they had studied English at four levels (kindergarten, primary, secondary and university) and whether they had studied additional English classes outside formal schooling. Only very few learners, 13 in all, claimed to have studied English at kindergarten age. Between 26% and 27% of learners on each of the three course types reported that they had studied English at primary school. Group differences emerged at secondary level, however, with a much higher proportion of pre-sessional students claiming that they had not studied English in secondary school: 13.5% compared to 1.0% on IELTS and 1.7% on combination courses. Combination course and pre-sessional students were more likely to have studied English at university (48% and 49% respectively) than IELTS preparation learners

Figure 5.5 Boxplot of learner scores (reversed) on Questionnaire A ('About how often you use English') Items 4 (Use of English at Work) and 5 (Use of English for socialising)

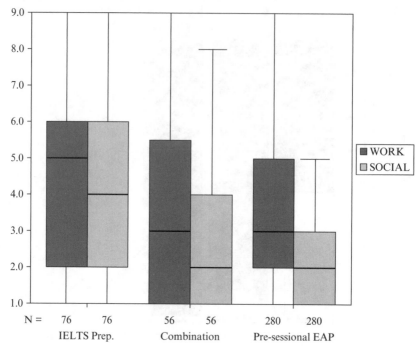

(36%), although this presumably reflects the higher proportion of younger, pre-university learners on IELTS preparation courses. A greater percentage of combination course students than of learners on other courses had studied extra English classes outside formal education (45% against 33% on IELTS and 32% on pre-sessional courses).

A larger proportion of IELTS preparation students (24.7%) reported studying English as a major subject at university than did combination (16.7%) or pre-sessional students (17.5%). However, 38.7% of learners on pre-sessional courses claimed some experience of English medium instruction on academic content courses. This was a higher percentage than on either combination or IELTS courses (21.2% and 25.0%).

Items 13 to 16 probed the frequency of English use in school classes and learners' experience of writing in their L1 (Figure 5.6). Learners most often reported having 'a few' (49.6%) or no (22.5%) L1 English-speaking teachers. There was a split in reported use of English in English language classes at school. Of learners, 30.4% stated that their English teachers used the target language all or more than half of the time. A further 43.3% reported that

Figure 5.6 Frequency of classes with L1 teachers, Use of TL English in class, Writing in English at school and Writing in L1 by Course Type (scored from 1 for least to 9 for most frequent)

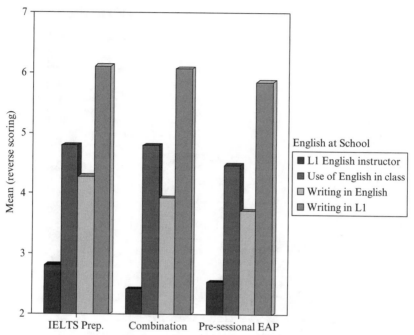

teachers had used English less than half of the time and 6.3% claimed that their English teachers never used the target language.

Writing in English was generally reported to be an occasional activity with the majority of learners (51.7%) reporting writing in less than half of their English classes with a further 5.3% reporting no writing practice, while 15% reported practising writing in more than half of their English classes.

Of learners, 66.2% reported writing essays or reports in their own language more than once a year with 21.3% writing as often as once a month. A small minority (3.4%) of learners reported never writing essays or reports in their L1. A non-parametric test of difference (Kruskal-Wallis) revealed no significant differences between course types on any of these four items.

On average, learners on pre-sessional courses reported spending the longest period studying English since leaving full-time education (Figure 5.7), but the fewest hours each week (2.3 hours per week compared with 4.8 hours per week for IELTS preparation students). Of combination course students, 28.6% and of pre-sessional students 34.5%, had previously studied on an IELTS preparation course, compared to 15.8% of those now entering IELTS preparation courses.

Figure 5.7 Years of English study since leaving full-time education by Course Type

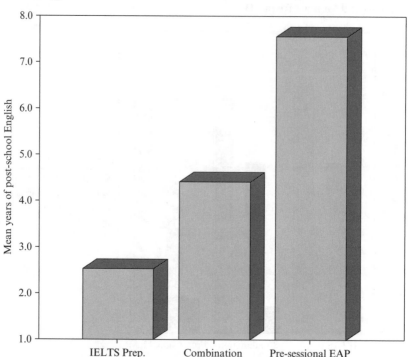

Learners were asked to indicate how long they had spent studying in an English-speaking country. Although 'English-speaking' as a description of a country may be a controversial term in applied linguistics, given debates over what constitutes a 'native' English speaker, the item was not questioned during piloting either by teachers or students and it was considered that any additional explanation of the term would be unnecessary, and possibly confusing, for the learners in the study.

Figure 5.8 shows that IELTS preparation students spent more time than others studying in English-speaking countries (a mean of 6.3 months compared with 3.2 months for combination, and 3.0 months for pre-sessional learners). The majority of learners on IELTS courses spent over three months in an English speaking country, while a high proportion of pre-sessional and combination course students were new arrivals with no previous experience of studying in L1 English countries at course entry (42.9% on combination and 58.8% on pre-sessional courses). The longest period spent in an English-speaking country by any student was four years (this was by a student on an IELTS preparation course).

Figure 5.8 Percentage of students spending time studying in an L1 English country by Course Type

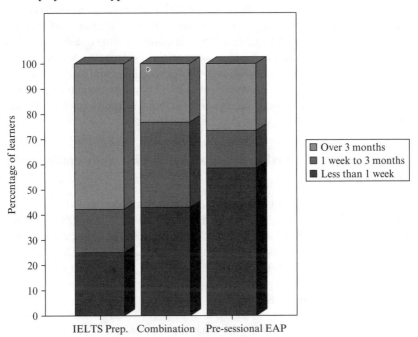

Questionnaire A Section 1: Reasons for choice of course

As many as 85.2% of learners on IELTS preparation courses and 69.6% of those on combination courses agreed with the statement 'I am taking this course because I want to get a good grade on IELTS or other test/ assessment'. In contrast, 50.9% of learners on pre-sessional courses disagreed with the statement and 45.9% agreed. Just 1.8% of learners on pre-sessionals, 9% of combination course and 17.1% of IELTS preparation students disagreed with the second statement 'I am taking this course to learn useful skills for university' (97.8%, 91.1% and 81.5% agreed).

Most learners asserted that they were studying to improve their general ability to use English, but a higher proportion of pre-sessional students expressed strong agreement (82.3%). The figures for combination and IELTS preparation course learners were 76.8% and 64.5%.

Of learners on IELTS courses 61% ranked item RE1 (I am taking this course to get a good grade on IELTS or other test) as the most important, while 21.9% of combination course learners and 6.5% of pre-sessional students also rated this item as the most important. Of pre-sessional learners 53.8% ranked RE2 (I am taking this course to learn useful skills for university) as most important,

171

compared with 45.5% of combination and 30.5% of IELTS preparation students. Whereas 23.1% of pre-sessional, 13.1% of IELTS preparation and 14.5% of combination course students rated RE3 (I am studying on this course because I want to improve my general ability to use English) most important.

Across courses, learners affirmed their intention to improve their English and to learn academic skills. It seems clear on this evidence, nonetheless, that the IELTS test was a particularly strong influence on the motivation of learners on IELTS preparation courses. Learners on combination courses recognised both the need to pass the test and the need to prepare for university study, the primary objective for pre-sessional learners.

Questionnaire A Section 2: Satisfaction with study context and self-confidence

Section 2 of the initial questionnaire addressed satisfaction with the study context, including Self-Confidence in English Writing Ability (SC01, SC03, SC05, SC06, SC07, SC09, SC12, SC14, SC15 and SC19); Orientation to the Study Context (the school and the wider host community) (SC02, SC04, SC08, SC11 and SC18) and Test Anxiety (SC10, SC13, SC16 and SC17) (see Box 5.1).

Box 5.1 Questionnaire A Section 2

SC01	People say that I am good at language learning.
SC02	I feel happy about living in an English speaking country.
SC03	I usually did better than other students at my school in English classes.
SC04	I do NOT really like the British way of life.
SC05	I am NOT good at writing in English.
SC06	I feel I will never really enjoy writing in English.
SC07	Writing classes are difficult for me.
SC08	I am pleased I chose to study at this school.
SC09	I like writing down my ideas in English.
SC10	If we had no tests, I think I would actually learn more.
SC11	I usually enjoy meeting British people.
SC12	I think learning languages is more difficult for me than for the average learner.
SC13	During an important test, I often feel so nervous that I forget facts I really know.
SC14	I DON'T think I write in English as well as other students.
SC15	It is easy for me to write good English essays.
SC16	Even when I'm well prepared for a test, I feel very worried about it.
SC17	I DON'T study any harder for final exams than for the rest of my course work.
SC18	I think the Writing classes will be useful for me.
SC19	I enjoy writing in English.

Reliability analysis indicated that item SC09 was making a negative contribution to the reliability of the Self-Confidence in English Writing Ability scale. Perhaps the inclusion of the word 'ideas' in item SC09 introduced an element unaddressed by other items. Following its elimination, the reliability (alpha) for the 9-item scale was .791.

Item SC18 made a negative contribution to the reliability of the Orientation to the Study Context scale. As most learners agreed with this statement (the mean rating was 3.75 of a possible 4), it contributed too little to the variance of the scale. Following its removal, the resulting scale reliability (Cronbach's alpha) was .594.

The Test Anxiety items did not appear to form a coherent scale, with only SC13 and SC16 showing consistency. These two items were therefore taken as an *ad hoc* indicator of Test Anxiety. This Test Anxiety scale was significantly (p<.05) correlated with student worry about taking the IELTS test as indicated on the Before the Writing Test questionnaire (Kendall's Tau .183), providing a degree of external support for the use of the scale in the analyses.

Analysis of covariance was undertaken with Self-Confidence in English Writing Ability as the dependent variable, Course Type, Gender and Region of Origin as fixed factors and IELTS Academic Writing Module (AWM) Score at Time One, Age, and Course Length as covariates. These variables were selected as key presage and process variables on the basis of an initial exploration of the results. The analysis revealed a significant (p<.05) effect for student Region of Origin and Gender, but not for Course Type. Of the four regional categories, the Other East Asia group had the lowest scores (see Figure 5.9).

Analysis of covariance with Orientation to the Study Context as the dependent variable, Course Type, Gender and Region of Origin as fixed factors and AWM score at Time One, Age, and Course Length as covariates showed no significant (p<.05) effects for either Candidate Region of Origin or Course Type. Similarly, analysis of covariance with Test Anxiety as the dependent variable revealed no significant (p<.05) between-subject effects.

Self-confidence in English writing ability at course exit

The items relating to the variables Self-Confidence in English Writing Ability and Orientation to the Study Context were administered again at course exit on Section 3 of Questionnaire B. The variable Self-Confidence in English Writing Ability was represented by:

IM02 (SC06) I feel I will never really enjoy writing in English.
IM04 (SC05) After studying on this course, I feel I am NOT good at writing in English.
IM06 (SC07) The Writing classes were difficult for me.

Figure 5.9 Means plot of self-confidence in English writing ability by student Region of Origin (Maximum score = 32)

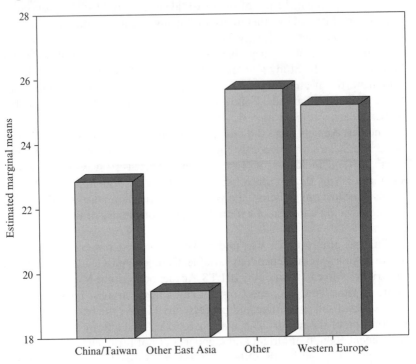

IM08	(SC19)	I enjoyed writing in English.
IM13	(SC14)	I DON'T think I write in English as well as other students.
IM15	(SC15)	It was easy for me to write good English essays.

IM07 (SC04) (I do NOT really like the British way of life), IM11 (SC08) (I am pleased I chose to study at this school), IM12 (SC11) (I usually enjoy meeting British people) and IM20 (SC02) (I feel happy about living in an English speaking country) addressed Orientation to the Study Context. Reliability analysis showed that both scales were acceptably reliable, with alphas of .705 for Self-Confidence in English Writing Ability and .605 for Orientation to the Study Context. Correlations between the two scales on Questionnaire B and the scales on Questionnaire A were .516 and .528 respectively.

Analysis of covariance with Self Assessed Aptitude at course exit as the dependent variable, Course Type, Gender and Region of Origin as fixed factors and AWM Score at Time One, Age, and Course Length as covariates again revealed no significant effect for Course Type, but did show a near-significant ($p<.05$) effect for Candidate Region of Origin. Orientation to the Study Context again showed no significant between-subject effects.

At the item level, students across Course Types gave the highest ratings to the same six items: SC02, SC08, SC09, SC11, SC18 and SC19. A Kruskal Wallis test revealed significant differences ($p<.05$) between Course Types for only three items: SC08 (I am pleased I chose to study at this school), SC10 (If we had no tests, I think I would actually learn more) (both rated higher by students on pre-sessional courses) and SC15 (It is easy for me to write good English essays) (rated higher by students preparing for IELTS).

The three items also showed significant differences between Course Types across student Region of Origin. When the test was repeated with the file broken down by region, only item SC10 displayed significant differences ($p<.05$) for Course Type across two regions (China/Taiwan and Other). These results suggest that students on the test-directed courses were somewhat more likely than their counterparts on EAP courses to believe that tests encouraged them to learn. However, the data cannot reveal whether the learners on test-directed courses had chosen their course because they were more heavily influenced by tests, or whether their courses had influenced them to believe in the motivational power of tests.

Region of Origin was associated with significant differences on nine items in all: SC01, SC05, SC06, SC08, SC10, SC11, SC12, SC15 and SC19. Learner background thus appears to be a more decisive factor in determining orientation to the study context than Course Type. The attitudes towards learning that learners bring with them to the classroom may have a greater influence on how the learning experience is constructed and experienced than the power of the test.

Questionnaire A Section 3 and Questionnaire B Section 3: Student expectations

Box 5.2 Questionnaire A Section 3/Questionnaire B Section 3: Student expectations

CE01	I expect to learn specialist vocabulary for my university subject.
CE02	I expect to learn general vocabulary.
CE03	I expect to learn about the kinds of writing tasks students do at university.
CE04	I expect to learn about differences between university education in my country and in Britain.
CE05	I expect to learn ways of improving my English Language test scores.
CE06	I expect to learn words and phrases for describing graphs and diagrams.

CE07   I expect to learn how to use evidence to support my written arguments.

CE08   I expect to learn how to organise an essay to help the reader to understand.

CE09   I expect to learn how to communicate my ideas effectively in writing.

CE10   I expect to learn grammar.

CE11   I expect to learn how to write university essays and reports.

CE12   I expect to learn how to find information from books to use in writing essays.

CE13   I expect to learn how to use quotations and references in academic writing.

CE14   I expect to learn how to edit and redraft my written work.

CE15   I expect to learn how to use ideas from text books or academic journals in my writing.

CE16   I expect to learn how to write long essays or reports of 1,000 words or more.

CE17   I expect to learn how to organise my time for studying.

CE18   I expect my teacher to correct my grammar mistakes in my written work.

CE19   I expect the activities we do in class will be similar to the ones on the IELTS test.

CE20   I expect to learn quick and efficient ways of reading books in English.

CE21   I expect to learn how to write successful test essays.

CE22   I expect to read books and articles about my specialist subject area.

CE23   I expect to learn how to write in a formal, academic style.

CE24   I expect to take practice tests in class.

Note: Items in this section were coded to reflect their position on three linked instruments. On Questionnaire A, all were prefixed CE for Course Expectations. On Questionnaire B, CO (Course Outcomes) was used. On the Teacher Questionnaire, CT (Course Teacher) was used. Wording of items was adapted to reflect the perspective of the survey: CO items typically beginning 'I learned' and CT items typically beginning 'Students learned'. The numerical coding of items was constant.

Expectations of course content were high for learners on all course types. Inevitably, students expected to learn most of the items listed. However, some differences did emerge between IELTS preparation and pre-sessional EAP in the average ratings given to items.

The three highest ranked items on both course types were:

CE18   I expect my teacher to correct my grammar mistakes in my written work.

CE09   I expect to learn how to communicate my ideas effectively in writing.

CE23   I expect to learn how to write in a formal, academic style.

On the other hand the following had a low average rating on all course types:

CE04   I expect to learn about differences between university education in my country and in Britain.

CE17   I expect to learn how to organise my time for studying.

CE22   I expect to read books and articles about my specialist subject area.

CE01   I expect to learn specialist vocabulary for my university subject.

Although many items received similar ratings from students on all course types, a non-parametric Kruskal Wallis analysis revealed a number of significant differences across groups. The following were rated significantly higher (p<.05) by learners on IELTS preparation courses:

CE24   I expect to take practice tests in class.

CE19   I expect the activities we do in class will be similar to the ones on the IELTS test.

The following were all ranked significantly higher by students entering pre-sessional EAP courses:

CE07   I expect to learn how to use evidence to support my written arguments.

CE11   I expect to learn how to write university essays and reports.

CE12   I expect to learn how to find information from books to use in writing essays.

CE16   I expect to learn how to write long essays or reports of 1,000 words or more.

Of these, items CE11, CE12, CE16, CE19 and CE24 also displayed significant differences for student Region of Origin. When the data was divided by student Region of Origin, there were significant (p<.05) differences between Course Types for two or more regional groups on items CE16 and CE19.

As course expectation items were generally given high ratings, making it difficult to compare ratings, students were also asked to indicate which of the 24 statements they felt would be most important to them. The item most often selected by IELTS preparation students was CE05 (I expect to learn ways of improving my English Language test scores), selected by 10 students (15.9% of responses). This item was also selected by nine (9.2%) learners on combination courses and by six (2%) on pre-sessional courses. CE24 (I expect to take practice tests in class) was chosen by nine (14.3%) on the IELTS courses, two (2%) on the combination courses and two (0.7%) on the pre-sessional EAP courses. CE23 (I expect to learn how to write in a formal, academic style) was selected most often by students on both pre-sessional and combination courses (12.4% and 12.1%) and was also popular with

IELTS students (11.1% – third most popular). CE14 (I expect to learn how to edit and redraft my written work) and CE15 (I expect to learn how to use ideas from text books or academic journals in my writing) were not selected by any IELTS or combination students. Despite its high ratings across course types, CE18 (I expect my teacher to correct my grammar mistakes in my written work) was the least popular choice for pre-sessional EAP students (it was selected by only one student). This suggests that although students generally expected grammar correction, it was not seen as a priority.

Table 5.1 Course expectation items selected by students as most important

Item	IELTS Frequency	%	Combination Frequency	%	Pre-sessional EAP Frequency	%
CE01	4	6.3%	12	12.2%	32	10.4%
CE02	0	0.0%	5	5.1%	8	2.6%
CE03	2	3.2%	1	1.0%	9	2.9%
CE04	1	1.6%	3	3.1%	3	1.0%
CE05	10	15.9%	9	9.2%	6	2.0%
CE06	2	3.2%	5	5.1%	4	1.3%
CE07	0	0.0%	3	3.1%	13	4.2%
CE08	0	0.0%	7	7.1%	11	3.6%
CE09	4	6.3%	9	9.2%	34	11.1%
CE10	2	3.2%	4	4.1%	3	1.0%
CE11	2	3.2%	3	3.1%	9	2.9%
CE12	0	0.0%	1	1.0%	12	3.9%
CE13	1	1.6%	1	1.0%	2	0.7%
CE14	0	0.0%	0	0.0%	9	2.9%
CE15	0	0.0%	0	0.0%	7	2.3%
CE16	5	7.9%	5	5.1%	24	7.8%
CE17	1	1.6%	2	2.0%	6	2.0%
CE18	1	1.6%	0	0.0%	1	0.3%
CE19	2	3.2%	2	2.0%	1	0.3%
CE20	1	1.6%	3	3.1%	11	3.6%
CE21	6	9.5%	4	4.1%	34	11.1%
CE22	3	4.8%	5	5.1%	28	9.1%
CE23	7	11.1%	12	12.2%	38	12.4%
CE24	9	14.3%	2	2.0%	2	0.7%
Total	63	100%	98	100%	307	100%

Course activities at course exit

At course exit, students were asked to rank the same activities and objectives once more. While at entry they had indicated what they were expecting to study, and were able to rate a list of skills that they would probably hope to acquire, now students were invited to rate what they felt they had learned during the course. As might be anticipated, because students were now reflecting back on and evaluating their experiences, the ratings were generally lower than at course entry.

Again, there were significant differences between course types. The following items were rated significantly ($p < .05$) higher by students on IELTS courses:

CO02 I learned general vocabulary.
CO05 I learned ways of improving my English Language test scores.
CO06 I learned words and phrases for describing graphs and diagrams.
CO10 I learned grammar.
CO17 I learned how to organise my time for studying.
CO19 The activities we did in class were similar to the ones on the IELTS test.
CO24 I took practice tests in class.

Items rated significantly higher by students on pre-sessional EAP courses included:

CO03 I learned about the kinds of writing tasks students do at university.
CO07 I learned how to use evidence to support my written arguments.
CO08 I learned how to organise an essay to help the reader to understand.
CO11 I learned how to write university essays and reports.
CO15 I learned how to use ideas from text books or academic journals in my writing.
CO16 I learned how to write long essays or reports of 1,000 words or more.
CO22 I learned to read books and articles about the specialist subject area I will study at university.

Ratings given by combination course students were intermediate between those for the IELTS and pre-sessional EAP courses, except in the case of CO10 (I learned grammar); CO24 (I took practice tests in class); CO17 (I learned how to organise my time for studying) and CO01 (I learned specialist vocabulary for my university subject), to which they gave the lowest average ratings.

Items also displaying significant differences across student Region of Origin included; CO01, CO02, CO08, CO16, CO17 and CO22, together with:

CO09 I learned how to communicate my ideas effectively in writing.
CO18 My teacher corrected my grammar mistakes in my written work.
CO21 I learned how to write successful test essays.
CO23 I learned how to write in a formal, academic style.

Of these items, CO08, CO16 and CO22 displayed significant differences across Course Type for two or more groups when the data was divided by student Region of Origin.

Comparisons between initial and exit ratings

Comparing the ratings given at course exit with those given at course entry using a Wilcoxon Signed Ranks test, almost all items, across Course Type, displayed significant ($p<.05$) changes. The exceptions were CO19 (The activities we did in class were similar to the ones on the IELTS test) (NS for all courses); CO06 (I learned words and phrases for describing graphs and diagrams); CO07 (I learned how to use evidence to support my written arguments); CO18 (My teacher corrected my grammar mistakes in my written work) (NS on IELTS and combination courses) and CO13 (I learned how to use quotations and references in academic writing) (NS on pre-sessional EAP and combination courses).

Although most were given lower ratings at course exit, the ordering of items at exit was broadly similar to that obtaining at course entry. CO18 (My teacher corrected my grammar mistakes in my written work) was now the highest ranked item on all Course Types. CO23 (I learned how to write in a formal, academic style) was now ranked third on the pre-sessional EAP courses, maintaining its position, and falling back by just two places – from second to fourth – on the IELTS and combination courses. However, CO09 (I learned how to communicate my ideas effectively in writing) was ranked lower, falling from second to sixth place on the IELTS-focused courses, from first to 12th place on the pre-sessional courses and from second to 15th on the combination courses.

Other items also shifted in rank at course exit. CO21 (I learned how to write successful test essays) was ranked lower by learners on all Course Types at exit than at entry, falling from fourth to 12th on the IELTS courses, from fifth to ninth on the combination courses and from seventh to 15th on the pre-sessionals. Students on pre-sessional courses also ranked the following items eight or more places lower at exit than at entry:

CO20   I learned quick and efficient ways of reading books in English. (4th to 19th)

CO09   I learned how to communicate my ideas effectively in writing. (1st to 12th)

On the other hand, for pre-sessional students, the following items moved up the order by eight or more places from their position at course entry:

CO13   I learned how to use quotations and references in academic writing. (13th to 5th)

CO03   I learned about the kinds of writing tasks students do at university. (14th to 6th)

CO04   I learned about the differences between university education in my country and in Britain. (22nd to 11th)

Learners on IELTS preparation courses ranked the following items at least eight places higher at course exit:

CO06   I learned words and phrases for describing graphs and diagrams.
CO17   I learned how to organise my time for studying.
CO19   The activities we did in class were similar to the ones on the IELTS test.

These moved from 10th to 2nd, from 24th to 15th and from 13th to 5th respectively – although the ratings for all three items at course exit were not significantly different from the ratings given at course entry.

At course exit the three highest ranked items for pre-sessional students, and for students on combined courses, were:

CO18   My teacher corrected my grammar mistakes in my written work.
CO08   I learned how to organise an essay to help the reader to understand.
CO23   I learned how to write in a formal, academic style.

CO18 and CO23 were in first and third place for the IELTS students at course exit; with second place occupied by CO06 (I learned words and phrases for describing graphs and diagrams).

The lowest ranked items for pre-sessional students were:

CO17   I learned how to organise my time for studying.
CO01   I learned specialist vocabulary for my university subject.
CO19   The activities we did in class were similar to the ones on the IELTS test.

For IELTS students the lowest ranking items were:

CO16   I learned how to write long essays or reports of 1,000 words or more.
CO22   I learned to read books and articles about the specialist subject area I will study at university.
CO01   I learned specialist vocabulary for my university subject.

Students on combined courses gave the lowest ratings to CO17, CO22 and CO01.

Teacher ratings

Teachers on the two course types differed in their objectives. The following items were all ranked eight or more places higher by IELTS than by pre-sessional teachers:

CT19   The class activities are similar to the ones on the IELTS test.
CT18   I correct students' grammar mistakes in their written work.
CT06   Students learn words and phrases for describing graphs and diagrams.
CT05   Students learn ways of improving their English language test scores.
CT20   Students learn quick and efficient ways of reading books in English.
CT21   Students learn how to write successful test essays.
CT24   Students take practice tests in class.

The following were placed eight or more ranks higher by pre-sessional teachers:

CT03   Students learn about the kinds of writing tasks they will do at university.
CT11   Students learn how to write university essays and reports.
CT12   Students learn how to find information from lectures or course-books to use in writing essays.
CT16   Students learn how to write long essays or reports of 1,000 words or more.
CT13   Students learn how to use quotations and references in academic writing.

Comparisons between teachers and students

Although students were in substantial agreement with teachers regarding what had been learned, there were some areas of disagreement. Teachers on pre-sessional courses ranked two items higher by at least eight places than their students:

CT09   Students learn how to communicate their ideas effectively in writing. (3rd and 12th)
CT17   Students learn how to organise their time for studying. (13th and 21st)

CT18 (I correct students' grammar mistakes in their written work), the highest ranked item for students on both courses, and the second ranked item for IELTS preparation teachers, was put in 14th position by teachers on pre-sessional EAP courses. Like the pre-sessional EAP teachers, IELTS teachers ranked CT08 (Students learn how to organise an essay to help the reader to understand) as the primary objective of their courses, but the IELTS students ranked this item 11th as a course outcome. The IELTS students put CO10 (I learned grammar) in 10th place as an outcome and teachers put its equivalent (CT10 Students learn grammar) in 18th place as an objective.

Between entry and exit, the ordering of items by students moves closer to the ordering of objectives assigned by teachers. Rank order correlations between the placing of items by teachers and by students at course exit are relatively high, while correlations between student expectations at course entry and teacher objectives are more modest (see Table 5.2). The significant level of agreement between pre-sessional and IELTS preparation learners concerning their expectations for their courses (rho = .476) is not repeated at course exit when students reflect on what they have learned (rho = .045).

The relationship between teacher ratings and student ratings at course entry and exit on selected items is illustrated in Figure 5.10. Item CE22 (I expect to read books and articles about my specialist subject area) was rated much higher by pre-sessional EAP than by IELTS teachers, but was given similar ratings by all students at course entry. At course exit, student ratings for this item fell across Course Types. However, relative to students on other courses those given by pre-sessional EAP students remained relatively high (and were similar to the teacher rating).

Item CE19 (I expect the activities we do in class will be similar to the ones on the IELTS test), on the other hand, was rated higher by IELTS than by pre-sessional EAP teachers. Student ratings of this item rose marginally at course exit across groups, but pre-sessional EAP students continued to give lower ratings than their counterparts on other courses.

Evidence from teachers and students regarding course expectations and outcomes is indicative of substantive differences between courses. Learners arrive on their courses with expectations of instruction which vary, to an extent, according to course aims, but which also reflect many shared intentions. Students leave with diverging beliefs about what they have learned, in keeping with the nature of the instruction they have received. Teachers on different course types adopt distinctive aims and students generally accommodate to these, reflecting the focus of instruction in their reports of course outcomes. Of particular interest are the course outcomes that were not anticipated, or at least were not prioritised by learners at course entry as these are suggestive of the influence of the teacher and the learning context on learners. On IELTS preparation courses these included the description of graphs and diagrams and time management; on pre-sessional courses they involved referencing, learning about university writing tasks and learning about differences in university study across cultures.

Questionnaire A Section 4: Learning style preferences

Section 4 of Questionnaire A targeted perceptual Learning Preferences including Auditory Preference, Visual Preference, Kinaesthetic/Tactile Preference, Group Preference and Individual Preference.

Table 5.2 Spearman Rho rank order correlations for Course Expectations and Course Content: student and teacher ratings

	CE/SIELTS	CE/SCOMB	CE/SEAP	CO/SIELTS	CO/SCOMB	CO/SEAP	C/TIELTS	C/TEAP
CE/SIELTS								
CE/SCOMB	0.708**							
CE/SEAP	0.476**	0.853**						
CO/SIELTS	0.803**	0.387	0.120					
CO/SCOMB	0.499*	0.494*	0.382	0.583**				
CO/SEAP	0.223	0.588**	0.645**	0.045	0.602**			
C/TIELTS	0.746**	0.475*	0.245	0.854**	0.618**	0.157		
C/TEAP	0.015	0.430	0.559**	−0.130	0.260	0.730**	0.042	

** Correlation is significant at the 0.01 level (2-tailed).
* Correlation is significant at the 0.05 level (2-tailed).
CE = Course Expectations; CO = Course Outcomes. S = Students, T = Teachers.

Figure 5.10 Comparison of initial student ratings with student ratings at course exit and teacher ratings for CE/O/T19 (class activities similar to IELTS test) and CE/O/T22 (read books and articles about specialist subject area) (Maximum score for each item = 4)

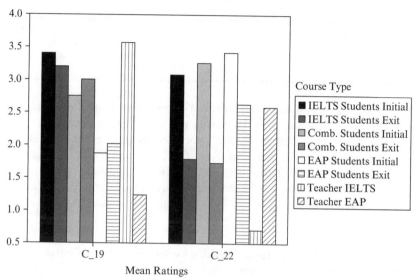

Reliability analysis revealed that one or two items in each scale were making a negative contribution to reliability. Item LP17 (I prefer to solve my problems by myself: When I have a problem, I usually ask for help from other people) involved problem solving outside the classroom and may indicate that a preference for group-based learning is not necessarily an indicator of a more general preference for seeking support from others. Items LP10 and LP19 both referred to 'reading for pleasure' and it may be that the word 'pleasure', carrying the implication of enjoyment, affected the ratings.

The Visual Preference Scale seemed to emerge more clearly in opposition to the Kinaesthetic/Tactile Scale than in opposition to the Auditory. Both of the divergent items on this scale – LP07 (I remember images and pictures: I remember things that I have heard people say) and LP15 (I understand better when someone tells me what to do: I understand better when I look at visual instructions) – opposed Visual Preference to Auditory. Following the elimination of items contributing negatively to reliability, the Group/ Individual Preference was the most reliable (α = .718) and the Visual Preference scale least reliable at α = .629.

Highest ratings across Course Types were given to the Kinaesthetic/ Tactile Preference, with moderately higher ratings for Visual over Auditory

Table 5.3 Reliability (alpha) for Learning Preference scales

Scale	All items retained			Items removed	
	No. of items	Alpha	Items removed	No. of items	Alpha
Group/Individual	4	.647	LP17	3	.718
Kinaesthetic/Tactile	11	.633	LP19	10	.638
Auditory	10	.602	LP18, LP10	8	.638
Visual	11	.558	LP15, LP07	9	.629

Preference on pre-sessional courses and Auditory over Visual Preference on IELTS courses (Figure 5.11). However, analyses of covariance with these scales as dependent variables, Course Type, Gender and Region of Origin as fixed factors and AWM Score at Time One, Age and Course Length as covariates showed no significant interaction between Course Type or student Region of Origin with any of the scales. There was a significant (p<.05) interaction between student gender and Visual Preference: women scored higher on this scale than men.

Figure 5.11 Boxplot of scores on Learning Preference scales by Course Type (Minimum rating = 1, Maximum = 9)

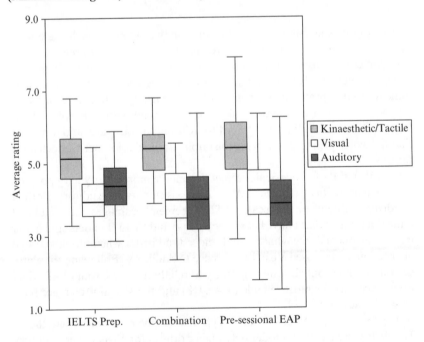

Questionnaire B Section 2: Learning strategies

Box 5.3 Questionnaire B Section 2: Learning strategies

PS01	I memorised English words by saying or writing them several times.
PS02	I tested my knowledge of new English words by using them in different ways.
PS03	I tried to find better ways of learning English.
PS04	I looked for words in my own language that look or sound similar to new words in English.
PS05	I tried to improve my writing by asking others (e.g. teachers, students, friends) to correct my mistakes.
PS06	I noticed mistakes in my writing, and used that information to help me do better.
PS07	I took IELTS Writing or other practice writing tests in my free time.
PS08	I tried to find grammar patterns in English.
PS09	I looked for people I could talk to in English.
PS10	I studied vocabulary in my free time.
PS11	I thought about my progress in learning English.
PS12	I studied extra English outside school.
PS13	I tested myself on new words or phrases I learned.
PS14	If I couldn't think of an English word, I used a word or phrase that means the same thing.
PS15	I reviewed my class notes or text book in my free time.
PS16	I tried to learn about the culture of English speakers.
PS17	I encouraged myself to use English even when I was afraid of making a mistake.
PS18	I read English without looking up every new word.
PS19	When reading in English, I tried to translate into my language to help me understand.
PS20	I studied grammar in my free time.
PS21	I was NOT sure how to improve my English skills.
PS22	I used new English words in sentences so I could remember them.
PS23	When I learned a grammar rule, I tested myself to make sure I really knew.
PS24	I tried to improve my writing by doing extra writing activities at home.
PS25	To understand unfamiliar English words, I tried to guess their meaning.
PS26	When writing in English, I tried to translate from my language.
PS27	I thought about the goals I wanted to achieve on this course.
PS28	Before studying, I planned what to do, so I could use my time well.
PS29	I tried to improve my writing by analysing the work of other writers.
PS30	When I received corrected work from the teacher, I thought about how to improve next time.

Learning Strategy items were treated individually and as an overall scale of strategy use. Reliability analysis revealed that five items were making a negative contribution to the reliability of this scale. These items, mostly relating to direct translation strategies, were PS4 (I looked for words in my own language that look or sound similar to new words in English), PS18 (I read English without looking up every new word), PS19 (When reading in English, I tried to translate into my language to help me understand), PS21 (with reverse scoring) (I was NOT sure how to improve my English skills) and PS26 (When writing in English, I tried to translate from my language). The differential performance of these items suggests that translation strategies run counter to general learning strategy use. After deleting these five items from the analysis, the remaining 25-item scale had a reliability (Cronbach's α) of .847.

Analysis of covariance with Learning Strategy Use as the dependent variable, student Region of Origin and Gender as fixed factors and Initial Writing Score, Age, and Course Length as covariates revealed that only student Region of Origin made a significant contribution ($p<.05$). Categorising students into three groups for strategy use (high, mid and low), it can be seen that students in the Other East Asia category claimed to make the least use of learning strategies (Figure 5.12). However, the use of learning strategies appears largely unrelated to Course Type.

Figure 5.12 Learning Strategy Use by Student Region of Origin

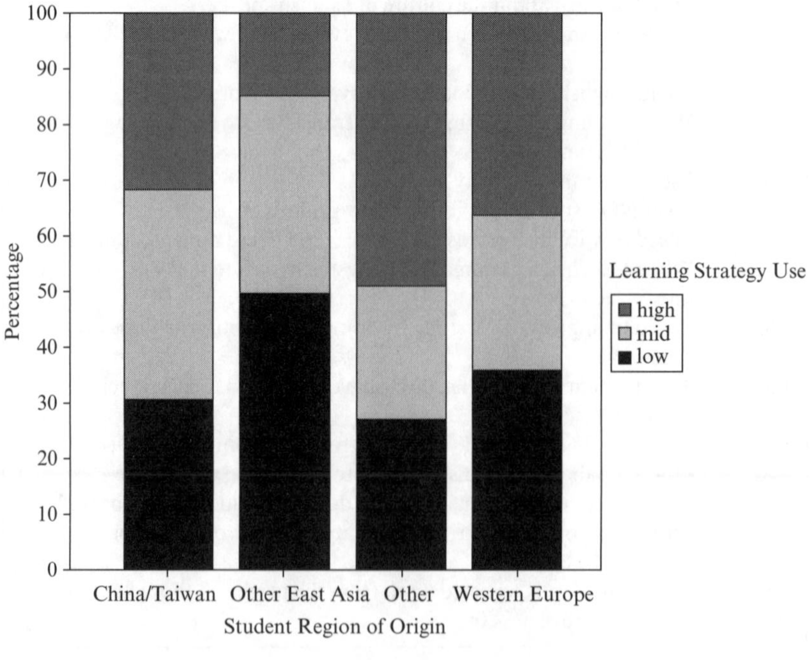

At the item level, Kruskal Wallis tests showed significant (p<.05) differences for Course Type, but not for Region of Origin for items PS07 (I took IELTS Writing or other practice writing tests in my free time), PS08 (I tried to find grammar patterns in English), PS09 (I looked for people I could talk to in English), PS15 (I reviewed my class notes or textbook in my free time) and PS24 (I tried to improve my writing by doing extra writing activities at home).

As displayed in Figure 5.13, these items were all scored higher by students on IELTS preparation courses than by those on pre-sessional EAP courses with combination course students scoring between the other two, except on PS08 (I tried to find grammar patterns in English), to which they gave the lowest mean ratings. To this extent, IELTS preparation does appear to encourage learning strategy use, including activities closely modelled on the test (practice Writing tests) and broader strategies aimed at increasing communication in the target language (seeking out opportunities to speak English).

Figure 5.13 Learning Strategy Items by Course Type (Maximum rating = 4)

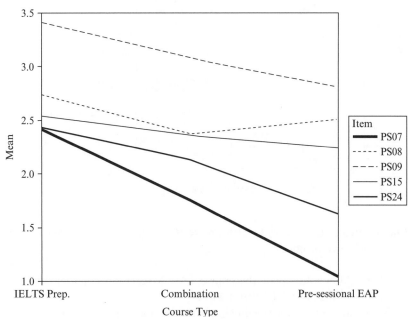

The highest ratings overall were given to metacognitive strategies: PS30 (When I received corrected work from the teacher, I thought about how to improve next time), PS06 (I noticed mistakes in my writing, and used that information to help me do better) and PS11 (I thought about my progress in learning English). The lowest ratings across courses were given to PS21 (I was NOT sure how to improve my English skills), PS26 (When writing in English, I tried to translate from my language) – both items that were eliminated from the strategy use scale – and PS20 (I studied grammar in my free time).

Questionnaire B Section 3: Self-assessment of improvement in writing

Figure 5.14 Distribution of self-assessed improvement in academic writing (Maximum score = 28)

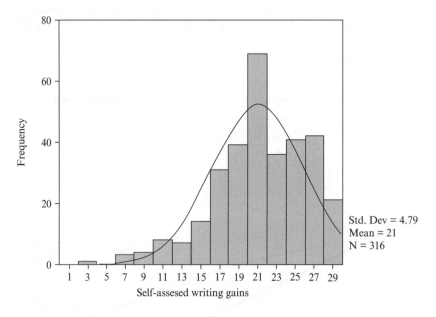

The following items from Questionnaire B, Section 3 required learners to assess their own progress:

IM01   After studying on this course, I would feel more confident about taking an IELTS Writing test.

IM03   My ability to write quickly in English has improved during this course.

IM05   My ability to organise my ideas in my written work has improved during this course.

IM09   I feel that my general ability to use English has improved during this course.

IM16   My ability to use evidence to support my written arguments has improved during this course.

IM17   After taking this course, I would feel more confident about writing assignments at university.

IM18   I feel that my ability to write in English has improved during this course.

IM19   My ability to use grammar and vocabulary in my writing has improved during this course.

IM21   My ability to write using information from books or articles I have read has improved during this course.

These items were combined to form a scale representing students' self-assessment of their improvement in academic writing ability.

Reliability analysis revealed that item IM01 (After studying on this course, I would feel more confident about taking an IELTS Writing test) made a negative contribution to the reliability of the scale for the population as a whole and for pre-sessional EAP or combination courses when analysed separately. However, this item made a positive contribution to reliability when IELTS courses were analysed separately. Item IM21 (My ability to write using information from books or articles I have read has improved during this course), on the other hand, made a negative contribution to reliability for the IELTS preparation group, but contributed to the reliability of the scale for the combined and pre-sessional EAP courses. Excluding Items IM01 and IM21, the remaining seven items formed a reliable scale with a Cronbach's α of .862.

Across all course types students reported that they had made gains in their writing ability (Figure 5.15). Analysis of covariance with Self-Assessed Improvement in Writing Skills as the dependent variable, Course Type, Gender and Region of Origin as fixed factors and AWM Score at Time One, Age and Course Length as covariates revealed that there was a significant difference ($p<.05$) in Self-Assessed Improvement in Writing Skills across Course Types (see Figure 5.15) with pre-sessional EAP students scoring highest and combined course students lowest. This suggests that the students on EAP courses believed that they had made greater improvements in their ability to write in English than their counterparts on IELTS preparation and combination courses.

At the item level, a Kruskal Wallis analysis for ranked data found significant differences ($p<.05$) for item IM19 (My ability to use grammar and vocabulary in my writing has improved during this course) across Course Types, but IM19 also varied significantly by student Region of Origin. A Mann Whitney test comparing IELTS and pre-sessional EAP groups on IM19 found significant differences ($p<.05$) on this item between China/Taiwan and Other, but no significant differences for Other East Asia or Western Europe.

Figure 5.15 Estimated marginal means of Self-Assessed Improvement in Writing Skills (Maximum score = 28) by Course Type, controlling for Course Length, Student Age, Initial IELTS AWM Score, 'Adjusted' AWM Score Gain, Course Type, Gender, and student Region of Origin

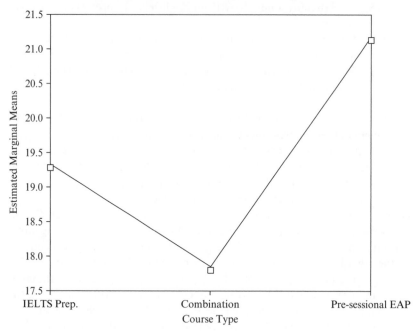

Among the remaining items in this section, IM01 (After studying on this course, I would feel more confident about taking an IELTS Writing test), IM06 (The Writing classes were difficult for me), IM07 (I do NOT really like the British way of life), IM15 (It was easy for me to write good English essays), IM20 (I feel happy about living in an English-speaking country) and IM21 (My ability to write using information from books or articles I have read has improved during this course) differed significantly (p<.05) across Course Types. Of these, IM01 and IM15 also displayed significant differences across regions. Independent Mann Whitney tests showed significant differences (p<.05) for IM01 between IELTS and pre-sessional EAP courses for China/Taiwan and Other. For IM15, the difference between these courses was significant only for the Other category. Items IM06, IM07 and IM15 attracted low ratings on all courses, being ranked among the five least popular items. However, all three items attracted higher ratings on the IELTS preparation courses than on the other two.

IELTS preparation students were least happy about living in an English-speaking country, ranking this item (IM20) in 12th place, while combination course students ranked it first and pre-sessional EAP students third. Items IM01 (After studying on this course, I would feel more confident about taking an IELTS Writing test) and IM19 (My ability to use grammar and vocabulary in my writing has improved during this course) were ranked higher by IELTS students than by those on other courses, while rankings for these items were similar on pre-sessional EAP and combination courses.

Questionnaire B Section 4: Expectations of tertiary education in the UK

Expectations of Tertiary Education in the UK were addressed through 15 items based on surveys conducted by Bloor and Bloor (1991) and Jordan (1993). On the basis of the washback model, it was anticipated that learners on the three course types would leave their courses with differing expectations of university study. To the extent that the IELTS Writing test offers a less complete reflection of university writing needs than do EAP pre-sessional courses, it follows that learners on IELTS-directed courses would have less knowledge of university writing requirements and of the role of writing in university study.

The analysis of the survey data in the Bloor and Bloor (1991) and Jordan (1993) studies did not involve validation of the instruments used. There was no investigation of reliability as called for by Alderson and Banerjee (2001), nor did the researchers explore the dimensionality of the data obtained. In order to address these issues and to reduce the data in preparation for further analysis, a factor analysis was undertaken of this section of the questionnaire.

Alpha factor extraction with varimax rotation was performed through SPSS FACTOR for the 15 Expectations of Tertiary Education items. Principal components extraction was used prior to alpha extraction to estimate the number of factors, absence of multi-colinearity and factorability of the correlation matrix. Following inspection of the scree plot of Eigenvalues, analyses were carried out with three, four and five factors. Extraction of three factors resulted in simple structure with all items loading on a factor (Table 5.4).

The three factors extracted, and the interpretation of each, were as follows:

Factor 1: Expectation for guidance and support (28 points)

EU02   I do NOT expect university teachers to show students examples of good essays and reports.

EU03   I expect university teachers to tell the students exactly which books they should read.

EU10   I expect my university subject teachers to correct the English grammar mistakes in my essays.

Table 5.4 Rotated factor matrix: Expectations of Tertiary Education in the UK

| | Factor | | |
	1	2	3
% of variance	21.6%	11.7%	11.6%
EU01			−0.321
EU02	−0.430		
EU03	0.515		
EU04		0.422	
EU05		0.402	
EU06			0.583
EU07			0.337
EU08		0.606	
EU09		0.592	
EU10	0.674		
EU11	0.430		
EU12	0.701		
EU13			0.690
EU14	0.355		
EU15	0.617		

Extraction method: alpha factoring.
Rotation method: varimax with Kaiser Normalisation.

EU11 I expect my university tests will follow a multiple-choice style – in multiple-choice questions you choose the correct answer from a list: a, b, c or d.

EU12 I expect university teachers to tell students exactly what to do when the students prepare an essay or report.

EU14 I expect the writing tasks students do at university are similar to the writing tasks I have done on this course.

EU15 I expect my university teachers will give me all the facts and information I need to get a good grade.

Factor 2: Expectation that grades come from following the teacher (16 points)

EU04 I expect students should read all the books their university teachers recommend.

EU05 To get a good grade for their writing at university, students must show that they have remembered facts from lectures.

EU08 To get a good grade in their writing, students should NOT criticise the work of their teachers or other experts in their specialist subject.

EU09 I expect my university grades will mostly come from tests or examinations rather than from essays or coursework.

Factor 3: Expectation of problems at university (16 points)

EU01   I feel that I have a good knowledge of what university study in Britain is like.

EU06   I expect I will have difficulties studying at university because of problems with the English language.

EU07   I expect the style of teaching at university will be different from the teaching in my country.

EU13   I expect I will have difficulties studying at university because the style of education in my country is different to the style of education in Britain.

Reliability analysis through SPSS RELIABILITY indicated that the Factor 1 scale had a reliability (α) of 0.737. Alphas for the Factor 2 and 3 scales were 0.597 and 0.506 respectively.

Figure 5.16 Marginal means plot of scores on EU Factor 1: (Expectation for guidance and support) by Course Type (Maximum score = 28 points)

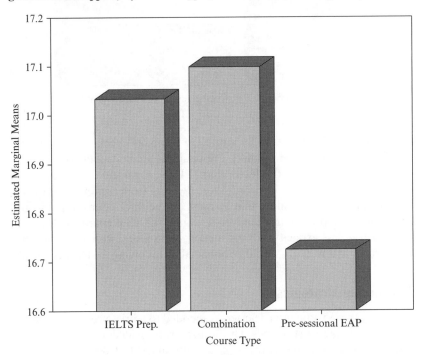

A 3 × 2 analysis of covariance was conducted with the three EU factors as dependent variables. Covariates were Initial Writing score, Course Length and Student Age. After adjustment by covariates, there was a significant

Figure 5.17 Marginal means plot of scores on EU Factor 2 (Expectation that grades come from following the teacher) by Course Type (Maximum score = 16 points)

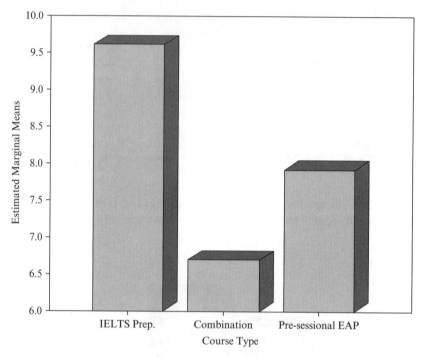

difference (p<.05) for Course Type on EU Factor 2 (Expectation that grades come from following the teacher). Pre-sessional students and combination students scored lower on this factor than IELTS preparation students.

These results support the proposition, deriving from the review of the literature and the pilot studies, that learners on the three course types would have differing expectations of university study. IELTS preparation learners, who received less explicit EAP instruction, were more likely to expect that good grades at university would be obtained by following the teacher's lead.

Test-taking strategies

Following the Writing tests, learners responded to a brief protocol targeting the use of test-taking strategies. The protocol was divided into two parts, the first three items targeting learners' perceptions of test task demands:

I understood the question.
I had enough ideas to write about this topic.
I had enough time to write about the question.

Figure 5.18 Marginal means plot of scores on EU Factor 3 (Expectation of problems at university) by Course Type (Maximum score = 16 points)

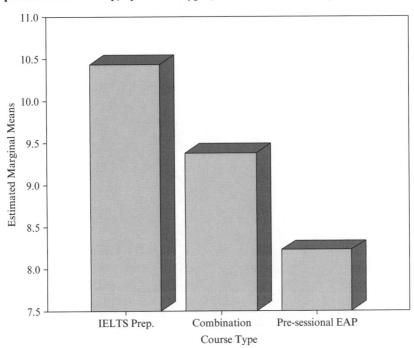

The remaining five items targeted test-taking strategies:

I read the question carefully and underlined or highlighted key words.

I made an outline plan before writing.

I tried not to write more than the required number of words.

I checked my answers for grammar and spelling mistakes.

I wrote a draft essay first, then wrote the essay again neatly.

The items were presented twice on each testing occasion, one set of items corresponding to each task on the Writing test. The two sets of items under Test Task Demands were combined to form one six-item scale and the items under Test-Taking Strategies were combined to form a second. Although it was intended that item 8, as a strategy disapproved by IELTS textbooks, would be scored negatively, it proved to be positively correlated with the other items on the scale. This item generally attracted low ratings (means ranged from 0.76 for Task 1 at exit to 0.87 for Task 2 at entry), but higher ratings were associated with higher ratings for other items on the scale.

Figure 5.19 Estimated marginal means of Test Strategy Use by student Region of Origin (Maximum score = 40 points)

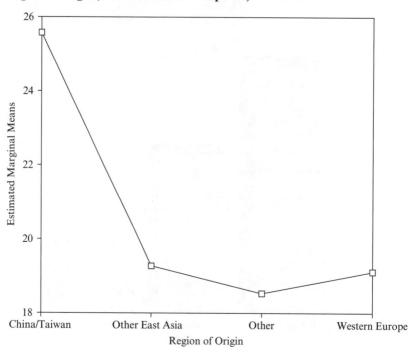

Reliability analysis showed that both the initial and exit Test Task Demands scales had a high level of reliability and that no items were making a negative contribution. Cronbach's α for the initial test strategy scale was .714 and for the exit measure it was .735. The reliabilities (α) of the Test-Taking Strategies Scales were .759 on the initial and .793 on the exit administration.

Pre-sessional students spent the least time on Task 1 and the longest on Task 2 on both tests. However, learners on the other course types reduced the time spent on Task 1 on the second testing occasion (Figure 5.20).

IELTS awareness and test strategy forms

When taking the IELTS test the learners were administered brief question-naires targeting their knowledge of the test and their use of test-taking strategies.

Test knowledge

Before responding to the Writing tasks, students were given brief tests of their knowledge of the IELTS Academic Writing Module. These tests consisted of

Figure 5.20 Time spent on Task 1 and Task 2 (self-estimated) on initial and exit Writing tests by Course Type. Sixty minutes are available for the test

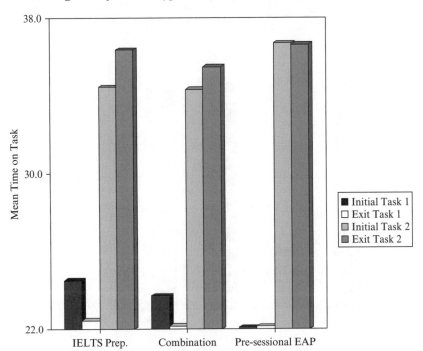

six statements about the test to which learners responded 'yes', 'no' or 'I don't know'. It was anticipated that learners preparing for IELTS would be more likely to improve their knowledge of the test during their courses and that gain in knowledge of test demands might contribute to improvements in scores.

Reliability analysis revealed that all six items making up the Test Knowledge Scale were making a positive contribution to reliability and discriminated well between students both on the entry and exit forms of the test. The initial Test Knowledge Scale had a reliability (Cronbach's α) of .887 and the exit Test Knowledge Scale had a reliability of .867.

There was an improvement of one third of a point in the mean score on the Test Knowledge scale for all students between testing occasions. Around one quarter of the students on the initial administration (28%) and one fifth of students at exit (22%) scored no points on the Test Knowledge measure, while on each occasion 19% achieved a perfect score of six points.

Analysis of covariance with Test Knowledge score gain as the dependent variable, Course Type, Gender and Region of Origin as fixed factors and AWM Score at Time One, Age, and Course Length as covariates revealed

Figure 5.21 Mean ratings of Test Task Demands on initial and exit test administrations (Maximum score = 24)

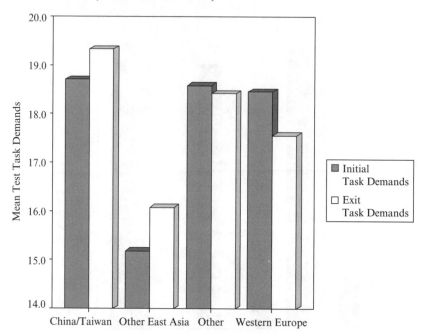

significant effects for Course Type and Region of Origin. IELTS-preparation students made significantly greater gains in their knowledge of the test than learners on the other two course types. Learners in the China/Taiwan cohort made the greatest gains and Western Europeans the least.

Pre-sessional students also made the most use of test strategies both on the initial and exit tests. IELTS preparation students, in keeping with the attention given to test-taking strategies on preparation courses, increased their Test Strategy Use scores by the greatest amount. However, combination course members made less increase in Test Strategy Use scores than did pre-sessional EAP learners. This suggests that direct instruction in test-taking strategies is not the only factor encouraging their increased use on the second Writing test.

Questionnaire B, Section 5: Approaches to Learning

Section 5 of Questionnaire B addressed Approaches to Learning and was made up of three scales, Meaning-Based Orientation (the M scale), Reproducing Orientation (the R scale) and Achieving Orientation (the A scale). These were adapted for use with English language learners from

Figure 5.22 Mean ratings of Test Strategy Use on initial and exit test administrations

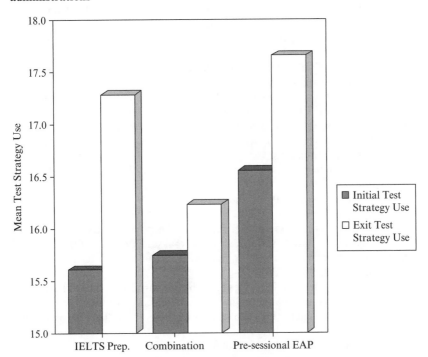

Entwistle's (1981) Approaches to Studying Inventory (ASI). Following the format used in other sections of the questionnaire, the 20 items were each accompanied by a 5-point Likert scale with options ranging from 0 (I definitely disagree) to 4 (I definitely agree) (see Box 5.4).

The three Approach to Learning Inventory scales (Meaning-Based Orientation, Reproducing Orientation and Achieving Orientation) were subjected to reliability analysis. The M scale (Meaning-Based Orientation) achieved had a reliability (α) of .576, with all items making a positive contribution. The R (Reproducing Orientation) scale was less reliable (α = .442) with one item (R07) making a negative contribution. R07 (I prefer courses that are structured and highly organised) addressed syllabus-boundedness (Entwistle 1981) or a preference for closely adhering to content provided by the teacher. This received the second highest average rating of the items in the section and was the highest rated item for Chinese learners. It may be that the lack of variance in the item, caused by the generally high ratings, limited the effectiveness of the item. On the other hand, it may be that a preference for highly structured courses is not indicative of a reproducing orientation to learning in this context; perhaps because a structured approach to language

Box 5.4 Questionnaire B Section 5: Approaches to Learning

A01	When I am doing an assignment, I try to think about exactly what the teacher of that class seems to want.
A02	I find it easy to organise my time for studying.
A03	It's important for me to do really well in this course.
A04	If the situation is not right for me to study, I usually manage to do something to change it.
A05	When I am doing a piece of work, I try to think about exactly what that particular teacher seems to want.
A06	It is important to me to do things better than my friends.
M01	When I am trying to understand new ideas, I often try to connect them to real-life situations.
M02	I often think about and criticise things that I hear in lessons or read in books.
M03	I need to read a lot about connected ideas before I am ready to write about a topic.
M04	I like to try to find several different ways of explaining facts.
M05	I usually try hard to understand things that seem difficult at first.
M06	I usually try to understand completely the meaning of what teachers ask me to read.
M07	I am very interested in puzzles or problems, particularly when I have to study the information carefully to reach a logical conclusion.
R01	When I am reading, I try to memorise important facts that may be useful later.
R02	I usually study very little except what I need for assignments or tests.
R03	Teachers seem to like making the simple truth more complicated.
R04	I find I have to memorise a lot of what we study.
R05	Teachers seem to want me to use my own ideas more.
R06	I like teachers to tell me exactly what I must do in essays or other coursework.
R07	I prefer courses that are structured and highly organised.

learning is preferred by most learners. When this item was removed, the resulting scale had a reliability (α) of .456.

The A scale (Achieving Orientation) had a reliability (α) of .583, but item A02 (I find it easy to organise my time for studying) was found to be making a negative contribution. A02 attracted the third lowest average rating in the section (2.40). The low ratings for the item, taken together with the low correlations with other A scale items, suggest that learners found time management challenging regardless of their desire for achievement. After removal of this item, the resulting A scale alpha was .611.

The highest rated items across courses included R01 (When I am reading, I try to memorise important facts that may be useful later); R07 (I prefer courses that are structured and highly organised); A03 (It's important for me to do really well in this course) and M06 (I usually try to understand completely the meaning of what teachers ask me to read). These items were among the six highest rated items on all three course types. The lowest rated item was R02 (I usually study very little except what I need for assignments or tests). Low ratings were also given to R03 (Teachers seem to like making the simple truth more complicated) and A02 (I find it easy to organise my time for studying). The ratings for these items were consistently low across courses.

Researchers using the Approaches to Learning Inventory and related instruments have suggested that the relationship between Achieving Orientation and the other two scales may be taken as an indicator of washback (Tang 1992, Watkins 1994, Tang and Biggs 1996). Where Achieving Orientation is identified with Reproducing Orientation, this suggests that Achieving-motivated learners receive cues that success can be gained by adopting a Reproducing Orientation. Conversely, high correlations between Meaning-Based and Achieving Orientations suggest that learners believe success derives from the Meaning-Based Orientation.

To investigate links between the three scales, the file was split by Course Type and a correlation analysis conducted for each group (Table 5.5). The highest correlation on all Course Types was that between Achieving and Meaning-Based Orientation. There was a high correlation between Achieving Orientation and Reproducing Orientation on IELTS preparation courses that was not matched on the other two course types. However, there was also a high correlation between Meaning-Based and Reproducing Orientations on IELTS preparation courses; there was no clear indication here that IELTS was encouraging a Reproducing Orientation.

Table 5.5 Intercorrelations between Approaches to Learning scales

Course Type		Meaning-Based Orientation
IELTS Prep.	Achieving Orientation	.584(**)
	Reproducing Orientation	.555(**)
Combination	Achieving Orientation	.445(**)
	Reproducing Orientation	.219(**)
Pre-sessional EAP	Achieving Orientation	.078(**)
	Reproducing Orientation	.142(*)

** *Correlation is significant at the 0.01 level (2-tailed).*
* *Correlation is significant at the 0.05 level (2-tailed).*

Correlations between the Approaches to Learning Inventory and other indicators of learning behaviour are displayed in Table 5.6. These correlations provide evidence of how Approaches to Learning were realised in learners' behaviour.

Table 5.6 Correlations between Approaches to Learning and Learning Strategy Use

		Achieving Orientation	Meaning-Based Orientation	Reproducing Orientation
Learning Strategy Use	Pearson Correlation	0.365	0.428	0.169
	Sig. (2-tailed)	0.000	0.000	0.003
English Study Outside Class	Pearson Correlation	0.180	0.079	0.045
	Sig. (2-tailed)	0.002	0.169	0.427
Exposure to English in Media	Pearson Correlation	0.113	0.125	0.125
	Sig. (2-tailed)	0.048	0.030	0.029
Use of L1	Pearson Correlation	−0.104	−0.148	0.096
	Sig. (2-tailed)	0.070	0.010	0.093
Speaking English to NS	Pearson Correlation	0.032	0.149	0.040
	Sig. (2-tailed)	0.574	0.010	0.486
Speaking English to NNS	Pearson Correlation	−0.029	0.106	−0.147
	Sig. (2-tailed)	0.611	0.067	0.010

Learning Strategy Use was significantly (p<.05) correlated with all three scales. The strongest correlation (0.428) involved the Meaning-Based Orientation and the weakest (0.169) Reproducing Orientation. The Achieving Orientation was the only one of the three scales significantly correlated with hours spent on English Study Outside Class. Exposure to English in the Media was significantly correlated with all three scales, while greater Use of L1 was negatively related to Meaning-Based Orientation.

Speaking English to NS was significantly (p<.05) correlated with Meaning-Based Orientation, while Speaking English to NNS was negatively correlated with Reproducing Orientation. Meaning-Based Orientation was correlated with Exposure to English in the Media, greater Use of English relative to L1, Speaking English to L1 English speakers and Learning Strategy Use. All three scales were positively correlated with Exposure to English in the Media and Learning Strategy Use, but the correlation was highest for Meaning-Based Orientation and lowest for Reproducing Orientation. The relationship between Meaning-Based Orientation and Learning Strategy Use was strongest for IELTS preparation students (r = .706) and was not significant (p<.05) for learners on combination courses (r = .269).

An analysis of covariance was carried out to further explore relationships between Course Type, student Region of Origin and Approaches to Learning, together with students' stated Intention to Take IELTS. This revealed significant interactions between student Region of Origin and both the Achieving Orientation and Meaning-based Orientation scales, but no significant interaction between Region of Origin and the Reproducing Orientation scale.

Non-parametric tests of difference (Kruskal Wallis) were used to investigate differences between groups by Course Type and Region of Origin at the item level. Three items showed significant (p<.05) differences between Course Types: R03 (Teachers seem to like making the simple truth more complicated); A02 (I find it easy to organise my time for studying); and M05 (I usually try hard to understand things that seem difficult at first). When the data were split by student Region of Origin, one of these (R03) displayed significant differences by Course Type for two groups (China/Taiwan and Other). The other two items (A02 and M05) showed significant differences by Course Type within the China/Taiwan group, but not for other regions.

The Approach to Learning scales showed that Course Type bore only a weak relationship to learners' orientation to their learning. Differences in the aims and content of the three Course Types revealed at the level of course design in Pilot Studies One and Five and at the level of delivery in Pilot Studies Two, Three and Four did not appear to give rise to great differences in the way learners approached their learning task.

Exposure to English outside class

IELTS Awareness Form B, administered at course exit, replaced questions on Form A relating to experiences before the course with items on the subject of extra-curricular exposure to English through extra-curricular study, use of the media and socialising in English.

The highest mean ratings for Items 15 and 16 on Form A, targeting anxiety about the IELTS test, came from students on IELTS preparation courses. 71.1% of learners on IELTS preparation courses and 66.7% of those on combination courses rated passing the test as 5 (very important) compared with 43.9% of those on the pre-sessional courses (Figure 5.23).

Worry about the test was also linked to course focus. 35.5% on IELTS courses, 27.1% on combination courses and 20.5% of those on pre-sessionals reported being very worried about taking the test, while 15.8%, 10.4% and 23.4% respectively claimed to be not at all worried by the test (Figure 5.24). As in Pilot Study Two, it is apparent that the test is not seen as important or as a cause of worry by all. However, even for pre-sessional students with no requirement to take the test, IELTS seems to be a residual cause of anxiety. The surprisingly high ratings given by pre-sessional learners might reflect both the minority of these learners intending to take the test, and a retrospective interpretation of the items by some learners. It may be that the test had been important and a cause of worry to them in the past.

Extra-curricular exposure to English

Section 2 of the of the IELTS Awareness Form administered at course exit addressed extra-curricular use of English. This had been nominated by course providers as a key variable predicting progress for EAP students (Pilot Study Five, Chapter 3). Items 4 to 10 asked respondents to estimate the number of hours they had spent each week in a range of activities and how

Figure 5.23 Bar chart showing mean responses to Item 15: 'How important is it for you to pass the IELTS test?' (5 = very important, 1 = not at all important)

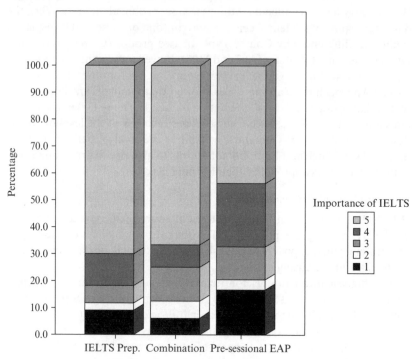

much of their time outside class they spent using English rather than their own language.

4. Outside class, about how many hours did you study English each week?
   _____ hours

5. How many hours each week did you watch TV/listen to the radio in English?
   _____ hours

6. Outside class, how much of the time did you use English or your own/other languages?
   Always English (1)   Always my language/other language (9)
   1   2   3   4   5   6   7   8   9

7. Outside class, for how many hours each week did you talk to native English speakers?
   _____ hours

Figure 5.24 Bar chart showing mean responses to Item 16: 'Do you worry about taking the IELTS test?' (5 = very much, 1 = not at all)

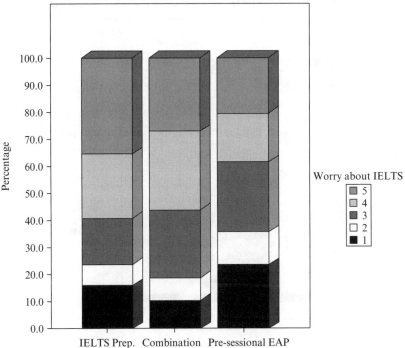

8. Outside class, how many hours a week did you talk in English to other non-native speakers?

＿＿＿＿＿＿ hours

9. How many hours each week do you read English newspapers, magazines or books for pleasure?

＿＿＿＿＿＿ hours

10. How many hours each week do you read about your specialist subject in English?

＿＿＿＿＿＿ hours

Figure 5.25 shows that the IELTS preparation students claimed to spend the most time speaking English rather than their L1. The relatively greater proportion of time spent using English by IELTS preparation students is also illustrated by Figure 5.26. IELTS preparation students claimed a mean of 9 hours per week speaking to native speakers of English and 8.9 hours per week speaking to fellow L2 English speakers. Combination and EAP course

Figure 5.25 Bar chart showing frequency of responses to Item 6: 'Outside class, how much of the time did you use English or your own/other language' (1 = Always English – 9 = Always my own language/other language)

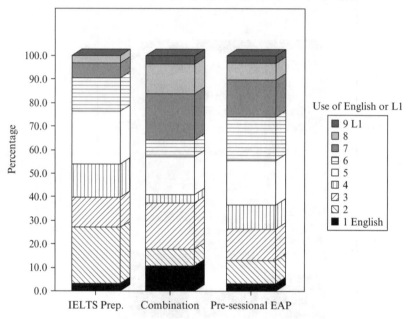

students claimed, respectively, 3.4 and 3.7 hours talking to L1 speakers and 9.2 and 8.7 hours talking to L2 speakers in English. The differences are probably attributable to differences in student accommodation. Those on IELTS preparation courses more often stayed in homestay accommodation, living with a local family, while those on pre-sessional courses were more likely to stay in university halls of residence among other students from the same country.

Pre-sessional students reported spending the most time studying outside class, while the IELTS students claimed the most exposure to English in the media, perhaps another effect of using homestay accommodation with local families. Learners on all course types spent comparatively little time reading about their academic subjects in English and it was, unexpectedly, the IELTS students who reported spending the most time, on average, on this activity. Again this suggests that preparing for the test does not necessarily exclude English study directed towards longer-term goals.

Figure 5.26 Bar chart of mean responses to items targeting time in hours spent using English outside class by students on three course types

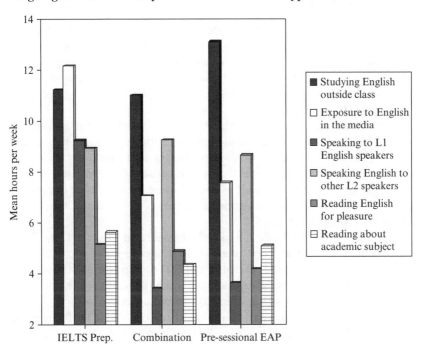

Summary

Analysis of the questionnaires revealed demographic differences between the learners populating the three course types. The IELTS preparation students were younger and were less likely than their counterparts to be East Asian, although the evidence from Pilot Study Five suggests that the regional origin of the participating IELTS preparation students may reflect the choice of institutions in the study rather than IELTS provision nationwide.

The responses from teachers and learners suggest that the delivery of IELTS preparation courses reflects the relatively narrow focus of their design revealed by Pilot Study Five. However, on these brief courses, going beyond matters of course content, the questionnaires did not reveal fundamental differences in how learners approached their learning across course types.

Regarding overlap, in comparison with IELTS preparation, the testimony of learners suggests that EAP courses reflect more of the features of academic writing suggested by the literature review (Chapter 2). IELTS courses involve less work on the use and integration of source materials and working on composing texts of longer than 250 words.

Asking: interviews with course directors, teachers and students

Questionnaires provided extensive evidence relating to group differences and of the extent of test influence on learner behaviours. However, a shortcoming of questionnaire methods, especially those involving selected response items, is that they are inflexible and tend to decontextualise the data; not allowing the researcher to probe in depth respondents' understanding of the context (Miles and Huberman 1994).

Following Alderson and Wall (1993) it is now widely recommended that washback studies should triangulate both data sources and methods of collection (see for example, Bailey 1999 and Turner 2001). Broad-based survey data is now routinely supplemented by semi-structured interviews, offering participants a forum for their views and allowing the researcher opportunities to pursue questions in greater depth (Burrows 1998, Cheng 2004, Hayes and Read 2004, Hawkey 2006).

On the basis of the washback models described in Chapter 1, the focus group interviews were designed to explore in greater depth, and from the perspective of the participants, perceptions of the overlap between the test and academic writing at university, beliefs about test demands and how best to meet them and questions of test difficulty and importance.

A list of questions was prepared as a resource to be used in the focus group interviews. This list was drawn from the pilot studies described in Chapter 3 and from the teacher and student survey instruments described in Chapter 4. However, as the intention was to explore areas of concern to participants, the interviews were not limited to this database of questions. Issues raised by participants were also pursued. The list, covering both teacher and student interviews, included the following items:

1. What is your name, age, home country, first language?
2. What experience do you have of IELTS, other English language tests, test-preparation classes, English for Academic Purposes?
3. What level of education have you completed? What subject do you plan to study? At what level?
4. What are your teaching qualifications? What is your role on the course? Are you free to select the course materials?
5. Do you think the IELTS is a fair screening test for university entrance? Why? What do you think are the main strengths and weaknesses of IELTS?
6. What do you think is easy/difficult about IELTS?
7. How is IELTS similar to/different from other English language tests you are familiar with?

8. To what extent do you believe it is possible to prepare for the IELTS Academic Writing tasks?
9. Is one task easier to prepare for than the other? (Why?)
10. What do you hope you/your students will learn from this course?
11. What do you enjoy/dislike about this course?
12. What would you like to do more of in class and why? What would you like to do less of in class and why?
13. Do you think this course will help you/your students in the future after you/they have finished? How?
14. How do you think the course could be improved to make it more useful for your/your students' needs?
15. What have been the most useful and least useful parts of the course?
16. What does a good/successful student do on this course that an unsuccessful one doesn't?
17. How is teaching/studying on this course different from other classes you have experienced?
18. To what extent do you feel studying on this course provides a suitable preparation for university study?
19. How far do you think the IELTS test influenced the content of this course?
20. What did you teach/learn that was most useful in improving your/your students' IELTS Writing scores?
21. How far did the IELTS test influence how you taught/studied on this course?
22. In terms of IELTS bands, how much improvement do you expect to make/do you expect your students to make in their writing during this course?
23. What factors contribute to or work against these improvements?

Researcher position

In qualitative research, the status of the researcher poses a potential threat to the validity of the results. In an interview, the researcher inevitably brings to each encounter a set of personal characteristics that shape the encounter and affect the nature of the data obtained. For example, an interviewer who enters an institution as an outsider may not understand responses that assume a level of inside knowledge, while one working in familiar surroundings may share assumptions regarding the interview topics with the interviewees and fail to attend to these.

It is possible to counter the first of these risks by sharing findings with interviewees and asking them to check their accuracy. The second can be addressed through triangulation of researcher perspectives. It may also be of use to provide relevant information that will allow the reader to judge how the position of the researcher might affect the data that is reported (Miles and Huberman 1994).

As a teacher of English, I was able to bring to the interviews experience of institutions in all three sectors addressed in the study (BALEAP, BASELT and ARELS). I had some experience of teaching on both IELTS preparation courses and university pre-sessional courses. Although none of the interview participants was known to me prior to the interviews, I was able to approach them as a colleague with some knowledge of the kinds of setting in which they were working. The focus group interviews were conducted in the interviewees' workplaces so that they were on familiar ground and I sought to establish a relaxed and informal atmosphere.

Teachers

A total of 21 teachers and course providers at eight institutions participated in the teacher focus groups (see Chapter 4, Table 4.5). The participating institutions were drawn from both the university and private language school sectors and were intended to provide examples of the range of course types on offer to learners, although it was accepted that obtaining a fully representative sample would be beyond the resources of this project.

Interviews were conducted before the start date for the focal courses and ahead of observation sessions carried out as the next phase of the case study (see below). In all but two focus groups, one of the interview participants had also responded to the survey in Pilot Study Five. Nine of the interview participants were also observed teaching classes in the next phase of the study. In the following discussion, figures in brackets refer to the number of interviews in which an issue was raised.

Test importance and difficulty: attitudes to IELTS as a screening test

Attitudes to the test varied, but there was a general acceptance among the focus groups that a mechanism is required for university screening and that IELTS, whatever its faults, is the best available test for this purpose.

Some questioned the ways in which the test is used in university admissions. On the one hand, admissions tutors were said to rely too heavily on IELTS for their decisions without considering other sources of evidence (2), on the other, there was concern that standards for admissions were not being adhered to consistently (3). Participants in two focus groups related anecdotes of students whom they considered well able to cope with academic study being rejected by institutions because of unexpectedly poor IELTS results, although teachers were able to attest to their readiness for academic study.

Two groups questioned whether admissions staff were well enough informed about the test, with one interviewee recalling instances of admissions staff requiring half-band scores in Writing and Speaking for entry – an impossibility for test takers as only whole-band scores are awarded for these two modules (though half bands did become possible from July 2007). One interviewee had a different concern about admissions policies, fearing that some universities might relax entry standards in pursuit of lucrative international student fees.

Several interviewees commented on the recent growth of IELTS, noting the increasing pressure on students to obtain an IELTS score. This was seen as something of a threat by one university course provider as institutions that had previously recognised their internally developed diploma would now only recognise IELTS. This encouraged more students to take the test, and so to take test preparation courses rather than broader-based EAP courses.

IELTS was regarded by all groups as a high-stakes test with important consequences for most students. Success on the test was said to be the primary, and for some interviewees the sole objective of the preparation courses for both teachers and students.

Although IELTS was acknowledged to be the *raison d'être* for the IELTS preparation courses (or IELTS course components), the need to pass the test was not necessarily the only motivation for students to attend. Two interviewees, both at private language schools, reported that students sometimes took their IELTS preparation courses because they liked the seriousness and 'focus' of the course and, in the view of one interviewee, felt dissatisfaction with General English classes. A third, also at a language school, named a student who was taking the test for personal reasons, as a 'motivator' without any intention of going to university. Other students at private language schools, although intending to take the test, were said to be uncertain of whether they would, in fact, go on to university and of what subject they might study. It seems likely that, for such students, the test might not carry particularly high stakes.

Four interviews touched on the issue of minimum levels for IELTS students. The interviewees agreed that a certain minimum level of general proficiency would be required for students to benefit from their IELTS preparation courses. This was said to be a 'good intermediate' (2) or 'strong upper-intermediate' (1) level, with one interviewee suggesting that only students of FCE level or above could really benefit from training. At one school it was reported that students were routinely diverted to General English classes until they reached the required level for IELTS preparation. However, as has been reported, by Read and Hayes (2003), in New Zealand, there was pressure from students to prepare for the test even though they were not judged by their teachers to be ready (2). Where numbers allowed, students were divided into classes on the basis of proficiency, permitting teachers to tailor course content to the needs of the students.

Although IELTS scores are reported on a 9-band scale, a concern was expressed that the test may be unsuitable for learners below a band score of 5 (4). Such learners might be unable to interpret the tasks in the writing test and so be unable to perform to the best of their ability.

The focus groups were divided on the question of whether the test would be less suitable for pre-university students than for undergraduates and post-graduates. Some considered it most suitable for postgraduates because it requires a certain level of maturity, while others felt the 'general interest' nature of the topics would be more suitable for undergraduate students.

Issues of test bias

While one interviewee was concerned that Task 1 (data description) would favour science students, a second felt that the choice of Task 2 topics favoured arts and social science students. However, a more persistent source of disquiet than method effects relating to student field of study was the cultural accessibility of the writing topics in Task 2 (5). Although intended to be culturally neutral, the topics were seen to work against learners from certain backgrounds: 'Some topics are simply non-issues for students from other cultures – like the Chinese with animal rights.' Differences of rhetorical tradition were also considered to favour Europeans and work against Asians, with three interviewees mentioning the argumentative essay tradition and two the description of graphs in this regard. For Japanese learners, this perceived cultural bias was regarded by one interviewee as a strength of the test, in terms of washback, as it meant that learners were inducted, through test preparation, into ways of thinking current in the UK.

Two other potential sources of bias were broached. The frequent occurrence of sport as a topic was seen by one interviewee to involve a gender bias, favouring males. Another mentioned issues in administering the test for candidates with special needs, with the timing of the test proving particularly problematic in the case of one dyslexic candidate.

Issues of practicality

The immediate practical need to reserve test places was an important concern for many interviewees, particularly in the London area, where there was felt to be a need for more centres. With the increasing demand for the test, course providers were having to book tests well in advance and sometimes needed to look beyond their local region to place their students in a session. The logistics of test provision were apparently also having an impact on the composition of the preparation courses. The shortage of test places meant that students would have to commit to a test date long before their readiness to take the test could be assessed, dictating a more liberal approach to course admissions (2).

A second practical issue was the requirement that students wait 90 days before repeating the test. For one centre this was considered an annoyance, a burden on students under pressure to obtain a university place and an incentive for students to take the TOEFL test instead of IELTS. Conversely, at another centre, a university, the 90-day period was considered an advantage for IELTS as it avoided the risk that results could be 'hit and miss'; students able to repeat the test might continue to take it until they managed to pass by luck. (The 90-day wait between test sittings no longer applies.)

Students were selected for IELTS preparation either on the basis of estimates of their proficiency, or by meeting the criteria for admission to pre-sessional EAP courses; although some did insist on joining preparation courses, even where their ability to succeed was in doubt. On one pre-sessional course, those taking the IELTS course were said to be 'borderline' cases who might need to apply to other institutions if they failed to meet the internal course requirements for admission. For these students IELTS would be a kind of 'insurance policy' against failure on the course.

One teacher described the IELTS as 'a difficult test' and a second described it as 'more difficult than TOEFL'. A third felt that the test had become easier since the revisions of 1995 when specialist modules were withdrawn. Of the modules, Writing was generally said to be the most difficult, with Reading in second place. Specific sources of difficulty mentioned included time pressures and the unfamiliarity of topics for some test takers.

Summary

In short, the consensus among focus groups was that IELTS is both challenging and important to learners, although clearly not uniformly so. The Writing Module was considered to be difficult for the target population – possibly too much so for those requiring overall scores of 5.0 or 5.5 for entry to foundation courses or similar who might have difficulty in comprehending the tasks – although this is not the intended population for the Academic Modules which are explicitly targeted at undergraduates, postgraduates and applicants for professional registration (IELTS 2005).

It was also felt that the test may disfavour East Asians (although some felt that this might reflect linguistic and cultural disadvantages for this group in the academic study context). Most students on these courses intended to study at universities in the UK – a goal which called for an IELTS score. Thus IELTS was considered to be a high-stakes test, although perhaps more so for the students than for course providers or teachers; there was no mention of rewards or sanctions related to IELTS in the form of funding allocations or salary awards.

Test design characteristics: IELTS as a test of EAP writing

Many of the comments on the strengths and weaknesses of the IELTS AWM addressed the extent to which the test reflected the participants' understanding of academic writing. These included the content and format of the test, the test conditions, the marking scheme and the raters.

Every group pointed to differences between the IELTS AWM and the writing tasks required at university. The general view was that IELTS did not fully reflect academic writing and that 'Writing 250 words is very different from writing a dissertation or a 3-hour exam essay.' Specific differences mentioned by interviewees included the following:

Academic writing involves more opportunities for editing

Academic writing allows for more reflection time and planning

Academic writing requires the selection and reduction of information (2)

Academic writing involves integration of source material and referencing (2)

Academic writing requires attention to theories and theoretical issues

Academic writing requires more demanding content and 'analytical knowledge' of the topic

Academic writing requires greater 'depth of argument'

IELTS essays require personal opinions (2)

IELTS essays are relatively restricted in genre (2)

In IELTS the ideas do not need to be good

IELTS essays are short in comparison to most academic writing (4)

IELTS essays are written under tighter time constraints (3)

IELTS requires handwriting, but most academic assignments are now typewritten

IELTS is a test of academic writing, but is scored by EFL teachers.

Additionally, there was widespread agreement that Task 2 was more reflective of academic writing skills than Task 1, and Task 2 was regarded as a better indicator of 'general ability'. Although one interviewee commented that describing data is a useful skill for university, many were less positive. Specific concerns relating to Task 1 included the following:

Task 1 requires only description where university lecturers would require interpretation and conclusions based on the information presented (2)

Task 1 does not reflect the needs of students in some disciplines: graphical information is not relevant to all (3)

Task 1 items inconsistently generate either too much or too little information to sustain a 150-word response.

The 1-hour time limit was regarded by some as an unreasonable constraint, with one interviewee describing the writing test as 'a race against the clock'. The time limits in the test were not felt to be a realistic reflection of the time constraints operating in most university work and placed an additional burden on candidates. However two interviewees felt that these time constraints generated a degree of positive washback on the learners, suggesting that the time pressure in IELTS could 'sharpen and speed up the skills of interpreting data' – an advantage in academic study – even though the test task was not considered to reflect real life.

Issues of test content

The content of IELTS was said to be predictable (6). Interviewees felt able to list 'typical' topics for Task 2, and Task 1 was felt to be quite restricted in scope. There was a suspicion on the part of one interviewee that, perhaps for operational reasons, the description of processes in Task 1 had been discarded as an item type, leaving the description of graphs or bar charts as the predominant item type. Task 2 topics were said to be limited to 'business' or 'social science' issues such as 'health, education and the role of government in various issues' or 'environment, alternative fuels etc.'; described by one interviewee as 'Headway issues', in reference to the popular EFL textbook series. One interviewee also commented that the topics would not include 'religion, hard science, contemporary politics and potentially upsetting issues'. As the predictability of topics and of essay types could allow for formulaic responses, one interviewee suggested that IELTS might be strengthened by a 'Use of English' paper targeting grammar and vocabulary knowledge, similar to those on the Cambridge Main Suite tests.

IELTS was thought to test something more than language: academic ability on the test as a whole, observational skill (3) on Task 1, world knowledge and a certain 'way of thinking' (5) on Task 2. Maturity and experience were felt to be important to success on Task 2, but were also 'difficult to teach in eight weeks'. Knowledge of the topic encountered on the day was felt to make an important contribution to test performance and many students were said to lack this (6). Task 1 was also felt to require a certain 'knack', and an ability to process graphic information which could be taught, but was easier for some learners than others (2).

At the same time, the direct testing of writing in IELTS was compared favourably with the multiple-choice approach adopted earlier in other tests such as the TOEFL test. A number of the abilities required for success on the test were felt to pervade all academic writing. In particular, the following items were mentioned as valuable both for success on IELTS and for academic writing in general:

structuring a logical argument (3)

organising an essay into an introduction, body and conclusion

paragraphing and topic sentences (2)

coherence.

In addition, some interviewees felt that some of the less authentic features of the test (less reflective of university writing tasks), such as the time constraints, or the restrictions on genre imposed by Task 1, would provide useful training for university by encouraging students to work faster and to work within the conventions of a set task.

Issues of scoring

For those with no experience as IELTS examiners, the confidentiality of the scale band descriptors was a concern (5). The IELTS partners published the criteria used by examiners, but did not publish the band descriptors. Where trained examiners were working with other teachers, it was clear that they shared their expertise with colleagues. Where such expertise was not available, the teachers were frustrated at the lack of access.

Questions were raised over the scoring procedures. One group, made up of trained examiners, reported problems in applying the scoring criteria, favouring provision of a specific 'set of points for inclusion' in an adequate response. They also expressed uncertainty about how 'academic' the language used in the responses would need to be. Another interviewee (also an examiner) believed that IELTS Writing scores might be inflated by the use of the analytic rating scale (in contrast to impression marking on the Cambridge Certificate in Advanced English (CAE). Attention to components could result in a higher score than an essay would merit if considered as a whole. Another interviewee questioned whether EFL/ESOL teachers (the population from which IELTS examiners are usually drawn) would be the best qualified judges of the quality of a piece of academic writing.

Two focus groups saw problems in the sensitivity of the rating scale. The distance between the band scores of 5 and 6 was described as 'a big jump' and a cause of problems where students were being asked to obtain an overall score of 5.5 or 6.5 for university admissions.

Summary

Although the direct testing of writing in the IELTS was considered an attraction of the test, the interviewees did not believe that the test was fully representative of academic writing. Test characteristics such as the selection and variety of topics; sources of data; test conditions, including the time limit and required essay lengths, the nature of the expected responses; the characteristics of the rating scale and the characteristics of the raters were considered by at least some interviewees to distort the picture of test takers' academic writing ability provided by the IELTS AWM. At the same time, interviewees spoke of the 'positive washback effect' of the test in encouraging the teaching and learning of writing skills (contrasting this with indirect, MCQ-based tests). It was also acknowledged that the IELTS essay tasks better reflected academic writing than the more 'social and literary' writing tasks included on Cambridge Main Suite tests such as CAE.

Washback to the classroom: How to prepare students for IELTS

The perception of limited overlap between the IELTS AWM and academic writing for university study suggests, on the basis of the washback model, that IELTS preparation courses are likely to provide instruction in writing skills, but restrict this to areas thought to be required by the test. For those providing both pre-sessional EAP and IELTS preparation, there was sometimes just such a tension between efficient IELTS preparation and the aim of readying students for academic study.

The interviewees were asked to compare the focal course with the other courses they had experienced and to give examples of successful teaching strategies for the IELTS test. There was a clear relationship between perceptions of the test demands and the strategies adopted by teachers in preparing students. Teaching points for the test included:

Language content
linking words, transition signals or discourse markers (3)
focus on the language of graphs, visual information, trends and
   comparisons (2)
familiarity with typical essay topics (3)
grammatical accuracy (focusing on specific test-relevant weaknesses) (2)

Techniques
making use of brainstorming and planning (5)
organising ideas in a coherent fashion (3)
rigorous paragraphing (4)
use of topic sentences and supporting ideas (4)
question analysis (2)
time management and writing at speed (2)

In preparing students for the test, there was an emphasis across courses on the structure of the essays deemed appropriate to each of the tasks; the need for an introduction, body and conclusion arranged into paragraphs with topic sentences and supporting evidence. Initial brainstorming would yield ideas that could then be organised to fit the essay template so that 'Preparation starts from the essay framework and expanding from topic sentences, building up essay structure and supporting ideas, emphasising accurate use of discourse markers' (course teacher).

Time management and the ability to work at speed could also be improved with training (2). Where students were allowed to choose activities (on the 'self study' course) they favoured timed essay writing practice, presumably in the same belief.

One interviewee suggested that grammar feedback could be focused on specific areas of weakness relating to the requirements of the test. On the other hand, overall knowledge of grammar and vocabulary were not expected to develop to any great extent. Rather the focus of the courses, especially where time was limited, tended to be on more trainable test-taking strategies.

It was suggested that students with relatively poor control of language could 'fake' a band score of 6 if given training in layout, writing the required number of words and 'connectiveness'. The interviewee who suggested this, an examiner, noted that cohesion is not required of an essay at Band 6.

Task 1 could be addressed by a focus on graphs, visual information, trends and comparisons and by providing vocabulary and structures to describe these. One teacher reported supplementing published preparation materials with graphics from *The Guardian* newspaper supplements to prepare for Task 1.

Familiarity with typical IELTS topics for Task 2 including knowledge of social science was encouraged (4). One interviewee reported teaching knowledge of British life to address a perceived cultural bias in the IELTS AWM towards British concerns. Another teacher reported encouraging students to read *The Economist* to build their general knowledge. There was also felt to be an element of 'cultural' training in encouraging students to produce three pros and three cons for any given topic, a skill the interviewee associated with British 'A' Levels.

Teaching methods

If test demands dictated course content, they did not appear to determine teaching methods. One interviewee welcomed teaching on the IELTS course because it provided opportunities to use knowledge about teaching writing that he had gained on an MA TEFL course. Although not required in the test, some teachers asked students to redraft essays or evaluate each others' work in the belief that this would build awareness of writing skills. Effective teaching activities for the IELTS AWM reported for another course included teacher reformulation of student work, matching topic sentences to paragraphs, analysing Task 2 questions and working back from a model essay to a title or graph.

The predictability both of the written genres required in the test and of the topics addressed seemed to encourage the teaching of organisational templates and of memorised phrases. Some felt that Task 1 was more open to training because it requires 'many linking words and verbs students have not previously been exposed to' or because it could be approached in a formulaic manner, allowing teachers to bypass some of the intrinsic difficulty of the tasks: 'Students may lack knowledge of graphic presentation, but this is formulaic; there are chunks they have to learn.' Although interviewees more often pointed to Task 1 as encouraging memorised phrases, some felt that both tasks were equally amenable to training and that formulaic responses to Task 2, based on 'chunked' language could also be successful.

Teaching materials

Although interviewees were not asked to name useful materials, two books were mentioned as valuable preparation texts: *A Book for IELTS* (McCarter, Easton and Ash 2000) – praised for conciseness and clarity of layout, and *Academic Writing Course* (Jordan 1990) – said to be 'good on study skills'. Other comments on available preparation materials included both the positive – the available books are useful – and the negative – complaints that they are generally 'dry' and uninspiring or that they required a 'high upper intermediate level' and are thus unsuitable for learners who are not yet at this level.

Issues of gain

Areas of gain

On shorter courses, there was a sense that little could be done in the limited time available to improve general grammar or vocabulary knowledge, but that the structuring of essays could be addressed. Areas of greatest improvement in students' work seen over the preparation courses closely reflected a focus on essay structure and included paragraphing (5), organisation (4) and planning (4), with linking words (2), time management (2), accuracy (2), topic familiarity and the language of trends and comparisons also being mentioned. Gains made during preparation courses that might not be reflected in IELTS AWM scores included improved general knowledge (3), greater self-confidence in using English (2) and an increased ability to work in groups and discuss topics in English.

Extent of gain

Interviewees were divided on how much gain on the AWM they would expect of students following their courses. On one (pre-sessional) course, the group would not have expected any measurable gain on the five-week module (given that IELTS Writing is measured in whole bands), but felt a one-band gain would be possible after eight weeks with this being perhaps an average gain over 18 weeks. A one-band increase would be a satisfactory gain after a one year foundation course. On another course, an average gain of two bands was expected over three months. Some felt that predictions of half a band per month were reasonable, although perhaps dependent on student motivation and adherence to test training; others felt that this was too optimistic.

It was suggested that test training provided a trump card that could be played only once. Relatively rapid score gains could be made on the test by applying a set of test-taking strategies, without large improvement in students' language ability (5). Although once these strategies had been acquired additional test training might bring diminishing returns.

Faster gains in AWM scores would be expected on dedicated test-preparation courses than on pre-sessional EAP courses, particularly where learners had no previous experience of test-strategy training. One interviewee related how 'foundation year' students (who spent a full year studying in preparation for university entrance) had generally made a one-band improvement by the end of their course, but suspected that four days of IELTS familiarisation may have contributed a good deal to this gain. Other interviewees agreed with this view that dedicated test training provided a real advantage to students.

Although training for the test could boost scores to some degree (estimates ranged between half a band and two bands), there were felt to be limits to its effectiveness. As noted above, a minimum level of proficiency was said to be required before students could benefit from training. There was also talk of a ceiling beyond which test training could not take students. One interviewee claimed that it was more difficult to move from a Band 6 to a Band 7 than from a Band 5 to a Band 6 and another intimated that students could only progress beyond a band of 6 or 7 if they had strong motivation and academic ability.

Variables promoting or hindering gain

A number of individual differences were cited as helping or hindering success in IELTS preparation. A persistent theme was regional origin: East Asians – and specifically the Chinese – were said to make slower progress than others (5). Personality was also felt to be important: self-discipline and motivation being key (3), with students who completed work set and worked outside class said to outperform their less committed peers. However, there was also talk of a 'factor X' (2) that allowed some learners to do better for no obvious reason. Additionally, some were said to perform well under the pressure of the test and to respond well to 'coming up against it' (2).

It was also reported that the best gains were made by those who learned to apply 'the formula' provided (2), while inflexible learners who could not adapt to a co-operative classroom style (1) or accept the need to follow a prescription (2) did not improve as much. Two interviewees spoke of students who had not been open to test training and so failed to improve their scores.

Assessing students

In response to the lack of published information on the content of the IELTS rating scales, teachers built up a sense of how essays would be evaluated as they gained experience of the scores students were awarded. They also looked for more information on the standards applied by examiners. One interviewee had sought access to examiner training, without intending to become an examiner, simply to learn about the band descriptors. Another interviewee, apparently unaware even of the published grading criteria, said that he graded work for 'vocabulary and range of expression and mechanical accuracy', but awarded scores on a 9-point scale as an indication to students of their approximate IELTS band score.

On the other hand, knowledge of the test gleaned from training gave rise to its own issues. One trained examiner felt a tension between her role as an examiner and her role as a teacher. Examiners have inside knowledge of test topics and of the features of task responses most valued by raters and there may be an ethical dilemma for individual teachers/examiners between providing the best possible preparation for students and avoiding any disclosure of privileged information.

Students on IELTS courses were said to be well-motivated (4), an attraction of these courses for the teachers (3). Attendance was better than on other courses, and better among students taking the test than those who were not (1), with IELTS being regarded as 'a great focuser of minds'. However, it was said that some students reacted better to the pressure imposed by the test than others (2).

The improved student motivation exacted costs on course content. Where courses included both IELTS preparation and other elements, IELTS could come to dominate, narrowing students' focus at the expense of other areas (2). One interviewee reported that students lobbied for test practice at the expense of other activities, more valued by the teacher. At the same time, the length of the course (11 weeks full time) allowed for a much wider range of activities than a 30-hour IELTS preparation course provided by the same institution. This reinforces the image gained elsewhere (Pilot studies Three and Four) of IELTS test training as a bounded package of skills requiring a limited period of instruction.

Students

Student focus groups involved the same database of questions as the teacher sessions. Again, the intention was exploratory and issues raised by participants were pursued. However, there were generally more participants in each group and less time available. As a result fewer questions could be explored in each session.

Importance and difficulty

The importance and difficulty of the test, identified by teachers during piloting as potentially sensitive topics for learners, were not, for this reason, explored in depth in the focus group sessions. Rather, the presence of students on the IELTS preparation courses together with their responses to the questionnaires and the interest they expressed in discussing the test bore testimony to the value they placed on it.

IELTS was clearly an important test for most of those interviewed. In the majority of cases, IELTS grades were required for entrance to UK universities. However, as the teachers had reported, a few students were undecided as to whether they would use their IELTS results for this purpose. One student said that he was taking the test just to check his level of English and another needed a certificate for employment purposes (in finance).

Student comments also suggested that they saw the test as difficult; and sometimes frustratingly so. Two students had previously prepared for the test by self-study, but had found they were unable to reach the required level and so had chosen to join a preparation course. A third had studied alone when requiring a band score of 5.5 to join a foundation course, but had joined a preparation course in order to obtain the more challenging 6.5 required for university study.

One student who had taken the test twice before reported that her grade had failed to improve, although she felt sure that her abilities had. She believed that the test had become more difficult over the intervening period. Others believed progressing from a band score of 5 to a score of 6 was easier than moving from 6 to 7. Students requiring scores of 7 or above seemed particularly frustrated by their progress (2). One student felt that IELTS requirements at his institution were too high. He was confident that his ability to understand and use English was adequate for university study, but could not obtain the band score of 7 required for his course.

The 90-day embargo on repeating the test was a further source of dissatisfaction (2). Candidates under pressure to obtain a given score felt that they were being denied the opportunity to obtain a better result and this exacerbated the difficulty of reaching the required standard. Such evidence that students take account of the perceived difficulty of the test in deciding how much to invest in preparation activities is supportive of the washback model.

Overlap between academic writing for university and IELTS AWM

Like the course providers and teachers, students commented on how far IELTS reflected their conception of academic writing ability. When asked to compare the IELTS to another test they had experienced, many chose to compare IELTS to the TOEFL test, remarking either that IELTS better represented language abilities, or that it was more readily available in the UK. Favourable comparisons included the testing of four skills on IELTS (5) as opposed to the use of multiple-choice grammar items on TOEFL (4). One student considered TOEFL writing to be easier as it involved just one writing task. Others considered that the use of multiple-choice questions made TOEFL the easier of the two tests (2). Several students said that they had chosen to take IELTS rather than TOEFL either because IELTS, but not TOEFL, preparation courses were available at their institution, or because an IELTS score had been requested by their intended university (4).

It was also said that IELTS more accurately reflected 'real' language abilities and that high scores on TOEFL could be obtained just through knowledge of grammar and vocabulary (4), so that 'a good score in TOEFL does not mean you can pass IELTS, but a good score in IELTS means you have a good level of English ability.' One student claimed to know people who had 'passed' TOEFL with scores of over 600 points and had entered university, yet had then been unable to follow lectures, something he felt would not happen with IELTS. Another (Chinese) student favoured IELTS because he believed that TOEFL, as a test of North American English, would not reflect British usage and would not therefore reflect the language he would encounter in the UK.

A major concern about IELTS Writing was the impact of the essay topic on performance. This was a question raised by every group, being encapsulated in one student's comment on the topic he had been presented with on the test, claiming that, 'Even in Chinese I don't know about this!' Most students commenting on the issue felt that they had been disadvantaged by topics that they knew too little about; although one recalled that he had been lucky on the test and had encountered a topic for which he had memorised an essay. This student felt that this had contributed to his success in obtaining a band score of 6 on the Writing test, which exceeded his expectations. Others agreed that the topics were predictable, citing education and the environment as common essay themes. One student felt that IELTS topics were of more general interest than those encountered in TOEFL, commenting that the issues were sometimes 'things that you've heard about.' A number of students said that they felt disadvantaged by topics outside their academic discipline; 'topics may come from other fields such as agriculture or geography – I would prefer to be able to choose the field as this would give me a better chance.'

Beyond the topic area, one group raised the importance of understanding the essay title. They complained that misinterpretation of a single word could completely misdirect the response and prevent the resulting essay from reflecting the true abilities of the writer. Unlike the teachers and course providers, the students did not submit that the test topics might be biased against learners from particular cultures or backgrounds. This may, however, simply reflect the narrower perspective of learners on cross-cultural issues; teachers may be better placed to make such comparisons.

While complaints about topics generally centred on Task 2, there was a sense expressed by some students that the kind of writing demanded by Task 1 did not reflect writing for the university (3). Two students with prior experience of university study in the UK remarked that Task 2 was a better reflection of the kinds of writing they had done. One, yet to enter university, commented of Task 1 that 'There is no academic writing like this in my area – financial markets – there are graphs, but we don't need to describe them'.

The speededness of the test was a further, if less pressing, cause of discontent (4). One mature student who had struggled with the timing suggested that younger people might be better able to 'think quickly' and generate ideas for the essays. Others complained that the limited time available for the test did not reflect the reality of academic writing outside the examination hall. In spite of these reservations, most students seemed to believe that the IELTS AWM provided a generally fair reflection of academic writing. One student suggested that scores were '80% fair and 20% luck in getting a topic you know about.'

Specific features of IELTS that were said to reflect academic writing included the use of an introduction, body and conclusion; the use of paragraphs and the use of topic sentences. The difficulty for some students in making this kind of comparison was pointed up by one student who considered that, as IELTS provided his only experience of academic writing in English, he was unable to make a comparison. This was probably true of many of the students on these courses, and these may, as a result, have relied on their teachers in shaping their constructions of academic writing.

Like their teachers, the students noted that IELTS required general knowledge (2) and personal opinions (2), and that these were less valued in academic writing. They noted that IELTS Writing is relatively brief (2), and one student felt that writing short essays of this kind would give only a very poor indication of whether an individual would be capable of writing a dissertation in English. One Japanese student felt that IELTS was similar in format to (Japanese medium) university entrance examinations in her country, which also comprised an academic essay and reading comprehension questions and were used to screen students for academic ability.

One group, made up of learners on an intensive IELTS preparation course, without previous experience of academic study in the UK, appeared to have generalised from IELTS in formulating their beliefs about academic writing in English. They seemed to believe that features of the IELTS test essays characterised all academic writing in English. One (Palestinian) student expressed the belief that in English there is only 'one way of writing' based on an introduction, body and conclusion, while Arabic allows for a wider variety of patterns. Others in the group (including Italian, Chinese and Russian students) agreed with each other that academic writing in their L1s was less 'superficial' than writing in English; content was more important than form, writing was more extended and time less of a constraint. These are all features that other focus groups saw as distinguishing academic writing from IELTS essays.

A more general comparison between L1 and IELTS writing involved differences in rhetorical patterns across cultures. Chinese, Japanese and Arabic-speaking students remarked that English writing was more direct, and involved the use of topic sentences. One Japanese student remarked that, in her language 'there is more for the reader to work out.' Some students observed that they had not received instruction in writing in their own languages and there was general agreement that writing in English, whether for IELTS or for university study, involved somehow 'thinking in a different way' from L1 writing.

Students, including the minority with experience of both, generally perceived a good deal of overlap between the IELTS AWM and writing in the university. Those studying on intensive IELTS preparation courses did not introduce the issues of input and integration of sources raised by teachers, although they did believe that academic writing would involve more 'professional' or specialist vocabulary.

Learning experiences

As four of the focus groups were studying on pre-sessional courses, they were able to compare their earlier experiences in IELTS preparation classes with the current experience of their pre-sessional. Differences between the two course types identified by students included the following:

IELTS essays involve more use of personal ideas, and so more use of 'I' and 'We' than essays on pre-sessionals.

You need to work out the length of the essay (number of words) on IELTS.

There is practice in coping with the time pressure of the test on IELTS courses.

Essay titles in academic writing are less restrictive; 'IELTS provides a clear thesis statement, university titles may be more free.'

Greater attention to subject-specific topics and vocabulary on the pre-sessionals:

'This course is for postgraduates who know what they will learn at college so is more focused on relevant topics. IELTS is more general in what you study.'

'There is no reading of law texts in IELTS class, but no chance to do this extensively in my own time.'

'Essay writing and presentations here are more relevant for university as most students are studying in the business field.'

Pre-sessionals involve learning IT and other study skills, 'Using computers and doing projects are very useful for my MSc. Tutors will assume that I know how to do these things and I do not expect much help (although I didn't have these skills before this course).'

Length of written assignments; and (for some) associated differences in text structure. 'Here the emphasis is on structuring long essays – not just 250 words, but over 3,000 words.' However, others disputed whether project work and brief essays would require different structures (to introduction/body/conclusion) – this was a point of disagreement in two focus groups.

Simulation on pre-sessional EAP courses of an academic study process. 'This course is more like university life as it includes seminar skills and project work.'

The use of sources and references in writing on pre-sessional courses.

All pre-sessional groups agreed that IELTS preparation and pre-sessional courses had a fundamental difference of purpose: 'Both are for academic study. With IELTS the purpose was very clear: to improve scores. The pre-sessional course teacher improves our level.'

The objective of passing the test was said to have both a motivational and a narrowing effect on student learning both in and out of class. Students agreed with each other that IELTS preparation might not involve the most appropriate preparation for their future studies; it was, first and foremost, directed at obtaining a higher score.

One student commented that she did work harder for IELTS, but useful language learning activities like watching television or reading the newspapers seemed like a waste of time when she was studying for the test. She said that she had focused on 'analysing' the exam and this was not the same as improving her level of English.

Another learner, who had taken the test on three occasions and was preparing for a fourth attempt, believed that IELTS preparation had a limited impact. It could improve scores, but not beyond a certain point: 'IELTS courses are all the same; they introduce the test. All test courses tell you the test style, but not really how to improve further.' This supports the view expressed by teachers that the test strategies provided by preparation courses add, for those students who have not previously been aware of them, a one-off premium to test scores, but that accelerated rates of gain cannot be sustained.

The perception of similarities among IELTS preparation courses was shared by other students who had previously studied on such courses elsewhere in the UK or prior to arrival. 'The IELTS course in Japan was on a smaller scale and was more intensive, but otherwise it was the same.'

Differences noted by students generally related to the teaching methods, rather than course content. For example, one student reported that in her previous class the teacher had spent more time answering test questions in class, while now the teacher gave more emphasis to test-taking strategies. Others noted differences in the composition of class groups; one reporting that in her own country the class had been more heterogeneous in level and that the teacher had concentrated on the lower-level students. Another had previously received less feedback from the teacher, who had just returned the writing with his marks. She felt that this had benefited higher-level students, but she had wanted more guidance in how to improve her own work.

Students were asked about the kinds of improvement they felt they had made on their IELTS courses, and what they had found most useful in preparing them for the test. Areas of improvement included the following:

Time management during the test.

Building general knowledge: 'For Task 2 you need to be interested in general matters; I prepared by reading newspapers, listening to the BBC, reading journals, and studying culture.'

Knowledge of the test method (question formats).

Learning steps for answering the question. Analysing the questions and so on.

Brainstorming a topic and dividing it into points.

Making plans (3).

Organising an IELTS essay: introduction, body, conclusion (4).

Organising paragraphs (2).

Using topic sentences and thesis statements with support (2).

Using English and not Chinese ideas; 'I learned about differences between Chinese and UK composition: Western writers put the main point first. In Chinese writing, it can be placed in the middle.'

Learning how to write formally (4).

Using more 'academic' words – such as 'athlete' not 'player' when discussing sport.

Linking words and increasing their repertoire of these compared to General English.

Starting new sentences (sentence divisions).

Understanding how to analyse graphs or charts (4): 'You need to practise analysing charts and think fast. It's not easy; sometimes your mind goes blank.'

'How to write the essay without understanding the topic; for example, we use strategies such as "I am not sure of the meaning of x, but as I understand it . . .".' We were taught by examiners who train students in the "tricks" and what is being looked for.'

Learning set expressions (for building responses to Tasks 1 and 2).

The language of description; phrases and vocabulary for Task 1 (3).

Collecting model essays and memorising them.

Memorising phrases/sentences/whole paragraphs (4).

This list reflects the emphasis reported by course providers in IELTS preparation on an essay writing process based on question analysis, brainstorming, planning and building from topic sentences, with attention given to time management. Many students placed a high value on memorisation, with some memorising paragraphs and even entire essays; although memorising useful phrases (typically for graph description or introductions) was more popular. On the other hand, one student found that memorisation had not helped her as she had simply forgotten all the phrases she had learned as soon as she entered the test room.

Students in all groups were asked to give examples of activities and strategies they had found most useful in preparation for the test. Their responses to this question included the following:

Doing the essays and getting your grammar corrected.

Learning about the structure of academic writing; we always split into two groups to debate the topic for brainstorming, and then we wrote practice tests.

'I learned essay style; categorising graphs and charts, and a way of thinking: logical thought. The test evaluates this kind of point.'

'Learning about topics (social problems/current affairs) and practising listing advantages and disadvantages.'

'I was told it's very important to finish both essays and to follow the word requirements. If you finish, you'll get at least a 5. If you add more formal words you gain more.'

'Learning about the structure of the essay, and timing. I sat IELTS before taking the intensive course and my score was low because I didn't know the style of the exam. I learned how to deal with the chart or graph – this is new to Japanese candidates.'

'I used model essays (for self-study), I tried to write on the topic, then compared my essay with the model. Some essays had Chinese translations. I compared the Chinese with the English versions and tried to memorise good essays.'

'Learning example essays; how to write an excellent sentence and use correct vocabulary. We read essays ten times, each time we focused on a different point to learn about the structure; how to combine nouns and adjectives; how to build words and so on.'

'The course helped to build my knowledge of the test. We spent the last week on test practice – this gave me an idea of the test. In the mornings we studied reading and writing with one teacher. In the afternoon we studied speaking and listening with another. We used practice tests.'

In terms of skills, students were divided on which area had benefited most from the preparation courses. Most felt that their writing had improved, and the largest number in all groups believed this was the most improved skill. This was especially true for those who lacked previous experience of extensive writing in English. Some students felt unable to assess whether their speaking or listening skills had improved, with one remarking that improvements in speaking skills could have occurred outside the classroom, while writing was limited to work on the course.

Although students were generally positive about the worth of their IELTS preparation courses, reservations were expressed about their value as preparation for academic work. Some of those preparing for IELTS seemed to expect that all academic writing in English would be similar to IELTS, others expressed uncertainty about how well prepared they would be for the demands of university study. One student summed up their concern thus: 'IELTS preparation teaches basics of academic writing. We use a one sentence introduction – a very basic technique. If I learn this method, I don't know if it's useful for academic writing such as a dissertation. I don't know how to write for an MA, but I think the basic idea is the same.' Others had come to realise that expectations of rapid score gains might be disappointed. Although test preparation could help, it remained true that 'Studying language takes a long time. Perhaps 10 weeks is not really long enough to reach the required level.'

Summary

Teachers and learners agreed that the IELTS test defined the objectives of their preparation courses. The stakes associated with the test seemed to encourage such training, despite misgivings about its value in developing academic writing skills. A picture emerged from the teacher interviews of a package of teaching strategies aimed at improving textual organisation through planning and paragraphing skills in the few weeks available. There was a focus on data comparison for Task 1 and argument structure for Task 2 with practice in managing the production of two essays within one hour.

Although IELTS was often favourably compared with the alternatives, learners believed that luck played an important role in success. Variations in topic, or in the wording of prompts, could impact on their ability to produce an adequate response. Both teachers and learners felt that, in addition to language ability, IELTS required a certain level of general knowledge and maturity.

There was a shared belief among participants that the training package provided learners with the best short-term opportunity for improving test scores. However, there was some disagreement about the amount of gain that could be expected. On the one hand, there was concern that learners required a certain level of ability to benefit from preparation courses, on the other, some participants considered that progress beyond a certain band score would be unlikely.

Watching: the observation schedule

Alderson and Wall (1993) point to the value of empirical data in washback studies. Only direct observation can allow the researcher to relate attitudes expressed in survey responses to teacher and learner behaviour in the classroom. The development of the observation schedule is described in Chapter 4.

Results: the observation schedule

Timing, episodes and activities

IELTS and Academic writing classes were of similar length. Scheduled IELTS classes observed ranged from 60 to 120 minutes, averaging 89 minutes, while the pre-sessional EAP writing classes observed ranged from 50 to 120 minutes and averaged 94 minutes. The ratio of episodes to activities was also very similar across course types; there were approximately 10 episodes to every three activities, with each activity taking up just under 17 minutes on average. IELTS classes accounted for both the longest and shortest average length of activities in a class. One IELTS class, involving test practice, had an average activity length of 38 minutes; another, involving a series of grammar exercises averaged 9 minutes per activity. In pre-sessional EAP writing classes the longest average activity length in a class was 25 minutes and the shortest was 10 minutes.

Participant organisation

The balance of participant organisation was similar across course types. The predominant form of participant organisation was Teacher – Students/Class, accounting for 56% of pre-sessional EAP classes and 54% of IELTS preparation classes. In this context, this form of organisation did not generally involve lengthy teacher monologues, but more typically involved interactions centred on the teacher.

The second most frequent form of organisation was individual students working on the same task. This took up 28% of IELTS classes and 26% of pre-sessional EAP classes. Third most popular was group work on the same task; 17% of the time on both IELTS and pre-sessional EAP classes. Other forms of participant organisation were rare; 6% of time on pre-sessional EAP classes involved individual students addressing the class for a minute or longer, and 2% involved groups of students undertaking different tasks. One per cent of the time on IELTS courses was taken up by individual students doing different activities.

Content: management

Discipline issues were very rare during these observations. Occasionally a teacher reminded students to speak English rather than their L1, but as no class period as long as a full minute was given over to disciplinary matters, discipline was not recorded as the main focus of any activity. For this reason, discipline was (under-)recorded as taking 0% of class time.

Procedural issues took up 9% of time on IELTS and 12% on pre-sessional EAP courses. Variation in the amount of time spent on procedures appeared to be a matter of teacher style, rather than of test focus. Teachers that were observed on more than one occasion were consistent in the amount of time given to procedural matters across classes, but there were sometimes wide differences between teachers. Recorded times for procedural matters ranged from a minimum of 0% to 20% of IELTS classes and from 2% to 29% of pre-sessional EAP classes, although, as noted above, the COLT disregards events of less than a minute and so tends to under-record brief procedural episodes.

Content: language

As much as 46% of IELTS class time involved a major focus on language form (grammar and vocabulary) as compared with 22% of pre-sessional EAP class time. Language function was the focus of 19% of IELTS and 12% of pre-sessional EAP classes. Discourse issues were a focus of 16% of IELTS and 40% of pre-sessional EAP classes. Sociolinguistic issues were a major focus of just 3% of pre-sessional EAP and 0% of IELTS class time.

Content: other

In all classes observed, topics were generally broad: relating to issues of general interest. In IELTS preparation classes 58% of time and in pre-sessional EAP classes 48% of time was spent working with topics in this category. Little time (4% of IELTS and 1% of pre-sessional EAP classes) was spent on immediate personal topics (and these typically occurred only during brief introductory episodes). Academic topics – those topics which became the focus of the class in their own right – occurred only in two pre-sessional EAP classes, making up just 2% of the total pre-sessional EAP class time observed. Typically, topics were limited to one or two class activities and switches of topic would occur with each change of task. Four pre-sessional EAP classes (29% of those observed) remained focused on a single topic for the duration of a class, while IELTS classes more typically switched topic frequently with only one IELTS class (5%) remaining with a single topic throughout. Eleven of the IELTS classes (50% of those observed) included more than five topics, while this was true of just three (21%) of the pre-sessional EAP classes.

References to the test

A good deal of attention was given to IELTS in the preparation classes; the test was mentioned by participants a total of 122 times during the IELTS classes, compared with just 10 times during pre-sessional EAP classes. Of these 10 mentions, nine were on combination courses (on which students were intending to take the test) where teachers mentioned how the class content could be applied to the test, or where students asked for information about the test. Specific test strategies or 'test taking tips' were provided by teachers on a total of 67 occasions, or just over three times per class on average. Just two of the 21 IELTS classes observed included no explicit mention of the IELTS test; although even here it remained the implicit focus for the class activities.

Tests other than IELTS were mentioned five times during pre-sessional EAP classes on courses unrelated to IELTS. One class accounted for four of these mentions. This class included 50 minutes of explicit test preparation for a course exit test to be held three days after the observation. The teacher introduced the test format, describing the timing and format of the tasks, and gave 25 minutes to a practice exercise.

Content control

The teacher or text in both IELTS and pre-sessional EAP classes most often held control of class content (82% of the time in IELTS and 73% of the time in pre-sessional EAP classes). Students did not hold sole control of content during any of the classes observed, but control was shared between teacher, text and students a little more often in pre-sessional EAP (27% of class time) than in IELTS classes (18% of class time).

Student modality

Modality was surprisingly similar across course types (Table 5.7). Listening (mostly teacher-centred activities such as calling on individual learners to answer questions) took up just over half of class time on both types of classes. Oral interaction between students took up around 10% of class time and a similar proportion was given to writing activities. Reading and writing, typically grammar or other textbook exercises, took up a further 10% of class time, with the remaining portion made up of group speaking and reading (paired or group reading) or speaking and writing (collaborative writing) activities.

Materials

Published materials used in IELTS classes generally included a reference to IELTS in their titles.

Fowler, H R and Aaron, J (2001) *The Little, Brown Handbook*, Harlow: Longman.

Hopkins, D and Nettle, M (1999) *Passport to IELTS*, Harlow: Pearson Education.

Jakeman, V and McDowell, C (2001) *Insight into IELTS: The Cambridge IELTS Course*, Cambridge: Cambridge University Press.

McCarter, S, Easton, J and Ash, J (2000) *A Book for IELTS*, Ford, Midlothian: IntelliGene.

Prodromou, L (1999) *Grammar and Vocabulary for First Certificate*, Harlow: Longman.

Sahanaya et al (1999) *IELTS Preparation and Practice*, Oxford: Oxford University Press.

Sellen, D (1982) *Skills in Action*, London: Hulton Educational.

Of the three items that included no reference in their title to the IELTS test, two were intended as preparation materials for other English language tests (5 and 7). The four IELTS titles were all coursebooks directed towards the test, rather than collections of test practice material.

On pre-sessional EAP courses the following published materials were observed:

Jordan, R R (1990) *Academic Writing Course*, London: Collins.

Table 5.7 A comparison of student modality in IELTS- and EAP- focused classes.

	Listening (to teacher or text)	Oral interaction	Speaking and Reading	Listening and Reading	Reading	Writing	Reading and Writing	Speaking and Writing
IELTS	51.8%	11.2%	2.7%	0.2%	14.4%	8.7%	10.2%	0.9%
EAP	51.1%	10.3%	2.0%	0.2%	14.8%	11.7%	10.0%	0.0%

Oshima, A and Hogue, A (1991) *Writing Academic English*, New York: Addison-Wesley.

Swales, J M and Feak, C B (1994) *Academic Writing for Graduate Students*, Ann-Arbor, Michigan: University of Michigan Press.

Trzeciak, J and Mackay, S (1994) *Study Skills for Academic Writing*, London: Prentice Hall.

None of these titles is intended primarily as an IELTS preparation text, although, as noted above, Jordan (1990) is widely used as a resource in IELTS courses.

Post-observation teacher interviews

Aims

Thirteen of the 14 IELTS classes for which interview data was available included mention of the IELTS Writing test as an aim of the class. The only IELTS preparation class that was said not to be influenced by the test came at the beginning of the course and was intended as a gentle introduction to the discursive essay; specifically the need to support ideas with evidence. The central activity (finding examples to support popular proverbs from students' countries) was intended as a means of preparing students for the demands of Task 2 without directly introducing test-like questions. Thus, although the teacher maintained that the test did not directly influence the class, it was clear that the demands of Task 2 were the ultimate goal.

Class aims on IELTS preparation courses included both practice in performing directly test-derived tasks (Task 1 or Task 2 Writing practice) and a wide variety of other activities intended to build relevant skills for the test. These aims included:

- gaining an overview of test demands
- building grammar and vocabulary related to test demands (such as sentences to describe graphs and processes or exercises related to common Task 2 issues)
- learning how to analyse questions for Task 2 and select data for Task 1
- learning about thesis statements, topic sentences and paragraph structure
- focusing on specific areas of difficulty through self or peer correction
- supporting propositions with evidence
- understanding the IELTS assessment criteria.

Some of the aims for pre-sessional EAP classes were similar to those for IELTS:

- learning how to describe processes
- learning how to construct paragraphs
- learning about the problem/solution essay structure
- reviewing the tense system
- debating an issue.

    Others seemed to have no parallel among the IELTS classes:

- learning how to write definitions
- learning about hedging in academic writing
- distinguishing one's own ideas from others'
- learning to integrate source material
- learning how to construct a bibliography.

Achievement of aims

Teachers on both course types were confident that their aims had been at least partially met, although comments on this question such as 'Will have a clearer picture after the homework' reflected the need for teachers to see students' written production before gaining a clear impression of how far the teaching points had been assimilated.

Comments during the interviews showed that teachers believed that most students in their classes had learned in the class, but that the difficulty of the materials was too great for some learners: 'Generally students got the idea, although one or two of the lower-level students could not get there' (IELTS teacher). This seemed to be true both of IELTS and of non-IELTS classes.

Location of class in instructional sequence

Both IELTS and pre-sessional EAP classes seemed to follow a similar cycle with input from the teacher, practice writing tasks and diagnostic feedback. It was the content of this cycle, not the process, which differentiated pre-sessional EAP from IELTS preparation classes. The IELTS preparation cycle was closely tied to test content: practice involved test tasks, with this apparently intensifying as the courses progressed. In the pre-sessional EAP classes, the courses built towards longer writing tasks, with students being given greater independence (for research activities and library work) as the courses neared completion. Where the courses involved a final test, there might be some attention given to this at the end of the course, with students being given opportunities for test practice.

On at least one combination course it was apparent that, as the test date approached, the IELTS exerted an influence on the content of classes beyond the identified IELTS component, with students requesting practice in test tasks. The cycle for IELTS preparation seemed to be based around the organisation of a successful response to the IELTS essay tasks; building up a toolkit of elements – selecting and describing data for Task 1, introducing and structuring a five-paragraph essay for Task 2. Equally, in pre-sessional EAP classes the cycle involved essay structure; building essays around problem-solution or comparison/contrast structures and incorporating functions such as definitions and process description. Attention was also given to information sources and incorporating source material into essays.

Typical class?

Most classes observed were said to be typical. When teachers mentioned differences between the observed classes and typical classes, these were often related to the behaviour of the students (that they had been quiet or lively), rather than to the content of the lesson.

Influence of IELTS

Teachers on IELTS courses usually claimed that the class content was entirely dictated by the IELTS test. Conversely, those on EAP courses either dismissed the idea that IELTS had any influence on their classes, or suggested that it served as a baseline for their teaching; they could assume that learners arrived on their courses with some knowledge of how to write a basic five-paragraph essay.

Student work

Teachers participating in the observations were asked to provide examples of student responses to writing tasks recently undertaken by their students, either in class or as homework, at the time of observation. The responses should be representative of three levels; one exemplifying the best work in the group, one intermediate and one weak in relation to the class. In all, 61 pieces of written student work were collected from nine courses. Of these 18 were taken from three EAP classes and the remainder came from six IELTS preparation classes.

An immediately apparent difference between IELTS and EAP work was the variety of tasks. All written work collected from IELTS classes consisted of responses to practice IELTS tasks with varying degrees of guidance from supporting materials. EAP tasks ranged from timed writing exercises to extended projects, which included tables of contents, references and bibliographies.

The tasks also differed in their presentation. All but two of the practice IELTS tasks were handwritten, while the work collected from pre-sessional EAP courses, with the exception of work done in class under time constraints, was all word processed. This points to an area of overlap given little attention in the literature, but raised by students during the interview sessions: the growing role of information technology in EAP writing.

As anticipated, there was a much greater range in the length of EAP task responses than of IELTS responses. IELTS tasks ranged in length from 98 to 445 words, while the pre-sessional EAP essays ranged from 128 to 3,495 words.

Of the six IELTS teachers, five marked student work using IELTS band scores, with one providing a breakdown of the score by the criteria used on the test. The five teachers giving scores often added a comment to the awarded score such as 'good 6' or '5.0+'. Two of the three EAP teachers provided scores (one as marks out of 20, the other as percentages) while the third made written comments, but did not give a score. One of the teachers giving scores used an analytical style of reporting with the criteria content and task achievement, organisation and coherence, range and accuracy of language and improvement between drafts.

Overall, the examples of student work supported the claims of teachers and students that IELTS coursework was closely directed towards the test. The extended Writing tasks undertaken in IELTS classes were all intended to mirror the tasks offered in the test. EAP tasks included timed writing practice on similar broad topics, but also included quite specific projects linked to learners' academic subjects.

Summary

The observations revealed broad similarities in teaching methods across courses. There was little variation associated with the type of course in participant organisation, content control or student modality. There was much in common in the activities occurring in the different classes regardless of the course focus.

Clearer differences emerged in the content of the classes. IELTS classes had a greater focus on form: on points of grammar and vocabulary. EAP classes were more concerned with discourse. IELTS classes involved more frequent changes of topic and topics appeared more incidental to the programme. In EAP classes single topics were more often maintained through a sequence of activities.

Above all, IELTS classes were dominated by the test. Classes were directed explicitly towards ensuring success on the test. There were frequent mentions of IELTS and of strategies for dealing with the test tasks. Most of the materials used were either taken from IELTS text books or chosen by the teacher to reflect the content of the test. Frequent essay writing practice involved test practice under timed conditions and completing tasks closely modelled on IELTS. Feedback was often provided in the form of IELTS band scores. In contrast, EAP classes generally involved little mention of tests and offered a wider range of teaching points. There was greater variety in the length of essays, including lengthy texts of over 3,000 words. Teachers did not regard IELTS preparation material as a useful resource for their EAP classes.

Grammar and vocabulary tests

Grammar and vocabulary tests were administered at course entry and at course exit. These provided a means of identifying group differences in grammatical and lexical knowledge as well as relating this knowledge to Writing score gains.

From the descriptive statistics displayed in Table 5.8, it is clear that most learners already possessed at least some knowledge of the majority of words on the Academic Word List with a mean score of 25 out of 30 points at course entry. As a result, the distributions of scores on the vocabulary test were strongly negatively skewed. However, composite scores composed of the sum of the vocabulary and grammar test scores were more normally distributed (Figure 5.27) and were used in the subsequent analyses.

Table 5.8 Descriptive statistics for grammar and vocabulary tests

	Initial vocabulary	Exit vocabulary	Initial grammar	Exit grammar
Mean	25.01	26.53	31.93	34.04
Median	27	28	32	34
Mode	29	30	33	32
Std. Deviation	5.40	4.23	6.75	6.43
Variance	29.15	17.88	45.53	41.38
Skewness	−1.57	−1.89	−0.22	−0.38
Kurtosis	2.18	3.97	−0.45	−0.12
Range	26	25	35	39
Minimum	4	5	13	11
Maximum	30	30	48	50

Paired sample t-tests showed significant gains (p<.01) across course types. As displayed in Figure 5.29, the highest average gains occurred on IELTS preparation courses. However, as these learners also had the lowest initial scores the difference may simply reflect entry status or a ceiling effect (an upper limit on the scores higher-level learners were able to reach).

Figure 5.27 Histogram (with normal curve) showing distribution of composite grammar vocabulary scores at course entry

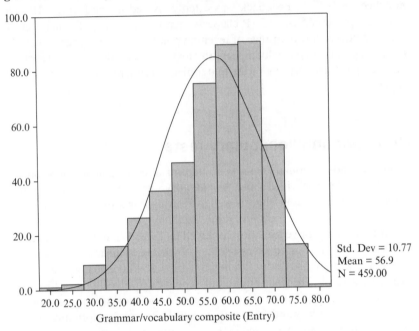

In order to investigate the contribution of intervening variables to grammar and vocabulary gains, a repeated measures analysis of covariance was carried out (Table 5.10). Course Type and Student Region of Origin were fixed factors and Course Length and Student Age were covariates. There was a significant effect for Course Type, Course Length and Student Age, but when covariates were taken into account, IELTS preparation students were seen to make the least gain in their grammar and vocabulary composite scores (Figure 5.30).

The surveys of teachers revealed that those on IELTS courses felt that they were directing more attention to grammar and vocabulary than their counterparts on other courses – perhaps in response to test demands expressed in the scoring rubric (Vocabulary and Sentence Structure is the only criterion for rating shared by both Task 1 and Task 2). However, these results suggest that learners on courses that include a more general EAP focus, with less explicit attention to grammar on the part of teachers, outperform those on IELTS courses in spite of the greater focus on grammar on the latter.

Figure 5.28 Histogram (with normal curve) showing distribution of composite grammar vocabulary scores at course exit

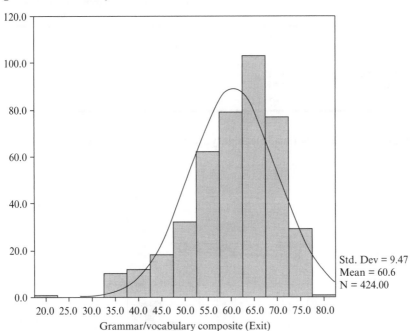

Std. Dev = 9.47
Mean = 60.6
N = 424.00

Grammar/vocabulary composite (Exit)

Summary

This chapter has pointed to a level of awareness among participants of discrepancies between IELTS preparation and the academic writing construct described in Chapter 2. Awareness of these discrepancies was greater among those with experience of pre-sessional EAP as well as IELTS. Questionnaire and interview data confirmed that, in their preparation classes, students expected test-taking practice and expected activities that emulated the IELTS test tasks. Reflecting areas of the academic writing construct under-represented in the IELTS test, pre-sessional EAP students were more likely to expect to write long texts and to use information from external sources in their writing.

At the end of their courses, students preparing for IELTS reported significantly more emphasis on taking practice tests, learning to describe graphs and diagrams, time management skills and learning of general vocabulary. Students on pre-sessional EAP courses, conversely, reported learning about the writing tasks they would encounter at university, using evidence to support arguments, taking notes from lectures, using ideas from sources in

Table 5.9 Descriptive statistics for grammar and vocabulary test score gains

	Vocab. score gain	Grammar score gain	Grammar/vocab. score gain
Minimum	−12	−13	−25
Maximum	25	15	26
Mean	1.318	1.879	3.138
Std. Deviation	3.341	4.065	5.348
Skewness	1.609	−0.075	0.119
Kurtosis	8.291	0.840	3.365

Figure 5.29 Grammar and vocabulary score gains by Course Type

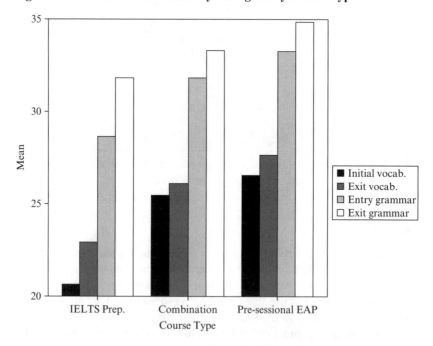

their writing, writing long reports and reading about their own subject areas. There was evidence for the influence of instruction in mediating washback to the learner in the convergence of student ratings with teacher reports on course content.

Although IELTS preparation students felt the most confident about taking an IELTS test at the end of their courses, those on pre-sessional EAP courses claimed to make the most gain in overall writing ability in English. Self-assessed gain in the ability to draw on written sources in composition was also greatest for pre-sessional learners. In addition, this group reported greater confidence about studying at university and appeared to have more

Table 5.10 Repeated Measures Analysis of Covariance. Tests of between-subjects effects

Source	Type III Sum of Squares	df	Mean Square	F	Sig.
Intercept	57720.264	1	57720.264	445.616	.000
Course Length	7229.365	1	7229.365	55.813	.000
Student Age	1604.121	1	1604.121	12.384	.000
Course Type	2057.286	2	1028.643	7.941	.000
Student Region of Origin	551.183	3	183.728	1.418	.237
Course Type Student Region of Origin	4654.717	6	775.786	5.989	.000
Error	46241.909	357	129.529		

Figure 5.30 Means plot of exit grammar/vocabulary scores (maximum score = 80) controlling for Initial GV Scores, Student Age, Course Length and student Region of Origin

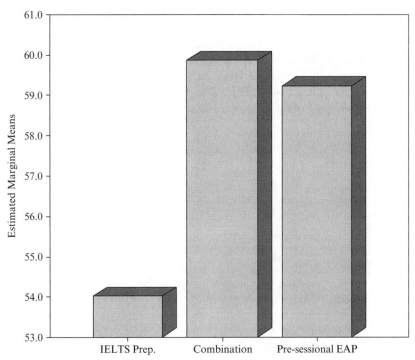

realistic expectations of the amount of support they could expect from university teachers. However, as more of these learners already had some experience of university study in their own countries, their greater awareness of the university context could have arisen from this prior experience rather than from the nature of their language courses.

Reflecting the emphasis on test-taking strategies reported by students and teachers, IELTS preparation students increased their knowledge of the test and their use of test-taking strategies at course exit. However, IELTS students made least gain in grammar and vocabulary test scores, despite reporting that they had learned grammar and vocabulary in their classes. It may be that the students were mistaken about the amount of grammar they were learning (teachers did not share their students' impression that more grammar was being studied on IELTS courses). Perhaps the narrow focus of the IELTS courses limited learning of grammar and vocabulary to items their teachers considered of relevance to the test, but that were not represented to the same extent in the test instrument used here.

The analyses described in this chapter have revealed differences in the content of courses and in the expectations participants bring to IELTS and pre-sessional EAP courses. It is clear on this evidence that the IELTS test has a strong influence on what participants choose to teach and study. The analyses have also revealed differences between individual learners on the focal courses. Learner background variables play a pivotal role in predicting how learners approach the task of studying English, regardless of whether the focus of their courses is on IELTS or EAP. The following chapter will examine the impact of the differences described above on Writing test scores.

6

Main study results II

Introduction

The third phase of the study set out to discover whether and how test preparation had in any way contributed to IELTS score gain for the participating students. Had there, as anticipated by participants in the pilot studies, been a quantifiable premium in terms of Writing score gain associated with taking IELTS preparation courses?

The washback literature reviewed in Chapter 1 also predicts that instruction directed towards test demands will result in higher, but less interpretable, scores. Was this the case for preparation courses directed towards the IELTS Academic Writing Test? How far did test preparation contribute to score gains when weighed with other salient variables?

In this chapter the improvement made by learners participating in the main study in Writing test performance is described. This improvement is expressed in terms of gain scores (the product of subtracting Initial Writing scores from Exit Writing scores). Next, a diagnostic model is described for the prediction of exit Writing scores on the basis of initial test scores and questionnaire data. The chapter concerns the amount of gain made by learners following instruction and relates these score gains to research questions four and five:

4. *Do instructional alternatives at points on a continuum from IELTS-driven to IELTS-unrelated EAP courses result in differential outcomes in terms of:*
   - *gains in scores on the IELTS Academic Module?*
   - *linguistic (lexico-grammatical) proficiency gains?*
   - *academic awareness and study skills gains?*
5. *Do facets of learners' individual differences interact with instructional differences in predicting outcomes?*

Results: Score gains on the IELTS Writing test

In an overview of language gain study methods, Ross (1998) sets out two assumptions that must be met to justify inferences of score gain. Firstly, that a significant gain in score values has occurred and second that the instruments used are reliable. If the inference of gains in criterion abilities is to be justified, further assumptions must also be fulfilled, but it is these two that are of immediate concern here.

Paired t-tests were used to investigate the first of these questions. The results (Table 6.1) indicated that a significant (p<.01) gain in Writing scores had indeed occurred on all three course types. Taken as a whole, the learners improved their Writing scores by an average of 0.207 of a band score. The mean score gains on the three course types were:

IELTS preparation: .187 (Initial: 5.129; Exit: 5.315)
Pre-sessional EAP: .191 (Initial: 5.3740; Exit: 5.5651)
Combination: .324 (Initial: 4.8818; Exit: 5.2053)

Table 6.1 Paired sample t-tests comparing initial and exit Writing scores on three Course Types. Paired Samples Test – Initial Writing: Exit Writing

			Course Type		
			IELTS	Combination	Pre-sessional
Paired differences	Mean		−.187	−.324	−.191
	Std. Deviation		.561	.685	.582
	Std. Error Mean		.061	.088	.032
	95% Confidence Interval of the Difference	Lower	−.308	−.501	−.254
		Upper	−.066	−.146	−.128
t			−3.071	−3.657	−5.973
df			84	59	330
Sig. (2-tailed)			.003	.001	.000

The second assumption, that the test instruments are reliable, is explained by Ross (1998). Although changes in language performances over time imply that there has been gain, this assumption rests on the reliability of the tests administered at both points in time. In order to estimate the reliability of the gain score, and given that there has been a significant gain, the internal consistency of both the pre-intervention and post-intervention measurements must be known. These reliability figures can be used in conjunction with the correlation between the pre- and post-intervention scores.

In order to estimate whether apparent score gains for individual learners might have occurred by chance, it is necessary to consider the reliability of the test instruments employed. Ross (1998) provides the following formula, derived from Zimmerman and Williams (1982) for computing the reliability of gain scores, taking into account the assumption that learners' scores show greater variation before instruction than after:

$$r_{dd} = \frac{\lambda_1 \, r_{xx} + \lambda_2 \, r_{yy} - 2r_{xy}}{\lambda_1 + \lambda_2 - 2r_{xy}}$$

r_{xx} is the internal consistency of the pre-test
r_{yy} is the internal consistency of the post-test
r_{xy} is the product moment correlation between the two tests
λ_1 is the ratio of pre- to post-test standard deviations
λ_2 is the ratio of post- to pre-test standard deviations

The multifaceted Rasch procedure described in Chapter 4 adjusts test scores to take account of error associated with differential task difficulty and rater severity. Nonetheless, the fair average scores obtained include an element of error variance, which limits the confidence we can place in the resulting scores. In applying the gain score reliability formula to the results of the Writing tests, the reliability estimate of .94 derived from the FACETS analysis, described in Chapter 4, was employed as an indicator of internal consistency. The standard deviations for the entry and exit test administrations (0.67 and 0.61) and the correlation between Initial Writing scores and Exit Writing scores (0.570), yielded .861 as an estimate of gain score reliability.

One of the advantages of estimating reliability in classical true score theory is that it enables us, through the standard error of measurement, to attach a confidence band to test scores and their derivatives, such as gain scores. Calculating a standard error of measurement on the basis of this reliability figure enables us to predict with a 95% probability that an individual's true gain score would fall within 0.422 of a band above or below their observed gain score. Thus, any Writing score gains greater than 0.630 of a band made by an individual learner are unlikely to be attributable to measurement error, but would indicate better performance, as measured against the IELTS criteria, on the second test.

Figure 6.1 shows that the scores on the Initial and Exit Writing tests were normally distributed, an assumption underlying the use of parametric statistical analyses such as the t-tests described above. The distribution of scores also demonstrates that the raters were making use of a range of levels – between Bands 3 and 8 on the IELTS scale – to score the scripts they were given.

The scores on the Exit Writing test were somewhat negatively skewed (see Figure 6.1). This is also consistent with improvement following instruction as learners who enter with lower scores, and study for longer, improve their test performance more at time two than do their initially higher scoring peers.

Taken as a whole, the score gains fell well short of the figure previously suggested by the IELTS partners of a half band for each month (100 hours) of study (the mean length of study here being 5.5 weeks or 130 hours).

Figure 6.1 Distribution of Initial and Exit Writing (AWM) scores

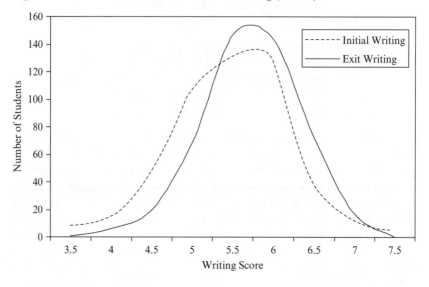

Figure 6.2 Distribution of Writing score gains

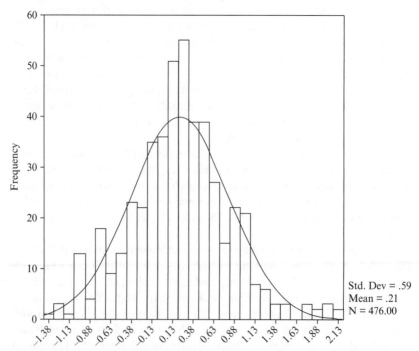

Although gains in FACETS fair average scores of as much as two bands were observed (the highest gain was 2.08 bands), these were exceptional, with just three of the 476 learners gaining by two bands or more and only 39 (8.2%) gaining by one band or more. The three highest gainers all had fair average scores below Band 4 on the initial test. All were studying for at least nine weeks on pre-sessional (2) or combination (1) courses, all came from East Asia (one Chinese, one Japanese and one Korean) and two of the three were intending to take an IELTS test.

As shown in Figure 6.3, the majority of the 39 students making gains of one band or more in their Writing scores were studying on courses with a course length of between eight and 10 weeks (that is between eight and 10 weeks between testing occasions), while just 13% were studying on courses with between two and four weeks between tests.

Figure 6.3 Period between Writing tests (in weeks) for learners making Writing score gains of one band or more

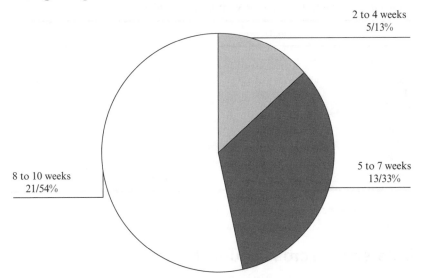

Most learners made gains, in terms of fair average scores, of less than one band, with 61% (66% on IELTS preparation, 57% on combination and 61% on pre-sessional courses) making an improvement of between zero and one band between time one and time two. As many as 31% of students had lower scores on the second test (31% on IELTS preparation, 32% on combination and 31% on pre-sessional EAP courses). The greatest score loss between testing occasions was 1.34 bands.

Five of the eight learners whose scores fell by a band or more had scored Band 6 or higher on the initial test. Seven of the eight were East Asian (three were Chinese, one Taiwanese, one Korean, one Japanese, one Thai and one Greek). Seven were studying on pre-sessional EAP courses and one on an IELTS preparation course (the only one of the group intending to take an IELTS test). Six of the eight were studying for four to five weeks with a total of between 80 and 115 hours of instruction (the other two were studying for periods of three and nine weeks between tests with, respectively, 69 and 207 hours of instruction). All but one were aged over 26 and intending to study at postgraduate level.

Table 6.2 shows that the highest score on the Exit Writing test was somewhat lower than that for the Initial Writing test, while the lowest score was much the same on both occasions. Again this is consistent with greater gains for learners on longer courses, with lower initial scorers gaining more than their counterparts with higher scores who were, typically, studying on shorter courses.

Table 6.2 Descriptive statistics for fair average scores on the Writing test at Time One and Time Two and for Writing score gains

	Initial score	Exit score	Writing score gain
N	476	476	476
Mean	5.27	5.48	0.21
Median	5.30	5.49	0.20
Mode	5.00	5.53	0.09[a]
Std. Deviation	0.67	0.61	0.59
Variance	0.44	0.37	0.35
Skewness	−0.24	−0.39	0.19
Kurtosis	0.57	0.45	0.54
Range	4.41	3.9	3.42
Minimum	3.06	3.09	−1.34
Maximum	7.47	6.99	2.08

[a] *Multiple modes exist. The smallest value is shown*

Differences across course types

On average, learners on combination courses, those including both EAP and avowedly IELTS directed content, made the most gain in their Writing scores (Figure 6.4) (from a mean band score of 4.88 to 5.21). The combination courses were also the most diverse both in the Initial Writing scores obtained by students (with a standard deviation of 0.81 compared to 0.69 on IELTS preparation and 0.53 on pre-sessional EAP courses) and in Course Length (standard deviation: 68.1 hours; IELTS preparation: 49.7 hours; pre-sessional EAP: 51.3 hours).

Ranking the learners into five groups of roughly equal size on the basis of their Writing score gains (see Table 6.4) provides for broad comparisons

Table 6.3 Descriptive statistics: Course Length (in weeks and hours) and Initial and Exit Writing scores by Course Type

Course Type		Minimum	Maximum	Mean	Std. Deviation
IELTS Prep.	Course Length (weeks)	3.00	10.00	4.84	1.17
	Course Length (hours)	8.00	230.00	92.28	49.74
	Initial Writing Score	3.61	7.47	5.13	.69
	Exit Writing Score	3.57	6.99	5.32	.66
Combination	Course Length (weeks)	3.00	9.00	5.92	2.71
	Course Length (hours)	63.00	225.00	132.92	68.10
	Initial Writing Score	3.06	6.26	4.88	.81
	Exit Writing Score	3.09	6.52	5.21	.77
Pre-sessional EAP	Course Length (weeks)	3.00	10.00	5.56	2.21
	Course Length (hours)	69.00	210.00	139.83	51.29
	Initial Writing Score	3.64	7.14	5.37	.60
	Exit Writing Score	3.81	6.97	5.57	.53

Figure 6.4 Initial and Exit Writing scores (on the 9-band IELTS scale) by Course Type

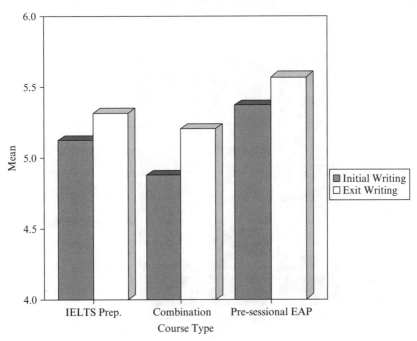

between course types. Plotting the proportion of learners on each of the course types falling into these fair average gain groups (Figure 6.5), it can be seen that the combination courses had the highest percentage of learners in both the high and low gain groups. However, there was no clear advantage in score gains for either IELTS or pre-sessional course types; similar proportions of learners on both course types were placed in each of the five groups.

The results of the analysis of covariance set out in Table 6.5 show that, when Initial Writing scores were taken into account, there was a significant

Table 6.4 Five levels of Writing score gain: divided at the 20th, 40th, 60th and 80th percentile ranks

IELTS Writing Gain	N	Minimum	Maximum	Mean	Std. Deviation
Low Gain	96	−1.34	−.25	−.62	.28
–	99	−.24	.09	−.05	.11
Medium Gain	93	.10	.32	.21	.06
–	96	.33	.65	.48	.10
High Gain	92	.66	2.08	1.06	.36

Figure 6.5 IELTS Writing gain by Course Type

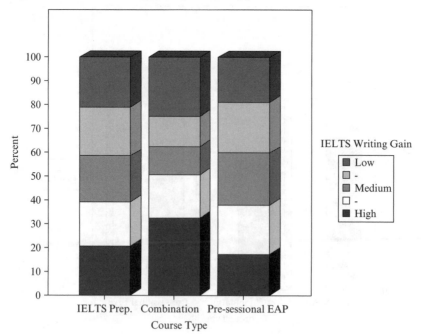

Table 6.5 Analysis of covariance: Writing gain by Course Type, controlling for Initial Writing score and Course Length (in hours). Tests of between-subjects effects

Source	Type III Sum of Squares	df	Mean Square	F	Sig.
Corrected Model	52.650[a]	4	13.162	53.720	.000
Intercept	32.417	1	32.417	132.303	.000
Initial Writing Score	39.007	1	39.007	159.199	.000
Course Length in Hours	1.631	1	1.631	6.655	.010
Course Type	.519	2	.259	1.058	.348
Error	115.404	471	.245		
Total	188.491	476			
Corrected Total	168.054	475			

[a] *R Squared = .313 (Adjusted R Squared = .307)*

effect for Course Length, but no significant effect for Course Type. There is little support here for the belief expressed by participants in the pilot studies described in Chapter 3 and the interviews in Chapter 5 that courses directed towards the IELTS test are more effective than broader-based EAP pre-sessional courses in boosting IELTS Writing scores.

Figure 6.6 shows Initial and Exit Writing scores by Course. As the numbers on many of the individual courses were limited, the variation in outcomes cannot be taken as an indication of relative effectiveness. However, gains did occur on all but one course (the exception, at College B, being a part-time IELTS familiarisation course and the briefest in the study in terms of contact hours). It is also notable that only one course (at University C) achieved average gains of over one band. This was a pre-sessional EAP, not an IELTS preparation course, and had the longest period between testing occasions (10 weeks).

In keeping with the general observation that those with the lowest scores on the initial test tended to make the greatest gains, the students on the University C course scored poorly on the initial test in comparison with those on other courses. Although the results for College B and University C were consistent with the trend observed elsewhere for lower scoring students on the initial test to make greater gains, the strength of the effect at these two centres is atypical. As each contributed just 12 students to the study, the small number of learners probably accounts for the somewhat unusual results. University C also participated in the observational phase of the study (see Chapter 5) and the observed classes were consistent with practices on courses of the same type at other universities.

Figure 6.6 Writing score gains by Course

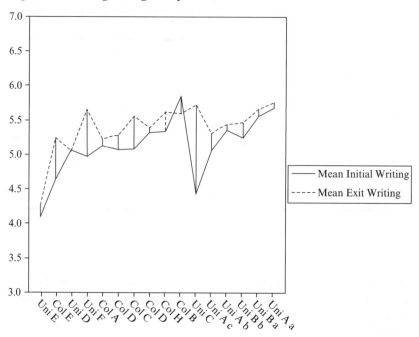

At Universities A and B, which each contributed more than one course to the study, gains were higher on the longer courses, which set lower entry demands for students. However, learners on the longer courses (nine to ten weeks between testing occasions) did not reach the same level at course exit as the students on the briefer courses (with three or six weeks between tests) in spite of the additional period of study.

Until 2003, the IELTS partners advised, as a broad guideline, that learners intending to study at higher education institutions in the UK should study for up to 200 hours to allow an improvement of one band on the IELTS test (IELTS 2001). This advice was taken up by BALEAP (Bool, Dunmore and Tonkyn 1999, Bool, Tonkyn, Schmitt and Ward-Goodbody 2003) in their advice to course providers and is commonly followed on university pre-sessional courses. These courses typically accept learners presenting IELTS scores half a band below the standard required for entry to academic courses for one month of intensive English study and those presenting scores one band below the entry standard for two months. However, in terms of Writing test scores, longer periods of instruction do not appear to compensate for lower entry scores to the extent anticipated in the partners' recommendations.

There are relationships between group differences and levels of gain. Writing score gains are connected with the status of learners at course entry.

Those with lower scores on entry are likely to make more substantial measured gains, while those scoring comparatively high at entry may make no improvement in their scores. Differences in Writing score gains between groups with different band scores at entry outweighed any differences between Course Types.

Consideration of the gains made on the three Course Types leads to the following conclusions:

Writing score gains occurred across Course Types. On average, learners on all three Course Types made significant gains in their Writing scores between Time One and Time Two.

There was no evidence of any substantial IELTS preparation effect in terms of test outcomes. There were no significant differences between Course Types in terms of Writing score gains.

Score gains were limited. Less than 10% of learners made gains of more than one band, while one third of all learners scored lower on the second test. Students, whether on IELTS-directed courses or not, did not generally appear to gain in their Writing scores at the rate of one band in 200 hours as had been suggested by the IELTS partners.

Score gains varied with Initial Writing scores. Recommendations for periods of study based on a single figure across skills for learners at different levels of ability are therefore likely to be misleading.

Prediction models

To address the question of whether variables other than Course Type contributed more to score gains, a predictive model was developed. Using the extensive database of information on each student provided by Questionnaires A and B, the IELTS Awareness Forms and Test Taking Strategy Inventories, constellations of variables were sought that would make possible the accurate prediction of Exit Writing scores. As outlined in Chapters 3 and 4, the questionnaires targeted:

presage variables – such as details of learners' backgrounds and their language proficiencies at course entry

process variables – such as course length, teaching objectives and learning strategies, and

product variables – course outcomes such as grammar and vocabulary test scores and self-ratings of gains in academic writing skills.

The first step in predicting Exit Writing scores on this basis was to identify those variables (or features as they are termed in neural network nomenclature) likely to contribute most to the prediction of Writing score gains.

The predictive models were based on two competing approaches; the first a traditional statistical approach employing linear regression and the second an artificial intelligence approach using a neural network. Given that both linear and neural network approaches impose limits on the number of variables or features that may be included in analysis (Green 1991, Garson 1998), an *a priori* selection process was required. In a preliminary phase, features demonstrating insufficient variance to contribute any meaningful information were eliminated. For example, only seven respondents to Questionnaire A (1.7% of respondents) claimed a NS parent, so this feature was excluded from further consideration.

Then, setting aside a proportion (20%) of the cases as a model-testing set to provide an estimate of the generalisability of the models (the same set in both cases), input features were correlated with gains in IELTS Writing scores. Features that displayed a significant correlation with Writing score gain were selected for further analysis. In order to identify non-linear relationships, the data was then plotted to explore patterns of association between features and Writing score gains. Where there appeared from the data plot to be a clear non-linear relationship between a feature and Writing score gains, the feature was also flagged for further analysis. Partial correlations, controlling for Initial Writing score were also calculated to provide additional insights into the likely contribution of features to prediction.

In this way a total of 17 presage and 17 process or product variables were identified as input features (independent variables), with Exit Writing score as the desired feature (dependent variable). These included category variables such as Level of Intended Study, which were each treated as multiple features, coded as one or zero for input to the network. Intended Level of Study thus provided four features:

Intended Level of Study = Pre-University

Intended Level of Study = Undergraduate

Intended Level of Study = Postgraduate

Intended Level of Study = Other

A student who intended to study at postgraduate level would be presented to the network as an input vector including a string of, '0010' corresponding to these four features. For the purposes of linear regression, it is customary to eliminate one of these dummy variables to avoid over determination (one of the dummy variables is redundant, as it is simply the negative of the sum of the others). However, in training a neural network, this is unnecessary.

There were a number of cases of missing records in the data, either because individuals had not completed the full set of questionnaire instruments, or because they had omitted one or more items on a questionnaire form. All such cases were replaced with mean values for the feature. In neural network models, mean values do not affect the network weights and are effectively ignored in training.

Presage features

Presage features identified as potential predictors of Writing score gains included those shown in Box 6.1. Correlations with Writing score gains are displayed for each feature, together with the partial correlation controlling for the effect of Initial Writing score. For individual questionnaire items, as these are ranked data, non-parametric correlations (Spearman's rho) are provided in brackets.

Box 6.1

Questionnaire A	r	partial r
Student Background		
2. Student Age	$-.176$	$-.115$
3. Student Region of Origin – China/Taiwan	$-.067$	$-.117$
Student Region of Origin – Western Europe	$-.042$	.120
4. Use of English at Work	.105 (.082)	.041
Section 1: Motivation for Study		
RE1 (*I am taking this course to get a good grade on IELTS or other test*)	.126 (.128)	.061
RE2 (*I am taking this course to learn useful skills for university*)	.112 (.058)	.147
Section 2: Orientation to the Study Context		
SC11 (*I usually enjoy meeting English people*)	.131 (.100)	.185
Self Confidence in English Writing Ability	.038	.184
Section 3: Expectations for Language Study		
CE24 (*I expect to take practice tests in class*)	.135 (.099)	$-.044$
Test Knowledge Form		
7. Level of Previous Education = Secondary School	.213	.054
11. Level of Intended Study = Undergraduate	.140	$-.165$
12. Previous IELTS Score	$-.133$	.110
13. Intention to Take IELTS	.103	$-.018$
Test Taking Strategies		
Time (minutes) spent on Task 2 on Initial Writing test	$-.130$	$-.013$
Initial Tests		
Initial Grammar Score	$-.149$	.035
Initial Vocabulary Score	$-.119$	.093
Initial Writing Score	$-.530$	

Negative correlations indicate that higher scores on the variable are associated with lower score gains

Although students in all age groups increased their scores from Time One to Time Two, in common with many studies of language gain (see reviews in Spolsky 1989, Ellis 1994, Ross 1998), younger learners were found to make greater improvements in their Writing scores. Although under-eighteens had the lowest scores at entry, the greatest gains were made by those aged between 19 and 22 years (Figure 6.7). Students in the 29 to 35 year-old cohort made the least improvement. Against the general trend, learners in the over 35 age group achieved the highest scores both at course entry and exit (although the small number of learners in this cohort – 24 – may help to explain their surprisingly high results, given the distribution of scores among other cohorts).

Figure 6.7 Mean Initial and Exit Writing score gains (on the 9-band IELTS scale) by Age

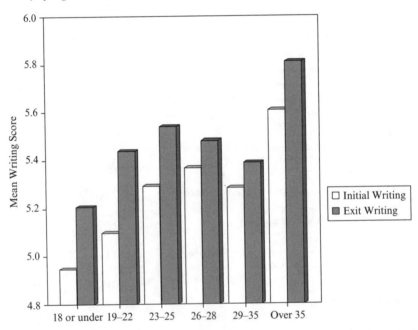

Under-eighteens experienced the lowest scores on both occasions. The poor performance of the youngest learners is consistent with the observation made by interview participants (Chapter 5) that maturity and knowledge of the world would be advantageous for IELTS candidates. However, as might be expected, the advantage did not appear to grow in linear fashion with increasing age. The 29 to 35 year-olds were outperformed on the Initial Writing test by 26 to 28 year-olds and were overtaken by 19 to 22 year-olds at

Exit. Similarly, 23 to 25 year-olds overtook 26 to 28 year-olds, achieving higher scores at Time Two.

Student Region of Origin (Figure 6.8) also appeared strongly related to Writing score gains. Membership of the China/Taiwan cohort and of the Western Europe cohort were both negatively correlated with score gains. Western Europeans outscored other groups on both occasions, but the China/Taiwan group fell from second place on the initial test to third place at exit. Although on average Western Europeans made less gain than learners in the Other and Other East Asian categories, when learners at a similar level of performance on the initial test are compared (Figure 6.8) it is clear that the Western Europeans outperformed their peers. A repeated measures analysis of covariance carried out on the model-building set (Table 6.6) confirms this impression, with Western Europeans making significantly greater gains than all three other groups when Initial Writing scores are taken into account.

Figure 6.8 Mean Writing score gain by student Region of Origin at Initial Writing Score 4.5 to 5.5 on the 9-band IELTS scale

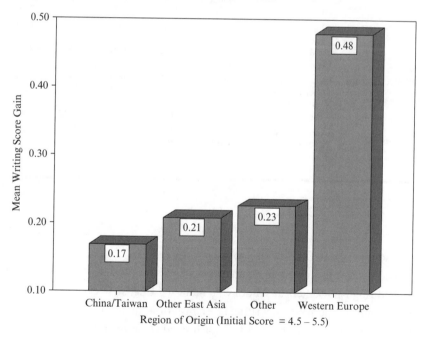

Learners scoring higher on both tests tended to be those who:

* had experience of using English at work or for socialising
* reported more frequent reading and writing in English

Table 6.6 Repeated measures analysis of covariance Measure: Initial Writing score: Exit Writing score

Transformed Variable: Average

Source	Type III Sum of Squares	df	Mean Square	F	Sig.
Intercept	15925.215	1	15925.215	26704.100	.000
Region of Origin	21.281	3	7.094	11.895	.000
Error	224.827	377	.596		

Post Hoc Bonferroni Tests

(I) Region of Origin	(J) Region of Origin	Mean Difference (I−J)	Std. Error	Sig.	95% Confidence Interval	
					Lower Bound	Upper Bound
China/Taiwan	China/Taiwan					
	Other East Asia	.0881	.07615	1.000	−.1138	.2901
	Western Europe	−.4862(*)	.08886	.000	−.7218	−.2505
	Other	−.0138	.08208	1.000	−.2315	.2039
Other East Asia	China/Taiwan	−.0881	.07615	1.000	−.2901	.1138
	Other East Asia					
	Western Europe	−.5743(*)	.10425	.000	−.8508	−.2978
	Other	−.1019	.09854	1.000	−.3633	.1594
Western Europe	China/Taiwan	.4862(*)	.08886	.000	.2505	.7218
	Other East Asia	.5743(*)	.10425	.000	.2978	.8508
	Western Europe					
	Other	.4724(*)	.10866	.000	.1842	.7606
Other	China/Taiwan	.0138	.08208	1.000	−.2039	.2315
	Other East Asia	.1019	.09854	1.000	−.1594	.3633
	Western Europe	−.4724(*)	.10866	.000	−.7606	−.1842
	Other					

Based on observed means.
* *The mean difference is significant at the .05 level.*

- had majored in English at university
- had studied in English medium classes
- had English teachers at school who had used English in class
- had more experience of writing in English or in their L1
- had not been taught by native English speakers in their own countries.

Of these features, only the use of English at work was significantly ($p < .01$) correlated with score gains. Those who had no experience of using English at work were able to make greater score gains. It may be that this correlation merely reflects other relationships in the data; these learners were younger and scored lower on the initial tests than their counterparts, both features associated with higher gains. However, there may be an implication that students with more experience of using English in academic and professional settings found it more difficult to improve their Writing scores.

Attitudes towards IELTS

A number of items on Questionnaire A and on the Test Knowledge Form addressed learners' attitudes and intentions towards the IELTS test. These included the question of whether students were intending to take an IELTS test, motivations for study, and expectations regarding the content of classes. Section 1 on Questionnaire A asked students to respond to statements about their motivations for study on a 5-point Likert scale, from 0 (I definitely disagree) to 4 (I definitely agree). Higher ratings for item RE1 (I am taking this course because I want to get a good grade on IELTS (or other test/assessment) were associated with both lower initial scores and higher score gains (Figure 6.9).

Figure 6.9 Mean Initial and Exit Writing scores by RE1 (*I am taking this course because I want to get a good grade on IELTS or other test/assessment*). Maximum score = 4

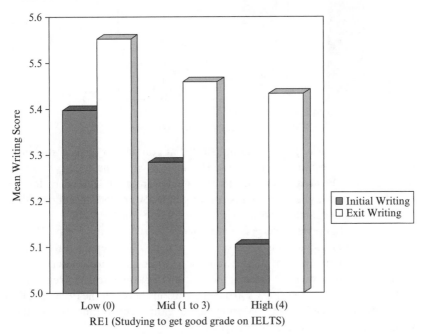

RE1 (Studying to get good grade on IELTS)

In Section 3, which followed the same format as Section 1, respondents rated statements about expectations of their courses. Item CE24 (I expect to take practice tests in class) was also associated with lower initial scores and higher score gains. As can be seen in Figure 6.10, mean Exit Writing scores were very similar across groups at approximately 5.47. However, this represented greater gain for those giving a rating of 4 to CE24 (0.29 of a band) than for those giving ratings of between 0 and 2 (0.11 of a band).

Figure 6.10 Mean Initial and Exit Writing Scores by CE24 (*I expect to take practice tests in class*). Maximum score = 4

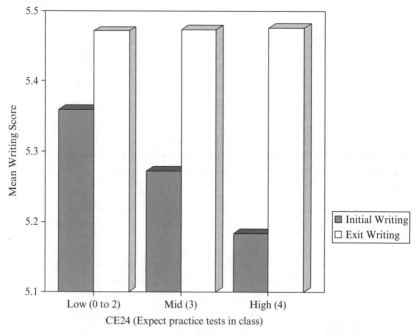

The Test Knowledge Form administered at course entry asked students whether they were intending to take an IELTS test within the next six months (Figure 6.11). Positive responses to this item were again linked to lower initial scores and higher score gains, although the lower scoring group on the initial test did not catch up with their higher scoring counterparts.

Although the correlations between students' motivation to take an IELTS test and greater score gains suggest that learners who prepare for the test make greater improvement, there are reasons to be cautious in interpreting this finding. Those with the greatest motivation to pass the test also tended to score lower on both occasions. Partial correlations between the three IELTS preparation indicators and Writing score gains, controlling for Initial Writing score, were not significant (p<.05).

Figure 6.11 Mean Initial and Exit Writing scores by Intention to Take IELTS

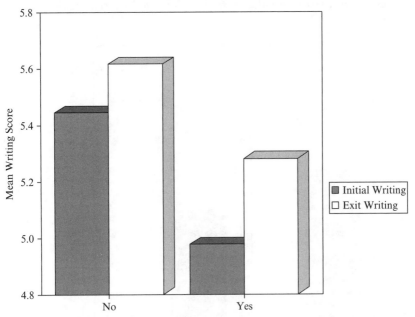

Other items addressing motivation for study which were positively cor-related with Writing score gains, but unrelated to the IELTS test, included RE2 (I am taking this course because I want to learn useful skills for study-ing at university) and SC11 (I usually enjoy meeting British people). These items also involved rating statements on a 5-point scale from 0 (I definitely disagree) to 4 (I definitely agree).

Figure 6.12 and Figure 6.13 show that those giving lower ratings to these items (I tend to agree, I tend to disagree or I definitely disagree) made less gain than those who gave the highest rating of four points (I definitely agree). These results support findings reported elsewhere (Hawkey 1982, Skehan 1989 for example) that sources of motivation other than the need to pass a test may be predictive of language gain.

Self Confidence in English Writing Ability was also positively associated with score gains (Figure 6.14). This was a scale made up of the following items; SC01 (People say that I am good at language learning), SC03 (I usually did better than other students at my school in English classes), SC05 (I am NOT good at writing in English – reversed), SC06 (I feel I will never really enjoy writing in English – reversed), SC07 (Writing classes are difficult for me – reversed), SC12 (I think learning languages is more difficult for me

Figure 6.12 Initial and Exit Writing Scores by RE2 (*I am taking this course because I want to learn useful skills for studying at university*). Maximum score = 4

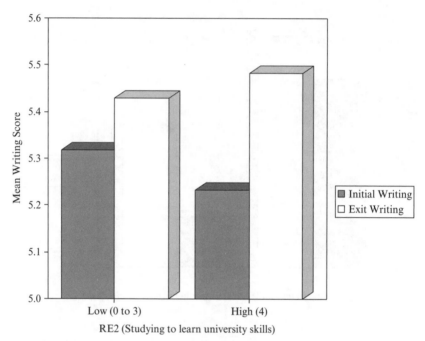

RE2 (Studying to learn university skills)

than for the average learner – reversed), SC14 (I DON'T think I write in English as well as other students – reversed), SC15 (It is easy for me to write good English essays) and SC19 (I enjoy writing in English). Dividing students into three groups on the basis of their scores on the Self Confidence scale, all three groups made a mean score gain of 0.203, but the mean Initial Writing score was highest for the most confident students (5.43) and lowest for the least confident (5.06). As score gains were generally lowest for those scoring highest at entry, there appears to be an advantage for students who are confident of their ability to write in English.

Test measures

Of the variables investigated, Initial Writing score provided the highest correlation with Exit Writing scores at r = 0.57. There was an almost equally strong negative correlation of r = −0.51 between Initial Writing and Writing score gains, while Exit Writing scores were correlated with Writing score gain at r = 0.41. In short, the higher the Initial Writing score, the less the Writing score gain.

Figure 6.13 Initial and Exit Writing scores by SC11 (*I usually enjoy meeting British people*). Maximum score = 4

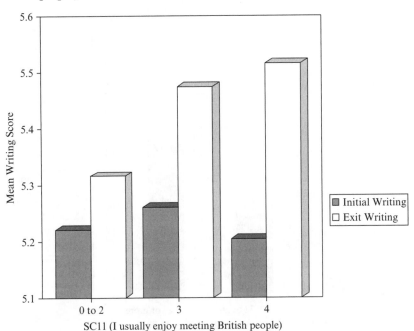

SC11 (I usually enjoy meeting British people)

The relationship between score gains and initial and exit measures is displayed in Figure 6.15, with the model-building set divided into five groups of equal size at the 20th, 40th, 60th and 80th percentiles. Those making the greatest gains scored below the mean on the Initial Writing test and above the mean at Exit, while those making losses of more than 0.25 of a band typically scored above the mean at Time One and below the mean at Time Two.

The variation in Writing scores between testing occasions, including score losses for one third of the sample, is indicative of measurement error. The multifaceted Rasch procedure adjusts scores for rater severity and task difficulty, thus minimising the contribution of these facets to the variance in the fair average scores. This suggests the influence of other sources of error in the data.

Insights into a possible source of this error were afforded by the self-report items administered after each Writing test. The second and third items on the forms asked learners to indicate how long (in minutes) they had spent on each of the two writing tasks. Those spending least time on Task 2 on the initial test achieved the lowest Initial Writing scores, but made the most gain (Figure 6.16). It seems that time management may be an important factor

Figure 6.14 Initial and Exit Writing scores by Self Confidence in English Writing Ability. Maximum score = 36

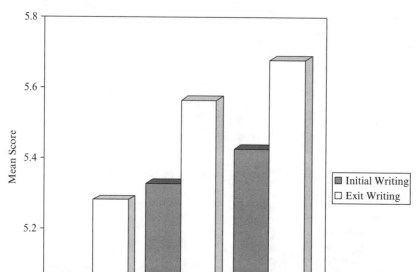

limiting the scores of those who under-perform on the test; too much time spent on the first task restricts the time available for the second. These learners on average spent longer on Task 2 on the second test (34.1 minutes compared with 28.1 on the first).

Students also rated statements on their perceptions of each test task on a scale ranging from 0 (I definitely disagree) to 4 (I definitely agree). The first three items included, (1) I understood the question; (2) I had enough ideas to write about this topic; and (3) I had enough time to write about the question. These six items (three items relating to Task 1 and three relating to Task 2) were combined to form two scales representing learners' perceptions of Test Task Demands on the initial and final tests. A low score on the scale would indicate that a learner found the test tasks challenging, while a high score would indicate confidence that the test tasks were manageable. The reliability (α) of the entry scale was .731; the reliability (α) of the exit scale was .735. The correlations between the Test Task Demands scales and Writing Test Scores are displayed in Table 6.7.

Table 6.8 shows how perceptions of test task demands may shift between testing occasions; 46% of the lowest scoring group on this variable were included in the higher scoring groups at course exit, including 18% in the

Figure 6.15 Mean Initial and Exit Writing scores at five initial score levels

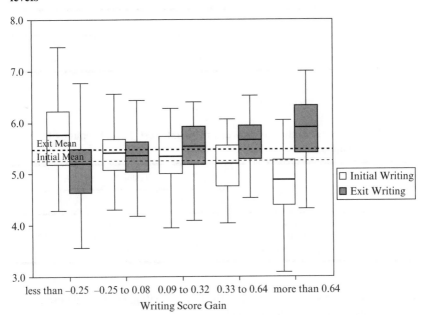

highest scoring group. At the same time, 40% of the highest scoring students at Time One were counted among the lower scoring groups at Time Two with some 10% joining the lowest scoring group at course exit. While it is to be expected that learners would find the test tasks easier to manage as their writing ability improved, it is clear that many found the second test more challenging than the first; although the FACETS analysis revealed that all four tasks were of equivalent difficulty for the total sample. It seems that tasks of apparently equal difficulty may be perceived by individual learners as presenting different levels of challenge and that more challenging tasks result in lower scores for the individuals affected.

The relationship between shifting perceptions of task difficulty and test scores is displayed in Figure 6.17. Those finding the tasks more challenging on the Exit Writing test did, on average, succeed in making gains, but made less gain than those who had found the Initial Writing test the more demanding. The latter group scored lower on the Initial and higher on the Exit Writing tests than their counterparts. Although IELTS topics are carefully selected to provide equal opportunity for all candidates to perform to the best of their ability, there is clearly a relationship between perceptions of test task demands, which vary with testing occasion, and Writing test performance.

Table 6.7   Correlation between Initial and Exit Task Demands and Initial and Exit Writing Test Scores

	Initial Writing Score	Exit Writing Score
Initial Test Task Demands	.179(**)	.199(**)
Exit Test Task Demands	.118(*)	.274(**)

** *Correlation is significant at the 0.01 level (2-tailed).*
* *Correlation is significant at the 0.05 level (2-tailed).*

Table 6.8   Cross-tabulation of scores on Initial Test Task Demands by Exit Test Task Demands

		Initial Test Task Demands		
		less than 15	15 to 19	more than 19
Exit Test Task	less than 15	54.2%	26.2%	10.1%
Demands	15 to 19	27.5%	32.6%	30.3%
	more than 19	18.3%	41.1%	59.6%

Figure 6.16   Time spent on Task 2 on the Initial Writing test (40 minutes is recommended in the test instructions)

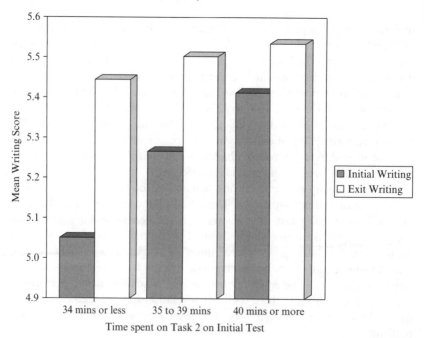

Figure 6.17 Initial and Exit Writing scores by Difference in Student Perceptions of Test Task Demands at Time One and Time Two

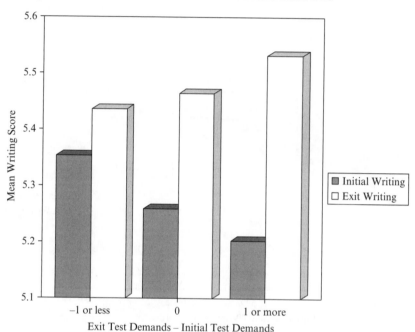

Exit Test Demands – Initial Test Demands

Figure 6.18 plots Writing scores at course entry and exit against composite Initial Grammar/vocabulary scores. The results are consistent with the observation made by Davies (1990) that Writing skills are dependent on lexico-grammatical competence. It is notable that, in contrast to the Initial/Exit comparison of Writing test scores, score gains on the Writing tests occur at all levels of lexico-grammatical competence and there is no drop in scores between Time One and Time Two at the higher levels. However, as Grammar/vocabulary scores increase, Writing score gains do become more modest. There appears to be a ceiling effect for learners scoring between 49 and 65 on the Initial Grammar/vocabulary test with all reaching a mean of around 5.5. Those scoring above 65 on the Grammar/vocabulary test were able to make average gains equalling those made by students scoring between 57 and 61 (0.15 of a band) and surpassing the lack of gain made by students scoring between 62 and 65.

Process features

Process features identified as potential predictors of Writing score gains included those shown in Box 6.2. Again, correlations with Writing score gains

Figure 6.18 Distribution of Initial and Exit Writing scores by five levels of Initial Composite Grammar/Vocabulary score. Maximum score = 80

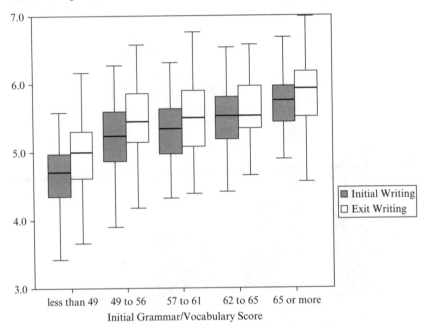

Initial Grammar/Vocabulary Score

are displayed for each feature, together with the partial correlation controlling for the effect of Initial Writing score. For individual questionnaire items, as these are ranked data, non parametric correlations (Spearman's rho) are provided in brackets.

Box 6.2 Process features

Course parameters	r	partial r
Course Length (weeks)	.269	.114
(Course Intensity – hours per week)	−.008	.073
Questionnaire B		
Section 1: Course Outcomes		
CO05 (I learned ways of improving my English Language test scores)	.162 (.185)	.128
CO06 (I learned words and phrases for describing graphs and diagrams)	.104 (.108)	.021
CO08 (I learned how to organise an essay to help the reader to understand)	.075 (.118)	.112

CO09 (I learned how to communicate my ideas effectively in writing)	.105 (.107)	.032
CO18 (My teacher corrected my grammar mistakes in my written work)	.093 (.083)	.022
CO19 (The activities we did in class were similar to the ones on the IELTS test)	.174 (.201)	−.050
Section 2: Learning Strategies		
Learning strategy use	.113	.085
Section 3: Self-Assessed Gain		
Self-assessed aptitude	.128	.175
Self-assessed Writing score gains	.179	.200
Satisfaction with study context	.115	.084
Section 5: Approaches to Learning		
Meaning-based approach scale	.083	.058
Test Knowledge Form		
Test knowledge gain	.057	.010
Change in test task demands	.155	.150
Test strategy use	.168	.271

Box 6.3 Outcomes features

Exit Tests	r	partial r
(Exit AWM score)	.407	
Exit Grammar score	−.167	.132
Exit Vocabulary score	−.096	.185

The relationship between these features and Writing score gains are depicted below.

Course length and intensity

Although course length was correlated with Writing score gain, there was no clear equivalence between period of study and increasing scores. When Writing score gains are plotted against course length and a distinction is made according to score at entry, it is apparent that the amount of gain depends very much on the latter. This is shown in Figure 6.19; Writing score gain varies relatively little with the length of the course, but is strongly related to Initial Writing score.

As shown in Figure 6.19, longer courses seemed most effective at improving scores for those with the lowest Writing scores at entry. For students with middle-ranking scores on the initial test, longer courses seemed less effective

Figure 6.19 Writing score gain by weeks between Writing tests and Initial Writing score

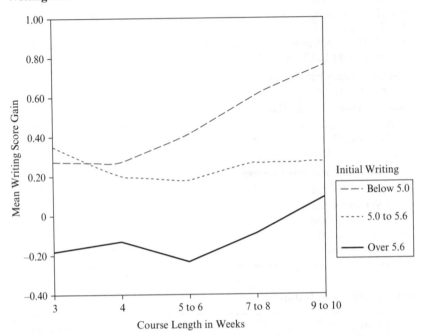

than shorter courses and for those with the highest Initial Writing scores, brief courses seemed to have a negative effect on their Writing scores, while even 10-week courses yielded only minimal gains.

The failure of higher scoring learners to register gains, even after 10 weeks, or 200 hours, of instruction (Figure 6.19), is probably explained, at least in part, by the effect of regression to the mean. The further a score falls from the mean on the initial testing occasion, the more likely, through the chance effects of measurement error, that the score will fall closer to the mean on retesting.

Mean scores on the initial test were lower on lengthier courses (see Figure 6.20); candidates on nine to 10-week courses who scored above 5.6 were over 0.7 of a band above the mean (or 1.08 standard deviations). Candidates scoring at the same level on a three-week course were just 0.14 of a band above the mean (or 0.22 of a standard deviation). The middle-ranking scorers on the initial test were generally scoring above the mean on the shorter courses, but below the mean on the longer courses, and this goes some way to explaining the anomaly of higher gains after three weeks than after ten weeks of instruction for those scoring between 5.0 and 5.6.

A similar picture emerges from the data provided by Cambridge ESOL on 15,343 candidates taking the official IELTS test on more than one occasion

Figure 6.20 Initial and Exit Writing scores by Total Hours on Course

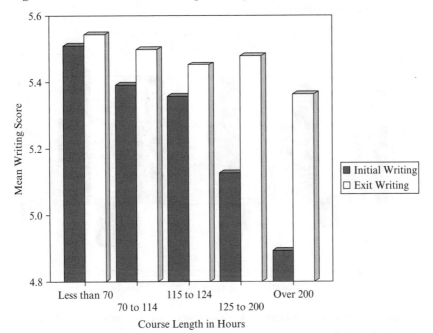

between 1998 and 2001. As noted above (Chapter 4) this data is not relatable to training histories in the intervening periods. It can be seen in Figure 6.21 that candidates scoring 6 or above were, as a group, unlikely to improve their IELTS Writing performance. As with the data generated in this research study, the greatest gains were made by those with the lowest scores on the earlier testing occasion. In this official IELTS data no half bands are awarded.

From this data (Figure 6.21), it seems clear that students cannot generally expect to make gains of a band in their IELTS Writing scores after 200 hours of instruction, as envisaged in recommendations made by the IELTS partners prior to 2002. Learners with different starting points – different score levels at entry – are apt to improve their scores at different rates.

Figure 6.22 shows that although 32.9% of learners on courses of 200 to 250 hours did make gains of a band or better (when fair average scores were rounded to the nearest half band), 41.5% made no substantial improvement on their Initial Writing score.

Learner perceptions of course outcomes

Learners' perceptions of course outcomes were addressed in both Sections 1 and 3 of Questionnaire B. As on Questionnaire A, statements were rated on a

Figure 6.21   Bar Chart of Official IELTS AWM mean score gains 1996–2001 for all repeating candidates

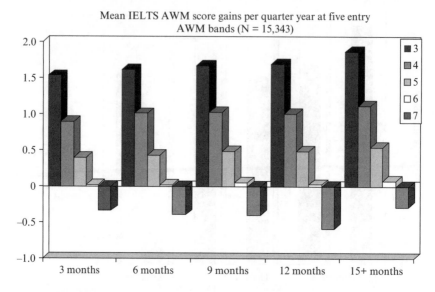

Figure 6.22   Stacked bar chart of Writing score gains (measured in half bands) by Course Length

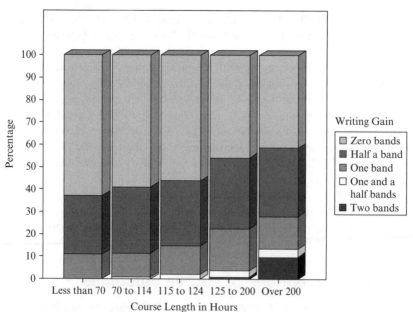

5-point scale from 'I definitely agree' to 'I definitely disagree'. Section 1 asked students about what they had learned in their classes, and Section 3 included self-assessment of Writing gains.

In Section 1, items CO05 (I learned ways of improving my English Language test scores); CO06 (I learned words and phrases for describing graphs and diagrams) and CO19 (The activities we did in class were similar to the ones on the IELTS test) were linked to test preparation (see Chapter 5) and were correlated with Writing score gains. There appears to be some advantage to students in strategies directed towards IELTS such as learning the language of data description and practice with activities similar to those on the test. Figure 6.23 to Figure 6.25 show that high ratings on all three items were associated with lower scores on the Initial Writing test and higher Writing score gains.

Figure 6.23 Bar chart of Initial and Exit Writing scores by CO05 (*I learned ways of improving my English language test scores*). Maximum score = 4

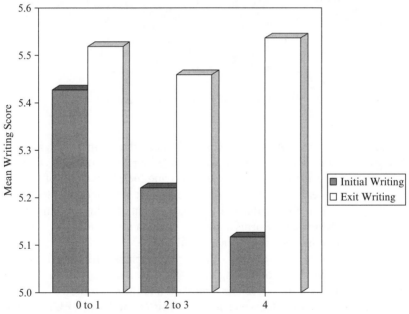

CO05 (I learned ways of improving my English language test scores)

Immediately before responding to each Writing test, learners completed Test Knowledge Forms (Chapter 4). The initial and exit forms each included the same six questions about the IELTS Writing test. Subtracting the scores obtained on the Initial IELTS Writing Test Knowledge items from those on the Exit form provided a measure of Test Knowledge Gain.

Figure 6.24 Bar chart of Initial and Exit Writing scores by CO06 (*I learned words and phrases for describing graphs and diagrams*). Maximum score = 4

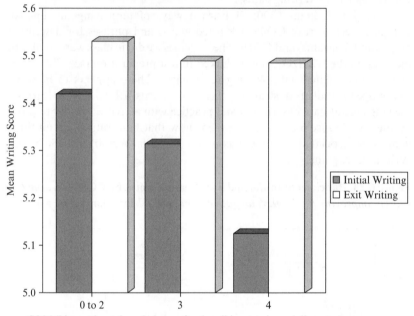

CO06 (I learned words and phrases for describing graphs and diagrams)

Like the Course Outcome items described above, increases in Test Knowledge scores were associated with greater Writing score gains (Figure 6.26). Again, the advantage for those improving their knowledge of the test was modest; a mean gain of 0.28 of a band against a mean of 0.21 for those reducing their Test Knowledge scores. Students maintaining the same score on both Test Knowledge Forms made least gain (a mean of 0.15 of a band), but were also the highest scorers on the initial test.

If a focus on the IELTS test on the part of learners during their courses appeared to contribute to Writing score gains, the learning of EAP skills unrelated to IELTS, such as referencing skills and the integration of sources, did not. However, some items which were consistent both with IELTS preparation and with broader EAP writing skills instruction, as described in Chapter 2, did seem to play a role.

Items CO08 (I learned how to organise an essay to help the reader to understand) and CO09 (I learned how to communicate my ideas effectively in writing) were associated with both EAP and IELTS preparation courses (see Chapter 5). High ratings for these items were related to higher Writing scores at Exit, despite lower scores on the Initial Writing test (Figure 6.27 and

Figure 6.25 Bar chart of Initial and Exit Writing scores by CO19 (*The activities we did in class were similar to the ones on the IELTS test*). Maximum score = 4

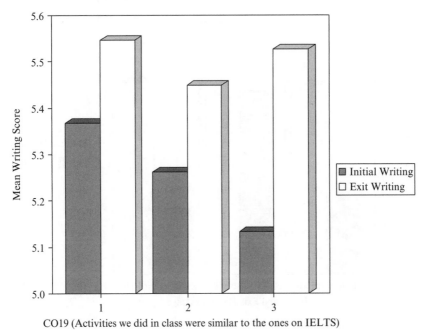

CO19 (Activities we did in class were similar to the ones on IELTS)

Figure 6.28). This suggests that the acquisition of discourse skills can make an important contribution to IELTS Writing score gains.

Section 3 of Questionnaire B included self-assessment of Writing skills gains. When combined into a scale (see Chapter 5), these items correlated with Writing score gains at r = 0.179.

Learners rating their own writing gains the highest were also those who made the most improvement in their Writing scores (Figure 6.29).

Another item positively correlated with Writing score gains was CO18 (My teacher corrected my grammar mistakes in my written work), a feature which was also associated with IELTS preparation courses (see Chapter 5). This suggests that a focus on form may be beneficial in improving IELTS Writing scores. However, item CO10 (I learned grammar) and IM19 (My ability to use grammar and vocabulary in my writing has improved during this course) were not significantly ($p < .05$) correlated with Writing score gains (although they were both significantly correlated with Grammar and Vocabulary score gains).

Questionnaire B Section 5 targeted approaches to learning (Chapter 4). Of the three Approaches to Learning scales (Meaning-Based Orientation;

Figure 6.26   Bar chart of Initial and Exit Writing scores by Test Knowledge Gain

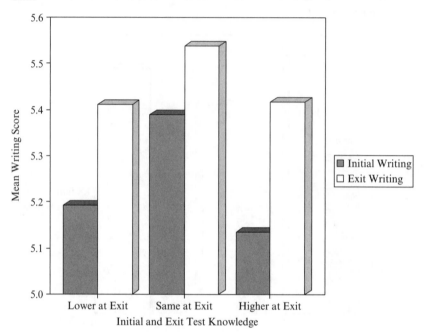

Reproducing Orientation and Achievement Orientation), only the Meaning-Based Orientation scale, involving comprehension learning and a deep approach to learning, was significantly correlated with score gains.

Figure 6.31 shows that higher scores on the Meaning-Based Approach scale were associated with higher Writing score gains. Reproducing Orientation, indicating an overdependence on memorisation and taught material, was negatively correlated with both Initial and Exit Writing scores (but not with score gains). However, the Reproducing Orientation was correlated with both Grammar ($r = 0.20$) and Vocabulary ($r = 0.118$) score gains.

Although test preparation has often been associated with such pathologies of learning as syllabus-boundedness and rote learning (Entwistle and Ramsden 1983, Biggs 1987a, Tang 1992), these do not seem to be rewarded by the IELTS Writing test. The highest gains were achieved by those adopting a Meaning-Based Approach to their learning. This tends to contradict the claim made by some participants that successful IELTS responses (and rapid gains in test scores) can be fashioned from memorised formulae (Chapter 5). Rather, the IELTS Writing test appears to reward a more analytic and exploratory approach to learning.

Figure 6.27   Bar chart of Initial and Exit Writing scores by CO08 (*I learned how to organise an essay to help the reader to understand*). Maximum score = 4

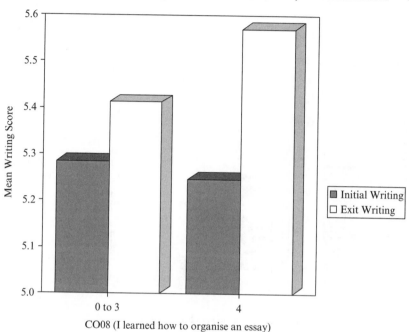

CO08 (I learned how to organise an essay)

Greater use of learning strategies (Questionnaire B: Section 2) was linked with Writing score gains (Figure 6.32). The Learning Strategy Use scale was made up of 25 items, each rated on a 5-point Likert scale offering responses ranging from 'Usually' to 'Never' (see Chapter 4).

Those learners making greatest use of learning strategies (scoring 70 or more points of the 100 available) made the greatest Writing score gains, scoring lowest on the Initial Writing test, but highest on the Exit Writing test. Among the learning strategy items included on the Learning Strategy Use scale, three were significantly partially ($p<.05$) correlated with Exit Writing score, controlling for Initial Writing score. These items relate to learning new grammar and vocabulary and might indicate an active engagement in learning new material: PS05 (I tried to improve my writing by asking others to correct my mistakes) r = .128; PS13 (I tested myself on new words or phrases I learned) r = .135; PS22 (I used new English words in sentences so I could remember them) r = .137.

Of the five items rejected from the Learning Strategy Use scale, three were negatively correlated with Exit Writing scores (partial correlations controlling for Entry Writing and significant at $p<.05$). These were items

Figure 6.28 Bar chart of Initial and Exit Writing scores by CO09 (*I learned how to communicate my ideas effectively in writing*). Maximum score = 4

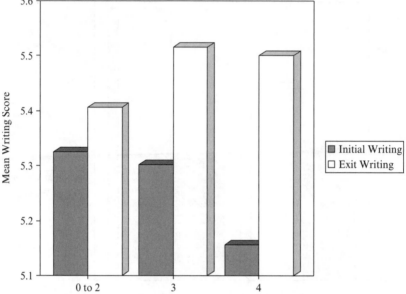

CO09 (I learned how to communicate my ideas effectively in writing)

PS19 (When reading in English, I tried to translate into my language to help me understand); PS21 (I was NOT sure how to improve my English skills) and PS26 (When writing in English, I tried to translate from my language). Translation strategies appear ineffective at boosting Writing scores.

Summary

The above data suggests that learners do profit, in terms of Writing score gains, from focusing on IELTS preparation activities, but that the additional benefit is very limited. Those claiming to have learned content and strategies specifically directed towards the test did seem to improve their scores as a result. However, there was little evidence of dramatic increases in scores on the part of learners as a result of explicit test preparation. The test score evidence seems to contradict some of the stronger claims for the value of intensive IELTS preparation made by participants (Chapters 3 and 4).

Figure 6.29 Bar chart of Initial and Exit Writing scores by Self-Assessed Writing Gain Scale. Maximum score = 28

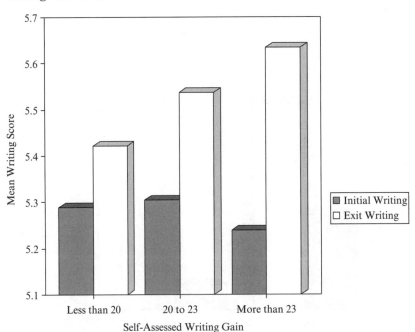

Prediction of writing gains: linear regression and neural network models

Having identified factors likely to contribute to prediction, the next step was to establish the extent of the relationship between these apparently salient background variables and gain on the IELTS Academic Writing Module (AWM) from Time One to Time Two. To do this, two methods of analysis were employed; a neural network method through NeuroSolutions 4.16 (NeuroDimension 2001) and traditional linear prediction through multiple regression in SPSS 11.5 for Windows (SPSS 2002). To test the generalisability of results obtained through these methods, 40% of the data was set aside to supply a cross-validation and a testing set each consisting of 95 cases or 20% of the data. In this way the performance of the predictive models could be checked against additional data. The same testing set was used with both methods.

Figure 6.30 Bar chart of Initial and Exit Writing scores by CO18 (*My teacher corrected my grammar mistakes in my written work*). Maximum score = 4

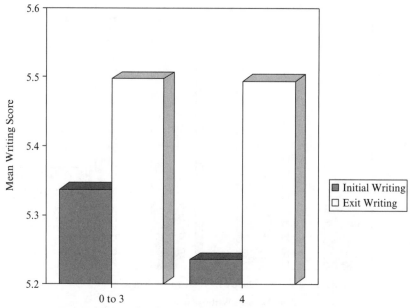

CO18 (My teacher corrected my grammar mistakes in my written work)

Linear regression models

For the prediction set of 34 variables, the ratio of cases to independent variables was acceptable, according to the criterion of $N \geq 50 + 8m$ (where m is the number of independent variables) proposed by Green (1991). As with the neural network (see below), category variables were converted to dummy variables with values of 1 or 0. All cases of missing data were converted to mean values. Again, as was the case for the neural network, and as is standard practice in traditional multiple regression studies (Cohen and Cohen 1983) a proportion of the cases were retained as a model-testing set to provide an estimate of the generalisability of the results. To provide for comparison between the performances of the two methods in prediction, the same testing set of 20% of cases was employed for this model and for the neural network.

A linear regression model was developed by progressively dropping variables from the prediction set. The results of the multiple regression are set out in Table 6.9.

On the basis of the linear regression, we can construct the following equation as a means of predicting course outcomes:

Figure 6.31 Bar chart of Initial and Exit Writing scores by scores on the Meaning-Based Approach Scale. Maximum score = 28

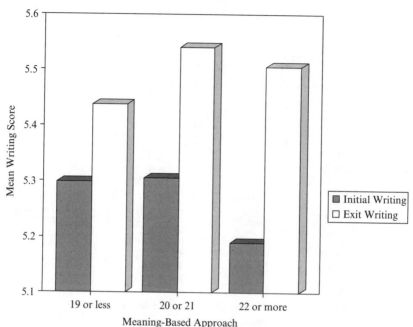

Exit Writing score =

1.184 (Constant) + .405 × Initial Writing score + .030 × Test Strategies at Course Exit + .018 × Initial Vocabulary score + .228 × Highest Level of Education Completed (Secondary School) + .038 × Course Length in Weeks + .011 × Self Confidence in English Writing Ability + .070 × SC11 (I usually enjoy meeting British people) + .054 × CO05 (I learned ways of improving my English Language test scores) + .010 × Initial Grammar score

The regression formula suggests that learners who have lower Writing, Grammar and Vocabulary scores at entry, study on longer courses in preparation for study in the UK, are educated beyond secondary level and believe that they are good at learning to write in English, will achieve the greatest Writing score gains. The model also indicates that there are advantages in having a positive orientation towards the host culture and, it appears, in learning how to improve one's Writing test scores.

A learner entering with a band score of 5, studying for 10 weeks, with grammar and vocabulary scores of 35 and 30 and scoring maximum points

Figure 6.32 Bar chart of Initial and Exit Writing scores by Learning Strategy Use Scale. Maximum score = 100

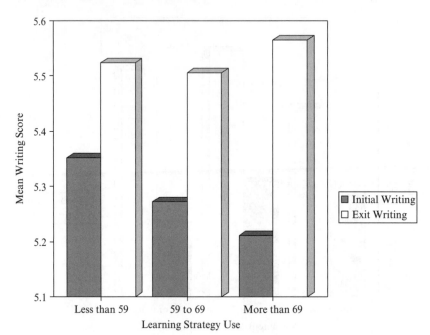

on the other criteria is predicted to score 6.3 at course exit, making a score gain of 1.3 bands. A second learner with the same score at entry, studying for four weeks with grammar and vocabulary scores of 25 and 20 and scoring at the lowest observed level on the other criteria is predicted to score 4.8 at course exit, making a loss of 0.2 of a band.

Neural network models

Figure 6.34 depicts a simple three-layer neural network with four input nodes (neurons), two nodes in the hidden layer and one output node. Each neuron in the input layer represents an input feature (assumed predictor variable). Input values are weighted (as indicated by the arrows marked W11 to W42 in Figure 6.34) and passed to the hidden layer (nodes U1 and U2). When the sum of the weighted inputs reaches a threshold level, the neuron fires and a signal is passed to the output layer (node O1). The output layer generates predicted values (Exit Writing scores) for each input. The network is trained by passing patterns (cases) through the network. When an input is accurately mapped to its expected output, existing weights are retained. When error occurs, network weights are adjusted.

Figure 6.33 Bar chart of Intial and Exit Writing scores by Item PS26 (*When writing in English, I tried to translate from my language*). Maximum score = 4

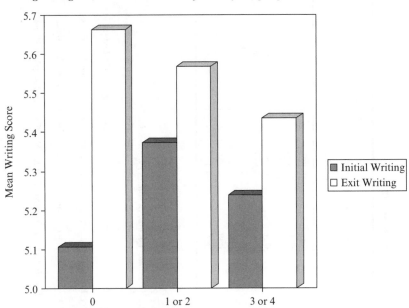

PS26 (When writing in English, I tried to translate)

Patterns are looped through the network until an optimal level of error is reached. A proportion of the data (the cross-validation set) is used to test generalisation as the network is trained. The optimal level of error is reached when the network achieves the most accurate level of prediction on this cross-validation set. If left unchecked, a network may overlearn a problem. Each input in the training set may be accurately mapped to output, but predictions based on the resulting model will not generalise well to the cross-validation set. For this reason, training is stopped when optimal levels are reached.

The most efficient network architecture was determined empirically, by running networks of different complexity through NeuroSolutions (NeuroDimension 2001) and comparing performance measures. Following selection, networks were each trained three times. Network weights derived from the run yielding the best results (the lowest mean square error on the cross-validation set) were retained and the testing set (the 20% of cases set aside for this purpose) was presented to the network.

Three performance measures are displayed in the tables below. The first is the correlation between the values of the Exit Writing scores predicted by the

Table 6.9 Multiple regression model predicting Exit Writing test scores – Model Summary

Model	R	R square	Adjusted R square	Std. Error of the estimate	Change Statistics				
					R square change	F change	df1	df2	Sig. F change
1	.559[a]	.312	.310	.49486	.312	128.786	1	284	.000
2	.602[b]	.363	.358	.47713	.051	22.498	1	283	.000
3	.625[c]	.390	.384	.46761	.027	12.648	1	282	.000
4	.641[d]	.411	.403	.46035	.021	9.958	1	281	.002
5	.652[e]	.425	.414	.45581	.014	6.632	1	280	.011
6	.662[f]	.439	.427	.45099	.014	7.015	1	279	.009
7	.669[g]	.448	.434	.44804	.009	4.685	1	278	.031
8	.675[h]	.456	.440	.44560	.008	4.058	1	277	.045
9	.681[i]	.464	.446	.44310	.008	4.127	1	276	.043

a Predictors: (Constant), Initial Writing score
b Predictors: (Constant), Initial Writing score, Test Strategy Use (Exit)
c Predictors: (Constant), Initial Writing score, Test Strategy Use (Exit), Entry Vocabulary score
d Predictors: (Constant), Initial Writing score, Test Strategy Use (Exit), Entry Vocabulary score, Secondary level Schooling
e Predictors: (Constant), Initial Writing score, Test Strategy Use (Exit), Entry Vocabulary score, Secondary Level Schooling, Course Length in Weeks
f Predictors: (Constant), Initial Writing score, Test Strategy Use (Exit), Entry Vocabulary score, Secondary Level Schooling, Course Length in Weeks, Self-Confidence in Writing
g Predictors: (Constant), Initial Writing score, Test Strategy Use (Exit), Entry Vocabulary score, Secondary Level Schooling, Length in Weeks, Self-Confidence in Writing, SC11
h Predictors: (Constant), Initial Writing score, Test Strategy Use (Exit), Entry Vocabulary score, Secondary Level Schooling, Length in Weeks, Self-Confidence in Writing, SC11, CO05
i Predictors: (Constant), Initial Writing score, Test Strategy Use (Exit), Entry Vocabulary score, Secondary Level Schooling, Length in Weeks, Self-Confidence in Writing, SC11, CO05, Entry Grammar score

Coefficients (a)

	Unstandardised coefficients		Standardised coefficients	t	Sig.	Correlations			Colinearity statistics	
	B	Std. Error	Beta			Zero-order	Partial	Part	Tolerance	VIF
(Constant)	1.184	.315		3.753	.000					
Initial Writing	.405	.053	.436	7.649	.000	.559	.418	.337	.597	1.676
Test Strategy Use	.030	.007	.197	4.273	.000	.287	.249	.188	.910	1.099
Initial Vocabulary	.018	.006	.164	2.920	.004	.410	.173	.129	.619	1.616
Secondary Level Schooling	.228	.085	.121	2.679	.008	.089	.159	.118	.952	1.050
Course Length (weeks)	.038	.013	.135	2.822	.005	-.099	.167	.124	.843	1.186
Self-Confidence in English Writing	.011	.006	.092	1.941	.053	.270	.116	.086	.859	1.164
SC11 (enjoy meeting British)	.070	.032	.099	2.195	.029	.181	.131	.097	.963	1.039
CO05 (learned to improve test scores)	.054	.026	.096	2.091	.037	.048	.125	.092	.930	1.075
Initial Grammar	.010	.005	.117	2.031	.043	.441	.121	.090	.587	1.704

a Dependent Variable: Exit Writing score

Figure 6.34 A Three-Layer Neural Network

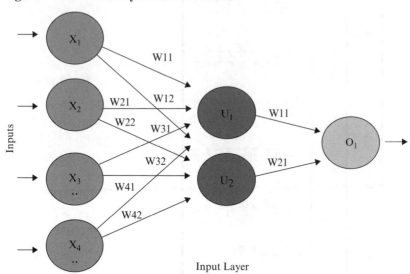

model and the observed values: the scores obtained by the participants. Because consistently high or low estimates on the part of the network could result in high correlations, masking poor model performance, a useful complementary indicator is the mean square error (MSE) of prediction, the average of the square of the difference between the desired output (the observed scores) and the actual network output. Low MSE is indicative of good model fit to the data.

Where there is noticeable variation in levels of correlation between testing runs then some degree of caution should be exercised in generalising from the results. Where results are similar across different runs then more confidence in the generalisability of the predictions can be had.

As in the multiple regression analysis, the single best predictor of Writing score gain was not Course Length, but Initial Writing score. This accounted for approximately 28% of the variance in the training set and generalised well to the testing set ($r = .597$). Course Length in Weeks, in contrast, accounted for just 8.4% of the variance in the training and 9.6% in the testing set.

Figure 6.35 depicts the process of learning. As each pattern is presented to the network, the difference is calculated between the output predicted by the network model and the desired value (the actual Exit Writing score awarded). With each iteration, error is reduced until convergence is achieved or the network training is stopped.

Tables 6.10 to 6.14 show the performance of models of different levels of complexity. In each case the performance of the non-linear model is

Table 6.10 Performance measures for prediction based on 34 process and presage features employing linear and non-linear methods of prediction (desired feature = Exit Writing score)

Set	34 presage and process features 1 hidden layer with 4 PEs r	mse	Error %
Training	0.725	0.049	6.112
Cross validation	0.602	0.079	7.750
Training	0.719	0.050	6.152
Cross validation	0.595	0.080	7.791
Training	0.715	0.051	6.116
Cross validation	0.595	0.080	7.802
Average training	0.720	0.050	6.127
Average cross validation	0.597	0.080	7.781
Testing	0.636	0.062	6.631
Linear training	0.710	0.052	8.009
Linear cross validation	0.561	0.085	6.109
Linear testing	0.642	0.061	6.878

Figure 6.35 Desired and predicted values plot: 17 presage features on the training set

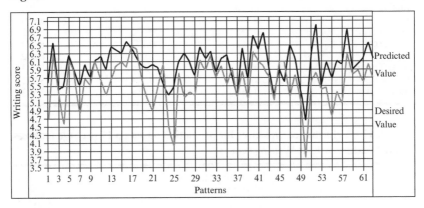

compared with its linear equivalent (estimated by running the network without a hidden layer).

It can be seen that a combination of the three Entry test measures (Grammar, Vocabulary and Writing) is capable of accounting for 38% of the variance in the Exit Writing scores in the testing set (Table 6.13), while the multiple regression model described above accounts for 39% and the full set of 34 predictors accounts for 41% (Table 6.10).

The addition of other presage variables to Entry test scores did not improve network performance (Table 6.12). Although the network more accurately mapped inputs to outputs, generalisation to the testing set was no more successful. Process features also appeared to perform rather poorly as predictors of Exit Writing (Table 6.11). The combination of 17 process features was capable of accounting for just 19% of the variance in Exit Writing scores in the testing set. When Initial Writing scores were excluded from the full set of predictors, the remaining 33 features were capable of accounting for 22% of the variance in the Exit Writing scores.

When used for prediction, the multiple regression equation given above is capable of accounting for 42% of the variance in the training set, but does not generalise quite as well to the testing set. Values predicted by the regression

Table 6.11 Performance measures for prediction based on 17 process features (desired feature = Exit Writing score)

Set	17 process features 1 hidden layer with 2 PEs		
	r	mse	Error %
Training	0.550	0.073	7.308
c.v.	0.424	0.101	8.527
Training	0.549	0.073	7.280
c.v.	0.408	0.103	8.630
Training	0.570	0.071	7.198
c.v.	0.406	0.103	8.804
Average Training	0.556	0.072	7.262
Average c.v.	0.413	0.102	8.654
Testing	0.399	0.089	8.062
Linear Training	0.529	0.075	7.343
Linear c.v.	0.396	0.104	8.715
Linear Test	0.436	0.084	7.943

Table 6.12 Performance measures for prediction based on 17 presage features (desired feature = Exit Writing score)

Set	17 presage features 1 hidden layer with 4 PEs		
	r	mse	Error %
Training	0.668	0.058	6.724
c.v.	0.605	0.078	7.646
Training	0.706	0.052	6.313
c.v.	0.646	0.079	7.760
Training	0.652	0.050	6.795
c.v.	0.610	0.077	7.584
Average Training	0.675	0.054	6.611
Average c.v.	0.621	0.078	7.663
Testing	0.619	0.064	6.571
Linear Training	0.658	0.059	6.774
Linear c.v.	0.614	0.077	7.592
Linear Test	0.618	0.064	6.611

model account for 39% of the variance in the Exit Writing scores in the testing set.

If the same set of features are used as input to a neural network with a hidden layer made up of three processing elements, prediction is marginally less successful for the training set, and the model does not generalise as successfully to the testing set, with predicted values accounting for 36% of the variance in the observed values. The percentage of error in prediction is marginally higher than for the linear model (Table 6.13).

This linear regression model predicted 42% of cases in the testing set to within a quarter of a band and 69% of cases to within half a band of their

Table 6.13 Three test features: Initial Writing, Vocabulary and Grammar tests

Set	3 test features (initial tests) 1 hidden layer with 2 PEs		
	r	mse	Error %
Training	0.592	0.068	7.201
c.v.	0.615	0.077	7.581
Training	0.594	0.068	7.182
c.v.	0.620	0.076	7.535
Training	0.593	0.068	7.199
c.v.	0.621	0.076	7.522
Average Training	0.624	0.063	6.475
Average c.v.	0.592	0.068	7.205
Testing	0.619	0.076	7.551
Linear Training	0.625	0.064	6.481
Linear c.v.	0.592	0.068	7.201
Linear Test	0.615	0.077	7.581

Table 6.14 Prediction model based on nine features (Desired Feature = Exit Writing score)

Set	9 presage and process features 1 hidden layer with 3 PEs		
	r	mse	Error %
Training	0.681	0.056	6.347
c.v.	0.592	0.080	7.969
Training	0.687	0.055	6.346
c.v.	0.602	0.078	7.863
Training	0.680	0.056	6.365
c.v.	0.602	0.078	7.862
Average Training	0.646	0.059	6.774
Average c.v.	0.683	0.056	6.353
Testing	0.599	0.079	7.898
Linear Training	0.682	0.056	6.330
Linear c.v.	0.594	0.079	7.893
Linear Test	0.623	0.063	6.929

observed Exit Writing scores. The most complete neural net model (with 34 prediction features: Table 6.10) was somewhat more accurate, predicting score gains to within a quarter of a band for 44% of cases in the testing set, and to within a half band for 74%. The neural net model predicted all but one of the scores obtained to within one band of the observed scores (the exception being out by 1.05 of a band score). Predictions based on mean Writing score gains were accurate in 39% of cases to within a quarter and 63% of cases to within a half band score. Predictions based on the mean were all accurate to within two bands, with 10.5% of predictions incorrect by over one band.

Summary

The predictive models described above have shown the importance of the Initial Writing score in predicting outcomes. Adding information relating to student background does improve prediction, but process variables including Course Length are not as useful in forecasting Exit Writing scores.

Score gains were far lower than the available advice had predicted. Even after 200 hours of instruction only a minority made the anticipated gain of one band. In fact the majority of learners in the study did not improve substantially on their Initial Writing score. The lack of improvement, especially at higher levels, could be attributed to a number of causes. It is probable that regression to the mean, associated with measurement error, accounts for at least some of the observed changes. Certainly, the learner's sense of the difficulty of the test task emerged as a contributing factor. At the same time it may be that learners are able to make more rapid progress through the IELTS bands at lower levels.

The observed decline in the scores awarded to some learners could also be explained in a number of ways. It has been observed by SLA researchers that language learning is non-accumulative. Learners may become less accurate as they begin to use more complex formulations in their writing. Such a loss of accuracy may be penalised, leading to lower scores. It is also possible that there were affective differences in the way the learners approached the two tests. Some may have become less motivated to succeed on the second occasion. Equally, tiredness or anxiety at Time Two might have contributed to declining scores. Again, greater task difficulty at Time Two experienced by the individual learner was probably a contributing factor.

It is notable that Course Type played no discernible role in determining outcomes. Following an IELTS preparation course rather than a pre-sessional EAP course did not seem to yield the rewards expected by participants. However, attention to the demands of the test on the part of the learner did seem to contribute, albeit marginally, to score gains. Learners who employed test-taking strategies and reported learning how to improve their test scores did tend to make greater score gains.

Chapters 5 and 6 have set out the results from the main study. Conclusions and implications to be drawn from these results will be considered in Chapter 7.

7 Conclusions and implications

Since 1989, when IELTS was first introduced, the test has undergone continuous modification and development. Although the constituent modules have remained the same since the last major revision in 1995, adjustments to the content and administration of the test are introduced on a regular basis. For an historical perspective on IELTS, the reader is referred to Davies (forthcoming). For regular updates on changes to the test as they occur, details are provided on the IELTS website at www.ielts.org and in the Cambridge ESOL publication, *Research Notes*. As pointed out in the chapters above, a number of such modifications have been introduced in the period since this study was carried out (in 2001 and 2002).

Over the intervening period, this study has itself contributed to the ongoing development of IELTS. The findings indicated a need for sensitivity to the relationship between test scores, periods of study and language gains. Recommendations made in the *IELTS Handbook* equating roughly 100 hours of intensive study to a half-band gain on the test have been removed. The findings also contributed to the revision of the Writing Module in 2005, in particular encouraging the rewording of task prompts, which no longer specify lecturers and educated non-specialists as the audiences for Task 1 and Task 2 responses.

The study indicated a more general need for wider access to information on the meaning of band scores. In response, public versions of the rating scales for both Writing and Speaking are now provided on the IELTS website and new tools such as the *IELTS Scores Explained* DVD have been developed by the IELTS partners to provide test users with interpretations and exemplification of the 9-band IELTS scale. Support for teachers engaged in preparing learners for the test is also being extended via the IELTS website.

The IELTS partners' concern with testing consequences is also an emergent, ongoing project of which the research reported in this volume forms one, relatively narrow strand. The broader IELTS Impact Study (IIS) initiated in 1995 by Cambridge ESOL was among the earliest investigations into consequential validity. The IIS, described in detail in Hawkey (2006), encompasses the influence of the test on a range of stakeholders, on test preparation materials and on receiving institutions. The study reported in this volume was conceived and initiated externally to the IIS, but proceeded in parallel and benefited from the experience of the other study as well as from the instruments developed.

Other volumes in this series (Cheng 2005, Wall 2005) have investigated washback in other settings, highlighting the complexity of the mechanisms through which washback occurs and the importance of teachers in mediating test influence. Both this study and the IIS (Hawkey 2006) applied this awareness to IELTS in exploring attitudes towards and practices informed by the test. Since this study was completed a number of IELTS-funded projects have also investigated test consequences. Rea-Dickins, Kiely and Yu (2005) looked at the consequences of using IELTS for learners after they have entered university and the effects on their receiving departments; Everett and Coleman (2003) investigated the content of IELTS preparation materials; Coleman, Starfield and Hagan (2003) surveyed test takers and users in the UK, Australia and China about their views and practices in relation to IELTS; Rao, McPherson, Chand and Khan (2003) explored the impact of the General Training Module on preparation programmes in Fiji, and Smith (2007) is investigating the effects in secondary schools of IELTS use.

This volume synthesised findings from earlier research to develop the washback model presented in Chapter 1. The model provides what should prove to be a useful framework for further studies in the emerging field of washback. Insufficient attention has been given in much recent research to issues of test design or of learning outcomes. As a result it has been difficult to relate behaviours to test design. This report has shown the value of investigating participants, processes and products together. It is hoped that this integrated approach will serve to inform future investigations.

This final chapter links the results of the study to the research questions set out in Chapter 2. Firstly, the research questions are revisited in turn, summarising the evidence from the various strands of the study. Following this analysis, implications are suggested for the immediate stakeholders in the research context of UK higher education and for the test developers themselves. As they arise, the response of the IELTS partners to each of the issues is briefly described. In the final section, this project is considered in the light of the developing field of washback/impact studies – including the three recent volumes in this series (Wall 2005, Cheng 2005, Hawkey 2006). Emerging questions and some possible future directions for washback/impact research are identified.

Research questions revisited

Research Question 1

Given the commonalities and discrepancies between IELTS and the EAP writing construct revealed in the literature review (Chapter 1), do students and teachers regard themselves as engaging in IELTS test preparation rather than university preparation and do such beliefs give rise to practices, in relation to IELTS, which fail to address the EAP writing construct?

The model of washback set out in Chapter 1 and the review of the IELTS Academic Writing Module (AWM) in Chapter 2, suggested that concentration on test demands would eclipse broader academic literacy concerns: notably the integration of sources, diversity of genres and academic register. Diverse sources of data including the survey of course providers described in Chapter 3; the surveys of teachers and students reported in Chapters 3 and 5 and the direct observation of classroom activities reported in Chapter 5 confirmed that most participants on IELTS courses did direct their efforts towards passing the test and that this was the defining objective of these courses for teachers and the majority of learners.

The interviews with teachers yielded consistent views on the question of overlap. Although they valued the direct testing of writing, teachers did not believe that IELTS was fully representative of the academic writing skills their learners would need for university study. Test design characteristics such as the choice and range of topics; sources of data; test conditions, including the time limit and required essay lengths; the kinds of responses expected of candidates; the nature of the rating scales and the characteristics of the raters were considered by at least some participants to limit or even distort the picture of test takers' academic writing ability provided by the IELTS AWM. At the same time, teachers saw what one described as a 'positive washback effect' in the way that the test encouraged the teaching and learning of writing skills (contrasting this with indirect, multiple-choice tests). It was also said that the IELTS essay tasks better reflected academic writing than the writing tasks on tests of general English proficiency.

Students, particularly those with experience of pre-sessional courses, shared some of their teachers' perceptions of limited overlap, although some expressed the view that the IELTS tasks, and particularly Task 2, were broadly reflective of their experience of academic writing. Students were more likely to be concerned about apparent mismatches between features of the IELTS AWM and the requirements of their specific disciplines, with Task 1 attracting some complaints on this score from students who did not believe they would need to describe graphs in their academic studies. There seemed to be a danger that those without pre-sessional experience might see the IELTS tasks as definitive of academic writing in English and might enter university with this misconception.

To summarise, participants identified discrepancies between the IELTS test and their beliefs about academic writing in the following areas, which were felt to be under-represented in the IELTS AWM:

- gathering and transformation of source data
- integration of sources in composition through summary or paraphrase
- referencing and acknowledgement of written sources
- variety of text type or genre
- composition and rhetorical organisation of lengthy texts
- composition of texts in learners' academic disciplines
- use of information technology for research and word processing in composition
- learning about the distinctive nature of student academic literacy in university
- learning about academic cultural differences.

Given that most teachers and learners identified success on the test as the primary goal of IELTS classes, and given the extent of overlap revealed in Chapter 2, the washback model predicted that IELTS preparation courses would under-represent the academic writing needs recognised by the EAP teaching profession.

Weigle's (2002) framework for the description of Writing test tasks (see Chapter 2), provides a means of relating the interview and observation data to features of the test. In this way it is possible, following the recommendation of Chapman and Snyder (2000) to trace participant behaviour to test design features (Table 7.1).

Interview and survey data showed that many participants regarded the test preparation courses in instrumental terms. The purpose of the courses was to ensure that students achieved the required grade by the most efficient means. If higher grades could be achieved by memorising answers or by relentless test practice, these practices were not regarded as unethical, but as part of 'playing the game'. If such strategies were rejected, it was because participants believed they were not the most effective methods for improving scores. However, as realised in the classes observed, IELTS preparation involved more than test-practice activities. Teachers set out to build the writing skills they believed were required by the test through skills-building activities.

The observations confirmed that IELTS-directed classes, across institutions, tended to involve activities with a direct relationship to the IELTS AWM tasks. The teaching cycle on these courses was directed towards test-practice activities and included question analysis, brainstorming ideas, forming an outline plan with topic sentences and sentence and paragraph building. In comparison with IELTS preparation, there was a greater variety of activities on EAP courses and these appeared to take account of more of the features of the processes of academic writing outlined in the literature review (Chapter 1). However, reflecting areas of overlap between the IELTS

Table 7.1 Framework relating test design features to participant behaviours and data sources. Based on Weigle (2002: 63)

Dimension	Teacher surveys/ interviews	Student surveys/ interviews	Observations
Subject matter	IELTS involves general rather than academic knowledge. Encourage reading of newspapers to build ideas about (British) current affairs topics. Brainstorming on variety of topics.	Topics not related to students' academic disciplines. Learning about general knowledge and typical IELTS topics. Reading *The Economist*. Preparing essays on common IELTS topics.	Lists of typical IELTS topics prepared for students. Topics were broad, not explored beyond task demands.
Stimulus	Look for input material that emulates IELTS Writing Tasks 1 (graphs and diagrams) and 2 (topics of general social concern).	IELTS class material included T1 and T2 tasks.	IELTS-like task stimuli heavily used on IELTS courses.
Genre	Teaching was directed towards genres required in the test.	Learned introduction, body, conclusion. 'Basic essay'. Studying (sometimes memorising) model essays.	IELTS classes limited to writing T1 and T2 type essays.
Rhetorical task	Classes focus on description. Frequently assign practice tests.	Learned description (of graphs) and argument. Took tests in and out of class.	Rhetorical tasks limited to those required for the test: description, hortation.
Pattern of exposition	Taught comparison/ contrast, process.	Increased awareness of cultural differences in IELTS argument structure.	IELTS classes limited to T1 and T2. EAP involved greater variety. E.g. classes on definition.
Cognitive demands	IELTS believed to encourage memorisation.	Expressed need to reproduce ideas in essays. Memorisation of phrases – creating a template.	IELTS classes about reproducing information: from graph or from personal knowledge.
Specification of: • audience	Looked for information on how examiners judge essays.	Learned about what examiners look for.	Some mention of university lecturers (the specified audience), but more attention given to examiner expectations. Teaching 'ways to impress the examiner'.

Table 7.1 (continued)

Dimension	Teacher surveys/ interviews	Student surveys/ interviews	Observations
• role	IELTS involves personal opinion. Encourage learners to generate opinions on any given topic.	IELTS involves personal opinion.	
• tone, style	Taught formal style.	Learned to write in a formal style.	Taught formal style, but not including such academic features as hedging.
Length	IELTS is relatively short. Counted words in writing tasks.	IELTS is short. Learned to write test essays, but not longer essays. Counting of words to satisfy T1 demands.	Essays for the IELTS classes were short (100–300 words). Students encouraged to count words. Teaching how to use more words – sentence expansion.
Time allowed	Taught time management – working within test constraints.	Complained that time is too short. Learned time management.	Timed essay practice activities more frequent in IELTS classes.
Prompt wording	Taught analysis of question prompts.	Learned how to analyse prompts, how to respond when unable to understand the prompt.	Question analysis based on the generic IELTS task prompt.
Choice of prompts	Preference for a choice of prompts.	Preference for choice to offset the negative effects of an unfamiliar topic or to reflect their own discipline.	Students were sometimes given a choice of topic for IELTS practice essays.
Transcription mode	Note that IELTS responses are handwritten, although most academic work is word processed.	Note that there was less use of IT in IELTS preparation.	Little word processing observed in IELTS Writing (and none in class).
Scoring criteria	Seeking information on the criteria. Teaching of cohesion, 'linking words', 'transition signals' or 'discourse markers'. Grammar and organisation. Informing students about the scoring criteria.	Learned vocabulary and grammar. Learned organisation and cohesive devices. Learned how to support arguments.	Feedback on essays in the form of band scores. Teaching organisational templates. Teaching grammar points relevant to test – error analysis/ useful structures. Encouraging use of more formal vocabulary.

test and the Academic Writing construct, there were also substantial areas of common practice between IELTS preparation and EAP courses. Excluding the references to the test, many of the activities in the IELTS classes observed would not have been out of place in the EAP classes.

Both class types involved brainstorming and planning and frequent practice with extensive writing, both encouraged a formal, objective style of writing, offered instruction in discourse-level organisation, were concerned with the requirements implicit in task instructions and involved work (often in the form of remediation) on grammar and vocabulary. Many of the differences between classes, such as the balance of time given to whole-class or group work, or the inclusion of peer assessment of essays, were linked to teacher beliefs about effective learning rather than the influence of the test.

It further emerged from the interviews and surveys that participants believed that IELTS courses developed skills with a value beyond the immediate requirement to pass the test. Teachers believed that their courses would improve their students' ability to think critically or to express their own opinions. Students believed that the courses improved their ability to write in English, their ability to organise their essays and their general language ability, as well as teaching them strategies that would help them to pass the test.

On the other hand the observations bore out the claims of teachers and students that test-design issues did impact on the design and delivery of preparation courses and on learners' engagement with them. Limitations on the selection of topics for Task 2 and the choice of data for presentation in Task 1 attracted a number of test-preparation strategies such as:

Teaching strategies

Providing lists of topics and encouraging learners to read about these in the media and to practice planning and writing essays on these themes.

Encouraging memorisation of formulaic phrases and teaching relevant vocabulary and structures (such as language for describing trends, and reporting on information in graphs and diagrams or encouraging students to learn past-tense forms of verbs).

Learning strategies

Attempting practice writing tests outside class.

Reviewing class notes at home.

Memorising phrases and, in a few cases, extended passages for the test.

Examples of student work supported the claims of teachers and students that IELTS coursework was closely directed towards the test. The extended Writing tasks undertaken in IELTS classes were all intended to mirror the tasks offered in the test. EAP tasks included timed writing practice on similar 'broad' topics, but also included quite specific projects linked to learners' academic subjects and involving independent data collection.

Evidence that the influence of the test on learners is mediated by teachers and course materials was provided by the responses to the course expectation and outcome items in Section 2 of Questionnaire A, Section 1 of Questionnaire B and on the Teacher Questionnaire. Student ratings shifted to reflect the objectives of their teachers. Where these did not match learner expectations at course entry, learners' ratings tended to shift at course exit to accommodate to the teacher objectives. On IELTS preparation courses these included the description of graphs and diagrams and time management; on pre-sessional courses they involved referencing, learning about university writing tasks and learning about differences in university study across cultures.

On the other hand, there was evidence that learners were not simply acceding to their teachers' priorities; that washback to the learner is not determined by washback to the teacher. There were areas where student reports of learning outcomes moved away from teacher objectives. On Questionnaire B, grammar correction of written work was the highest ranked learning outcome for students on all course types, although it was not given priority as an objective by teachers.

In conclusion, there was substantial evidence both for washback and for the complexity of the phenomenon. There was variation between participants in how the effects of the test were realised. Although strategies were adopted to accommodate to the demands of the test, the relationship between these strategies and test characteristics was not always transparent. Indeed, participants did not always agree about which strategies would bring success; teachers generally favoured a focus on organisation, learners placed more emphasis on learning grammar.

Research Question 2

Do practices on courses which are not driven by IELTS better reflect this construct?

Participant interviews and surveys and observation of classes all suggested that EAP courses included in this study exposed learners to a wider range of academic writing tasks than did IELTS preparation courses. The teaching and learning cycle on EAP courses included stages that were not typically featured in IELTS preparation including the collection and integration of source material, referencing and routine redrafting. Attention was given in EAP classes to issues of plagiarism and the compilation of bibliographies.

Teachers and students on pre-sessional courses, and IELTS preparation teachers with experience of both, believed that EAP courses better reflected academic writing needs. Questionnaire data relating to course outcomes suggested that EAP courses encouraged learning of academic literacy skills and engendered greater confidence among EAP learners that they were prepared for university study.

The EAP classes observed better reflected academic writing needs as currently understood. However, there were restrictions on how far these classes could be said to embody the academic writing construct delineated in Chapter 2. There was, for example, evidence in the selection of topics for these classes for the limits on the level of subject specificity that can be accommodated on courses for learners entering diverse academic disciplines.

Analysis of questionnaire data revealed a significant difference ($p<.05$) in self-assessed improvement in writing ability across course types. Pre-sessional EAP students scored highest and combined course students scored lowest. This suggests that more students on EAP courses believed that they had made greater improvements in their ability to write in English than their counterparts on IELTS preparation and combination courses.

The results also supported the proposition, deriving from the review of the literature and the pilot studies (see Chapter 3), that learners on the three course types would have differing expectations of university study. IELTS preparation learners, who received less explicit EAP instruction, were more likely to expect support and guidance from university teachers; to expect that good grades at university would be obtained by following the teacher's lead; and to expect that they would experience problems with studying at university. Pre-sessional students seem to have felt better prepared for university study and to have had more realistic expectations of academic work.

Research Question 3

What are the characteristics of learners on different courses and how do these relate to the characteristics of the IELTS test-taking population?

As revealed by the learner questionnaires, the learners on the various courses differed on a number of the variables addressed in the study. For example, learners on IELTS preparation courses were generally younger, and had completed lower levels of education than their counterparts on other courses. The proportion of learners from different regions also varied between groups. The demographic differences may suggest variation in language-learning aptitude or intelligence across groups that would restrict the generalisability of the results from this study. There is therefore a need to extend the research approach presented here to encompass other settings and other populations of test takers.

The Approaches to Learning scales showed that Course Type bore only a weak relationship to learners' orientation to their learning. Differences in the aims and content of the three course types revealed at the level of course design in Pilot Studies One and Five and at the level of delivery in Pilot Studies Two, Three and Four did not appear, insofar as these could be captured by the available instruments, to give rise to great differences in the way learners approached their learning task.

It is interesting that IELTS preparation students gave higher mean ratings to item PS09 (I looked for people I could talk to in English) on Questionnaire B. This may reflect the differences between the circumstances of students on the different courses outside classes. The pre-sessional students were more often housed with large numbers of fellow students in on-campus accommodation, while IELTS preparation students more often lodged with local families, perhaps affording them more opportunities to meet English L1 speakers.

In relation to the UK IELTS test-taking population, the participants in this study were more likely to intend entry to higher education. The highest proportion of UK test takers in 2001/2 came from East Asia and this was reflected in the study population. On the other hand, there were very few South Asians in the study and relatively few learners from regions other than East Asia and Western Europe. Mean Writing scores for the study population fell within the range of means for Academic Module forms of 5.33 to 5.86 (IELTS 2003: 8). Attention should be paid to the differences between the wider IELTS test-taking population and participants in the study in generalising from these results.

Research Question 4

Do instructional alternatives at points on a continuum from IELTS-driven to IELTS-unrelated EAP courses result in differential outcomes in terms of gains in scores on the IELTS Academic Module?

There is little support here for the belief expressed by participants in the pilot studies described in Chapter 3 and the interviews in Chapter 4 that courses directed towards the IELTS test are more effective than broader-based EAP pre-sessional courses in boosting IELTS Writing scores.

Before this study, the IELTS partners advised that learners intending to enter higher education institutions should prepare by studying the language for at least 200 hours to allow an improvement of one band on the IELTS test. This advice was taken up by BALEAP (Bool, Dunmore and Tonkyn 1999) and is commonly followed on university pre-sessional courses which accept learners presenting IELTS scores half a band below the standard required for entry to academic courses for one month of intensive English study and those presenting scores one band below the entry standard for two months. However, in terms of Writing test scores, longer periods of instruction do not appear to compensate for lower entry scores to the extent anticipated in the recommendations and these are no longer published in the *IELTS Handbook*.

Score gains typically fell well short of the IELTS partners' suggested figure of a half band for each month (100 hours) of study (the mean length of study here being 5.5 weeks or 130 hours). Although gains in FACETS fair average scores of as much as two bands were observed (the highest gain was 2.08 bands), these were exceptional, with just 3 of the 476 learners gaining by two bands and only 39 (8.2%) gaining by one band or more. It remains to be seen whether this would be equally true of other components of the test.

Differences between learner groups were related to score gains. Higher scores at entry were associated with lower score gains. This emerged as the most important difference in predicting score outcomes and the distinction between learners with different band scores at entry proved more influential in predicting gain than any observed differences between course types.

In brief, the picture to emerge of Writing score gains was as follows:

Writing score gains occurred across course types. Learners on all three course types made significant Writing score gains.

There was no evidence of any substantial IELTS preparation effect in terms of test outcomes. There were no significant differences in Writing score gains between course types.

Only one in 10 learners made gains of more than one band, while one third scored lower on the second test. Only exceptionally did learners improve their Writing test scores by a full band in 200 hours. Score gains varied with Initial Writing scores; the higher the Initial Writing score, the lower the gain. Recommendations for periods of study based on a single figure for learners at different levels of ability would seem to be inappropriate.

The longer courses were more effective at improving scores for those with low Initial Writing scores. For those with middle-ranking scores on the initial test, the longer courses actually seemed less effective than shorter courses. These learners included those with the lowest scores on short courses and those with the highest of the scores on longer courses. It seems likely that this is attributable to a degree of regression to the mean. For those with the highest Initial Writing scores, brief courses seemed to have a negative effect on their Writing scores, while even 10-week courses yielded only minimal gains.

The data suggested that learners can profit, in terms of Writing score gains, from giving attention to IELTS preparation activities, but that the additional benefit is surprisingly limited. Those who reported learning content and strategies specifically directed towards the test did seem to improve their scores as a result. However, there was little evidence of dramatic increases in scores on the part of learners as a result of explicit test preparation in their courses. The test-score evidence seems to contradict some of the stronger claims for the value of intensive IELTS preparation made by participants (Chapter 3).

Linguistic (lexico-grammatical) proficiency gains?

Sources of data on grammar and vocabulary gains were in conflict. Responses to the teacher survey suggested that EAP and IELTS-preparation teachers gave an equal amount of attention to these features, but results were different on the student surveys. EAP and IELTS learners both reported that teachers provided grammar correction, but IELTS learners were more inclined to agree with the statements, 'I learned grammar [on this course]' and 'I learned general vocabulary.'

However, analysis of test results suggested that it was the pre-sessional learners who made the greatest gains in their grammar and vocabulary scores. A speculative interpretation of this result is that although teachers on IELTS courses paid at least as much attention to grammar as their EAP peers, this was in relation only to a restricted body of test-relevant structures which were not reflected in the grammar test used in this study. Further investigation of the grammar and vocabulary taught in IELTS-preparation classes might reveal whether this was indeed the case.

Academic awareness and study skills gains?

As noted above, EAP learners' self-assessments indicated that they believed they had learned more about the university context than their IELTS counterparts. They also reported greater gains in areas such as using evidence to support arguments, taking notes from lectures, integrating sources and learning about university expectations for academic writing.

Interviews with learners and teachers supported the contention that those with pre-sessional experience would be better prepared for academic study. Students with experience of both course types felt that pre-sessionals offered a more complete preparation. Further research into the relative preparedness of students entering universities by satisfying test requirements or through pre-sessional programmes is urgently required.

Research Question 5

Do facets of learners' individual differences interact with instructional differences in predicting outcomes?

The study has demonstrated that it is possible to substantially improve on predictions of score gains by taking into account both instructional differences such as course length and individual differences such as student age and region of origin.

However, course-related variables contributed comparatively little to the predictive models. In both the multiple regression and neural network approaches the most accurate predictions of Writing score gain were provided not by Course Length, but by Initial Writing score. This feature alone accounted for approximately 25% of the variance in Writing score gain in the training set for both linear and non-linear (neural network) models. Course Length in Weeks, in contrast, accounted for just under 8% of the variance.

The regression formula suggested that learners who had low Writing and Grammar scores at entry, studied on longer courses in preparation for study in the UK, were educated beyond secondary level and believed that they were good at learning to write in English, would achieve the highest Writing score gains. The model also indicated that there were advantages in having a positive orientation towards the host culture and, it appears, in learning how to improve Writing test scores.

The contribution of test preparation as an approach to instruction appears to be minimal in this setting. Learners pursuing a test-preparation course do not obtain a significant advantage in test performance. However, learners intending to take the test, whether on EAP or IELTS courses, do make measurably greater gains than their counterparts. In this context, it seems to be washback to the learner, rather than washback to the programme, which has the greater relevance to outcomes.

The attitudes towards learning that learners bring with them to the classroom may have a greater influence on how the learning experience is constructed and experienced than the power of the test. Evidence from the student and teacher questionnaires suggest that participants' approaches to teaching and learning were influenced more by beliefs brought to the course than by the demands of the test. Echoing findings elsewhere (Alderson and Hamp-Lyons 1996, Watanabe 1996), course content was very clearly influenced by the test, but any influence on teaching and learning methods was less obvious and was mediated by participant beliefs.

Although test preparation has been associated with surface approaches to learning (Chapter 4), these did not seem to be rewarded by the IELTS Writing test. The highest gains were achieved by those espousing a Meaning-Based Approach. This weighs against the contention that improved IELTS responses might be constructed from an assemblage of memorised formulae (Chapter 2). Rather the IELTS Writing test appears to reward a more analytic and exploratory approach to learning.

Implications for stakeholders

In the following section, possible implications of the study are extracted for groups of IELTS stakeholders.

Implications for teachers and course providers

Allow more time for EAP instruction.

A clear finding of this study was that longer periods of instruction would be required for learners to make substantive gains in their Writing skills, as measured by the IELTS Academic Writing test, than envisaged in the recommendations current at the time. Most learners do not make a gain of one band on the IELTS test, in Writing at least, after 200 hours of instruction. This conclusion is supported by the work of Elder and O'Loughlin (2003) in Australia, who found limited gains across skills following three months of preparation.

This study provides an empirical basis for more realistic recommendations regarding the time necessary to make specified gains on the IELTS Academic Writing Module and points to factors likely to have a substantive bearing on rates of gain. These include the age, origin and motivation of learners and their adaptability to the host culture as well as their initial level. Language instruction calls for an investment that stakeholders are understandably reluctant to make, but evidence of the kind provided here may help to correct overly optimistic assumptions about the resources required.

It is very clear that blanket recommendations across proficiency levels are misguided. Targeted recommendations would need to be sensitive to the individual's level on entry to a particular preparation programme. Students entering below a band score of 5 are likely to make more rapid gains in Writing test scores than students who are already at Band 6 and above on entry. It seems highly likely that this latter group will require a greater amount of time to progress.

More fundamentally, given the differences between the content of the IELTS test and the objectives of pre-sessional EAP courses, the relationship between test scores and recommendations for periods of study may need to be reconsidered. There is a need for greater understanding on the part of all involved of the purpose of IELTS and its limitations as an indicator of study skills or academic ability. Learners fulfilling the demands of IELTS may still have much to learn about language and even more to learn about academic conventions. It is incumbent on pre-sessional course providers and language support staff to demonstrate the value of their courses in affording learners learning opportunities that IELTS preparation does not.

The same issue gives rise to the next recommendation:

Introduce IELTS in the context of EAP.

For learners intending to pursue higher education in the UK, it is important that the degree of overlap between IELTS and the construct of academic writing is made explicit. The demands made by the IELTS test are not equivalent to the requirements for academic writing made on university courses. Unless this is made apparent to learners, there may be an assumption that the features of IELTS Writing tasks are representative of all academic writing in English.

At the same time, where IELTS is integrated into brief EAP courses, there is a danger that the high stakes perceived to be associated with the test may cause a narrowing of focus. Students with limited resources of time and money may regard intensive IELTS preparation as the most efficient method of gaining entry to university and assume that reaching the level required indicates readiness. Course providers and teachers have a responsibility to make the possible hidden costs of this strategy clear to learners.

Inform students of relevant research findings.

Course providers and teachers have direct contact with learners and are a key source of guidance for them. Findings from the present study, and studies such as Deakin (1996), Read and Hayes (2003) and Coleman, Starfield and Hagan (2003) provide a valuable resource for teachers and course providers regarding the impact of the IELTS test and its relationship to academic writing needs. Students can be informed of the findings both informally, by teachers in class, and formally through promotional literature and course materials. It is important that learners understand that an IELTS band score at a given level does not imply that they have nothing further to learn about academic writing in English.

Implications for students

If teachers sometimes claim that learners pressure them to focus on test preparation, it is equally true that teachers are key informants for students about the implications of IELTS for their learning and might help to educate them about the role of IELTS.

Realistic expectations of gains in Writing scores over time.

Findings from the present study should prove a helpful source of information for learners about how long they might realistically take to make specified gains in their IELTS Writing scores. They should also serve as a reminder of the limitations of prediction in relation to language learning and test scores. In particular those students who enter courses at Band 6 and above need to be made aware that further score gains may be a longer-term process than had previously been thought.

Understand limitations and seek opportunities to go beyond the demands of the test.

The necessary restrictions of the IELTS tasks as a representation of academic writing suggest that learners will need to pass beyond the immediate requirements of the test if they are to be adequately prepared for academic study. If learners are aware of the limitations of IELTS in this regard, they will be able to make better informed choices about how to prepare themselves for university study. IELTS should not be the only element in this preparation.

Implications for receiving institutions

Be aware of the relationship between the IELTS test and EAP.

The restricted function of IELTS as a test of English language ability must also be an important consideration for receiving institutions. Receiving institutions should understand that the international student experience will be enhanced if ongoing language support is provided to manage the transition from meeting the generic demands of the IELTS tasks to meeting the specific demands of the appropriate academic discourse community in the immediate context of study.

As a corollary, it may no longer be sufficient to base admissions decisions on a simple formulaic approach relating a band score to a fixed period of tuition. The evidence produced in this study points to the complexity of language gain and its measurement and clearly shows the dangers of such an approach.

It is important to take on board the recommendation that interpretation of test scores by institutions should be made with full reference to local conditions. These conditions would include consideration of available support mechanisms in a particular institution, from formal instruction to tutorial support, balanced against the demands of a particular course with regard to writing.

Provide additional support to international students.

Given the length of time that may be required for improvement from a Band 6 level in writing to a recommended Band 7 for postgraduate entry purposes, it may be necessary to rethink the nature of ongoing support for international students. Such improvement in test scores may not be possible prior to registration through traditional pre-sessional approaches but could more readily be addressed by an integrated language and academic support programme over the first few years of PhD study. The solution for one-year Masters students may involve an even heavier amount of such institutional support in a concerted time frame.

Implications for the test developers

Test design implications

One implication of this study is that the IELTS partners, in future revisions of the test, might give serious thought to whether positive washback might be enhanced by increasing the range of task types and other performance conditions covered by the Academic Writing Module, i.e. further improve both its context and cognitive validity (Shaw and Weir 2007). However, this needs to be approached with due consideration to the use of the test in admissions procedures and the theoretical bases for testing English for specific purposes as well as to the practical logistic implications. Questions have been raised about the appropriacy of basing screening tests on a target situation analysis and the literature review in Chapter 1 points to the possibility of tension between desirable forms of preparation and test fairness.

In the short term, consideration is being given to making the tasks less predictable by varying the type and format of non-verbal input to Task 1 and by broadening the range of topics covered and text types required in Task 2. This work is reflected in recent revisions to the Writing prompts and in the test-construction cycle. The impact of memorisation strategies on Writing scores is being investigated through the IELTS-funded research programme (Wray and Pegg 2007) and further security measures have been taken to ensure that writing prompts cannot be predicted or anticipated by candidates.

Provision of information to stakeholders

Institutions

Stakeholders are already advised to take account of local context when interpreting IELTS scores (IELTS 2005). This message needs to be reinforced and further warnings provided on the relationship between gain scores and periods of study in line with the findings of this research. A clear message coming from stakeholders is that more information about the test is required. This has led to the development of new tools for test users such as the *IELTS Scores Explained* DVD intended to provide examples of test material and performance to build awareness of the test and to inform standards setting exercises.

Teachers and learners

Teachers and learners rightly look to examining boards for explicit specifications to guide them in their preparations for tests. Greater explicitness in publishing and publicising the operations and performance conditions involved in the test was called for. The confidential nature of the rating scales at the time of the study left open the suspicion that participants with access to the rating scales were unfairly advantaged. This issue has been addressed through the publication of the scales for Speaking and Writing: public versions of these are now available for download from the IELTS website.

Further guidance on the nature of the relationship between IELTS test content and the demands of the academic discourse community would facilitate decisions on course content and make clear where additional training with respect to academic writing is advisable for those with experience of IELTS preparation. The findings of this study have been publicised through conference presentations and research reports (Green 2003, 2005) and this volume represents a further step in the dissemination process.

A research agenda

The case study approach to washback adopted by Wall (2005) in the early 1990s and followed by Cheng (2005) and others is now well established as a methodology and has proved particularly fruitful in highlighting the role of teachers in moderating test influence. We now have a number of situated examples of how teachers and, to a more limited extent learners, respond to tests. The washback model presented here attempts to capture some of the key lessons from this work. However, it is true to say that our understanding of washback remains partial and restricted and this is partly attributable to limitations of method.

One limitation that this study sought to overcome was the failure to take up Messick's (1996) call and to establish evidential links between tests and behaviours. Differences in test design do seem to play an important role in participant behaviours. However, it is equally clear that there are restrictions on what can be predicted from test design, even where this is well known to participants. If it is apparent that teachers do often follow test format quite closely in specific settings, it is not always so clear, as Alderson (2004) observes, why they choose to do this. Why is it that the TOEFL teachers observed by Alderson and Hamp-Lyons (1996) seemed to put aside the teacherly virtues of lesson and course planning in test-preparation classes while those observed in this study and by Hawkey (2006) did not? Are such differences linked indirectly to test-design issues? Methods that focus closely on individual experiences of test preparation might begin to suggest answers, perhaps by pursuing in greater depth the teacher and learner interview strands of this and other studies.

Importance of outcomes

This study has demonstrated the need to relate perceptions of teachers and learners to measurable outputs. It has often been asserted that narrowing of the curriculum in response to test demands contributes to distortion in the interpretability of test results. By considering product variables together with presage and process variables such assertions are opened to empirical investigation. Indeed, the volume of data assembled for the current study could in itself constitute a valuable resource for future studies.

The study has also pointed to the important distinction between test score gains and any inferences to be drawn about gains in underlying abilities. The washback model suggests that it is possible to exploit test-design characteristics to convey the impression of improvements in underlying abilities by focusing on features of the test rather than on the focal construct: it may be possible to improve scores without improving target abilities. This has obvious implications for the use of test scores in the measurement of gains.

However, in the context of IELTS preparation, this study has cast doubt on the power of dedicated test preparation to deliver the promised yields. Future research into washback, by taking outcomes into account, will provide more grounded accounts of test impact and its implications for test validity.

Centrality of the learner

Washback to the learner is an area that has been under-investigated in the literature. There is evidence here to suggest that variability at the individual level is central to an understanding of the complex process of washback and that the nature and extent of washback to learners does not bear a transparent relationship to washback to the teacher. The response of the individual learner to the demands of the test and to other features of the learning context appear to influence outcomes to a greater extent than their choice of course and the content of their classes.

Just as the work carried out in the 1990s highlighted the role of teachers in promoting or resisting washback, longitudinal studies of how individual learners understand and respond to test demands could provide insights into the complexities of the interaction between learner beliefs and test influence. This work may have equally valuable implications for teachers, learners and test designers.

Impact

Within the broader framework of impact, this study indicates a need to explore the influence of IELTS on the performance of learners after they have entered university and the consequences for those who fail to reach the required level. In particular, research is urgently needed into how far preparation courses assist learners entering university to cope with the language and other demands of academic life. Are learners who pursue pre-sessional programmes in EAP better able to cope with these demands than those accepted on the basis of proficiency test scores alone? This question has attracted some interest in Canada (Matthews 1998, Berman and Rourke 2003), and work such as Banerjee (2003) and Rea-Dickins et al (2005) has shown that the question of how receiving institutions interpret and use IELTS scores is a promising avenue for research. On the basis of such studies it might be possible to discover how far dedicated EAP instruction can assist learners to overcome or to compensate for shortcomings in language proficiency.

While there is no doubt considerable scope for further situated case studies of test preparation, including studies of IELTS preparation for parts of the test and in settings other than those addressed here, wider questions of the social impact of tests also need to be taken up. Comparative studies of how similar test instruments are used and of how their influence is realised in different societies may be of particular value in exploring such questions. Does a test like IELTS encourage similar responses from teachers and learners in a variety of culturally distinct settings?

Value of the washback model

There is sufficient evidence to lay claim to the applicability of the washback model advocated in this study as a framework for identifying areas of washback of interest to the researcher and for investigating the effects of a test on teaching and learning. It relates test design issues to participant attributes, beliefs and behaviours. It extends relationships to curriculum delivery, social context and test outcomes.

Further refinement of the model is needed, particularly in the area of washback variability. This study has considered whether participants gain an advantage through concentrating their efforts on the characteristics of a test. The washback model has provided a useful framework for predicting the forms of preparation that might spring from such a strategy. Given the lack of any clear dividend in this context, however, it is not clear why participants are so attracted to test preparation. It is apparent from the evidence provided here that many participants bring to their classes a belief in the value of test preparation; they believe that scores can be boosted and adapt their behaviour to test demands as the model predicts. Future research might usefully seek explanations from participants for this faith. Longitudinal studies are required exploring how and why learners react to tests and the origins of beliefs about the benefits of test preparation.

Appendix 1 Research questions and methods summary

1) *Given the commonalities and discrepancies between IELTS and the EAP writing construct revealed in the literature review, do students and teachers regard themselves as engaging in IELTS test preparation rather than university preparation and do such beliefs give rise to practices, in relation to IELTS, which fail to address the EAP writing construct?*	**Survey *phase 1a:***		
	Questionnaire to providers	IELTS preparation courses involve narrower range of activities than recommended in EAP literature	Questionnaire administered to BALEAP, BASELT, ARELS members
	Case study phase 1b:		
	Personal Construct Psychology repertory grid interviews	Teachers and students concerned with limited strategies for passing the test rather than preparing for study, not broadly reflective of EAP	Structured PCP interviews with limited sample of teachers and students relating to IELTS driven courses
	Case-study interviews, questionnaires		Interviews with case study participants
	Observations	Activities restricted to those regarded as relevant for IELTS, not broadly reflective of EAP	Observation of sample classes employing adapted COLTeap observation scheme
	Analysis of classroom artefacts	Activities restricted to those regarded as relevant for IELTS, not broadly reflective of EAP	Analysis of artefacts (learner essays, course-books, internally developed worksheets, tests etc.) used in observed classes

2) Do practices on courses which are not driven by IELTS better reflect the EAP writing construct?	**Survey *phase 1a:***		
	Questionnaire to centres	EAP courses involve narrower range of activities than recommended in EAP literature	Questionnaire administered to BALEAP, BASELT, ARELS members
	*Case study **phase 1b:***		
	PCP repertory grid interviews	Teachers and students concerned with limited strategies for passing the course rather than preparing for study, not broadly reflective of EAP	Structured PCP interviews with limited sample of teachers and students relating to EAP driven courses
	Case-study interviews, questionnaires		
	Observations	Activities restricted to those regarded as relevant for passing the course, not broadly reflective of EAP	Observation of sample classes employing adapted COLT observation scheme
	Analysis of artefacts	Activities restricted to those regarded as relevant for passing the course, not broadly reflective of EAP classroom	Analysis of artefacts (learner essays, course-books, internally developed worksheets, tests etc.) used in observed classes
3) What are the characteristics of learners on different courses and how do these relate to the characteristics of the IELTS test-taking population?	*Survey **phase 2:***		
	Learner background questionnaires	Presage and process features are equivalent across course types and reflect wider population of IELTS test takers	Learner background questionnaires

4) Do instructional alternatives at points on a continuum from IELTS-driven to IELTS-unrelated EAP courses result in differential outcomes?	Case study *phase 3:* Quasi-experimental	In predictive model generated by neural network, course type is not predictive of differential outcomes	Course typology derived from phase 1 Pre- and post-test measures of lexico-grammatical competence, IELTS Academic Writing administered to case study participants
5) Do facets of learners' individual differences interact with instructional differences in predicting outcomes?	Case study *phase 3:* Quasi-experimental	In predictive model generated by neural network, either individual difference features alone or instructional features alone are predictive of success: accuracy of prediction is not enhanced by their combination	Pre- and post-measures combined with learner background survey data and course typology

Appendix 2 IELTS Awareness Form A

Before the Writing Test

Before you take the Writing test, we would like to ask you a few questions about yourself.
We are interested in finding out more about how international students prepare for university.
We will not use your name in our reports and we will not tell anyone about your personal answers.

SECTION 1 – About you

1. What is your name? _____   _____
    (Family name)   *(Given names)*

2. Age:_____   3. Sex: ❑ MALE   ❑ FEMALE   4. Nationality: _____

5. What is your first language (the language you usually use at home in your country)? ____

6. What other languages can you use to have a conversation (apart from English)? _____

7. What level of education have you finished (mark your highest level)?

    ❑ School up to 16   ❑ School 16-19 years

    ❑ Undergraduate: first university/college degree   ❑ Postgraduate

SECTION 2 – Your future plans

8. Are you planning to study at a college or university in Britain or other English speaking country?

    ❑   NO ➜   9. What is your reason for taking this course (please write your reason here)?
    _____

    Now go on to SECTION 3

    ❑   YES ➜   10. What subject are you planning to study? _____
                11. At what level are you planning to study after this course (choose one)?
    ❑ Pre-university   ❑ Undergraduate   ❑ Postgraduate   ❑ Other: _____
    (A level, Foundation,   (BA/BSc)   (MA, MSc, PhD)
    Preparation)

SECTION 3 – English language tests

12. Have you ever taken an official IELTS test?
    ❑ YES - What is your most recent test date and score?   ❑ NO (→ GO TO 13)
    → Month ____   Year ____   IELTS Score ____   Name of Test Centre _____

13. Are you intending to take an IELTS test within the next 6 months?   ❑ YES   ❑ NO

14. What IELTS score do you need to get?

    ❑ I don't need an IELTS score   ❑ I don't know   ❑ 4.5 ❑ 5 ❑ 5.5 ❑ 6 ❑ 6.5 ❑ 7 ❑ 7.5

    Very important (5)   Not at all important (1)

15. How important is it for you to pass the IELTS test?

5	4	3	2	1

    Very much (5)   Not at all (1)

16. Do you worry about taking the IELTS test?

5	4	3	2	1

    Very much (5)   Not at all (1)

17. Do you worry about passing this course?

5	4	3	2	1

Are the following statements about the IELTS Writing Test true?   Yes   No   I don't know

18. The IELTS Writing test is 60 minutes long.   ❑   ❑   ❑

19. There are two sections in the Writing test.   ❑   ❑   ❑

20. The Writing test is worth more marks than the Speaking test.   ❑   ❑   ❑

21. The topic for one of the Writing tasks comes from one of the
    texts in the Reading test.   ❑   ❑   ❑

22. The Writing test also has some grammar questions.   ❑   ❑   ❑

23. In Task 1, you should write 150 words.   ❑   ❑   ❑

Appendix 2

After the Writing Test

Please tell us what you did during the test.　　Name: _____

At the beginning, did you plan how much time to spend on each
section of the test?　　　　　　　　　　　　　　　　　　　❏ YES　　❏ NO

| The test takes 60 minutes, about how many minutes did you spend on TASK 1? | _____ minutes |
| The test takes 60 minutes, and about how many minutes did you spend on TASK 2? | _____ minutes |

*About **Task 1** (describing a diagram or table)*

Tick (✓) the boxes on the right to show how far
you agree with each statement.

If you definitely agree, tick 4.

If you definitely disagree, tick 0.

		I definitely agree	I tend to agree	I tend to disagree	I definitely disagree	I don't know / I cannot answer this question
1	I understood the question	4	3	1	0	2
2	I had enough ideas to write about this topic	4	3	1	0	2
3	I had enough time to write about the question	4	3	1	0	2
4	I read the question carefully and underlined or highlighted key words	4	3	1	0	2
5	I made an outline plan before writing	4	3	1	0	2
6	I tried not to write more than the required number of words	4	3	1	0	2
7	I checked my answers for grammar and spelling mistakes	4	3	1	0	2
8	I wrote a draft essay first, then wrote the essay again neatly	4	3	1	0	2

*About **Task 2** (written argument)*

		I definitely agree	I tend to agree	I tend to disagree	I definitely disagree	I don't know / I cannot answer this question
1	I understood the question	4	3	1	0	2
2	I had enough ideas to write about this topic	4	3	1	0	2
3	I had enough time to write about the question	4	3	1	0	2
4	I read the question carefully and underlined or highlighted key words	4	3	1	0	2
5	I made an outline plan before writing	4	3	1	0	2
6	I tried not to write more than the required number of words	4	3	1	0	2
7	I checked my answers for grammar and spelling mistakes	4	3	1	0	2
8	I wrote a draft essay first, then wrote the essay again neatly	4	3	1	0	2

Appendix 3 IELTS Awareness Form B

Before the Writing Test

Before you take the Writing test, we would like to ask you a few questions about your studies.
We are interested in finding out more about how international students prepare for university.
We will not use your name in our reports and we will not tell anyone about your personal answers.

SECTION 1 - About you

1. What is your name? _____   _____
   (Family name)   *(Given names)*

2. How old are you? _____   3. Where is your home country? _____

SECTION 2 - During this course . . .

4. Outside class, about how many hours did you *study*
   English each week?   _____ hours

5. How many hours each week did you watch TV/listen
   to the radio in English?   _____ hours

6. Outside class, how much of the time did you use English
   or your own/other languages?

   Always English (1)   Always my language/other language (9)

1	2	3	4	5	6	7	8	9

7. Outside class, for how many hours each week did
   you talk to native English speakers?   _____ hours

8. Outside class, how many hours a week did you talk in
   English to other non-native speakers?   _____ hours

9. How many hours each week do you read English
   newspapers, magazines or books for pleasure?   _____ hours

10. How many hours each week do you read about your
    specialist subject in English?   _____ hours

11. Please give details of any English text books you use outside school to study English
    (including books written mostly in your own language).

Title and Writer	Why did you choose this book?

SECTION 3 - English language tests

12. Have you taken an official IELTS test in the last 3 months?
    ❏ YES - What was your test date and score?   ❏ NO (→ *GO TO 13*)
    ❏ Month _____   Year _____   IELTS Score _____
    Name of Test Centre _____

13. Are you intending to take an IELTS test within the next 6 months?   ❏ YES   ❏ NO

14. What score will you need?
    ❏ I don't need an IELTS score ❏ I don't know ❏ 4.5 ❏ 5 ❏ 5.5 ❏ 6 ❏ 6.5 ❏ 7 ❏ 7.5

Are the following statements about the IELTS Writing Test true?   Yes   No   I don't know

15. The IELTS Writing test is 60 minutes long.   ❏   ❏   ❏

16. There are two sections in the Writing test.   ❏   ❏   ❏

17. The Writing test is worth more marks than the Speaking test.   ❏   ❏   ❏

18. The topic for one of the Writing tasks comes
    from one of the texts in the Reading test.   ❏   ❏   ❏

19. The Writing test also includes some grammar questions.   ❏   ❏   ❏

20. In Task 1, you should write 150 words.   ❏   ❏   ❏

After the Writing Test

Please tell us what you did during the test.   Name: _____

At the beginning, did you plan how much time to spend on each
section of the test?   ❏ YES   ❏ NO

The test takes 60 minutes, about how many minutes did you spend on TASK 1?	_____ minutes
and about how many minutes did you spend on TASK 2?	_____ minutes

*About **Task 1** (describing a diagram or table)*

Tick (✓) the boxes on the right to show how far
you agree with each statement.

If you definitely agree, tick 4.
If you definitely disagree, tick 0.

		I definitely agree	I tend to agree	I tend to disagree	I definitely disagree	I don't know / I cannot answer this question
1	I understood the question	4	3	1	0	2
2	I had enough ideas to write about this topic	4	3	1	0	2
3	I had enough time to write about the question	4	3	1	0	2
4	I read the question carefully and underlined or highlighted key words	4	3	1	0	2
5	I made an outline plan before writing	4	3	1	0	2
6	I tried not to write more than the required number of words	4	3	1	0	2
7	I checked my answers for grammar and spelling mistakes	4	3	1	0	2
8	I wrote a draft essay first, then wrote the essay again neatly	4	3	1	0	2

*About **Task 2** (written argument)*

		I definitely agree	I tend to agree	I tend to disagree	I definitely disagree	I don't know / I cannot answer this question
1	I understood the question	4	3	1	0	2
2	I had enough ideas to write about this topic	4	3	1	0	2
3	I had enough time to write about the question	4	3	1	0	2
4	I read the question carefully and underlined or highlighted key words	4	3	1	0	2
5	I made an outline plan before writing	4	3	1	0	2
6	I tried not to write more than the required number of words	4	3	1	0	2
7	I checked my answers for grammar and spelling mistakes	4	3	1	0	2
8	I wrote a draft essay first, then wrote the essay again neatly	4	3	1	0	2

Appendix 4 Teacher Questionnaire

EAP/IELTS Course End Teacher Questionnaire

About your professional background		
Name	Age	Sex

Professional qualifications	
1.	2.
3.	4.
5.	6.

Experience		
Years experience in EFL.	Experience of IELTS preparation courses.	Experience of other EAP teaching.

Do you have experience of IELTS? ❑ YES-Please answer these questions
❑ NO-Please turn over to the next page

Have you received any training in teaching IELTS preparation? Give details.

How much experience, if any, do you have as an IELTS . . .

examiner	item writer	other (e.g. examiner trainer)

Do you consider the IELTS to be a fair screening test for university? Why?

How is teaching IELTS preparation different from other classes you have taught?

To what extent do you believe it is possible to prepare students for the IELTS Academic Writing tasks?

Is one task easier to prepare for than the other? (why?)

What would be your strongest criticism of the IELTS Academic Writing module?

What do you regard as the greatest strength of the IELTS Academic Writing module?

Your feelings about this course

What do you enjoy about teaching this course?

What do you dislike about teaching this course?

Is it easier or more difficult to teach than other courses? Why?

	Very suitable		Unsuitable		Don't know
To what extent do you feel studying on this course provides a suitable preparation for . . .					
postgraduate study	4	3	1	0	2
undergraduate study	4	3	1	0	2
pre-university study	4	3	1	0	2

Comment:

Course topics and content

1. Topics were academic   Topics were of personal/general interest

   9   8   7   6   5   4   3   2   1

2. Teacher/syllabus controlled the   Students controlled course content
   course content

   9   8   7   6   5   4   3   2   1

3. Classes followed the book   Classes did not follow the book or syllabus

   9   8   7   6   5   4   3   2   1

4. Students asked for content relating   Students did not ask for
   to IELTS   IELTS content

   9   8   7   6   5   4   3   2   1

5. To what extent do you think the topics and content of these classes were influenced by the IELTS test?

    Very much   Not at all

9	8	7	6	5	4	3	2	1

6. How did IELTS influence the choice of course content and topics?

7. What other factors influenced the choice of course content and topics?

8. Comments

Assessment on the course

1. Students evaluated each others work Students did not evaluate each others work

9	8	7	6	5	4	3	2	1

2. Students assessed their own work   Students did not assess their own work

9	8	7	6	5	4	3	2	1

3. The teacher graded all student work   The teacher did not grade student work

9	8	7	6	5	4	3	2	1

4. To what extent do you think the assessment of student work was influenced by the IELTS test?

    Very much   Not at all

9	8	7	6	5	4	3	2	1

5. Did you give feedback to students in the form of IELTS-equivalent bandscores?

    Always   Not at all

9	8	7	6	5	4	3	2	1

6. How else did IELTS influence the assessment of student work?

7. What other factors influenced the assessment of student work?

8. Comment

Appendix 4

Student attitudes

1. Class was well motivated, on-task   Class was unmotivated, off-task

9	8	7	6	5	4	3	2	1

2. Students ask for extra homework   Students do not work outside class

9	8	7	6	5	4	3	2	1

3. To what extent do you think student effort was influenced by the IELTS test?
    Very much   Not at all

9	8	7	6	5	4	3	2	1

4. How did IELTS influence student effort?

5. What other factors influenced student effort?

Comment

Balance of skills development

1. Discourse level skills   Sentence level skills

9	8	7	6	5	4	3	2	1

2. Memorised language   Communication strategies

9	8	7	6	5	4	3	2	1

3. Skills with a use beyond the course   Training just for test/course requirements

9	8	7	6	5	4	3	2	1

4. Study skills   Language skills

9	8	7	6	5	4	3	2	1

5. Skills taught were conceptually unfamiliar   Conceptually familiar skills
    to students

9	8	7	6	5	4	3	2	1

6. To what extent do you think the balance of skills development was influenced by the IELTS test?

Very much   Not at all

9	8	7	6	5	4	3	2	1

7. How did IELTS influence the balance of skills development in the class?

8. What other factors influenced the balance of skills development in the class?

9. Comment

Class organisation

How frequent were the following groupings in class?

		Most classes								No classes
1.	Individual work	1	2	3	4	5	6	7	8	9
2.	Pair work	1	2	3	4	5	6	7	8	9
3.	Small group work	1	2	3	4	5	6	7	8	9
4.	Whole class activity	1	2	3	4	5	6	7	8	9
5.	Teacher lectures to class	1	2	3	4	5	6	7	8	9
6.	Other:	1	2	3	4	5	6	7	8	9

7. To what extent do you think the organisation of the class was influenced by the IELTS test?

Very much   Not at all

9	8	7	6	5	4	3	2	1

8. How did IELTS influence the organisation of the class?

9. What other factors influenced the organisation of the class?

Comment

Quantity and types of student writing

1. How often did students write essays (or sections of essays) in class?

Every class   Never

9	8	7	6	5	4	3	2	1

2. How many written assignments, on average, did students submit each month?

   _____

3. How long were the essays *expected* to be? shortest _____ longest _____

What kinds of writing task have you focused on during the course (e.g. lab reports, discursive essays etc.)?

What aspects of writing have you focused on during the course (e.g. organisation, writing from sources, cohesion, grammatical accuracy etc.)

4. To what extent do you think the choice of writing activities was influenced by the IELTS Academic Writing test?

   Very much   Not at all

9	8	7	6	5	4	3	2	1

6. How did IELTS influence essay writing activities?

7. What other factors influenced the choice of writing activities?

8. Comment.

Student learning

How far do you think the following statements characterise the kinds of student learning **required** for **success on this course**?

Student learning on this course involved . . .

	Critical to success		Unnecessary to successs		Don't know/unclear
1. Collecting new information provided by the teacher	4	3	1	0	2
2. Changing as a person	4	3	1	0	2
3. Assessing the relative value of theories and evidence	4	3	1	0	2
4. Being able to use and apply information in new contexts	4	3	1	0	2
5. Remembering/recalling facts and information	4	3	1	0	2
6. Understanding by giving knowledge a personal meaning	4	3	1	0	2
7. Seeing patterns: recognising the organisation or classification of information	4	3	1	0	2

8. Overall, what would you hope students have learned from this course?

Learning objectives

1. To what extent do the following statements represent learning objectives for this class?

	I definitely agree	I tend to agree	I tend to disagree	I definitely disagree	I don't know / I cannot answer this question
CT01 Students learn technical vocabulary for their university subjects.	4	3	1	0	2
CT02 Students learn general vocabulary.	4	3	1	0	2
CT03 Students learn about the kinds of writing tasks they will do at university.	4	3	1	0	2
CT04 Students learn about differences between university education in their countries and in Britain.	4	3	1	0	2
CT05 Students learn ways of improving their English language test scores.	4	3	1	0	2
CT06 Students learn words and phrases for describing graphs and diagrams.	4	3	1	0	2
CT07 Students learn how to use evidence to support their written arguments.	4	3	1	0	2
CT08 Students learn how to organise an essay to help the reader to understand.	4	3	1	0	2
CT09 Students learn how to communicate their ideas effectively in writing.	4	3	1	0	2
CT10 Students learn grammar.	4	3	1	0	2
CT11 Students learn how to write university essays and reports.	4	3	1	0	2
CT12 Students learn how to find information from lectures or course books to use in writing essays.	4	3	1	0	2
CT13 Students learn how to use quotations and references in academic writing.	4	3	1	0	2
CT14 Students learn how to edit and redraft their written work.	4	3	1	0	2
CT15 Students learn how to use ideas from text books or academic journals in their writing.	4	3	1	0	2
CT16 Students learn how to write long essays or reports of 1,000 words or more.	4	3	1	0	2

		4	3	1	0		2
CT17	Students learn how to organise their time for studying.	4	3	1	0		2
CT18	I correct students' grammar mistakes in their written work.	4	3	1	0		2
CT19	The class activities are similar to the ones on the IELTS test.	4	3	1	0		2
CT20	Students learn quick and efficient ways of reading books in English.	4	3	1	0		2
CT21	Students learn how to write successful test essays.	4	3	1	0		2
CT22	Students read books and articles about their specialist subject areas.	4	3	1	0		2
CT23	Students learn how to write in a formal, academic style.	4	3	1	0		2
CT24	Students take practice tests in class.	4	3	1	0		2
CT25	Students learn about the expectations of university supervisors.	4	3	1	0		2
CT26	Students learn the full process of writing (planning, drafting, revising).	4	3	1	0		2
CT27	Student receive grammar correction on written work.	4	3	1	0		2
CT28	Students do individual or group project work.	4	3	1	0		2
CT29	Students memorise phrases and structures.	4	3	1	0		2
CT30	Students learn subtechnical academic vocabulary (vocabulary found in academic texts across disciplines, but less frequent in general English contexts).	4	3	1	0		2
CT31	Students read material in their intended subject areas.	4	3	1	0		2
CT32	Students copy out models of good writing.	4	3	1	0		2

Other learning objectives of relevance to Academic Writing

CT33	_____	4	3	1	0		2
CT34	_____	4	3	1	0		2

2. How did IELTS influence the learning objectives on the course?

Very much   Not at all

9	8	7	6	5	4	3	2	1

3. What other factors influenced the learning objectives?

4. Comment.

If you have any additional comments about the course, or about this questionnaire, please write them here:

Appendix 5 Student Questionnaire A

STUDENT QUESTIONNAIRE A

In this questionnaire, we would like to find out about your experience of studying English, about what you expect to study on this course and about how you like to learn

*We hope these questions will also help **you** to think about how you study and about how to be successful*

The questions usually take about 20 minutes to answer

We will not use your name in our reports and we will not tell anyone about your personal answers, but we do need these details to help us to organise the information

If you have any trouble understanding a question, please ask your teacher or use a dictionary to help you. Thank you.

➔ **About you**
1. What is your name? _____   _____
   (Family name)   (Given names)
2. How old are you? _____   3. Where is your home country?_____

➔ **About how often you use English**
4. In your country, or before moving to Britain, how often have you used English in your work (including all the jobs you have done)?
   I have worked mainly in English (1)   I have not used English at work (9)

1	2	3	4	5	6	7	8	9

5. At home or at work, in your country, how often do you use English for socialising (talking to friends)?
   I usually socialise in English (1)   I usually socialise using my own/other language (9)

1	2	3	4	5	6	7	8	9

6. At home or at work, in your country, how often do you write in English?
   I write in English every day (1)   I never write in English (9)

1	2	3	4	5	6	7	8	9

7. At home or at work, in your country, how often do you read in English?
   I read in English every day (1)   I never read in English (9)

1	2	3	4	5	6	7	8	9

→ **About studying English**

8. As a child, did you live with a parent, guardian or other close relation who was a native speaker of English (English was their first language)? ☐ YES ☐ NO

9. As a child, did you live with a parent, guardian or other close relation who could have a conversation in English (although English was not their first language)?
☐ YES ☐ NO

10. Did you study English in . . .
Kindergarten (age 3–6) ☐ Primary school (7–11) ☐
University/college ☐ Secondary school (12–17) ☐
Extra language classes outside school ☐

11. Did you study English as your main/major subject at university?
☐ YES ☐ NO ☐ I have not been to university

12. Have you ever been taught other subject classes (for example science or maths) in English?
☐ Yes, at school ☐ Yes, at university ☐ Never

13. How many of your English lessons in your country were given by native speakers of English?

Most classes (1)　　More than half　　About half (5)　　Less than half　　A few　　None (9)

1	2	3	4	5	6	7	8	9

14. How much of the time in class did your English teachers speak to you in English?

All the time (1)　　More than half　　About half the time (5)　　Less than half　　Never (9)

1	2	3	4	5	6	7	8	9

15. How often did you practise writing in English in your classes?

In most classes (1)　　More than half　　About half (5)　　Less than half　　Never (9)

1	2	3	4	5	6	7	8	9

16. How often do you usually write essays and reports in your own language?

Often (about once a month) (1)　　Quite often　　Sometimes (once a year) (5)　　Occasionally　　Never (9)

1	2	3	4	5	6	7	8	9

17. Since leaving school/university have you studied English with a teacher in your own country?
☐ YES for ___ *years* ☐ NO (→ *GO TO 19*)
↓

18. Since leaving school/university, in your country, how many hours did you study English with a teacher each week?
about _____ *hours*

19. Have you stayed in any English speaking countries for more than two weeks (including this trip, if you are in Britain now)?
    ☐ YES for a total of _____ *years,* _____ *months*   ☐ NO (➔ *GO TO 22*)
    ⬇

20. How long have you studied English in any English speaking countries (including this school, if you are in Britain now)?
    For a total of _____ *years,* _____ *months*

21. If you studied English in an English speaking country, how many hours did you study each week on average?
    about _____ *hours*

22. Have you ever studied on an IELTS preparation course before?
    ☐ YES for _____ weeks   ☐ NO

Before you begin the rest of the questionnaire, please look at this example question.

Look at the statements below.

If you definitely agree with a statement mark 4 (I definitely agree).
If you definitely disagree mark 0 (I definitely disagree).
Do not mark 2 unless you cannot understand, or really cannot give an answer to the question.

Please mark your answers in the boxes on the right.

	I definitely agree	I tend to agree	I tend to disagree	I definitely disagree	I don't know / I cannot answer this question
a) I enjoy listening to music while I study.	④	3	1	0	2

In the example question, the student usually likes listening to music while she studies, so she has marked 4, 'I definitely agree'.

➔ **SECTION 1**

In this section, we would like to find out about your reasons for taking this course and for studying in an English speaking country.

	I definitely agree	I tend to agree	I tend to disagree	I definitely disagree	I don't know / I cannot answer this question
RE1 I am taking this course because I want to get a good grade on IELTS (or other test/ assessment called: _____).	4	3	1	0	2
RE2 I am taking this course because I want to learn useful skills for studying at university.	4	3	1	0	2
RE3 I am studying on this course because I want to improve my general ability to use English.	4	3	1	0	2

RE4   I am required to take the course by my employer, my parents, or other authority. (_____)

| 4 | 3 | 1 | 0 | | 2 |

RE5   I have a different reason for taking this course (write your reason here): (my reason is: _____).

| 4 | 3 | 1 | 0 | | 2 |

RE6   Which reason for taking this course (RE1 – RE5) is most important for you (circle one)?

RE1 RE2 RE3 RE4 RE5

RE7   I am going to college/university in an English speaking country to improve my English.

| 4 | 3 | 1 | 0 | | 2 |

RE8   I am going to college/university in an English speaking country to help me get a good job in the future.

| 4 | 3 | 1 | 0 | | 2 |

RE9   I am going to college/university in an English speaking country to study a subject that interests me.

| 4 | 3 | 1 | 0 | | 2 |

RE10 I am required to attend university/college by my employer, my parents, or other authority.(_____)

| 4 | 3 | 1 | 0 | | 2 |

RE11 I have a different reason for going to college/university in an English speaking country: (my reason is: _____).

| 4 | 3 | 1 | 0 | | 2 |

RE12 Which reason for going to college (RE7– RE11) is most important for you (circle one)?

RE7 RE8 RE9 RE10 RE11

→ SECTION 2

In this section, we would like to find out how you feel about learning languages and about taking tests.

	I definitely agree	I tend to agree	I tend to disagree	I definitely disagree		I don't know / I cannot answer this question
SC01 People say that I am good at language learning.	4	3	1	0		2
SC02 I feel happy about living in an English speaking country.	4	3	1	0		2
SC03 I usually did better than other students at my school in English classes.	4	3	1	0		2
SC04 I do NOT really like the British way of life.	4	3	1	0		2
SC05 I am NOT good at writing in English.	4	3	1	0		2

SC06	I feel I will never really enjoy writing in English	4	3	1	0		2	
SC07	Writing classes are difficult for me.	4	3	1	0		2	
SC08	I am pleased I chose to study at this school.	4	3	1	0		2	
SC09	I like writing down my ideas in English.	4	3	1	0		2	
SC10	If we had no tests, I think I would actually learn more.	4	3	1	0		2	
SC11	I usually enjoy meeting British people.	4	3	1	0		2	
SC12	I think learning languages is more difficult for me than for the average learner.	4	3	1	0		2	
SC13	During an important test, I often feel so nervous that I forget facts I really know.	4	3	1	0		2	
SC14	I DON'T think I write in English as well as other students.	4	3	1	0		2	
SC15	It is easy for me to write good English essays.	4	3	1	0		2	
SC16	Even when I'm well prepared for a test, I feel very worried about it.	4	3	1	0		2	
SC17	I DON'T study any harder for final exams than for the rest of my course work.	4	3	1	0		2	
SC18	I think the Writing classes will be useful for me.	4	3	1	0		2	
SC19	I enjoy writing in English.	4	3	1	0		2	

Comments on your feelings about learning English and taking tests.

→ SECTION 3

In this section, we would like to learn about what you want to study during this course, and what you expect to do in your classes.

		I definitely agree	I tend to agree	I tend to disagree	I definitely disagree		I don't know / I cannot answer the question
CE18	I expect my teacher to correct my grammar mistakes in my written work.	4	3	1	0		2

CE19   I expect the activities we do in class will be similar to the ones on the IELTS test. | 4 | 3 | 1 | 0 | | 2 |

CE04   I expect to learn about differences between university education in my country and in Britain. | 4 | 3 | 1 | 0 | | 2 |

CE03   I expect to learn about the kinds of writing tasks students do at university. | 4 | 3 | 1 | 0 | | 2 |

CE09   I expect to learn how to communicate my ideas effectively in writing. | 4 | 3 | 1 | 0 | | 2 |

CE14   I expect to learn how to edit and redraft my written work. | 4 | 3 | 1 | 0 | | 2 |

CE12   I expect to learn how to find information from books to use in writing essays. | 4 | 3 | 1 | 0 | | 2 |

CE08   I expect to learn how to organise an essay to help the reader to understand. | 4 | 3 | 1 | 0 | | 2 |

CE17   I expect to learn how to organise my time for studying. | 4 | 3 | 1 | 0 | | 2 |

CE07   I expect to learn how to use evidence to support my written arguments. | 4 | 3 | 1 | 0 | | 2 |

CE15   I expect to learn how to use ideas from text books or academic journals in my writing. | 4 | 3 | 1 | 0 | | 2 |

CE13   I expect to learn how to use quotations and references in academic writing. | 4 | 3 | 1 | 0 | | 2 |

CE23   I expect to learn how to write in a formal, academic style. | 4 | 3 | 1 | 0 | | 2 |

CE16   I expect to learn how to write long essays or reports of 1,000 words or more. | 4 | 3 | 1 | 0 | | 2 |

CE21   I expect to learn how to write successful test essays. | 4 | 3 | 1 | 0 | | 2 |

CE11   I expect to learn how to write university essays and reports. | 4 | 3 | 1 | 0 | | 2 |

CE20   I expect to learn quick and efficient ways of reading books in English. | 4 | 3 | 1 | 0 | | 2 |

CE02   I expect to learn general vocabulary. | 4 | 3 | 1 | 0 | | 2 |

CE10   I expect to learn grammar. | 4 | 3 | 1 | 0 | | 2 |

CE01   I expect to learn specialist vocabulary for my university subject. | 4 | 3 | 1 | 0 | | 2 |

CE06   I expect to learn words and phrases for describing graphs and diagrams. | 4 | 3 | 1 | 0 | | 2 |

CE05   I expect to learn ways of improving my English Language test scores. | 4 | 3 | 1 | 0 | | 2 |

CE22   I expect to read books and articles about my specialist subject area. | 4 | 3 | 1 | 0 | | 2 |

CE24   I expect to take practice tests in class.

| 4 | 3 | 1 | 0 | | 2 |

Other points you expect to study.

CE25 _____

| 4 | 3 | 1 | 0 | | 2 |

CE26 _____

| 4 | 3 | 1 | 0 | | 2 |

CE27   Which of these items (CE01 – CE24) do you think is most important for you?

_____

Comments on your expectations of this class:

➔ **SECTION 4**

In this section, we are interested in finding out about your general approach to studying (how you usually study). Do you learn best by seeing or doing, by reading or listening? Do you like to learn in a group or by yourself?

Instructions for Section 4.

You will see two sentences. Please decide which sentence better describes you.
Mark your choice on the scale.
If the first sentence describes you much better than the second sentence, mark 1.
If the second sentence describes you better, mark 9.
If both sentences are equally true about you, or if neither sentence is true for you, mark 5.

Example   I like listening to music while I study   I like to study in silence

| 1 | 2 | ③ | 4 | 5 | 6 | 7 | 8 | 9 |

The student usually likes to listen to music while she studies, but sometimes she likes to study in silence so she has marked 3.

LP01   I prefer to study by making or   I prefer to study by looking at charts,
       building things   maps or diagrams

| 1 | 2 | 3 | 4 | 5 | 6 | 7 | 8 | 9 |

LP02   I learn better when the teacher   I learn better when I can touch the things
       tells me something   I am learning about

| 1 | 2 | 3 | 4 | 5 | 6 | 7 | 8 | 9 |

LP03   I learn better when I work alone on assignments   I learn better when I work on group projects

| 1 | 2 | 3 | 4 | 5 | 6 | 7 | 8 | 9 |

LP04   I understand things better when I practise a new skill   I understand things better when the teacher gives a lecture

| 1 | 2 | 3 | 4 | 5 | 6 | 7 | 8 | 9 |

LP05   I understand more when I work on an assignment with two or three classmates   I understand more when I work by myself on assignments

| 1 | 2 | 3 | 4 | 5 | 6 | 7 | 8 | 9 |

LP06   I learn better by participating in role plays   I learn better when the teacher tells me something

| 1 | 2 | 3 | 4 | 5 | 6 | 7 | 8 | 9 |

LP07   I remember images and pictures   I remember things that I have heard people say

| 1 | 2 | 3 | 4 | 5 | 6 | 7 | 8 | 9 |

LP08   I understand better by reading books   I understand better by doing experiments or practical activities

| 1 | 2 | 3 | 4 | 5 | 6 | 7 | 8 | 9 |

LP09   I learn more when I write down my ideas   I learn more when I build something for myself

| 1 | 2 | 3 | 4 | 5 | 6 | 7 | 8 | 9 |

LP10   I enjoy reading for pleasure   I enjoy listening to people talking on the radio or on tape

| 1 | 2 | 3 | 4 | 5 | 6 | 7 | 8 | 9 |

LP11   I remember things better when I work with other students   I remember things better when I work independently

| 1 | 2 | 3 | 4 | 5 | 6 | 7 | 8 | 9 |

LP12   I learn more when someone tells me instructions   I learn more when I can make something for a class project

| 1 | 2 | 3 | 4 | 5 | 6 | 7 | 8 | 9 |

LP13   I learn when I write down my ideas   I learn more when the teacher gives a lecture

| 1 | 2 | 3 | 4 | 5 | 6 | 7 | 8 | 9 |

LP14   I prefer listening to the teacher   I prefer doing things in class

| 1 | 2 | 3 | 4 | 5 | 6 | 7 | 8 | 9 |

LP15   I understand better when someone tells me what to do   I understand better when I look at visual instructions

| 1 | 2 | 3 | 4 | 5 | 6 | 7 | 8 | 9 |

LP16   I remember better when I do experiments or practical activities   I remember better when I look at diagrams or pictures

| 1 | 2 | 3 | 4 | 5 | 6 | 7 | 8 | 9 |

LP17   I prefer to solve my problems by myself   When I have a problem, I usually ask for help from other people

| 1 | 2 | 3 | 4 | 5 | 6 | 7 | 8 | 9 |

LP18   I understand better when the teacher gives a lecture   I understand better when I read books

| 1 | 2 | 3 | 4 | 5 | 6 | 7 | 8 | 9 |

LP19   I enjoy making models or doing crafts   I enjoy reading for pleasure

| 1 | 2 | 3 | 4 | 5 | 6 | 7 | 8 | 9 |

LP20   I understand better by writing about a topic   I understand better by doing activities in class

| 1 | 2 | 3 | 4 | 5 | 6 | 7 | 8 | 9 |

Comments on how you like to learn:

Did you find any questions difficult to understand? Please write the numbers here.

That is the end of the questionnaire. Thank you very much for your help. If you have any other comments you would like to make please write them here.

Thank you very much for your help and co-operation.
This survey was prepared by:
Centre for Research in Testing, Evaluation and Curriculum, Erasmus House, Digby Stuart College, University of Surrey, Roehampton, Roehampton Lane, London SW15 5PU

Appendix 6 Student Questionnaire B

STUDENT QUESTIONNAIRE B

In this questionnaire, we would like to find out about what you have studied on this course.

We hope the questions will help you to think about what you have learned on the course and about what to expect from studying at university in Britain.

The questions usually take about 20 minutes to answer.

We will not use your name in our reports and we will not tell anyone about your personal answers, but we do need your name to help us to organise the information.

If you have any trouble understanding a question, please ask your teacher or use a dictionary to help you. Thank you.

➔ About you

1. What is your name? _____ _____
   (Family name) *(Given names)*

2. How old are you? _____ 3. Where is your home country? _____

Before you begin the rest of the questionnaire, please look at this example question.

Look at the statements below.

If you definitely agree with a statement mark 4 (I definitely agree).
If you definitely disagree mark 0 (I definitely disagree).
Do not mark 2 unless you cannot understand, or really cannot answer the question.

Please mark your answers in the boxes on the right.

	I definitely agree	I tend to agree	I tend to disagree	I definitely disagree		I don't know / I cannot answer this question
a) I enjoy listening to music while I study.	④	3	1	0		2

In the example question, the student usually likes listening to music while she studies, so she has marked 4 'I definitely agree'.

➔ SECTION 1

In this section, we would like to find out about what you learned on this course.

		I definitely agree	I tend to agree	I tend to disagree	I definitely disagree		I don't know / I cannot answer this question
CO03	I learned about the kinds of writing tasks students do at university.	4	3	1	0		2
CO07	I learned how to use evidence to support my written arguments.	4	3	1	0		2
CO20	I learned quick and efficient ways of reading books in English.	4	3	1	0		2
CO08	I learned how to organise an essay to help the reader to understand.	4	3	1	0		2

CO15 I learned how to use ideas from text | 4 | 3 | 1 | 0 | | 2 |
books or academic journals in my writing.

CO10 I learned grammar. | 4 | 3 | 1 | 0 | | 2 |

CO04 I learned about differences between | 4 | 3 | 1 | 0 | | 2 |
university education in my country
and in Britain.

CO17 I learned how to organise my time | 4 | 3 | 1 | 0 | | 2 |
for studying.

CO05 I learned ways of improving my | 4 | 3 | 1 | 0 | | 2 |
English Language test scores.

CO06 I learned words and phrases for | 4 | 3 | 1 | 0 | | 2 |
describing graphs and diagrams.

CO23 I learned how to write in a formal, | 4 | 3 | 1 | 0 | | 2 |
academic style.

CO24 I took practice tests in class. | 4 | 3 | 1 | 0 | | 2 |

CO14 I learned how to edit and redraft my | 4 | 3 | 1 | 0 | | 2 |
written work.

CO19 The activities we did in class were similar | 4 | 3 | 1 | 0 | | 2 |
to the ones on the IELTS test.

CO11 I learned how to write university | 4 | 3 | 1 | 0 | | 2 |
essays and reports.

CO18 My teacher corrected my grammar | 4 | 3 | 1 | 0 | | 2 |
mistakes in my written work.

CO21 I learned how to write successful | 4 | 3 | 1 | 0 | | 2 |
test essays.

CO01 I learned specialist vocabulary for my | 4 | 3 | 1 | 0 | | 2 |
university subject.

CO16 I learned how to write long essays | 4 | 3 | 1 | 0 | | 2 |
or reports of 1,000 words or more.

CO22 I learned to read books and articles | 4 | 3 | 1 | 0 | | 2 |
about the specialist subject area I will
study at university.

CO13 I learned how to use quotations and | 4 | 3 | 1 | 0 | | 2 |
references in academic writing.

CO02 I learned general vocabulary. | 4 | 3 | 1 | 0 | | 2 |

CO09 I learned how to communicate my | 4 | 3 | 1 | 0 | | 2 |
ideas effectively in writing.

CO12 I learned how to find information | 4 | 3 | 1 | 0 | | 2 |
from lectures or course books to use
in writing essays.

Other points you learned.

CO25 _____ | 4 | 3 | 1 | 0 | | 2 |

CO26 _____ | 4 | 3 | 1 | 0 | | 2 |

Comments on what you learned in this class:

➔ **SECTION 2**

In this section, we would like to find out
*about **how** you learned during this course*
and your feelings about your studies.

How often did you do the following? Mark
your answer from 4 (usually) to 0 (never).

Column headers: Usually | Quite often | Occasionally | Never | I don't know / I cannot answer this question

Code	Statement	4	3	1	0	2
PS01	I memorised English words by saying or writing them several times.	4	3	1	0	2
PS02	I tested my knowledge of new English words by using them in different ways.	4	3	1	0	2
PS03	I tried to find better ways of learning English.	4	3	1	0	2
PS04	I looked for words in my own language that look or sound similar to new words in English.	4	3	1	0	2
PS05	I tried to improve my writing by asking others (e.g. teachers, students, friends) to correct my mistakes.	4	3	1	0	2
PS06	I noticed mistakes in my writing, and used that information to help me do better.	4	3	1	0	2
PS07	I took IELTS Writing or other practice writing tests in my free time.	4	3	1	0	2
PS08	I tried to find grammar patterns in English.	4	3	1	0	2
PS09	I looked for people I could talk to in English.	4	3	1	0	2
PS10	I studied vocabulary in my free time.	4	3	1	0	2
PS11	I thought about my progress in learning English.	4	3	1	0	2
PS12	I studied extra English outside school.	4	3	1	0	2
PS13	I tested myself on new words or phrases I learned.	4	3	1	0	2
PS14	If I couldn't think of an English word, I used a word or phrase that means the same thing.	4	3	1	0	2
PS15	I reviewed my class notes or text book in my free time.	4	3	1	0	2
PS16	I tried to learn about the culture of English speakers.	4	3	1	0	2
PS17	I encouraged myself to use English even when I was afraid of making a mistake.	4	3	1	0	2

PS18   I read English without looking up every | 4 | 3 | 1 | 0 | | 2 |
new word.

PS19   When reading in English, I tried to | 4 | 3 | 1 | 0 | | 2 |
translate into my language to help
me understand.

PS20   I studied grammar in my free time. | 4 | 3 | 1 | 0 | | 2 |

PS21   I was NOT sure how to improve my | 4 | 3 | 1 | 0 | | 2 |
English skills.

PS22   I used new English words in sentences so | 4 | 3 | 1 | 0 | | 2 |
I could remember them.

PS23   When I learned a grammar rule, I tested | 4 | 3 | 1 | 0 | | 2 |
myself to make sure I really knew it.

PS24   I tried to improve my writing by doing | 4 | 3 | 1 | 0 | | 2 |
extra writing activities at home.

PS25   To understand unfamiliar English words, | 4 | 3 | 1 | 0 | | 2 |
I tried to guess their meaning.

PS26   When writing in English, I tried to | 4 | 3 | 1 | 0 | | 2 |
translate from my language.

PS27   I thought about the goals I wanted to | 4 | 3 | 1 | 0 | | 2 |
achieve on this course.

PS28   Before studying, I planned what to do, so | 4 | 3 | 1 | 0 | | 2 |
I could use my time well.

PS29   I tried to improve my writing by analysing | 4 | 3 | 1 | 0 | | 2 |
the work of other writers.

PS30   When I received corrected work from | 4 | 3 | 1 | 0 | | 2 |
the teacher, I thought about how to
improve next time.

Other ways you learned.

PS31   _____ | 4 | 3 | 1 | 0 | | 2 |

PS32   _____ | 4 | 3 | 1 | 0 | | 2 |

Comments on what you did to help you learn in this class:

→ SECTION 3

*In this section, we would like to find out about
how much progress you have made and how
satisfied you are with the course.*

I definitely agree	I tend to agree	I tend to disagree	I definitely disagree		I don't know / I cannot answer this question

IM01   After studying on this course, I would | 4 | 3 | 1 | 0 | | 2 |
feel more confident about taking an
IELTS Writing test.

IM02   I feel I will never really enjoy writing in English   4 | 3 | 1 | 0   2

IM03   My ability to write quickly in English has improved during this course   4 | 3 | 1 | 0   2

IM04   After studying on this course, I feel that I am not good at writing in English.   4 | 3 | 1 | 0   2

IM05   My ability to organise my ideas in my written work has improved during this course.   4 | 3 | 1 | 0   2

IM06   The Writing classes were difficult for me.   4 | 3 | 1 | 0   2

IM07   I do **NOT** really like the British way of life.   4 | 3 | 1 | 0   2

IM08   I enjoyed writing in English.   4 | 3 | 1 | 0   2

IM09   I feel that my general ability to use English has improved during this course.   4 | 3 | 1 | 0   2

IM10   I think the Writing classes were useful for me.   4 | 3 | 1 | 0   2

IM11   I am pleased I chose to study at this school.   4 | 3 | 1 | 0   2

IM12   I usually enjoy meeting British people.   4 | 3 | 1 | 0   2

IM13   I DON'T think I write in English as well as other students.   4 | 3 | 1 | 0   2

IM14   I like to write down my ideas in English.   4 | 3 | 1 | 0   2

IM15   It was easy for me to write good English essays.   4 | 3 | 1 | 0   2

IM16   My ability to use evidence to support my written arguments has improved during this course.   4 | 3 | 1 | 0   2

IM17   After taking this course, I would feel more confident about writing assignments at university.   4 | 3 | 1 | 0   2

IM18   I feel that my ability to write in English has improved during this course.   4 | 3 | 1 | 0   2

IM19   My ability to use grammar and vocabulary in my writing has improved during this course.   4 | 3 | 1 | 0   2

IM20   I feel happy about living in an English speaking country.   4 | 3 | 1 | 0   2

IM21   My ability to write using information from books or articles I have read has improved during this course.   4 | 3 | 1 | 0   2

Other ways you have improved or changed during this course.

IM22 _____   4 | 3 | 1 | 0   2

IM23 _____   4 | 3 | 1 | 0   2

Comments on how you have improved or changed during this course:

→ **SECTION 4**

In this section, we are interested in your expectations of studying at university in an English speaking country.

	I definitely agree	I tend to agree	I tend to disagree	I definitely disagree	I don't know / I cannot answer this question

EU01 I feel that I have a good knowledge of what university study in Britain is like.
4 | 3 | 1 | 0   2

EU02 I do **NOT** expect university teachers to show students examples of good essays and reports.
4 | 3 | 1 | 0   2

EU03 I expect university teachers to tell the students exactly which books they should read.
4 | 3 | 1 | 0   2

EU04 I expect students should read all the books their university teachers recommend.
4 | 3 | 1 | 0   2

EU05 To get a good grade for their writing at university, students must show that they have remembered facts from lectures.
4 | 3 | 1 | 0   2

EU06 I expect I will have difficulties studying at university because of problems with the English language.
4 | 3 | 1 | 0   2

EU07 I expect the style of teaching at university will be different from the teaching in my country.
4 | 3 | 1 | 0   2

EU08 To get a good grade, in their writing, students should **NOT** criticise the work of their teachers or other experts in their specialist subject.
4 | 3 | 1 | 0   2

EU09 I expect my university grades will mostly come from tests or examinations rather than from essays or coursework.
4 | 3 | 1 | 0   2

EU10 I expect my university subject teachers to correct the English grammar mistakes in my essays.
4 | 3 | 1 | 0   2

EU11 I expect my university tests will follow a **multiple choice** style (in multiple choice questions you choose the correct answer from a list: a, b, c or d).
4 | 3 | 1 | 0   2

EU12 I expect university teachers to tell `4 | 3 | 1 | 0` `2`
students exactly what to do when the
students prepare an essay or report.

EU13 I expect I will have difficulties studying `4 | 3 | 1 | 0` `2`
at university because the style of education
in my country is different to the style of
education in Britain.

EU14 I expect the writing tasks students do at `4 | 3 | 1 | 0` `2`
university are similar to the writing tasks
I have done on this course.

EU15 I expect my university teachers will give `4 | 3 | 1 | 0` `2`
me all the facts and information I need
to get a good grade.

Other expectations of university study.

EU16 _____ `4 | 3 | 1 | 0` `2`

EU17 _____ `4 | 3 | 1 | 0` `2`

Comments on your expectations of university:

➔ **SECTION 5**

*In this section, we are interested in finding out
about your attitude to studying
When you answer, please think about your
experience on* **this course**

		I definitely agree	I tend to agree	I tend to disagree	I definitely disagree		I don't know / I cannot answer this question

R01 When I am reading, I try to memorise `4 | 3 | 1 | 0` `2`
important facts that may be useful later.

R02 I usually study very little except what `4 | 3 | 1 | 0` `2`
I need for assignments or tests.

A01 When I am doing an assignment, I try to `4 | 3 | 1 | 0` `2`
think about exactly what the teacher of
that class seems to want.

R03 Teachers seem to like making the simple `4 | 3 | 1 | 0` `2`
truth more complicated.

M01 When I am trying to understand new `4 | 3 | 1 | 0` `2`
ideas, I often try to connect them to
real-life situations.

R04 I find I have to memorise a lot of what `4 | 3 | 1 | 0` `2`
we study.

A02 I find it easy to organise my time `4 | 3 | 1 | 0` `2`
for studying.

A03   It's important for me to do really well in this course. | 4 | 3 | 1 | 0 | | 2 |

R05   Teachers seem to want me to use my own ideas more. | 4 | 3 | 1 | 0 | | 2 |

M02   I often think about and criticise things that I hear in lessons or read in books. | 4 | 3 | 1 | 0 | | 2 |

R06   I like teachers to tell me exactly what I must do in essays or other coursework. | 4 | 3 | 1 | 0 | | 2 |

M03   I need to read a lot about connected ideas before I am ready to write about a topic. | 4 | 3 | 1 | 0 | | 2 |

A04   If the situation is not right for me to study, I usually manage to do something to change it. | 4 | 3 | 1 | 0 | | 2 |

M04   I like to try to find several different ways of explaining facts. | 4 | 3 | 1 | 0 | | 2 |

A05   When I am doing a piece of work, I try to think about exactly what that particular teacher seems to want. | 4 | 3 | 1 | 0 | | 2 |

M05   I usually try hard to understand things that seem difficult at first. | 4 | 3 | 1 | 0 | | 2 |

R07   I prefer courses that are structured and highly organised. | 4 | 3 | 1 | 0 | | 2 |

A06   It is important to me to do things better than my friends. | 4 | 3 | 1 | 0 | | 2 |

M06   I usually try to understand completely the meaning of what teachers ask me to read. | 4 | 3 | 1 | 0 | | 2 |

M07   I am very interested in puzzles or problems, particularly when I have to study the information carefully to reach a logical conclusion. | 4 | 3 | 1 | 0 | | 2 |

Comments on your attitude to studying

Did you find any of the questions in this questionnaire difficult to understand? Please write the numbers here.

That is the end of the questionnaire. Thank you very much for your help. If you have any other comments you would like to make please write them here.

Thank you very much for your help and co-operation.

Appendix 7 Observation schedule

IELTS-EAP Observation Schedule Part 1: Classroom observation.

Sheet number: _____   Centre: _____   Date: _____

Time	Activities & Episodes		Participant Organisation							Content									Test refs		Content control			Student modality				Materials			Notes/ Comments
			Class			Grp		Ind		Mgmt		Lang.				Broad		Other														
	Teacher actions	Student actions	T-C/S	S-C/S	Char	Same	Diff	Same	Diff	Proc	Dsc	Form	Funct	Dsc	Soc	Imm	Broad	Acad	ELTS	Other	Strat	T/Text	T/S/Text	Student	List	Spea	Read	Writ	Other	Ref	Page	Act	
	1	2	3	4	5	6	7	8	9	10	11	12	13	14	15	16	17	18	19	20	21	22	23	24	25	26	27	28	29	30	31	32	33	34

IELTS-EAP Observation Schedule Part 2: Materials used during observation (*attach copies wherever possible*).

Date: Observation Name:

School: Teacher's Name:

Item	Material		Mode						Source				Extent
	If unpublished indicate whether: a) internal course material b) teacher made c) student made	If published - Give Title and Author or Publisher	Ch/pp/sec	Written	Audio	Visual	IT		LT/NNS	L2/NS	L2/NS Ad	Stu	
1													
2													

Appendix 8 IELTS AWM scoring criteria and descriptors for Writing Tasks 1 and 2 (1995–2005)

Task 1

Band	Task Fulfilment	Coherence and Cohesion	Vocabulary and Sentence Structure
9	The writing fulfils the task in a way which satisfies all requirements.	The message can be followed effortlessly. Coherence and cohesion are so skilfully managed that they attract no attention.	A wide range of vocabulary and sentence structures is used accurately and appropriately.
8	The writing fulfils the task in a very satisfactory manner.	The message can be followed with ease. Coherence and cohesion are very good.	The range of vocabulary and sentence structures used is good, and well controlled for accuracy and appropriacy. There are no significant errors in word formation or spelling.
7	The writing generally addresses the task relevantly, appropriately and accurately, however it could be more fully developed.	The message can be followed throughout and usually with ease. Information is generally arranged coherently, and cohesion within and between sentences is well managed.	A satisfactory range of vocabulary and sentence structures occurs, usually used appropriately. There are only occasional minor flaws in word formation and in control of sentence structure. Spelling errors may occur, but they are not intrusive.
6	The writing mostly addresses the task. However, the reader notices some irrelevant, inappropriate or inaccurate information in areas of minor importance. Minor details may be missing.	The message can be followed throughout. Information is generally arranged coherently, but cohesion within and/or between sentences may be faulty with misuse, overuse or omission of cohesive devices.	Vocabulary and sentence structures are generally adequate and appropriate, but the reader may feel that control is achieved through the use of a restricted range. In contrast, examples of the use of a wider range of structures are not marked by the same level of accuracy. Some errors in word choice, word formation and spelling may occur, but they are only slightly intrusive.

Task 1 (continued)

Band	Task Fulfilment	Coherence and Cohesion	Vocabulary and Sentence Structure
5	The writing is generally adequate, but the inclusion of irrelevant, inappropriate or inaccurate material in key areas detracts from its fulfilment of the task. There may be some details missing.	The message can generally be followed, although sometimes with difficulty. Both coherence and cohesion may be faulty.	The range of vocabulary and the appropriacy of its uses are limited. There is a limited range of sentence structures and the greatest accuracy is achieved on short, simple sentences. Inappropriate choice of word and errors in areas such as agreement of tenses or subject/verb agreement are noticeable. Word formation and spelling errors may be quite intrusive.
4	The writing attempts to fulfil the task but is prevented from doing so adequately by omission of key details, and by irrelevance, inappropriacy or inaccuracy.	The message is difficult to follow. Information is not arranged coherently, and cohesive devices are inadequate or missing.	The range of vocabulary is often inadequate and/or inappropriate and limited control of sentence structures, even short, simple ones, is evident. Choice of words can cause significant problems for the reader. Errors in such areas as agreement of tenses or subject/verb agreement, word formation and spelling can cause severe strain for the reader.
3	The seriousness of the problems in the writing makes it difficult to judge the task.	There are only occasional glimpses of a message. Neither coherence nor cohesion are apparent.	Control of vocabulary and sentence structure is evident only occasionally and errors predominate.
2	The writing does not appear to be related to the task.	There is no recognisable message.	There is little or no evidence of control of sentence structure, vocabulary, word form or spelling.
1	The writing appears to be by a virtual non-writer, containing no assessable strings of English writing. Answers of less than two lines are automatically scored as Band 1.		
0	Should only be used where a candidate did not attend or attempt the question in any way or where there is proof that a candidate's answer has been totally memorised.		

Task 2

Band	Arguments, Ideas and Evidence	Communicative Quality	Vocabulary and Sentence Structure
9	A clear point of view is presented and developed. The argument proceeds logically through the text, with a very clear progression of ideas. There is plentiful material.	The reader finds the writing completely satisfactory.	A wide range of vocabulary and sentence structure is used accurately and appropriately.
8	A clear point of view is presented and developed. The argument proceeds logically through the text with a clear progression of ideas.	The reader finds the writing communicates fluently.	The range of vocabulary and sentence structures used is good, and well controlled for accuracy and appropriacy. There are no significant errors in word formation or spelling.
7	A generally clear point of view is presented. The argument has a clear progression overall, and ideas and evidence are relevant and sufficient, although there may be minor isolated problems in these areas.	The reader finds the writing satisfactory in that it generally communicates fluently with only occasional lapses.	A satisfactory range of vocabulary and sentence structures occurs, usually used appropriately. There are only occasional minor flaws in word formation and in control of sentence structure. Spelling errors may occur, but they are not intrusive.
6	A point of view is presented although it may become unclear in places. The progression of the argument is generally clear. The relevance of some ideas or evidence may be dubious and more specific support may seem desirable.	The reader finds the writing mainly satisfactory in that it communicates with some degree of fluency. Although there is occasional strain for the reader, control of organisational patterns and devices is evident.	Vocabulary and sentence structures are generally adequate and appropriate, but the reader may feel that control is achieved through the use of a restricted range. In contrast, examples of the use of a wider range of structures are not marked by the same level of accuracy. Some errors in word choice, formation and spelling may occur, but they are only slightly intrusive.
5	The writing introduces ideas,	The writing sometimes causes strain for the	The range of vocabulary and the appropriacy of its

Task 2 (continued)

Band	Arguments, Ideas and Evidence	Communicative Quality	Vocabulary and Sentence Structure
	although they may be limited in number or insufficiently developed. A point of view may be evident, but arguments may lack clarity, relevance, consistency or support.	reader. While the reader is aware of an overall lack of fluency, there is a sense of an answer which has an underlying coherence.	use are limited. There is a limited range of sentence structures and the greatest accuracy is achieved on short, simple sentences. Inappropriate choice of words and errors in areas such as agreement of tenses or subject/verb agreement are noticeable. Word formation and spelling errors may be quite intrusive.
4	There are signs of a point of view, but main ideas are difficult to distinguish from supporting material and the amount of support is inadequate. Such evidence and ideas as are presented may not be relevant. There is no clear progression to the argument.	The writing attempts communication but the meaning may come through only after considerable effort by the reader.	The range of vocabulary is often inadequate and/or inappropriate and limited control of sentence structures, even short, simple ones, is evident. Choice of words can cause significant problems for the reader. Errors in such areas as agreement of tenses or subject/verb agreement, word formation and spelling can cause severe strain for the reader.
3	The writing has few ideas and no apparent development. Such evidence and ideas as are presented are largely irrelevant. There is little comprehensible point of view.	The seriousness of the problems in the writing prevents meaning from coming through more than spasmodically.	Control of vocabulary and sentence structures is evident only occasionally and errors predominate.
2	There may be a glimpse of one or two ideas without development.	The writing displays almost no ability to communicate.	There is little or no evidence of control of sentence structure, vocabulary, word form or spelling.
1	The writing appears to be by a virtual non-writer, containing no assessable strings of English writing. Answers of less than two lines are automatically scored as Band 1.		
0	Should only be used where a candidate did not attend or attempt the question in any way or where there is proof that a candidate's answer has been totally memorised.		

References

Airasian, P W (1988) Measurement driven instruction: a closer look, *Educational Measurement: Issues and Practice* 7 (4), 1–11.

Alderson, J C (1981) Report on the discussion on testing English for specific purposes, in Alderson, J C and Hughes, A (Eds) *Issues in Language Testing*, London: The British Council, 123–134.

Alderson, J C (1986) Innovations in language testing? in Portal, M (Ed.) *Innovations in Language Testing*, Windsor: NFER–Nelson, 93–10.

Alderson, J C (1988) Testing English for specific purposes: how specific can we get? in Hughes, A (Ed.) (1988) *Testing English for University Study. ELT Document 127*, London: Modern English Publications, 16–28.

Alderson, J C (1993) Judgments in language testing, in Douglas, D and Chapelle, C (Eds) *A New Decade of Language Testing Research*, Alexandria, Virginia: TESOL, 46–57.

Alderson, J C (2000) Testing in EAP: Progress? Achievement? Proficiency? in Blue, G M (Ed.) *Assessing English for Academic Purposes*, Bern, Switzerland: Peter Lang European Academic Publishers, 21–48.

Alderson, J C (2004) Foreword, in Cheng, L, Watanabe, Y, and Curtis, A (Eds) *Washback in Language Testing: Research Contexts and Methods*, Mahwah, New Jersey: Lawrence Erlbaum Associates, ix–xii.

Alderson, J C and Banerjee, J (2001) Impact and washback research in language testing, in Elder, C et al (Ed.) *Experimenting with Uncertainty: Essays in honour of Alan Davies*, Cambridge: Cambridge University Press, 150–161.

Alderson, J C and Clapham, C M (1992) *Examining the ELTS Test: An account of the First Stage of the ELTS Revision Project*, Cambridge: The British Council, UCLES, IDP Australia.

Alderson, J C and Hamp-Lyons, L (1996) TOEFL preparation courses: a study of washback, *Language Testing* 13 (3), 280–297.

Alderson, J C and Wall, D (1993) Does washback exist? *Applied Linguistics* 14 (2), 115–129.

Altenberg, B (1998) On the phraseology of spoken English: the evidence of recurrent word combinations, in Cowie, A P (Ed.) *Phraseology: Theory, Analysis, and Applications*, Oxford: Clarendon Press, 101–122.

American Educational Research Association (1999) *Standards for Educational and Psychological Testing*, Washington: American Educational Research Association.

Archibald, A (2001) Managing L2 writing proficiencies: areas of change in students' writing over time, *International Journal of English Studies* 1 (2), 153–174.

Bachman, L F (1990) *Fundamental Considerations in Language Testing*, Oxford: Oxford University Press.

Bachman, L F and Palmer, A S (1996) *Language Testing in Practice*, Oxford: Oxford University Press.

Bailey, K M (1996) Working for washback: a review of the washback concept in language testing, *Language Testing* 13 (3), 257–279.

Bailey, K M (1999) *Washback in Language Testing*, Princeton, New Jersey: Educational Testing Service.

Bailey, P, Onwuegbuzie, A J and Daley, C E (2000) Using learning style to predict foreign language achievement at the college level, *System* 28 (1), 115–133.

Baker, D (1989) *Language Testing: A Critical Survey and Practical Guide*, London: Edward Arnold.

Bakhtin, M (1981) *The Dialogic Imagination: Four Essays of M M Bakhtin*, Austin: University of Texas Press.

Ballard, B and Clanchy, J (1991) Assessment by misconception: cultural influences and intellectual traditions, in Hamp-Lyons, L (Ed.) *Assessing Second Language Writing*, Norwood, New Jersey: Ablex, 19–36.

Bamforth, R (1992) Process versus genre: anatomy of a false dichotomy, *Prospect* 8 (1), 89–99.

Banerjee, J (1996) *The design of the classroom observation instruments*, unpublished report, Cambridge.

Banerjee, J (2000) *Using English language screening tests in your institution*, paper presented at the BALEAP Professional Issues Meeting, Nottingham Trent University, 20 May 2000.

Banerjee, J (2003) *Interpreting and using proficiency test scores*, unpublished PhD thesis, University of Lancaster.

Bartlett, B J (1932) *Remembering: A Study in Experimental and Social Psychology*, Cambridge: Cambridge University Press.

Bazerman, C (1988) *Shaping Written Knowledge: The Genre and Activity of the Experimental Article in Science*, Madison, Wisconsin: University of Wisconsin Press.

Becher, A (1989) *Academic Tribes and Territories*, Milton Keynes: Open University Press.

Beglar, D and Hunt, A (1999) Revising and validating the 2000 Word Level and University Word Level Vocabulary Tests, *Language Testing* 16 (2), 131–162.

Belanoff, P and Dickson, M (Eds) (1991) *Portfolios: Process and Product*, Portsmouth: Boynton Cook.

Belcher, D and Braine, G (Eds) (1995) *Academic Writing in a Second Language*, Norwood, New Jersey: Ablex.

Benesch, S (1996) Needs analysis and curriculum development in EAP: an example of a critical approach, *TESOL Quarterly* 30 (4), 723–738.

Benson, M J (1991) University ESL reading: a content analysis, *English for Specific Purposes* 10 (2), 75–88.

Bereiter, C and Scardamalia, M (1987) *The Psychology of Written Composition*, Hilsdale, New Jersey: Lawrence Erlbaum.

Berkenkotter, C and Huckin, T (1995) *Genre Knowledge in Disciplinary Communication*, Hilsdale, New Jersey: Lawrence Erlbaum.

Berman, R and Rourke, L (2003) *To what extent does EAP instruction work?* paper presented at the bi-annual conference of the British Association of Lecturers in English for Academic Purposes (BALEAP), Southampton, England, April 2003.

Berry, V (1994) Current assessment issues and practices in Hong Kong: a review, in Nunan, D, Berry, R and Berry, V (Eds) *Bringing About Change in Language*

Education, Hong Kong: The University of Hong Kong, Department of Curriculum Studies, 31–34.

Biber, D (1988) *Variations across Speech and Writing*, Harlow: Longman.

Biggs, J B (1987a) *Student Approaches to Learning and Studying*, Melbourne: Australian Council for Educational Research.

Biggs, J B (1987b) *Study Process Questionnaire Manual*, Melbourne: Australian Council for Educational Research.

Biggs, J B (1993) What do inventories of students' learning really measure: a theoretical review and clarification, *British Journal of Educational Psychology* 63 (1), 3–19.

Biggs, J B (1996) Western misconceptions of the Confucian-heritage learning culture, in Watkins, D A and Biggs, J (Eds) *The Chinese Learner*, Hong Kong: CERC/ACER, 45–68.

Biggs, J B and Collis, K F (1982) *Evaluating the Quality of Learning: The SOLO Taxonomy*, New York: Academic Press.

Biglan, A (1973) The characteristics of subject matter in different academic areas, *Journal of Applied Psychology* 57 (3), 195–203.

Bizzell, P (1987) Language and literacy, in Enos, T (Ed.) *A Sourcebook for Basic Writing Teachers*, New York: Random House, 125–137.

Black, P and Wiliam, D (1998) 'Inside the Black Box', Raising Standards Through Classroom Assessment, *Phi Delta Kappan* 80 (2), 139–144.

Bloch, J and Chi, L (1995) A comparison of the use of citations in Chinese and English academic discourse, in Belcher, D and Braine, G (Eds) *Academic Writing in a Second Language*, Norwood: Ablex, 231–274.

Bloom, B S (Ed.) (1956) *Taxonomy of Educational Objectives*, New York: Longman.

Bloor, M and Bloor, T (1991) Cultural expectations and socio-pragmatic failure, in Adams, P, Heaton, B and Howarth, P (Eds) *Socio-cultural Issues in English for Academic Purposes*, London: Macmillan, 1–13.

Blue, G M (1988) Individualising academic writing tuition, in Robinson, P (Ed.) *Academic Writing: Process and Product*, London: Modern English Publications, 95–99.

Blue, G M (1991) Language learning within academic constraints, in Adams, P, Heaton, B and Howarth, P (Eds) *Socio-cultural Issues in English for Academic Purposes*, London: Macmillan, 101–117.

Blue, G M (Ed.) (1993) *Language, Learning and Success: Studying Through English*, London: Macmillan.

Blue, G M (Ed.) (2000) *Assessing English for Academic Purposes*, Bern, Switzerland: Peter Lang European Academic Publishers.

Blue, G and Archibald, A (1999) The Europeanisation of the EAP classroom, in Bool, H and Luford, P (Eds) *Academic Standards and Expectations: The Role of EAP*, Nottingham: Nottingham University Press, 37–48.

Boldt, R F and Ross, S (1998) *Scores on the TOEIC (Test of English for International Communication) test as a function of training time and type*, Princeton, New Jersey: The Chauncey Group International.

Bool, H, Dunmore, D and Tonkyn, A (1999) *The BALEAP Guidelines on English Language Proficiency Levels for International Applicants to UK Universities*, London: British Association of Lecturers in English for Academic Purposes.

Bool, H and Luford, P (Eds) (1999) *Academic Standards and Expectations: The Role of EAP*, Nottingham: Nottingham University Press.

Bool, H, Tonkyn, A, Schmitt, D and Ward-Goodbody, M (2003) *The BALEAP Guidelines on English Language Proficiency Levels for International Applicants to UK Universities*, London: British Association of Lecturers in English for Academic Purposes.

Bourdieu, P (1991) *Language and Symbolic Power*, Cambridge: Polity Press.

Bracey, G W (1987) Measurement-driven instruction: catchy phrase, dangerous practice, *Phi Delta Kappan* 68 (9), 683–686.

Braine, G (1989) Writing in Science and Technology: an analysis of assignments from ten undergraduate courses, *English for Specific Purposes* 8 (1), 3–15.

Brew, A (1980) Responses of overseas students to different teaching styles, in Greenall, G M and Price, J E (Eds) *Study Modes and Academic Development of Overseas Students*, London: The British Council, 115–125.

Bridgeman, B and Carlson, S (1983) *Survey of Academic Writing Tasks Required of Graduate and Undergraduate Foreign Students*, Princeton, New Jersey: Educational Testing Service.

Brindley, G (1998) Outcomes-based assessment and reporting in language learning programmes: A review of the issues, *Language Testing* 15 (1), 45–85.

Brindley, G and Ross, S (2001) EAP assessment: issues, models and outcomes, in Flowerdew, J and Peacock, M (Eds) *Research Perspectives on English for Academic Purposes*, Cambridge: Cambridge University Press, 148–168.

Broadfoot, P (1996) *Education, Assessment, and Society*, Milton Keynes: Open University Press.

Brookes, A, Grundy, P and Young-Scholten, M (1996) Tutor and student evaluation of activity design and purpose, in Hewings, M and Dudley-Evans, T (Eds) *Evaluation and Course Design in EAP*, Review of English Language Teaching 6 (1), Hemel Hempstead: Phoenix ELT, 36–45.

Brown, G and Yule, G (1983) *Discourse Analysis*, Cambridge: Cambridge University Press.

Brown, J D (1991) Do English and ESL faculties rate writing samples differently? *TESOL Quarterly* 25 (4), 587–603.

Brown, J D (1996) *Testing in Language Programs*, Upper Saddle River, New Jersey: Prentice-Hall Regents.

Brown, J D (2000) University entrance examinations: strategies for creating positive washback on English language teaching in Japan, *Shiken JALT Testing and Evaluation SIG Newsletter* 3 (2), 4–8.

Brown, J D H (1998) An investigation into approaches to IELTS preparation, with particular focus on the Academic Writing component of the test, in Wood, S (Ed.) *IELTS Research Reports* (Volume 1), Sydney: ELICOS/IELTS Australia, 20–37.

Brown, J D and Hudson, T (2002) *Criterion-Referenced Language Testing*, Cambridge: Cambridge University Press.

Brown, J D and Yamashita, S O (1995) English language entrance examinations at Japanese universities: What do we know about them? *JALT Journal* 17 (1), 7–30.

Buck, G (1988) Testing listening comprehension in Japanese university entrance examinations, *JALT Journal* 10 (1), 15–42.

Bude, U (1989) *The Challenge of Quality in Primary Education in Africa*, Bonn: Education, Science and Documentation Center, German Foundation for International Development.

Bullinaria, J A (1995) Neural network learning from ambiguous training data, *Artificial Intelligence and Cognitive Research* 7 (2), 99–122.

Burchfield, S and Allen, T (1995) *An Analysis of the 1994 Common Entrance Examination, Jamaica, Primary Education Assistance Project*, Cambridge, Massachusetts: Harvard Institute for International Development.

Burr, V and Butt, T (1997) Interview method and PCP, in Denicolo, P and Pope, M (Eds) *Sharing Understanding and Practice*, Farnborough: EPCA Publications, 98–105.

Burrows, C (1998) *Searching for washback: an investigation of the impact on teachers of the implementation into the Adult Migrant English Program of the assessment of the Certificates in Spoken and Written English*, unpublished PhD thesis, Macquarie University, Sydney.

Cammish, N (1997) Through a glass darkly: the problems of studying at advanced level through the medium of English, in McNamara, D and Harris, R (Eds) *Overseas Students in Higher Education: Issues in Teaching and Learning*, London: Routledge, 143–155.

Campbell, C (1990) Writing with others' words: using background reading texts in academic composition, in Kroll, B (Ed.) *Second Language Writing: Research Insights for the Classroom*, Cambridge: Cambridge University Press, 211–230.

Campion, M E and Elley, W B (1971) *An Academic Vocabulary List*, Wellington: New Zealand Council for Educational Research.

Canagarajah, S (2001) Addressing issues of power and difference in ESL academic writing, in Flowerdew, J and Peacock, M (Eds) *Research Perspectives on English for Academic Purposes*, Cambridge: Cambridge University Press, 117–131.

Canale, M and Swain, M (1980) Theoretical bases of communicative approaches to second language teaching and testing, *Applied Linguistics* 1 (1), 1–47.

Candlin, C N and Hyland, K (Eds) (1999) *Writing: Texts, Processes and Practices*, Harlow: Longman.

Candlin, C N and Plum, G A (1999) Engaging with the challenges of academic writing: researchers, students and tutors, in Candlin, C N and Hyland, K (Eds) *Writing: Text, Processes, and Practices*, Harlow: Longman, 193–217.

Canesco, G and Byrd, P (1989) Writing required in graduate courses in business administration, *TESOL Quarterly* 23 (2), 305–321.

Cannell, J J (1988) Nationally normed elementary achievement testing in America's public schools: how all 50 states are above the national average, *Educational Measurement: Issues and Practice* 7 (2), 5–9.

Carroll, B J (1981) Specifications for an English Language Testing Service, in Alderson, J C and Hughes, A (Eds) *Issues in Language Testing*, London: The British Council.

Casanave, C P (1995) Local interactions: Constructing contexts for composing in a graduate sociology program, in Belcher, D and Braine, G (Eds) *Academic Writing in a Second Language*, Norwood, New Jersey: Ablex, 83–110.

Casanave, C P and Hubbard, P (1992) The writing assignments and writing problems of doctoral students: faculty perceptions, pedagogical issues, and needed research, *English for Specific Purposes* 11 (1), 33–49.

Celestine, C and Ming, C S (1999) The effects of background disciplines on IELTS scores, in Tulloh, R (Ed.) *IELTS Research Reports (Volume 2)*, Canberra: IELTS Australia, 36–51.

Chalhoub-Deville, M and Turner, C E (2000) What to look for in ESL admission tests: Cambridge certificate exams, IELTS, and TOEFL, *System* 28 (4), 523–539.

Chapelle, C and Douglas, D (1993) Foundations and directions for a new decade of language testing, in Douglas, D and Chapelle, C (Eds) *A New Decade of Language Testing Research*, Arlington, Virginia: TESOL publications, 1–22.

Chapman, D W and Leven, M (1997) *Suriname Education Sector Study*, Washington DC: Inter-American Development Bank.

Chapman, D W and Snyder, C W (2000) Can high stakes testing improve instruction: re-examining conventional wisdom, *International Journal of Educational Development* 20 (6), 457–474.

Charge, N and Taylor, L (1997) Recent developments in IELTS, *ELT Journal*, 51 (4), 374–380.

Cheng, L (1997) *The washback effect of public examination change on classroom teaching: an impact study of the 1996 Hong Kong Certificate of Education in English on the classroom teaching of English in Hong Kong secondary schools*, unpublished PhD thesis, University of Hong Kong, Hong Kong.

Cheng, L (2004) The washback effect of an examination change on teachers' perception towards their classroom teaching, in Cheng, L, Watanabe, Y and Curtis, A (Eds) *Washback in Language Testing: Research Contexts and Methods*, Mahwah, New Jersey: Lawrence Erlbaum, 147–170.

Cheng, L (2005) *Changing Language Teaching through Language Testing: A washback study*, Studies in Language Testing 21, Cambridge: UCLES/Cambridge University Press.

Cheng, L and Watanabe, Y (Eds) (2004) *Context and Method in Washback Research: The Influence of Language Testing on Teaching and Learning*, Hilsdale, New Jersey: Lawrence Erlbaum.

Cheng, Y, Horwitz, E and Schallert, D (1999) Language anxiety: differentiating writing and speaking components, *Language Learning* 49 (3), 417–446.

Chudowsky, N and Behuniak, P (1997) *Establishing Consequential Validity for Large-Scale Performance Assessments*, Chicago, Illinois: National Council of Measurement in Education.

Cizek, G J (2001) More unintended consequences of high-stakes testing, *Educational Measurement: Issues and Practice* 20 (4), 19–27.

Clanchy, B and Ballard, B (1992) *How to Write Essays*, Harlow: Longman.

Clapham, C (1996) *The Development of the IELTS: A Study of the Effect of Background Knowledge on Reading Comprehension*, Cambridge: Cambridge University Press.

Clapham, C (1997) The Academic Modules: Reading, in Clapham, C and Alderson, J C (Eds) *Constructing and Trialling the IELTS Test*, London: UCLES, The British Council, IDP Australia, 49–68.

Clapham, C (2000) Assessment for academic purposes: where next? *System* 28 (4), 511–521.

Clapham, C and Alderson, J C (Eds) (1997) *Constructing and Trialling the IELTS Test*, London: UCLES, The British Council, IDP Australia.

Clarke, J and Saunders, C (1999) Negotiating academic genres: the double burden for international students, in Bool, H and Luford, P (Eds) *Academic Standards and Expectations: The Role of EAP*, Nottingham: Nottingham University Press, 67–74.

Cmejrkova, S (1996) Academic writing in Czech and English, in Ventola, E and Mauranen, A (Eds) *Academic Writing: Intercultural and Textual Issues*, Amsterdam: John Benjamins, 137–152.

Cohen, A D (1994) *Assessing Language Ability in the Classroom*, Boston, Massachusetts: Newbury House/Heinle and Heinle.

Cohen, J and Cohen, P (1983) *Applied Multiple Regression/Correlation Analysis for the Behavioural Sciences*, Hilsdale, New Jersey: Lawrence Erlbaum.

Coleman, D, Starfield, S and Hagan, A (2003) Stakeholder Perceptions of the IELTS Test in three countries, in *IELTS Research Reports (Volume 5)*, Canberra: IELTS Australia, 159–235.

Coleman, H (1991) The testing of 'appropriate behaviour' in an academic context, in Adams, P, Heaton, B and Howarth, P (Eds) *Socio-cultural Issues in English for Academic Purposes*, London: Macmillan, 14–24.

Collins (1979) *Collins English Dictionary*, London: Collins.

Comrey, A L and Lee, H B (1992) *A First Course in Factor Analysis*, Hilsdale, New Jersey: Lawrence Erlbaum.

Connor-Linton, J (1995) Looking behind the curtain: what do L2 composition ratings really mean? *TESOL Quarterly* 29 (4), 762–65.

Corbett, H D and Wilson, B L (1991) *Testing, Reform and Rebellion*, Hillsdale, New Jersey: Ablex.

Cortazzi, M (1990) Cultural and educational expectations in the language classroom, in Harrison, B (Ed.) *Culture and the Language Classroom*, London: Macmillan, Modern English Publications and the British Council, 4–65.

Cortazzi, M and Jin, L (1997) Communicating for learning across cultures, in McNamara, D and Harris, R (Eds) *Overseas Students in Higher Education: Issues in Teaching and Learning*, London: Routledge, 76–90.

Coulthard, M and Sinclair, J (1975) *Towards an Analysis of Discourse*, Oxford: Oxford University Press.

Coxhead, A (1998) *An Academic Word List*, Wellington: Victoria University of Wellington.

Coxhead, A (2000) A new academic word list, *TESOL Quarterly* 34 (2), 213–238.

Coxhead, A and Nation, I S P (1998) The specialised vocabulary of English for academic purposes, *Wellington Occasional Papers in Applied Linguistics* 1 (1), 31–55.

Creme, P and Lea, M R (1999) Student writing: challenging the myths, in Thompson, P (Ed.) *Academic Writing Development in Higher Education: Perspectives, Explorations and Approaches*, Reading: University of Reading, 1–13.

Cresswell, A (2000) The role of portfolios in the assessment of student writing on an EAP course, in Blue, G M (Ed.) *Assessing English for Academic Purposes*, Bern, Switzerland: Peter Lang European Academic Publishers, 205–220.

Criper, C and Davies, A (1988) ELTS Validation Project Report, London: The British Council and the University of Cambridge Local Examinations Syndicate.

Cronbach, L J (1963) Course improvements through evaluation, *Teachers College Record* 64, 672–683.

Crooks, T J (1988) The impact of classroom evaluation practices on students, *Review of Educational Research* 58 (4), 43–481.

Cummins, J (1984) Wanted: a theoretical framework for relating language proficiency to academic achievement among bilingual students, in Rivera, C (Ed.) *Language Proficiency and Academic Achievement*, Clevedon: Multilingual Matters, 2–19.

Cunningham, J W and Moore, D W (1993) The contribution of understanding academic vocabulary to answering comprehension questions, *Journal of Reading Behavior* 25 (2), 171–180.

Currie, P (1998) Staying out of trouble: apparent plagiarism and academic survival, *Journal of Second Language Writing* 7 (1), 1–18.

Daborn, E and Calderwood, M (2000) Collaborative assessment of written reports: electrical engineering and EFL, in Blue, G M (Ed.) *Assessing English for Academic Purposes*, Bern, Switzerland: Peter Lang European Academic Publishers, 79–96.

Davies, A (1985) Follow my leader: is that what language tests do? in Lee, Y P, Fok, A C Y L, Low, R and Low, G (Eds) *New Directions in Language Testing*, Oxford: Pergamon, 3–13.

Davies, A (1990) *Principles of Language Testing*, Oxford: Blackwell.

Davies, A (2001) The logic of testing Languages for Specific Purposes, *Language Testing* 18 (2), 133–148.

Davies, A (forthcoming) *Assessing Academic English: Testing English proficiency 1950–2005 – the IELTS solution*, Studies in Language Testing 23, Cambridge: UCLES/Cambridge University Press.

Davies, A, Brown, A, Elder, C, Hill, K, Lumley, T and McNamara, T (1999) *A Dictionary of Language Testing*, Cambridge: Cambridge University Press.

Deakin, G (1996) IELTS in context: issues in EAP for overseas students, *EA Journal* 15 (2), 7–28.

Dörnyei, Z (2001) *Teaching and Researching Motivation*, Harlow: Longman.

Douglas, D (2000) *Assessing Languages for Specific Purposes*, Cambridge: Cambridge University Press.

Douglas, D and Chapelle, C (Eds) (1993) *A New Decade of Language Testing Research*, Alexandria, Virginia: TESOL.

Dunkin, M J and Biddle, B J (1974) *The Study of Teaching*, New York: Holt, Rinehart and Winston.

Dunn, R, Dunn, K and Price, G E (1991) *Productivity Environmental Preference Survey*, Lawrence, Kansas: Price Systems, Inc.

Eggington, W (1987) Written academic discourse in Korean: implications for effective communication, in Connor, U M and Kaplan, R (Eds) *Writing Across Languages: Analysis of L2 texts*, Reading, Massachusetts: Addison Wesley, 153–167.

Ehrman, M E and Oxford, R (1995) Cognition plus: correlates of language learning success, *The Modern Language Journal* 79 (1), 67–89.

Eisemon, T O (1990) Examination policies to strengthen primary schooling in African countries, *International Journal of Educational Development* 10, 69–82.

Elbow, P (1991) Reflections on academic discourse: how it relates to freshmen and colleagues, *College English* 53, 135–155.

Elder, C and O'Loughlin, K (2003) Investigating the relationship between intensive EAP training and band score gain on IELTS, in Tulloh, R (Ed.) *IELTS Research Reports (Volume 4)*, Canberra: IELTS Australia, 207–254.

Ellis, R (1994) *The Study of Second Language Acquisition*, Oxford: Oxford University Press.

Elman, J L (1996) *Rethinking Innateness: A Connectionist Perspective on Development*, Cambridge, Massachusetts: MIT Press.

Entwistle, N J (1981) *Styles of Learning and Teaching: An Integrated Outline of Educational Psychology for Students, Teachers, and Lecturers*, Chichester: Wiley.

Entwistle, N J and Ramsden, P (1983) *Understanding Student Learning*, London: Croom Helm.

Everett, R and Coleman, J (2003) A Critical Evaluation of Selected IELTS Preparation Materials, in *IELTS Research Reports (Volume 5)*, Canberra: IELTS Australia, 1–84.

Ewer, J R and Hughes-Davies, G (1971) Further notes on developing an English programme for students of Science and Technology, *English Language Teaching* 26 (1), 269–273.

Fathman, A K and Walley, E (1990) Teacher response to student writing: focus on form versus content, in Kroll, B (Ed.) *Second Language Writing: Research Insights for the Classroom*, Cambridge: Cambridge University Press, 178–190.

Flower, L (1994) *The Construction of Negotiated Meaning: A social cognitive theory of writing*, Carbondale: Southern Illinois University Press.

Flower, L S and Hayes, J R (1981) A cognitive process theory of writing, *College Composition and Communication* 32 (4), 365–387.

Flower, L S and Hayes, J R (1984) Images, plans and prose: the representation of meaning in writing, *Written Communication* 1 (1), 120–160.

Flowerdew, J (1993) An educational or process approach to the teaching of professional genres, *ELT Journal* 47 (4), 305–316.

Flowerdew, J and Miller, L (1995) On the notion of culture in L2 lectures, *TESOL Quarterly* 29 (2), 345–373.

Flowerdew, J and Peacock, M (Eds) (2001a) *Research Perspectives on English for Academic Purposes*, Cambridge: Cambridge University Press.

Flowerdew, J and Peacock, M (2001b) Issues in EAP: a preliminary perspective, in Flowerdew, J and Peacock, M (Eds) *Research Perspectives on English for Academic Purposes*, Cambridge: Cambridge University Press, 8–24.

Fowler, H R and Aaron, J (2001) *The Little, Brown Handbook*, Harlow: Longman.

Fredericksen, J R and Collins, A (1989) A systems approach to educational testing, *Educational Researcher* 18 (9), 27–32.

Fredericksen, N (1984) The real test bias: the influence of testing on teaching and learning, *American Psychologist* 39 (3), 193–202.

Fulcher, G (1999) Assessment in EAP: putting content validity in its place, *Applied Linguistics* 20 (2), 221–236.

Fullan, G M and Stiegelbauer, S (1991) *The New Meaning of Educational Change*, London: Cassell Educational.

Gardner, H (1989) Assessment in context: the alternative to standardized testing, in Gifford, B and O'Conner, M C (Eds) *Changing Assessments: Alternative Views of Aptitude, Achievement and Instruction*, Boston: Kluwer Academic Publishers, 77–119.

Gardner, R C (1985) *Social Psychological and Second Language Learning: The Role of Attitudes and Motivation*, London: Edward Arnold.

Gardner, R C, Tremblay, P F and Masgoret, A-M (1997) Towards a full model of second language learning: an empirical investigation, *The Modern Language Journal* 81 (3), 344–362.

Garson, G D (1998) *Neural Networks: An introductory guide for social scientists*, London: Sage.

Gates, S (1995) Exploiting washback from standardized tests, in Brown, J D and Yamashita, S O (Eds) *Language Testing in Japan*, Tokyo: Japan Association for Language Teaching, 101–106.

Geisler, C (1994) *Academic Literacy and the Nature of Expertise*, Hilsdale, New Jersey: Lawrence Erlbaum.

Geoghegan, G (1983) *Non-Native Speakers of English at Cambridge University*, Cambridge: Bell Educational Trust.

Geranpayeh, A (1994) Are score comparisons across language proficiency test batteries justified?: An IELTS-TOEFL comparability study, *Edinburgh Working Papers in Applied Linguistics* 5, 50–65.

Gerot, L and Wignell, P (1994) *Making Sense of Functional Grammar*, Cammeray, New South Wales: Antipodean Educational Enterprises.

Ghadessy, M (1979) Frequency counts, word lists, and materials preparation: a new approach, *English Teaching Forum* 17 (1), 24–27.

Gibbs, G (1992) *Improving the Quality of Student Learning*, Bristol: Technical and Educational Services.

Gipps, C (1994) *Beyond Testing: Towards a theory of educational assessment*, London: The Falmer Press.

Goldstein, H (1989) Psychometric test theory and educational assessment, in Elliott, J and Simons, H (Eds) *Rethinking Appraisal and Assessment*, Milton Keynes: Open University Press, 140–148.

Grabe, W and Kaplan, R B (1996) *Theory and Practice of Writing*, Harlow: Longman.

Gramsci, A (1971) *Selections from the Prison Notebooks*, London: Lawrence and Wishart.

Granger, S and Tyson, S (1996) Connector usage in the English essay writing of native and non-native EFL speakers of English, *World Englishes* 15 (1), 17–28.

Green, A (2003) *Goals and gains: washback from IELTS writing on teaching, learning and outcomes*, paper presented at the Language Testing Research Colloquium, University of Reading, 22 July 2003.

Green, A (2005) EAP study recommendations and score gains on the IELTS Academic Writing test, *Assessing Writing* 10 (1), 44–60.

Green, F (1991) How many subjects does it take to do a regression analysis? *Multivariate Behavioural Research* 26 (3), 449–510.

Greenall, G M and Price, J E (Eds) (1980) *Study Modes and Academic Development of Overseas Students*, London: The British Council.

Groom, N (2000) Attribution and averral revisited: three perspectives on manifest intertextuality in academic writing, in Thompson, P (Ed.) *Patterns and Perspectives: Insights for EAP Writing Practice*, Reading: CALS, The University of Reading, 15–26.

Guilford, J P and Fruchter, B (1978) *Fundamental Statistics in Psychology and Education*, Singapore: McGraw-Hill.

Haertel, E H (1999) Validity arguments for high-stakes testing: in search of the evidence, *Educational Measurement: Issues and Practice* 18 (4), 5–9.

Haladyna, T M, Nolen, S B and Haas, N S (1991) Raising standardised achievement test scores and the origins of test score pollution, *Educational Researcher* 20 (5), 20–25.

Hale, G, Taylor, C, Bridgeman, B, Carson, J, Kroll, B and Kantor, R (1996) *A Study of Writing Tasks Assigned in Academic Degree Programs*, Princeton, New Jersey: Educational Testing Service.

Hamp-Lyons, L (1987) *Testing second language writing in academic settings*, unpublished PhD thesis, University of Edinburgh, Edinburgh.

Hamp-Lyons, L (1990) Second language writing: assessment issues, in Kroll, B (Ed.) *Second Language Writing: Research Insights for the Classroom*, Cambridge: Cambridge University Press, 69–87.

References

Hamp-Lyons, L (1991) Reconstructing 'academic writing proficiency', in Hamp-Lyons, L (Ed.) *Assessing Second Language Writing*, Norwood, New Jersey: Ablex, 23–329.

Hamp-Lyons, L (1997) Washback, impact and validity: ethical concerns, *Language Testing* 14 (3), 295–303.

Hamp-Lyons, L (1998) Ethical test preparation practice: the case of the TOEFL, *TESOL Quarterly* 33 (2), 329–337.

Hamp-Lyons, L and Henning, G (1991) Communicative writing profiles: an investigation of the transferability of a multiple trait scoring instrument across ESL writing assessment contexts, *Language Learning* 41 (3), 337–373.

Hamp-Lyons, L and Kroll, B (1997) *TOEFL 2000 Writing: Composition, Community and Assessment*, Princeton, New Jersey: Educational Testing Service.

Hamp-Lyons, L and Zhang, B (2001) World Englishes: issues in and from academic writing, in Flowerdew, J and Peacock, M (Eds) *Research Perspectives on English for Academic Purposes*, Cambridge: Cambridge University Press, 101–116.

Hanson, F A (1993) *Testing, Testing: Social Consequences of the Examined Life*, Berkeley, California: University of California Press.

Harris, J (1989) The idea of community in the study of writing, *College Composition and Communication* 40 (1), 11–22.

Harris, R and Thorp, D (1999) Language, Culture and Learning: Some missing dimensions to EAP, in Bool, H and Luford, P (Eds) *Academic Standards and Expectations: The Role of EAP*, Nottingham: Nottingham University Press, 5–18.

Hartill, J (2000) Assessing postgraduates in the real world, in Blue, G M (Ed.) *Assessing English for Academic Purposes*, Bern, Switzerland: Peter Lang European Academic Publishers, 117–130.

Hatch, E and Lazaraton, A (1991) *The Research Manual: Design and Statistics for Applied Linguistics*, New York: Newbury House.

Hawkey, R A (1982) *Investigation of interrelationships between cognitive/affective and social factors and language learning*, unpublished PhD thesis, Institute of Education, University of London, London.

Hawkey, R (2006) *Impact Theory and Practice: Studies of the IELTS test and Progetto Lingue 2000*, Studies in Language Testing 24, Cambridge: UCLES/ Cambridge University Press.

Hayes, B and Read, J (2004) IELTS test preparation in New Zealand: preparing students for the IELTS academic module, in Cheng, L, Watanabe, Y, and Curtis, A (Eds) *Washback in Language Testing: Research Contexts and Methods*, Mahwah, New Jersey: Lawrence Erlbaum Associates, 97–111.

Hayes, B and Watt, L (1998) An IELTS preparation course for Asian learners: when practice doesn't make perfect, *EA Journal* 16 (1), 15–21.

Hazenberg, S and Hulstijn, J H (1996) Defining a minimal receptive second language vocabulary for non-native university students: an empirical investigation, *Applied Linguistics* 17 (2), 145–163.

Heaton, J B (1990) *Classroom Testing*, Harlow: Longman.

Heiman, J D (1994) Western culture in EFL language instruction, *TESOL Journal* 3 (3), 4–7.

Henning, G (1987) *A Guide to Language Testing: Development, Evaluation, Research*, Rowley, Massachusetts: Newbury House.

Herbert, A J (1965) *The Structure of Technical English*, Harlow: Longman.

Herington, R (1996) *Test-taking strategies and second language proficiency: is there a relationship?* unpublished MA thesis, University of Lancaster, Lancaster.

Hermann, J L and Golan, S (1993) The effects of standardized testing on teaching and schools, *Educational Measurement: Issues and Practice* 12 (4), 20–25, 41–42.

Heyneman, S P and Ransom, A W (1990) Using examinations and testing to improve educational quality, *Educational Policy* 4 (3), 177–192.

Hinds, J (1983) Linguistics and contrastive studies in particular languages: English and Japanese, *Text 3*, 78–84.

Hinds, J (1987) Reader vs writer responsibility: a new typology, in Connor, U M and Kaplan, R (Eds) *Writing Across Languages: Analysis of L2 Texts*, Reading, Massachusetts: Addison Wesley, 141–152.

Hinds, J (1990) Inductive, deductive, quasi-inductive: expository writing in Japanese, Korean, Chinese and Thai, in Connor, U and Johns, A (Eds) *Coherence in Writing: Research and Pedagogical Perspectives*, Alexandria, Virginia: TESOL, 87–110.

Hinkel, E (1994) Native and nonnative speakers' pragmatic interpretation of English text, *TESOL Quarterly* 28 (2), 353–376.

Holmes, E (1911) *What Is and What Might Be*, London: Constable and Co.

Hopkins, D and Nettle, M (1993) *Passport to IELTS*, London: Macmillan.

Hopkins, K D, Stanley, J C and Hopkins, B R (1990) *Educational and Psychological Measurement and Evaluation*, Englewood Cliffs, New Jersey: Prentice-Hall.

Horowitz, D M (1986a) What professors actually require: academic tasks for the ESL classroom, *TESOL Quarterly* 20 (3), 445–462.

Horowitz, D M (1986b) Essay examination prompts and the teaching of examination writing, *English for Specific Purposes* 5 (2), 107–120.

Hughes, A (1988) Introducing a needs-based test of English into an English-medium university in Turkey, in Hughes, A (Ed.) *Testing English for University*, Oxford: Modern English Publications, 134–153.

Hughes, A (1993) *Backwash and TOEFL 2000*, unpublished manuscript, Reading: University of Reading.

Hughes, A (2003) *Testing for Language Teachers*, Cambridge: Cambridge University Press.

Hughes, A, Porter, D and Weir, C (Eds) (1988) *ELTS Validation Project: proceedings of a conference held to consider the ELTS Validation Project Report*, London: The British Council and the University of Cambridge Local Examinations Syndicate.

Hughes-Wilhelm, K (1997) Use of an expert system to predict language learning success, *System* 25 (3), 317–334.

Hughes-Wilhelm, K (1999) Building an adult knowledge base: an exploratory study using an expert system, *Applied Linguistics* 20 (4), 425–459.

Hyland, K (1994) Hedging in academic writing and EAP textbooks, *English for Specific Purposes* 13 (3), 239–256.

Hymes, D (1972) On communicative competence, in Pride, J B and Holmes, J (Eds) *Sociolinguistics*, Harmondsworth: Penguin, 269–293.

IELTS (2000) *Writing Assessment Guide*, Cambridge: UCLES, The British Council, IELTS Australia.

IELTS (2001) *The IELTS Handbook 2001*, Cambridge: UCLES, The British Council, IDP Australia.

IELTS (2002) *IELTS Annual Review*, Cambridge: UCLES, The British Council, IELTS Australia.

IELTS (2003) *IELTS Annual Review*, Cambridge: UCLES, The British Council, IELTS Australia.

IELTS (2005) *The IELTS Handbook 2005*, Cambridge: UCLES, The British Council, IDP Australia.

Imber, B P and Parker, M (1999) Teaching socio-professional discourse: a needs analysis approach, in Bool, H and Luford, P (Eds) *Academic Standards and Expectations: The Role of EAP*, Nottingham: Nottingham University Press, 75–80.

Jakeman, V and McDowell, C (2001) *Insight into IELTS: The Cambridge IELTS Course*, Cambridge: Cambridge University Press.

Jenkins, S, Jordon, M and Weil, P (1993) The role of writing in graduate engineering education: a survey of faculty beliefs and practices, *English for Specific Purposes* 12 (1), 51–67.

Johns, A M (1990) L1 composition theories: implications for developing theories of L2 composition, in Kroll, B (Ed.) *Second Language Writing: Research Insights for the Classroom*, Cambridge: Cambridge University Press, 24–35.

Jones, M G, Jones, B D, Hardin, B, Chapman, L, Yarborough, T and Davis, M (1999) The impact of high stakes testing on teachers and students in North Carolina, *Phi Delta Kappan* 81 (3), 199–203.

Jones, S and Tetroe, J (1987) Composing in a second language, in Matsuhashi, A (Ed.) *Writing in Real Time*, Norwood, New Jersey: Ablex, 34–57.

Jordan, R R (1990) *Academic Writing Course*, London: Collins.

Jordan, R R (1993) Study skills: experience and expectations, in Blue, G M (Ed.) *Language, Learning and Success: Studying through English*, London: Macmillan.

Jordan, R R (1997) *English for Academic Purposes*, Cambridge: Cambridge University Press.

Kane, M B, Khattri, N, Reeve, A L and Adamson, R J (1997) *Assessment of Student Performance*, Washington DC: Office of Educational Research and Improvement, US Department of Education.

Kaplan, R (1966) Cultural thought patterns in intercultural education, *Language Learning* 16 (1), 1–20.

Kellaghan, T and Greaney, V (1992) *Using Examinations to Improve Education: A study of fourteen African countries*, Washington, DC: The World Bank.

Kellaghan, T, Madaus, G and Airasian, P (1982) *The Effects of Standardized Testing*, Boston, Massachusetts: Kluwer-Nijhoff Publishers.

Kember, D and Gow, L (1991) A challenge to the anecdotal stereotype of the Asian student, *Studies in Higher Education* 16 (1), 117–128.

Kenyon, D M (1995) An investigation of the validity of task demands on performance-based tests of oral proficiency, in Kunnan, A J (Ed.) *Validation in language assessment: selected papers from the 17th Language Testing Colloquium*, Long Beach, Mahwah, New Jersey: Lawrence Erlbaum, 19–40.

Khaniya, T R (1990) *Examinations as Instruments for Educational Change*, unpublished PhD thesis, University of Edinburgh, Edinburgh.

Khattri, N, Kane, M B and Reeve, A L (1995) How performance assessments affect teaching and learning, *Educational Leadership* 53 (3), 80–83.

Kinnell, M (Ed.) (1990) *The Learning Experiences of Overseas Students*, Bristol: Open University Press.

Kobayashi, H and Rinnert, C (1996) Factors affecting composition evaluation in an EFL context: cultural rhetorical pattern and readers' background, *Language Learning* 46 (3), 397–437.

Koretz, D (1988) Arriving at Lake Wobegon: Are standardized tests exaggerating achievement and distorting instruction? *American Educator* 12 (2), 8–15, 46–52.

Koretz, D, Barron, S, Mitchell, K and Stecher, B (1996) *Perceived effects of the Kentucky Instructional Results Information System (KIRIS)*, unpublished report, Santa Monica, California: Institute on Education and Training, RAND Corporation.

Koretz, D, Linn, R L, Dunbar, S B and Shepard, L A (1991) The effects of high-stakes testing: preliminary evidence about generalization across tests, in Linn R L (chair), *The Effects of High Stakes Testing*, symposium presented at the annual meetings of the American Educational Research Association and the National Council on Measurement in Education, Chicago, Illinois, April 1991.

Krapels, A R (1990) An overview of second language writing process research, in Kroll, B (Ed.) *Second Language Writing: Research Insights for the Classroom*, Cambridge: Cambridge University Press, 37–56.

Kuhn T S (1970) *The Structure of Scientific Revolutions*, Chicago, Illinois: Chicago University Press.

Lane, S and Parke, C (1996) *Consequences of a mathematics performance assessment and the relationship between the consequences and student learning*, paper presented at the annual meeting of the National Council on Measurement in Education, New York, April 1996.

Larsen-Freeman, D (1997) Chaos/Complexity Science and Second Language Acquisition, *Applied Linguistics* 18 (2), 141–165.

Larsen-Freeman, D and Long, M (1991) *An Introduction to Second Language Acquisition Research*, Harlow: Longman.

Laufer, B (1992) How much lexis is necessary for reading comprehension? in Arnaud, P and Béjoint, H (Eds) *Vocabulary and Applied Linguistics*, London: Macmillan, 126–132.

Lea, M and Street, B (1999) Writing as academic literacies: understanding practices through texts, in Candlin, C N and Hyland, K (Eds) *Writing: Text, Processes, and Practices*, Harlow: Longman, 62–81.

Lee, W O (1991) *Social Change and Educational Problems in Japan, Singapore and Hong Kong*, London: Macmillan.

Leki, I (1995) Good writing: I know it when I see it, in Belcher, D and Braine, G (Eds) *Academic Writing in a Second Language*, Norwood, New Jersey: Ablex, 23–46.

Leki, I and Carson, J (1994) Student Perceptions of EAP writing instruction and writing needs across disciplines, *TESOL Quarterly* 28 (1), 81–101.

Lewis, M and Starks, D (1997) Revisiting examination questions in tertiary academic writing, *English for Specific Purposes* 16 (3), 197–210.

Lewkowicz, J A (2000) Authenticity in language testing: some outstanding questions, *Language Testing* 17 (1), 43–64.

Linacre, J M (1988) *A User's Guide to FACETS, Rasch Measurement Computer Programme*, Chicago, Illinois: MESA.

Linn, R L (1994) Performance assessment: policy promises and technical measurement standards, *Educational Researcher* 23 (9), 4–14.

Linn, R L (2000) Assessments and accountability, *Educational Researcher* 29 (2), 4–16.

References

Linn, R L, Baker, E L and Dunbar, S B (1991) Complex, performance-based assessment: expectations and validation criteria, *Educational Researcher* 20 (8), 15–21.

Linn, R L, Graue, M E and Sanders, N M (1990) Comparing state and district results to national norms: The validity of the claims that everyone is above average, *Educational Measurement: Issues and Practice* 9 (3), 5–14.

Liu, J and Nesi, H (1999) Are we teaching the right words? A study of students' receptive knowledge of two types of vocabulary: 'subtechnical' and 'technical', in Bool H and Luford P (Eds) *Academic Standards and Expectations: The Role of EAP*, Nottingham: Nottingham University Press.

London, N (1997) A national strategy for system-wide curriculum improvement in Trinidad and Tobago, in Chapman, D W S, Mählck, L O and Smulders, A (Eds) *From Planning to Action: Government initiatives for improving school-level practice*, Paris: International Institute for School Level Planning, 133–146.

Lumley, T (2002) Assessment criteria in a large-scale writing test: what do they mean to the raters? *Language Testing* 19 (3), 227–245.

Mabry, L (1999) Writing to the rubric: lingering effects of traditional standardized testing on direct writing assessment, *Phi Delta Kappan* 81 (9), 673–679.

Madaus, G F (1988) The influence of testing on the curriculum, in Tanner, L N (Ed.) *Critical Issues in Curriculum*, Chicago, Illinois: Chicago University Press, 83–121.

Makaya, P and Bloor, T (1987) Playing safe with predictions: hedging, attribution and conditions in economic forecasting, *British Studies in Applied Linguistics* 2, 55–69.

Markee, N (1993) The diffusion of innovation in language teaching, *Annual Review of Applied Linguistics* 13, 229–243.

Marton, F and Saljo, R (1976a) On qualitative differences in learning, I: outcome and process, *British Journal of Educational Psychology* 46, 4–11.

Marton, F and Saljo, R (1976b) On qualitative differences in learning: II, *British Journal of Educational Psychology* 46, 115–127.

Matthews, E (1998) *Benchmarking UIEP Success: The role of the TOEFL*, Montreal: Embry-Riddle Language Institute.

Mauranen, A (1993) Contrastive ESP rhetoric: metatext in Finnish–English Economics texts, *English for Specific Purposes* 12 (1), 3–22.

Mayor, B, Hewings, A and Swann, J (2003) *An Analysis of the Linguistic Features of Output from IELTS Academic Writing Tasks 1 and 2*, London: British Council/IDP Australia.

McCarter, S, Easton, J and Ash, J (2000) *A Book for IELTS*, Ford, Midlothian: IntelliGene.

McDonnell, L M and Choisser, C (1997) *Testing and teaching: local implementation of new state assessments*, CSE Technical Report 442, Santa Barbara, California: CRESST/University of California.

McNamara, D and Harris, R (Eds) (1997) *Overseas Students in Higher Education: Issues in Teaching and Learning*, London: Routledge.

McNamara, T F (1996) *Measuring Second Language Performance*, Harlow: Longman.

McNamara, T F (2000) *Language Testing*, Oxford: Oxford University Press.

McNamara, T F and Lumley, T (1995) Rater characteristics and rater bias: implications for training, *Language Testing* 12 (1), 54–71.

Mehrens, W A (1998) Consequences of assessment: What is the evidence? *Education Policy Analysis Archives* 6 (13).

Mehrens, W A and Kaminsky, J (1989) Methods for improving standardized test scores: fruitful, fruitless or fraudulent, *Educational Measurement: Issues and Practice* 8 (1), 14–22.

Mellix, B (1998) From outside, in, in Zamel, V and Spack, R (Eds) *Negotiating Academic Literacies: Teaching and Learning Across Cultures*, Mahwah, New Jersey: Erlbaum, 61–70.

Merriam-Webster (2000) *Merriam-Webster's Collegiate Dictionary*, Springfield, Massachusetts: Merriam-Webster.

Messick, S (1989) Validity, in Linn, R (Ed.) *Educational Measurement*, New York: ACE/Macmillan, 13–103.

Messick, S (1994) The interplay of evidence and consequences in the validation of performance assessments, *Educational Researcher* 23 (2), 13–23.

Messick, S (1996) Validity and washback in language testing, *Language Testing* 13 (3), 241–256.

Mickan, P and Slater, S (2003) Text analysis and the assessment of academic writing, in *IELTS Research Reports Volume 5*, Canberra: IELTS Australia, 59–88.

Miles, M B and Huberman, A M (1994) *Qualitative Data Analysis*, Thousand Oaks, California: Sage.

Milton, J and Tsang, E (1993) A corpus-based study of logical connectors in EFL students' writing: directions for future research, in Pemberton, R and Tsang, E (Eds) *Studies in Lexis*, Hong Kong: Hong Kong University of Science and Technology, 215–246.

Mitchell, R and Myles, F (1998) *Second Language Learning Theories*, London: Arnold.

Miyahara, A (1986) A need for culture-particular criteria for observation and evaluation of persuasiveness in public communication: The case of Japan, *Studies in English Language and Literature* 37 (1), 85–102.

Mohan, B A and Lo, W A-Y (1985) Academic writing and Chinese students: transfer and developmental factors, *TESOL Quarterly* 19 (3), 515–534.

Moore, T and Morton, J (1999) Authenticity in the IELTS Academic Module Writing Test: A comparative study of Task 2 items and university assignments, in Tulloh, R (Ed.) *IELTS Research Reports Volume 2*, Canberra: IELTS Australia, 64–106.

Morley, J (2000) The Chaplen Test revisited, in Blue, G M (Ed.) *Assessing English for Academic Purposes*, Bern, Switzerland: Peter Lang European Academic Publishers, 49–62.

Morrow, K (1986) The evaluation of tests of communicative performance, in Portal, M (Ed.) *Innovations in Language Testing*, Windsor: NFER-Nelson, 1–13.

Moss, P A (1992) Shifting conceptions of validity in educational measurement: implications for performance assessment, *Review of Educational Research* 62 (3), 229–258.

Munby, J (1978) *Communicative Syllabus Design*, Cambridge: Cambridge University Press.

Myers, G (1988) The social construction of science and the teaching of English: an example of research, in Robinson, P (Ed.) *Academic Writing: Process and Product*, London: Modern English Publications, 143–150.

References

Myers, G (1999) Interaction in writing: principles, and problems, in Candlin, C N and Hyland, K (Eds) *Writing: Text, Processes and Practices*, Harlow: Longman, 40–61.

Myford, C M and Wolfe, E W (2000) *Monitoring and Evaluating Sources of Variability Within the Test of Spoken English Assessment System*, Princeton, New Jersey: Educational Testing Service.

Nation, I S P (1990) *Teaching and Learning Vocabulary*, New York: Newbury House.

Nation, I S P and Hwang, K (1995) Where would general service vocabulary stop and special purposes vocabulary begin? *System* 23 (1), 35–41.

National Committee of Enquiry into Higher Education (1997) *Higher Education in the Learning Society: Final Report of the National Committee of Enquiry into Higher Education (The Dearing Report)*, London: Her Majesty's Stationery Office.

Nettle, M (1997) Teaching for IELTS, *Modern English Teacher* 6 (1), 59–62.

NeuroDimension Inc. (2001) *NeuroSolutions 4*, Gainesville, Florida: NeuroSolutions Inc.

Nunan, D, Berry, R and Berry, V (Eds) (1996) *Bringing About Change In Language Education*, Hong Kong: The University of Hong Kong, Department of Curriculum Studies.

O'Malley, J M and Chamot, A (1990) *Learning Strategies in Second Language Acquisition*, Cambridge: Cambridge University Press.

Oshima, A and Hogue, A (1991) *Writing Academic English*, New York: Addison-Wesley.

Ostler, S (1980) A survey of academic needs for advanced ESL, *TESOL Quarterly* 14 (4), 489–502.

O'Sullivan, B (2002) Investigating variability in a test of second language writing ability, *Research Notes* 7, 14–17.

Oxford, R L (1990) *Language Learning Strategies: What Every Teacher Should Know*, New York: Newbury House.

Oxford, R L (Ed.) (1996) *Language Learning Strategies around the World: Cross-Cultural Perspectives*, Manoa, Hawaii: University of Hawaii.

Oxford University Press (2000) *Shorter Oxford English Dictionary*, Oxford: Oxford University Press.

Parry, K (1993) Too many words: learning the vocabulary of an academic subject, in Huckin, T H, Coady, M and Coady, J (Eds) *Second Language Reading and Vocabulary Learning*, Norwood, New Jersey: Ablex, 46–64.

Peacock, M (2001) Language learning strategies and EAP proficiency: teacher views, student views and test results, in Flowerdew, J and Peacock, M (Eds) *Research Perspectives on English for Academic Purposes*, Cambridge: Cambridge University Press, 268–297.

Pearson, I (1988) Tests as levers for change, in Chamberlain, D and Baumgartner, R (Eds) *ESP in the Classroom: Practice and evaluation*, Oxford: Modern English Publications, 98–107.

Peirce, B N (1992) Demystifying the TOEFL Reading Test, *TESOL Quarterly* 26 (4), 665–689.

Pennycook, A (1994) *The Cultural Politics of English as an International Language*, Harlow: Longman.

Pennycook, A (1996) Borrowing others' words: text, ownership, memory, and plagiarism, *TESOL Quarterly* 30 (2), 201–229.

Perkins, K, Gupta, L and Tammana, R (1995) Predicting item difficulty in a reading comprehension test with an artificial neural network, *Language Testing* 12 (1), 34–53.

Popham, W J (1987) Two-plus decades of educational objectives, *International Journal of Educational Research* 11 (1), 31–41.

Portal, M (Ed) (1986) *Innovations in Language Testing*, Windsor: NFER-Nelson.

Powers, D E (1993) Coaching for the SAT: A summary of the summaries and an update, *Educational Measurement: Issues and Practice* 12 (2), 24–30.

Prodromou, L (1995) The washback effect: from testing to teaching, *ELT Journal* 49, 13–25.

Prodromou, L (1999) *Grammar and Vocabulary for First Certificate*, Harlow: Longman.

Purpura, J E (1999) *Learner Strategy Use and Performance on Language Tests: A Structural Equation Modeling Approach*, Cambridge: Cambridge University Press.

Purves, A (1984) In search of an internationally valid scheme for evaluating compositions, *College Composition and Communication* 35 (4), 426–438.

Radecki, P and Swales, J (1988) ESL students' reactions to comments on their written work, *System* 16 (3), 355–365.

Rafferty, E A (1993) *Urban teachers rate Maryland's new performance assessments*, paper presented at the annual meeting of the American Educational Research Association, Atlanta, Georgia, April.

Raimes, A (1985) What unskilled writers do as they write: a classroom study of composing, *TESOL Quarterly* 19 (2), 229–258.

Ramirez, A (1999) Assessment-driven reform: the emperor still has no clothes, *Phi Delta Kappan* 81 (3), 204–208.

Rao, C, McPherson, K, Chand, R and Khan, V (2003) Assessing the Impact of IELTS preparation programs on candidates' performance on the General Training Reading and Writing Test Modules, in *IELTS Research Reports Volume 5*, Canberra: IELTS Australia, 237–262.

Rea-Dickins, P, Kiely R and Yu, G (2005) *Student identity, learning and progression: with special reference to the affective and academic impact of IELTS on 'successful' IELTS students*, unpublished IELTS research report.

Read, J (2000) *Assessing Vocabulary*, Cambridge: Cambridge University Press.

Read, J and Hayes, B (2003) The impact of the IELTS test on preparation for academic study in New Zealand, in *IELTS Research Reports* Volume 5, Canberra: IELTS Australia, 153–206.

Reid, J M (1987) The learning style preferences of ESL students, *TESOL Quarterly* 21 (1), 87–111.

Reid, J M (1990a) Responding to different topic types: a quantitative analysis from a contrastive rhetoric perspective, in Kroll, B (Ed.) *Second Language Writing: Research Insights for the Classroom*, Cambridge: Cambridge University Press, 191–211.

Reid, J M (1990b) The dirty laundry of ESL survey research, *TESOL Quarterly* 24 (1), 323–338.

Resnick, L B and Resnick, D P (1992) Assessing the thinking curriculum: new tools for educational reform, in Gifford, B G and O'Conner, M C (Eds) *Changing Assessments: Alternative views of aptitude, achievement and instruction*, Boston, Massachusetts: Kluwer Academic Publishers, 37–75.

Richards, J C, Platt, J and Platt, H (1992) *Dictionary of Language Teaching and Applied Linguistics*, Harlow: Longman.

References

Richardson, J T E (1992) A critical evaluation of a short form of the Approaches to Studying Inventory, *Psychology Teaching Review* 1, 34–45.

Richardson, J T E (1994) Using questionnaires to evaluate student learning: some health warnings, in Gibbs, G (Ed.) *Improving Student Learning – Theory and Practice*, Oxford: Oxford Centre for Staff Development.

Rignall, M and Furneaux, C (2002) *The effect of standardisation training on rater judgements for the IELTS Writing Module, British Council/IDP Australia IELTS Research Report*, unpublished IELTS Research Report, London: British Council/IDP Australia.

Ross, S (1998) *Measuring Gain in Language Programs: Theory and Research*, Sydney: National Centre for English Language Teaching and Research (NCELTR), Macquarie University.

Rumelhart, D E and McClelland, J (Eds) (1986) *Parallel Distributed Processing: Explorations in the Microstructure of Cognition*, Cambridge, Massachusetts: MIT Press.

Sahanaya, W, Lindeck, J and Stewart, R (1999) *IELTS Preparation and Practice*, Oxford: Oxford University Press.

Santos, T (1988) Professors' reactions to the academic writing of nonnative speaking students, *TESOL Quarterly* 22 (1), 69–90.

Sarason, I G (1980) *Test Anxiety: Theory, Research, and Applications*, Hilsdale, New Jersey: Lawrence Erlbaum Associates, Inc.

Sasaki, M and Hirose, K (1996) Explanatory variables for EFL students' expository writing, *Language Learning* 46 (1), 137–174.

Schiefelbein, E (1993) The use of national assessments to improve primary education in Chile, in Chapman, D W and Mahlck, L O (Eds) *From Planning to Action: Government Initiatives for Improving School-Level Practice*, Paris: International Institute for Educational Planning.

Schmitt, N, Schmitt, D and Clapham, C (2001) Developing and exploring the behaviour of two new versions of the Vocabulary Levels Test, *Language Testing* 18 (1), 55–88.

Scollon, R (1995) Plagiarism and ideology: identity in intercultural discourse, *Language in Society* 24 (1), 1–28.

Scouller, K (1998) The influence of assessment method on students' learning approaches: multiple-choice examination versus assignment essay, *Higher Education* 35 (4), 453–472.

Selinker, L (1979) On the use of informants in discourse analysis and language for specialized purposes, *International Review of Applied Linguistics* 17 (3), 189–215.

Sellen, D (1982) *Skills in Action*, London: Hulton Educational.

Shaw, P and Liu, E (1998) What develops in the development of second-language writing? *Applied Linguistics* 19 (2), 225–254.

Shaw, S D and Weir, C J (2007) *Examining Second Language Writing: Research and Practice,* Studies in Language Testing 26, Cambridge: UCLES/Cambridge University Press.

Shen, F (1998) The classroom and the wider culture: identity as a key to learning English composition, in Zamel, V and Spack, R (Eds) *Negotiating Academic Literacies: Teaching and Learning Across Cultures*, Mahwah, New Jersey: Erlbaum, 123–133.

Shepard, L A (1991) Will national tests improve student learning? *Phi Delta Kappan* 73 (3), 232–238.

Shepard, L A (1993) Evaluating test validity, *Review of Research in Education* 19, 405–484.

Shepard, L A, Flexer, R J, Hiebert, E H, Marion, S F, Mayfield, V and Weston, T J (1996) Effects of introducing classroom performance assessments on student learning, *Educational Measurement: Issues and Practice* 15 (3), 7–18.

Shi, L (2001) Native- and non-native speaking EFL teachers' evaluation of Chinese students' writing, *Language Testing* 18 (3), 303–325.

Shohamy, E (1992) Beyond proficiency testing: a diagnostic feedback testing model for assessing foreign language learning, *The Modern Language Journal* 76 (4), 513–521.

Shohamy, E (1993) *The Power of Tests*, Washington DC: National Foreign Language Center.

Shohamy, E (2001) *The Power of Tests: A critical perspective of the uses of language tests*, Harlow: Longman.

Shohamy, E, Donitsa-Schmidt, S and Ferman, I (1996) Test impact revisited: washback effect over time, *Language Testing* 13 (3), 298–317.

Silva, T (1993) Towards an understanding of the distinct nature of L2 writing: the ESL research and its implications, *TESOL Quarterly* 27 (4), 657–677.

Skehan, P (1989) *Individual Differences in Second Language Learning*, London: Arnold.

Skehan, P (1991) Individual differences in second language learning, *Studies in Second Language Acquisition* 13 (2), 275–298.

Skehan, P (1998) *A Cognitive Approach to Language Learning*, Oxford: Oxford University Press.

Smith, J (2007) *Accessibility of IELTS GT Modules to 16/17 year old students studying English in selected Asian countries*, unpublished research report, IDP: IELTS Australia.

Smith, M L (1991a) Put to the test: the effects of external testing on teachers, *Educational Researcher* 20 (5), 8–11.

Smith, M L (1991b) Meanings of test preparation, *American Educational Research Journal* 28 (3), 521–542.

Smith, M L, Noble, A, Heinecke, W, Seck, M, Parish, C, Cabay, M et al (1997) *Reforming Schools by Reforming Assessment: Consequences of the Arizona Student Assessment Program (ASAP)*, Los Angeles: National Center for Research on Evaluation, Standards, and Student Testing.

Snyder, C W, Prince, B, Johanson, G, Odaet, C, Jaji, L and Beatty, M (1997) *Exam Fervor and Fever: Case Studies of the Influence of Primary Leaving Examinations on Uganda Classrooms, Teachers and Pupils* (volume one), Los Angeles, California: Academy for Educational Development, University of California, Los Angeles.

Spack, R (1997) The acquisition of academic literacy in a second language: a longitudinal case study, *Written Communication* 14 (1), 3–62.

Spada, N and Fröhlich, M (1995) *COLT Observation Scheme: Coding Conventions and Applications*, Sydney: National Centre for English Language Teaching and Research (NCELTR), Macquarie University.

Spolsky, B (1989) *Conditions for Second Language Learning: Introduction to a General Theory*, Oxford: Oxford University Press.

Spolsky, B (1995) *Measured Words: The development of objective language testing*, Oxford: Oxford University Press.

Spolsky, B (1996) The examination-classroom backwash cycle: some historical cases, in Nunan, D, Berry, R and Berry, V (Eds) *Bringing About Change in Language Education*, Hong Kong: The University of Hong Kong, Department of Curriculum Studies, 55–66.

SPSS, Inc. (2002) *SPSS 11 for Windows*, Chicago, Illinois: SPSS Inc.

Starfield, S (2001) 'I'll go with the group': Rethinking 'discourse community' in EAP, in Flowerdew, J and Peacock, M (Eds) *Research Perspectives on English for Academic Purposes*, Cambridge: Cambridge University Press, 132–147.

Stecher, B M and Mitchell, K J (1995) *Portfolio-driven reform: Vermont teachers' understanding of mathematical problem solving and related changes in classroom practice*, CSE Technical Report 400, Los Angeles, California: CRESST/Graduate School of Education and Information Studies, University of California.

Stiggins, R J (1999) Assessment, student, confidence, and school success, *Phi Delta Kappan* 81 (3), 191–198.

Sutarsyah, C, Nation, P and Kennedy, G (1994) How useful is EAP vocabulary for ESP? A corpus based study, *RELC Journal* 25 (2), 34–50.

Swain, M (1985) Large-scale communicative language testing: a case study, in Lee, Y P, Fok, A C Y L, Low, R and Low, G (Eds) *New Directions in Language Testing*, Oxford: Pergamon, 35–46.

Swales, J M and Feak, C B (1994) *Academic Writing for Graduate Students*, Ann Arbor, Michigan: University of Michigan Press.

Tabachnik, B G and Fidell, L S (2000) *Using Multivariate Statistics*, Boston: Allyn and Bacon.

Tang, C (1992) Perceptions of task demand, strategy attributions and student learning, *Research and Development in Higher Education* 15, 474–481.

Tang, C and Biggs, J (1996) How Hong Kong students cope with assessment, in Watkins, D A and Biggs, J (Eds) *The Chinese Learner*, Hong Kong: CERC/ACER, 159–182.

Taschman, G N (1993) *A neural network model for spoken word recognition*, unpublished PhD thesis, University of Pennsylvania, Philadelphia.

Taylor, L (2002) Review of Recent Validation Studies, *Research Notes* 10, 22–23.

Taylor, L (2007) Impact of the Joint-funded Research Studies on the IELTS Writing Module, in Taylor, L and Falvey, P (Eds) *IELTS Collected Papers: Research in speaking and writing assessment,* Studies in Language Testing 19, Cambridge: UCLES/Cambridge University Press.

Teasdale, A and Leung, C (2000) Teacher assessment and psychometric theory: a case of paradigm crossing? *Language Testing* 17 (2), 165–186.

Thompson, P (Ed.) (1999) *Academic Writing Development in Higher Education: Perspectives, Explorations and Approaches*, Reading: CALS, The University of Reading.

Thompson, P (2001) *A pedagogically-motivated corpus-based examination of PhD Theses: macrostructure, citation practices and uses of modal verbs*, unpublished PhD thesis, University of Reading, Reading.

Thompson, P and Tribble, C (2001) Looking at citations: using corpora in English for Academic Purposes, *Language Learning and Technology* 5 (3), 91–105.

Thorndike, E L (1921) *Measurement in Education, Teachers College Record* 22, 378.

Thorp, D and Kennedy, C (2003) What makes a 'Good' IELTS Answer in Academic Writing? *IELTS Research Report*, London: British Council/IDP Australia.

Traynor, R (1985) The TOEFL: an appraisal, *ELT Journal* 39 (1), 43–47.

Trzeciak, J (1996) *Cultural Factors in English Academic Writing: The Problems of Non-Native Speaker Students*, Reading: University of Reading.

Trzeciak, J and Mackay, S (1994) *Study Skills for Academic Writing*, London: Prentice Hall.

Tsao, F (1983) Linguistics and written discourse in particular languages, *Annual Review of Applied Linguistics* 3, 99–117.

Tulloh, R (Ed.) (1999) *IELTS Research Reports Volume 2*, Canberra: IELTS Australia.

Tulloh, R (Ed.) (2003) *IELTS Research Reports Volume 4*, Canberra: IELTS Australia.

Turner, C (2001) The need for impact studies of L2 performance testing and rating: identifying areas of potential consequences at all levels of the testing cycle, in Brown, A et al (Eds) *Experimenting with Uncertainty: Essays in Honour of Alan Davies*, Studies in Language Testing 11, Cambridge: UCLES/Cambridge University Press, 138–149.

Turner, J (1999) Problematising the language problem, in Bool, H and Luford, P (Eds) *Academic Standards and Expectations: The Role of EAP*, Nottingham: Nottingham University Press, 59–66.

University of Cambridge Local Examinations Syndicate (ongoing) *The IELTS Impact Project*.

Valette, R M (1967) *Modern Language Testing*, New York: Harcourt, Brace and World Inc.

Vann, R, Meyer, D E and Lorenz, F (1984) Error gravity: a study of faculty opinions, *TESOL Quarterly* 18 (4), 427–440.

Ventola, E and Mauranen, A (1991) Non-native and native revising of scientific articles, in Ventola, E (Ed.) *Functional and Systemic Linguistics*, Berlin: Mouton de Gruyter, 457–492.

Ventola, E and Mauranen, A (Eds) (1996) *Non-native and Native Revising of Scientific Articles*, Amsterdam: John Benjamins.

Vernon, P E (1956) *The Measurement of Abilities*, London: University of London Press.

Volosinov, V I (1973) *Marxism and the Philosophy of Language*, New York: Seminar Press.

Wall, D (1996) Introducing new tests into traditional systems: insights from general education and from innovation theory, *Language Testing* 13 (3), 334–354.

Wall, D (1997) Impact and washback in language testing, in Clapham, C and Corson, D (Eds) *Language Testing and Assessment*, Amsterdam: Kluwer Academic Publishers, 291–302.

Wall, D (2000) The impact of high stakes testing on teaching and learning, *System* 28 (4), 483–499.

Wall, D (2005) *The Impact of High-Stakes Testing on Classroom Teaching: A case study using insights from testing and innovation theory*, Studies in Language Testing 22, Cambridge: UCLES/Cambridge University Press.

Wall, D and Alderson, J C (1993) Examining washback: the Sri Lankan impact study, *Language Testing* 10 (1), 41–69.

Wall, D, Nickson, A, Jordan, R R, Allwright, J and Houghton, D (1988) Developing student writing: a subject tutor and writing tutors compare points of view, in Robinson, P (Ed.) *Academic Writing: Process and Product*, London: Modern English Publications, 117–129.

Wallace, C (1997) IELTS: global implications of curriculum and materials design, *ELT Journal* 51 (4), 370–373.

Watanabe, Y (1992) Washback effects of college entrance examination on language learning strategies, *JACET Bulletin* 23, 175–194.

Watanabe, Y (1996) Does grammar translation come from the entrance examination? Preliminary findings from classroom-based research, *Language Testing* 13 (3), 318–333.

Watanabe, Y (1997) *The washback effects of the Japanese university entrance examinations of English-classroom-based research,* unpublished PhD thesis, University of Lancaster, Lancaster.

Watanabe, Y (2004) Methodology in washback studies, in Cheng, L and Watanabe, Y (Eds) *Context and Method in Washback Research: The Influence of Language Testing on Teaching and Learning,* Hilsdale, New Jersey: Lawrence Erlbaum, 19–36.

Waters, A (1996) *A Review of Research into Needs in English for Academic Purposes of Relevance to the North American Higher Education Context,* Princeton, New Jersey: Educational Testing Service.

Watkins, D (1994) Student evaluations of university teaching: a cross-cultural perspective, *Research in Higher Education* 35 (2), 251–266.

Watkins, D A and Akande, A (1992) Assessing the approaches to learning of Nigerian students, *Assessment and Evaluation in Higher Education* 17 (1), 11–20.

Watkins, D A and Biggs, J (Eds) (1996) *The Chinese Learner,* Hong Kong: CERC/ACER.

Weigle, S C (2002) *Assessing Writing,* Cambridge: Cambridge University Press.

Weir, C J (1983) *Identifying the language problems of overseas students in tertiary education in the UK,* unpublished PhD thesis, Institute of Education, University of London, London.

Weir, C J (1984) The Associated Examining Board's Test in English for Academic Purposes (TEAP), in Williams, R, Swales, J and Kirkman, J (Eds) *Common Ground: Shared interests in ESP and Communication Studies,* Oxford: Pergamon, 145–158.

Weir, C J (1990) *Communicative Language Testing,* Hemel Hempstead: Prentice Hall.

Weir, C J (1993) *Understanding and Developing Language Tests,* Hemel Hempstead: Prentice Hall.

Wen, Q and Johnson, R K (1997) L2 learner variables and English achievement: a study of tertiary-level English majors in China, *Applied Linguistics* 18 (1), 27–48.

Wesche, M (1987) Second language performance testing: The Ontario Test of ESL as an example, *Language Testing* 4 (1), 28–47.

Wesdorp, H (1982) *Backwash Effects of Language Testing in Primary and Secondary Education,* Amsterdam: Stichting Centrum voor onderwijsonderzoek van de Universiteit van Amsterdam.

West, M (1953) *A General Service List of English Words,* London: Longman, Green and Co.

Widdowson, H G (1983) *Learning Purpose and Language Use,* Oxford: Oxford University Press.

Widdowson, H G (1989) Knowledge of language and ability for use, *Applied Linguistics* 10 (2), 128–137.

Wiggins, G P (1998) *Educative Assessment,* San Francisco, California: Jossey-Bass Publishers.

Wiliam, D (1996) National curriculum assessments and programmes of study: Validity and impact, *British Educational Research Journal* 22 (1), 129–141.

Wilkinson, A (1968) The testing of oracy, in Davies, A (Ed.) *Language Testing Symposium: A psycholinguistic perspective*, Oxford: Oxford University Press.

Williams, R, Swales, J and Kirkman, J (Eds) (1984) *Common Ground: Shared Interests in ESP and Communication Studies*, Oxford: Pergamon.

Wintergest, A C, DeCapua, A and Itzen, R C (2001) The construct validity of one learning styles instrument, *System* 29 (3), 385–404.

Wise, S L (1985) The development and validation of a scale measuring attitudes towards statistics, *Educational and Psychological Measurement* 45 (2), 401–405.

Wiseman, S (Ed.) (1961) *Examinations and English Education*, Manchester: Manchester University Press.

Wood, S (Ed.) (1998) *IELTS Research Reports Volume 1*, Sydney: ELICOS/ IELTS Australia.

Wray, A and Pegg, C (2007) *The effect of memorization in the writing scripts of Chinese IELTS test takers*, British Council/IDP Australia IELTS Research Report, unpublished IELTS Research Report, London: British Council/IDP Australia.

Wright, B and Linacre, J (1994) Reasonable mean-square fit values, *Rasch Measurement Transactions* 8 (3), 370.

Xue, G and Nation, P (1983) A University Word List, *Language Learning and Communication* 3 (2), 215–229.

Zamel, V (1982) Writing: the process of discovering meaning, *TESOL Quarterly* 16 (2), 195–209.

Zamel, V (1983) The composing processes of advanced ESL students: six case studies, *TESOL Quarterly* 17 (2), 165–187.

Zamel, V (1998) Strangers in academia: the experiences of faculty and ESL students across the curriculum, in Zamel, V and Spack, R (Eds) *Negotiating Academic Literacies: Teaching and Learning Across Cultures*, Mahwah, New Jersey: Erlbaum, 249–264.

Zamel, V and Spack, R (Eds) (1998) *Negotiating Academic Literacies: Teaching and Learning Across Cultures*, Mahwah, New Jersey: Erlbaum.

Zimmerman, D W and Williams, R H (1982) Gain scores in research can be highly reliable, *Journal of Educational Measurement* 9 (2), 149–154.

Index

Index

Walley, E, 36
washback
  and IELTS, 64–69
  and test design, 6–17, 73–81
  definition, 1–5
  direction, 6–17
  intensity, 6, 21–25
  methods for investigation, 25–30
  model, 1, 13, 16–17, 24, 25, 30, 32, 58, 59,
    65–66, 68–69, 71, 82, 91, 193, 210, 219,
    225, 314–315
  validity, 3
  variability, 17–21
  to the learner/ to the programme, 1, 3, 6,
    9, 20, 24, 25, 26, 219, 314
Watanabe, Y, 5, 6, 19–20, 22, 25, 27, 28, 30,
    58, 71, 107, 137, 138, 308
Watkins, DA, 129, 130, 131, 203
Watt, L, 61
Weigle, SC, 1, 49, 50, 50, 299
Weir, CJ, 3, 5, 12–13, 32, 40, 40, 52, 53,
    57, 57, 59, 101, 106, 145, 150, 151, 154,
    312
Wesche, M, 4
Wesdorp, H, 6, 23
West, R, 145

Mann-Whitney test, 160, 191, 192
Widdowson, HG, 42, 49, 146
Wiggins, GP, 15
Wignell, P, 56
Wilcoxon, F, 160, 263
Wiliam, D, 5, 7, 8, 10, 21
Wilkinson, A, 1, 5
Williams, R, 248
Wilson, 6, 7
Wintergest, AC, 115
Wiseman, S, 6
Wray, A, 312
Lake Wobegon effect, 8, 23, 29
Wolfe, EW, 155, 157

X
Xue, G, 36, 145, 147

Y
Yamashita, SO, 19
Young-Scholten, M, 69
Yule, G, 37

Z
Zamel, V, 36
Zhang, B, 58
Zimmerman, DW, 248